Praise for **THE AGELE**

"We all need this book — women, men, Gen X, Y, Boomers, everyone — to remind us that what we expect, we get. Sands points the way to a new expectation of thriving throughout our ages and stages together in the Longevity Economy."

~ Elsie Maio, founder of Humanity, Inc./The SoulBranding℠ Institute

"It's all here. Everything you need to know about being an over-50 woman today and the prospects of becoming the best you can be as you grow older. Karen Sands is the ideal guide across this uncharted territory. She shares her own story and also the story of our generation. She offers statistics and inspirational insights, encouragement and advice about health, activism, business, priorities, and relationships, especially the importance of moving ahead together."

~ Suzanne Braun Levine, author of *Inventing the Rest of Our Lives, Fifty IS the New Fifty, How We Love Now,* and *You Gotta Have Girlfriends*

"Applause! I love this book! Karen Sands has created a trusted guide and masterful approach to the future rooted in sound knowledge, cutting-edge ideas, rich insights, and provocative questions throughout. This work is timeless evidence that can shape vibrant, intergenerational futures founded on Ageless vision."

~ Joyce Cohen, president, Life Planning Network,

"Brava to Karen Sands for weaving together powerful storytelling with spot-on insights. While Sands speaks specifically to women, this book will be invaluable for anyone crossing the threshhold into the second half of life."

~ Marc Freedman, CEO/founder Encore.org and author of The Big Shift

"Karen Sands has done it again! She stirs us up with her uncanny vision that age cannot wither, while also weaving a refreshing new perspective forecasting that women entrepreneurs (especially 40-plus) will be redefining growing older, catalyzing a transformation of the business of aging around the world."

~ Anne Garland, executive managing director, eWomenNetwork, Hartford & Shoreline

"Given our rapidly changing world, *The Ageless Way* couldn't be better timed! With a comprehensive overview of contemporary women's history in a well-structured framework with thoughtful commentary, Karen Sands aims to help us navigate midlife and aging. If you're seeking a path for reflection, renewal, and restructuring your life, you've come to the right book."

~ Cyma Shapiro, MidlifeMothers.org, MotheringintheMiddle.com, author of The Zen of Midlife Mothering

Praise for THE AGELESS WAY

"Just as a focus on wellness is now the norm for forward-thinking healthcare, so *The Ageless Way* overturns our culture's bleak perspective on growing older and replaces it with a positive template for being fully alive in every stage of life. Filled with humor, heart, and hard-won wisdom, *The Ageless Way* is a handbook for evolutionary aging. It should be read and recommended by every healthcare practitioner whose work touches those in the middle years of life and beyond."

~ Debra Gibson, N.D., naturopathic physician and writer

"Karen Sands rewrites the stereotypical—and, frankly, inaccurate—narrative of female aging as a journey toward irrelevance and decrepitude as the joyous, productive, and dynamic stage of life that it can be. Using a lively combination of stories, analysis, and provocative questioning, Karen persuasively shows how life and work after 40 may be the most satisfying years of our lives."

~ Amy Zalman, Ph.D., CEO World Future Society

"Karen Sands writes passionately about the possibilities for purpose and fulfillment throughout life. *The Ageless Way* is a guidebook for Baby Boomers and others searching for a new model of aging."

~ Paul Irving, chairman of the Milken Institute Center for the Future of Aging and distinguished scholar in residence at the University of Southern California Davis School of Gerontology

"*The Ageless Way* is an enthusiastic, provocative, and highly informative yet authentically personal book. Filled with growth promoting, consciousness raising exercises, the book asks us to creatively consider our future life direction, discussing the stories we tell ourselves about our past, present, and future—and how to reassess and reconfigure these stories to open new possibilities in our lives."

~ Tom Lombardo, Ph.D., futurist, psychologist, philosopher, and science fiction scholar, director of the Center for Future Consciousness and The Wisdom Page

"*The Ageless Way* beautifully and eloquently dismantles old perceptions of aging, unveiling a new paradigm for living longer, healthy, joyful, independently financial lives. Karen is the everlasting past, present, and future mother, encouraging women of all ages to take a giant leap into self-discovery and empowerment, to rightfully take their place in a vast, fast-changing universe."

~ Mary Madeiras, three-time Emmy-winning television director

"Congratulations on *The Ageless Way*! Karen's second chapter, "Agelessness Across Generations," grabbed my attention—and this book kept it until the end. Thank you for reminding me of the importance of intergenerational conversations and collaboration in my own life and in my workplace!"

~ Jonna Kurucz, staff vice president, health and wellness, Anthem

Praise for THE AGELESS WAY

"After *Visionaries Have Wrinkles*, Sands continues to redefine and more so to transform our cultural perspective on aging. As a GeroFuturist, she emerges as the grandmother of the 21st century women's movement, sharing her wisdom in a new interactive book, which encourages reflection and multigenerational conversation on the journey toward positive aging."

~ Irene J. Dabrowski, Ph.D., associate professor of sociology, St. John's University, and co-coordinator of the New Jersey Chapter of the World Future Society

"In *The Ageless Way*, Karen Sands sounds a clarion call to ditch denial and embrace the power of "positive aging." Rich in resources, expansive in scope, and brimming with wisdom, this book is both inspirational bible of feminine benchmarks and practical primer on how to leave "the same old 'old' " in the dust."

~ Jeanne Lombardo, futurist, editor and co-author of Mind Flight: a Journey into the Future

"*The Ageless Way* is a unique addition to humanity's greatest journey, the defeat of death and the growing attempt to radically extend the length of life to 100 and then 800 years long. This book answers the central question of meaningful inner advances, with its powerful personal, psychological, spiritual, and professional dimensions. Karen asks us, "Who will you become when you extend your life?"

~Dan Abelow, patented inventor, author, speaker, consultant

"*The Ageless Way* provides an invitation to remember our past, to be fully alive in the present, and to look ahead toward the future. Karen Sands gifts readers an abundance of opportunities for deeper wisdom and gracious understanding as we aim to create meaning throughout the stages of life."

~ Sharona Silverman, MPH, Director, Deutsch Family Shalom Center, Temple Chai, Phoenix, Arizona

"If you didn't know your age, how old would you be? How do you function, act, perform, execute, move, think, and feel? Chronological Age is crap, is Karen's message. In all of her work, and especially now in *The Ageless Way*, she tells us how to focus on our Functional Age and become a healthy and happy centenarian!"

~ Helen Harkness, Ph.D., Career Design Associates Inc., author of *The Career Chase*, *Don't Stop the Career Clock* and *Capitalizing on Career Chaos*

To say thanks for joining me on *The Ageless Way*,

Download the
FREE COMPANION WORKBOOK
The Ageless Way Reflections Journal

to delve more deeply into the Reflections with room to doodle as well as write.

Enjoy! – Karen

Download *The Ageless Way Reflections Journal* at:
KarenSands.com/the-ageless-way/workbook

THE
AGELESS
WAY

KAREN SANDS>

ILLUMINATING THE
NEW STORY OF OUR AGE

Discover Timely Truths & Tools to Radically Reinvent Growing Older

Broad Minded Publishing

PO Box 43

Roxbury, CT 06783-0043

Cover Design, Interior Design & Illustrations: Gloria Owens, Fish Cat Design
Back cover photo by Mary Madeiras. Author profile photo by Lisa Levart / LUSH Photography

Library of Congress Control Number: 2015955818

Sands, Karen
    Library of Congress Cataloging-in-Publication Data
    ISBN: 978-0-9849260-4-6

Disclaimers

Want to use excerpts in your e-zine/newsletter, blog, or website?

OTHER TITLES BY KAREN SANDS

An Ageless Story

Crossing the Canyon

The Greatness Challenge

Mastering Reinvention

Visionaries Have Wrinkles

Visionaries Have Wrinkles Reflections Card Deck

Visionaries Have Wrinkles Reflections Journal

A Glimpse of Tomorrow's Promise

The Ageless Way Reflections Journal

A FREE GIFT FROM KAREN

Download a FREE COPY of *The Ageless Way Reflections Journal*
(companion workbook to *The Ageless Way*) at
KarenSands.com/the-ageless-way/workbook

Watch Karen speak about being Ageless
and welcome you to *The Ageless Way!*
KarenSands.com/ageless

DEDICATIONS

To my numinous Ancient Future
who shined a light so I could learn and embrace *The Ageless Way*—
you connected me to my own Agelessness and welcomed me
on the Ageless Quest that has led to this book.
I thank you deeply, eternally.

To my grandmother, Sara,
my mom, Adelaide, my daughter, Dawn
my daughter-in-law, Paige
my first granddaughter, Arielle,
and my second granddaughter, Finley,
and the generations of women who connect me
to the distant past and to Ancient Future
with enduring love.

To Mark, my dear, beloved husband
Thank you for being my "Mr. Sunshine," always encouraging
me to keep on keepin' on my Ageless Quest.
You are everything I wish to be and more.

To all my readers, this one is for you.

The only people for me are the mad ones,
the ones who are mad to live,
mad to talk, mad to be saved,
desirous of everything at the same time,
the ones who never yawn or say a commonplace thing,
but burn, burn, burn, like fabulous yellow roman candles
exploding like spiders across the stars
and in the middle you see the blue centerlight pop
and everybody goes "Awww!"

~Jack Kerouac

Watch Karen speak about being Ageless
and welcome you to *The Ageless Way!*
KarenSands.com/ageless

Table of Contents

Gratitudes i

Foreword by Sandra Yancey. iii

Preface ～ Setting The Ageless Scene: From The Old Story to New . 1

Introduction ～ The New Story of Our Age 13

About The Ageless Way Reflections. 28

CHAPTERS:

1. The Ageless Way. 31
2. Agelessness Across Generations. 53
3. Positive Aging. 69
4. Ageless Women. 109
5. Ageless Attraction 119
6. Women Shaping The New Story of Our Age. 141
7. Gray is The New Green 173
8. The Longevity Economy 211
9. Ageless Reinvention 247
10. Letting Go 285
11. Ageless Homes and Communities. 315
12. Ageless Elderhood 329
13. Ageless Future 335

Afterword by Howard R. Moody, Ph.D.. 345

THE AGELESS WAY RESOURCES:

You've Always Known You Were Meant for More 349

How to Create Your Ageless Way Group, Pod, or Circle 352

"Aging vs. Ageless" Comparison Chart. 353

Dar Williams Lyrics. 354

Index. 355

About Karen Sands 363

GRATITUDES

Reading between the lines of any book will reveal the fingerprints of many people. This book is no exception. I would like to first thank my family for believing in the work I'm doing. My phenomenal husband, Mark, continues to support me throughout my Ageless Quest, always reflecting back how he sees me, and providing new insights as I birth this new book. Our adult children, Dawn and Brett, our daughter-in-law Paige, and our nephew, Larry, were also behind me cheering me on from book to book. The love and appreciation I feel for all of you is beyond words.

I am also grateful to the remarkable women and men whose shoulders I stand on, and whose pioneering work shaped my thinking and encouraged me to sound the clarion call to those who follow in my footsteps in the sands of time. There are too many to name here, but a few I am compelled to thank: Harry R. Moody, Ph.D., my long ago post-graduate advisor and now valued colleague; Marion Woodman, my beloved mentor whom I carry in my heart always; Nelson Broms, "social entrepreneur extraordinaire," who honed me into the global thinker, strategist, and futurist I've become; my dear friend and gerontologist role model, Cecelia Hurwich, Ph.D.; Dr. W. Edwards Deming, who catapulted my thinking to a whole new level; Peter Senge and Marshall Thurber, who introduced me to visionary leadership; Bob and Mallie Mandel and Sandra Ray, who brought me back to spirit; Anna Ivara, Brugh Joy, M.D., Carolyn Conger, Ph.D., and Sidra and Hal Stone, Ph.D.s, who ushered me through my own midlife "dark night of the Soul" onto an Ageless Quest that has led me into my own Elderhood.

I worked with many gifted professionals along the way. My deep gratitude goes to graphic artist Gloria Owens of Fish Cat Design for the stunning cover and book page design; to Melanie Mallon for her invaluable expertise and guidance when this manuscript was first taking shape; to Susan Leah Eller for her editing and patience as she shepherded this manuscript to completion; and to Nancy Cohen for her dedication and fortitude in her painstaking final reviews as the manuscript became a book. Last but not least, thank you to Julie Van Keuren for saving the day and creating a reader-friendly index.

And, through it all, I am fortunate to have enduring friends, Maria Stokes, Jane Purcell, and Dr. Debra Gibson, N.D., who challenge my thinking and encourage my evolving work. Special thanks to Mary Madeiras, Christine Sposato, Lisa Smartt, and Joan and Bill Spear for their belief in my work. To those others who are part of my feedback loop, always there to listen and share their opinions, I thank you for your support and belief in *The Ageless Way.* Thank you all for always being there. ❯

FOREWORD BY SANDRA YANCEY

If your dreams don't scare you, you're not thinking big enough.
~ Sandra Yancey, Founder & CEO, eWomenNetwork, Inc.

We are at a distinct moment in history when our sheer numbers give women unprecedented voting power and financial clout with which to change the conversation around aging, the future of women of all ages, and the future of our planet.

It is such an exciting time to be a woman. The same women who shattered the glass ceiling are ready to break through the silver ceiling—and not just in the workplace but also on the forefront of entrepreneurship.

There are no road maps to the new terrain of being older women (40+) who matter and make a difference. What I know for sure, no matter what your age and circumstances, it's how you show up and approach your life that determines if you will fulfill your destiny by standing in your own truth. Two main limits to being fulfilled and truly successful are your own fears and the subsequent resistance to what is possible.

What I love most about *The Ageless Way* is that it's about "possibilities." It is about courageously pioneering a new frontier, a way through the old negative story of growing older to a new definition of what it means to be 40 (70, 90…) and older. It's about how you can fully recognize and manifest all that you are truly capable of while shoring up your resiliency to begin again and again. This is the path Karen Sands opens up for all of us in *The Ageless Way*.

Karen illuminates both the new story about the upside of growing older and also the importance of women entrepreneurs in creating a new conversation around aging across generations. As a leading Educational GeroFuturist, she forecasts that women entrepreneurs (especially 40+) will redefine aging around the world, playing a major role in the new movement to monetize and transform the business of aging based on women supporting other women. This makes me especially excited about the future and the economic impact women will make across the globe! The world will become a stronger and better place because of this powerful shift.

Based on decades of work and study concerning the future of women, entrepreneurship, and the graying of the globe, Karen weaves in the collective and connective wisdom garnered from multiple generations to offer a new vision for a way forward with tools to forge our desired futures and create our new brave stories.

I am among those embracing the new story of *The Ageless Way*. I started my business, eWomenNetwork, when I turned 40. Today it is a multimillion-dollar global enterprise. And I am not alone! We women are leading our best lives post-40 after having intentionally reinvented ourselves based on our desire to live authentically and give back to the world.

Instead of falling victim to the culturally ingrained restricting story of how I couldn't (or shouldn't) start my own business since I had passed a certain age (though Karen asks what is *that* age, exactly?), I reflected upon what I wanted to do differently in the second half of my life.

Despite a strong discomfort with networking, and fear about venturing into unknown territory, I worked to build a community and establish a new kind of networking forum in which women entrepreneurs share connections, resources, ideas, contacts, leads, and customers. I went from feeling awkward at networking to heading a global company offering a new model to enhance the success of women entrepreneurs around the world.

From the start, when I met Karen at an eWomenNetwork Success Summit, it was clear there were many parallels in our respective visions for entrepreneurs and the global community of women. As with eWomen-Network, *The Ageless Way* espouses the values of being true to your heart, showing up, being open to profound transformation, lifting other women as you climb, and finding your tribe. When we show up to serve and help each other (as we say in eWomenNetwork "give first—share always"), everyone benefits from that generosity and reciprocity.

I invite you to join me on this journey with Karen Sands, a gifted storyteller, in an exploration of past, present, and future stories, from the ancient oracles to modern trends in everything from entrepreneurship and the economy to science and technology, health and beauty, community and politics. These stories and trend forecasts are illuminating the new Ageless story, revealing timely truths and tools to radically reinvent growing older for every age. Life is full of endings, transitions, and new beginnings. You don't always need answers at the outset, just great questions and thirst to discover.

In *The Ageless Way*, Karen asks the questions that enable those new perspectives. And she doesn't stop at personal mastery. Instead, she also opens us up to new opportunities for entrepreneurial mastery by sharing what we need to know about what she calls "the Longevity Economy." Throughout, Karen illuminates the changing story of women and entrepreneurship as the core driver of the New Story of Our Age. Like me, you will feel inspired and empowered!

Each chapter of *The Ageless Way* contains information to spur new conversations across generations on all aspects of life as we change the way we do business and conduct our daily lives. Following each chapter are reflections for enhancing awareness, clarifying what you want or want to change as you move into midlife and beyond, while inspiring transformative action to unfold what's next. It is a resource you can utilize on your own, with a friend, or for sharing in a group.

I recommend you take time to meander through this valuable resource and guide to the New Story of Our Age. Let it serve as a companion on your trek to engaging your power, your vision, and your voice for a life of deeper meaning, impact, authentic connection, and success as you embrace your very own "Ageless Way." Return often to this Ageless resource to leverage its wisdom on your future and discover new ways to monetize the business of aging so everyone benefits.

When you dream big enough, as inevitably happens when we discover our true purpose, passions and destiny, don't be surprised if the universe opens further doors to spur that momentum.

No matter the reason you picked up this book, know that in these pages you will find the inspiration, wisdom, timely truths, and tools to radically reinvent how you grow older.

 Let the transformations begin!

Sandra Yancey

Founder and CEO, eWomenNetwork, Inc. International award-winning entrepreneur, movie producer, best-selling author, speaker, coach, philanthropist, and CNN "American Hero."

So I'm going to steal out
with my paint and brushes
I'll change the directions,
I'll hit every street
It's the Tinseltown scandal,
the robin hood vandal
She goes out and steals
the king's English
And in the morning
you wake up and
the signs point to you

~ Dar Williams
"You're Aging Well," written and performed by Dar Williams,
1993, Honesty Room, Razor & Tie (lyrics owned by Dar Williams)

PREFACE:

SETTING THE AGELESS SCENE:
FROM THE OLD STORY TO NEW

Make the most of yourself by fanning the tiny,
inner sparks of possibility into flames of achievement.

~ Golda Meir, first woman prime minister of Israel

Four decades ago, when I was leaving my twenties, I lost my mom to the ravages of early onset Alzheimer's at age 59. This heart-rending loss catapulted me into a lifelong search to understand what it was like to become an older woman—an older woman who mattered and made a difference. Like most of our generation, I had very few positive role models as a girl.

As I entered middle school and upper grades, I kept searching for positive role models in my everyday world. I learned about the greats, the famous and celebrated. Early on, I adored and gobbled up anything I could read on visionary women like my revered Marie Curie, which no doubt led me to train as a biologist and to become a science educator in my early twenties.

Don't get me wrong. We had a richness of guides and role models in many areas, from Susan B. Anthony and Harriet Beecher Stowe to Harriet Tubman and other great women. In my adolescence I read all I could by Eleanor Roosevelt and Golda Meir. These women clearly informed my philosophical development, my world view. But they were too few, too far removed from my real time reach…they were in the rarefied out-of-reach uber world of the rich and famous superstars and movers and shakers.

I didn't know where I fit. Yet I always knew that I was meant for more. Is that true for you too?

All I could conjure up for my idealized older woman was based on what I didn't want. There were no road maps into the future and no women to guide me on my way.

Until one day. It was 1971. I was a 26-year-old new mom of a toddler girl, an ex-educator, living overseas in a posh London neighborhood as a corporate spouse. I loved my daughter, spent every waking moment with her. We took great family vacations abroad; I had culture and history at my fingertips, no worries…but something was missing, something I had no name for. I was searching for answers.

As my almost-2-year-old napped, I was flipping through my mail from back home in the United States when a brown paper–wrapped one-shot preview edition of Ms. magazine slipped out of the pile. I couldn't resist reading it cover to cover. That was a pivotal, life-changing moment for me—and for my family.

For those of you unfamiliar with Ms. magazine, it is an American liberal feminist magazine that was a big-deal risk-taking endeavor back in the early 1970s, which ushered the nascent Second Wave Feminist movement onto the American scene. Second Wave Feminists Gloria Steinem and Dorothy Pitman Hughes courageously co-founded Ms. and hired Letty Cottin Pogrebin as a founding editor and Suzanne Braun Levine as its first editor. In her own words, Steinem shares how it all started: "I realized as a journalist that there really was nothing for women to read that was controlled by women, and this caused me along with a number of other women to start Ms. magazine." Pogrebin described Ms. as the translation of the women's movement into a magazine.

Let's take a walk through women's history in the United States for a moment so you know why I'm using terminology like First, Second, and Third Wave Feminist movements and each group's place in our "Herstory"— our history, told from a women's perspective, without the usual patriarchal filtering. Each generation contends with the issues of its time. Understanding generational narratives about feminism, and their history and context, is crucial to how women's future story arc will evolve. Otherwise, we will forget to remember.

First Wave Feminism equates to Suffrage-era feminism between the 1880s and WWI (the early part of the twentieth century) and ends with the success of women's suffrage in 1920 with passage of the Nineteenth Amendment to the U.S. Constitution. As a result of the Suffragettes' challenge to social convention, these women can be considered our feminist foremothers, our visionary sisters.

Second Wave Feminism of the late 1960s and early 1970s revitalized feminism in the United States and continued a sociopolitical movement from the past. These women and men feminists placed their efforts not only on retaining voting rights, but also extended their focus to "Victim Feminism" (e.g., the dangers of rape), women's health rights, freedom of choice, and women's lack of agency. The World Bank defines "agency" as "an individual's (or group's) ability to make effective choices and to transform those choices into desired outcomes. Agency can be understood as the process through which women and men use their endowments and take advantage of economic opportunities to achieve desired outcomes."

Women born on the end cusp of the Second Wave have often viewed feminism as something passé since so many of women's rights were already in place by the time they were raised. The 1980s are considered by many to be a post-feminist decade because of the lack of externalized feminist activism. That moniker, however, does not accurately reflect the reality. Instead of taking to the streets as their forebears had done, many participants in this movement headed to academia via the creation of women's studies programs, with equal opportunity and freedom becoming the accepted norm.

The next generation of feminists, Third Wave Feminism of the 1990s, was led by new thought leaders like Naomi Wolf, Rene Denfeld, Katie Roiphe, and Rebecca Walker. These leaders celebrated a woman's right to pleasure, and power over their victimization. Wolf referred to Second Wave Feminists as "…literally mother figures to the third wave." She defined Third Wave Feminism's evolved mission in saying, "It would have to make joy, rowdiness, and wanton celebration as much a part of its project as hard work and bitter struggle." Though earlier feminists (who developed the wave metaphor) spoke about feminism as a generational phenomenon, authors Dicker and Piepmeier in *Catching a Wave* assert, "We no longer live in the world that Feminists of the Second Wave faced." Third Wave Feminists, they continue, "are therefore concerned not simply with 'women's issues' but with a broad range of interlocking topics."

What is important to recognize and celebrate in the morphing of feminism today is that now, because of these waves of activists from multiple eras, there are increasing possibilities for cross-generational identification with the range of human issues addressed by all feminists and citizens, women and men. This notion is supported by Alyssa Zucker and Abigail Stewart (2007), as reported in their study of 333 university alumnae, which asserted that feminism is internalized quite differently depending on the developmental stage in our lives. Going forward, feminism will no longer be solely based on chronological age or generational biases, but on a shared ideology. This new ideology transforms the old feminist story and firmly implants a new re-storying arc for the future of the human race and for *The Ageless Way.*

I refer to us all as "Clio Feminists," for our stories through the ages matter. In the Greek pantheon, Clio was the historian, archivist, one of the revered nine Muses. Considered the Goddess of History, Clio is a perfect archetypal representation of her modern-day feminist daughters' search for their past by archiving the Herstory of women and our feminist revolution and continuing evolution.

Gertrude Stein's words speak to what our quest as Clio Feminists is all about: "And how do you look backward? By looking forward. And what do you see? As they look forward, they see what they had to do before they could look backward. And there we have it all."

Now back to my Boomer story and our journey together as Clio Feminists who are creating our new story(ies) together.

In the early spring of 1972, my daughter and I returned stateside to the Northeast to find a new family home so I could set it up to coincide with the close of our family's two-and-a-half-year overseas corporate assignment. I was excited to be home again, eager to find friends for us in our new community, and to discover what my professional future might look like after our daughter got to be school age. We were perfectly situated in an upscale professional family community just outside of Manhattan. After settling in, I sought out women who were like me. I saw it as taking on the hummingbird totem and going out in search of women's nectar. I dipped into many different groups of women, from the Junior League and the

American Association of University Women to women's clubs and more. Finally, I realized that although these were organizations of great value, none could give me what I sought. I sought a one-stop haven, a safe place where I could discover my Womanself in the company of other women, where I could co-create futures that would matter for women, where women could show up and make a positive difference wherever our hearths and hearts were called.

So I started my own organization with a handful of friends. We called it the Summit Women's Center, and in our first year we grew to a membership of over one thousand women. What really blew us away was that most of our husbands, (albeit not mine), male friends, and colleagues showed up wanting more of the same. Clearly, they were our evolving brethren on this journey with us. We morphed into an adult growth center for women and the men in our lives.

It was here among these birds of a feather that I gained my wings. I learned who I was at the core and allowed myself to envision my aspirational future. I was in my late twenties, now with a girl and a boy, who to this day are the ones who matter most to me. (Well, that's not entirely true. Now my grandkids have eclipsed their parents!) I was encouraged to tear down my untrue limitations, break through the "I'm not enough" to a mantra of "I'm always more than enough!" and give myself permission to unleash my own Signature Greatness DNA (our unique innate divine-given gift, which everyone has. It is what makes each of us unique and enables us to be conscious human beings with something special to offer in the world which, when shared, helps ignite others' own genius within themselves and those they touch). It was here that I trained and became certified as a career counselor and life planner. I found my new voice as a woman. I learned early on as a science and health teacher that I would always be an educator, with teaching in my cells. I also realized that I would make the greatest possible difference by leveraging myself as a guide for other women on this bold and transformative journey to raise our consciousness, tap into unrealized potential, and change the conversation around who we are as women at every age and for the ages. I can thank Gloria Steinem and Ms. magazine for my life course redirection. Now I had a guide, a role model to whom I could relate.

I went on to create a woman-owned, women-run, and women-staffed company serving other women. My driving mission was to bring other women—moms-at-home, divorcees and widows, single professionals, grandmas—back into the workforce on their own terms. It was a grand success.

What I treasured the most about my involvement in the early days of the Second Wave Feminist Movement of the 1970s was that together we women broke the accepted rules defining a women's place, especially for moms-at-home, that continued to keep most women confined, psychically imprisoned, and suppressed with only one option open to us: to be stay-at-home housewives and moms.

Many of the suburban women in my northern New Jersey community of the early 1970s were company wives and moms with underutilized college degrees. Only a handful had started careers outside the home, but predominantly those women didn't choose to have kids. Others found themselves involved with charity work and volunteering. Most of us back then in the early 1970s were the prototypical transplanted suburban corporate wives, as depicted in the 2008 film *Revolutionary Road* with Kate Winslet and Leonardo diCaprio. Sadly, like the 1940s April, played by Winslet, a large percentage of women, even in the early 1970s, were as frustrated, bored, and depressed as research shows our stay-at-home mothers were before us. Not all, but a great number, of my cohort housewives were popping prescription pills and/or getting through their stultifying days with alcohol.

But not so for some of us, like me and my closest friends, who wanted to break out, to have a life outside the home, and to be independent, able to create our lives, unleash our own potential, and find our place at the kitchen table and in the boardroom. We outliers were on the cusp of the changing times for women. It wasn't easy, but together we proved our value as women, as entrepreneurs, and as working moms.

For those of you today who bypassed the constraints of my coming-of-age years, you may take your women's rights for granted, but please don't. It is only forty-five years or so since we women of the 1970s couldn't get a credit card in our own name. Women could not get a business loan or credit line without a co-signer, typically our husbands. We certainly had a lot of rules to break back then.

And we broke them, for ourselves and for all sisters and daughters in the future. We thought about feminism generationally, the "ages of women" in history and for both our female and male descendants in the future, our daughters and sons. We had you, reader, in mind from the very beginning.

I became a rebel with a cause with my Clio Sisters, wanting to change the world for no other reason than wanting to live a full, and fulfilling, life.

Yet it is a big responsibility to lift the veil of denial and step into our own shoes to change the world, to question the old stories we have lived by, which inform our current life stories. It takes guts and a deep commitment to embrace and carry the wild wisdom of the Inner Visionary Wise Woman into the outer world. In so doing, we risk suffering great losses and facing mighty challenges, as my children and I did.

My initiation into the bowels of the "old story" patriarchal underworld came during the mid-1970s in the midst of the vicious United States judicial backlash against women's liberation. Those of us women, especially mothers and wives who "went astray" by making choices that defied the old story of a woman's place (like the creation of the women's center or working outside our homes), were to be shown our place by those in charge. We were punished for stepping out, stripped down for being empowered and empowering others. Whereas women were almost automatically given child custody rights before this time, the backlash came in the form of removing those rights from mothers who did not automatically play second fiddle to their husbands or went against the patriarchal status quo in any form.

Mine was one of those families torn apart by this old, destructive story.

In the early 1970s, my then-husband dishonored the marital vows that were the foundation of our 1965 post-college-graduation nuptials. If that weren't bad enough, the other shoe dropped a few years after the birth of our second child, a son, when, unbeknownst to me and in spite of our agreement to not move out of the country again, he requested and got an overseas corporate assignment without a return end date. I was left with only one acceptable choice by the powers that be: become the epitome of a perfect corporate spouse. That meant giving up my own life with my kids, my thriving business, my community, my birth family, and the center I founded to follow him around the world. Brought up to believe it was

> Those of us women, especially mothers and wives, who "went astray" by making choices that defied the old story of a woman's place (like the creation of the women's center)...were to be shown our place.

7

my responsibility as a wife and mother to keep my family together, I was determined to stand by my man and our young family.

It didn't work. The marriage couldn't be resuscitated.

A gruesome, vicious, and tragic international custody case ensued, making the 1979 movie *Kramer vs. Kramer* (which won five Academy Awards in 1980) seem like child's play. Due to my "hubris" in not bowing down to the whims of the patriarchy—right in the midst of its ruthless backlash against women (above all feminist mothers)—I was condemned by a male judge known to rule against feminist mothers to suffer the most futile and hopeless life…for a mother to be without custody of her children, and they without me, for almost ten excruciating long years. We were caught between the anti-feminist courts and the emerging children's rights movement of the early 1980s.

I lost my connection to my Soul at that time. I became invisible, having to re-collect my disparate inner parts to make my Soul visible again. I had to face the horrific tragedy that befell my children and me.

In these worst of times, my adopted mantra, as it was for many Clio Feminists, was Helen Reddy's 1971 song "I Am Woman," the lyrics of which gave me a hold on life as the life I had known and cherished was swept away from me. Her lyrics, "I am strong, I am invincible," kept me keepin' on…even today.

Refusing to be suppressed by this patriarchal decision, I committed to three promises that day: 1) I would accept the here and now, 2) I would transcend our separation by re-storying the end of our family story, 3) I swore to the heavens that I would prove to my kids that no one can keep us down and apart. I knew we would rise triumphantly because our fate is in our own hands. And we did.

Those were the 1970s. It was a time of upheaval between the good-girl, good-wife 1950s and early 1960s mores to the free-wheeling, no-holds-barred mid-1960s and into the era of "sex, drugs, and rock 'n' roll"—which begat open marriage, increasing divorce rates, and plummeting wedding vows. This is the story of coming of age for the Leading Edge Boomers as epitomized by Crosby, Stills & Nash's song "Love the One You're With." The rest is history.

For a long while, I asked what purpose this devastating loss had. Now, nearly fifty years later, I can see that this tragic rupture in my early womanhood was my first experience of learning to live in between time and timelessness, chaos and order, space and spacelessness, the living world and the spirit world…only to surface again as the phoenix which rises from the ashes. Most of us think the story of the phoenix ends there. But the best part of this teaching story is that the phoenix gets to sing just one more song. It sings the song of creation. It ushers us into what's next.

My woman's story is a Baby Boomer story (those *born 1943-1967), a teaching story for all of us no matter our chronological age or life cycle. Too many Boomer women have a story to tell about how they were wronged by their partner, their "BFF," their boss, and the patriarchal system. Storytelling is what connects us over the millennia. Sharing our stories is how Boomer women "raised consciousness"—the question is, what use should we make of those "victim" stories and experiences now? What purpose does the Boomer women's story of courage against all odds serve?

Our stories shatter us into compassion and action. Now that we are in catastrophic times, it is only in story that we can find what J.R.R. Tolkien calls our "eu-catastrophe," the possibility for new life, which comes to us only after all hope is lost.

I had weathered the losses and mined the gold from the dross of lost hope. Against all odds, I had risen to prominence in the financial services and direct marketing industry, married my true love and reunited with my kids. But something was still missing. Now in my late thirties, confronting

> **My woman's story is a Baby Boomer story.**

---

* Never hold Boomers to fixed definitions. We have a propensity to self-contradict and change the rules as we evolve (e.g., "Don't trust anyone over thirty!"). So don't waste your time constraining us by rigid cohort groups. A wide spectrum of opinions exist on what *is* a Baby Boomer, demographically, historically, and culturally. The U.S. Census Bureau brackets Boomers based on the spike (boom) in birthrate from 1946 to 1964. Perhaps because this is an easy range to recall, it has garnered widespread popularity. However, I find myself in the camp embracing 1943 as the starting and 1967 as the last year of the Baby Boomer generation. I'm in good company with Landon Jones, in his book *Great Expectations: America & the Baby Boom Generation* (1980). Authors William Strauss and Neil Howe, creators of the Strauss-Howe generational theory, also define the social genera-tion of Boomers inclusive of those born starting in 1943. No matter which generation we are referring to it is important to soften the boundaries of our definitions so that we are inclusive of less defined beginnings and endings to allow for the gray areas.

the coming big 40, my desire to understand what it means to become an older woman who mattered and made a positive difference moved back into the forefront of my thoughts. But I hadn't a clue what to do about it. After all, I finally "had it all," so why bother to shake things up again? It is when we least expect it that our true life purpose reveals itself like an encrypted message long engraved in our book of life.

It happened out of the blue.

As I was readying myself for a wedding, I glanced once more in the antique gilded mirror. As I looked at my reflected image, I gasped and held my breath. My youthful joie de vivre image had transformed before my eyes into an old, old, old woman shrouded in black. She was me, but was not. She had more wrinkles than I had ever seen. Her gaze appeared to go through me into eternity and back again. I was overwhelmed with awe.

She cackled and crowed. Her sounds called to me. Sounds that vibrated within. I felt a quickening that pierced my soles, moved up from my toes, through my spine and into my pelvis. I was a cauldron of fire, the vapors spreading within. I was moved to dance, to swirl. As I turned in a dervish of sacred dance, I looked again into the mirror.

This old woman's dark eyes penetrated, staring through me. No words formed on her lips. Instead her eyes spoke to me. Yet I could feel her message as if she were speaking out loud, reflecting both my ancestral maternal line and our collective heritage. She told me that my time was coming. "Prepare yourself! You will be needed to awaken this energy…to bring the light… to ignite." Then, as quietly and mysteriously as she had appeared, she was gone. (Thank goodness my soon-to-be new husband had witnessed this exchange, or I would have thought I was hallucinating or going mad!) This old, old one—the Crone—was a messenger of what was yet to come.

She is my Inner Ageless Visionary, the womansoul, womenself within me whose eyes see all ages of woman I come from, I am in my living present, and I will be in my future. I call her Ancient Future.

Edward Edinger, psychologist, helped me to understand this was a numinous experience by explaining, "An experience is numinous when it carries an excess of meaning or energy, transcending the capacity of the conscious personality to encompass or understand it."

> My youthful joie de vivre image had transformed before my eyes into an old, old, old woman shrouded in black. She was me, but was not. She had more wrinkles than I had ever seen.

Ancient Future's appearance was life changing, a calling.

The old story of aging women in our culture was one of derision, that crones were "frightening aged hags." (Even www.merriam-webster.com defines a crone as "a cruel or ugly old woman.") Despite having grown up hearing that interpretation, I recognized her as a representative of an even more ancient archetypal story (and now part of the new story), someone who had reached an age of great wisdom and power, trusted her inner knowing, and had valuable knowledge to share. Had I ignored her, I would have most likely stayed stuck in my own old story with limiting beliefs about my capabilities and options. She ushered me along a new career path. I had gone into and left Corporate America at the peak of a career revered by our culture. Despite the odds for a woman in Corporate America in the 1980s, I became a visionary leader, change agent, and expert in the Graying of America and its impact on the future.

Ancient Future was my portal to now. She embodied age and transcended age; she was my visionary, and a visionary, a seer of and for the ages, calling me to become an Ageless Visionary like she was.

Her visitation compelled me to return to post-graduate school in my early forties to become an educational gerontologist specializing in creative living and Conscious Aging across the life course. My renewed life's mission is to sound the clarion call that it's time to create new models of aging that will rock our age! I've also become a champion for intergenerational conversations on our future and the future of aging. Leveraging my many years as a serial entrepreneur and intrapreneurial start-up and turnaround pro, I continue to consult and coach on the business of aging and women's role in leading the evolution of aging in the marketplace, the workplace, and your place.

Along the way, I continue to be blessed to witness the unfolding of women's personal and professional lives (also of the men in their lives) and the rise of the Conscious Feminine power within them as they move through the cycles and along the spirals of the continuum of life into death and the afterlife. But there is more…

Ancient Future's sudden and startling appearance beckoned me into my coming of age and my future old and old, old age. She gave me the

Don't hold us back,
we're the story you tell,"
And no sooner than spoken,
a spell had been broken
And the voices before her
were trumpets and tympani
Violins, basses and woodwinds
and cellos, singing
We're so glad that you
finally made it here
You thought nobody cared,
but we did, we could tell
And now you'll dance
through the days
while the orchestra plays
And oh, you're aging well.

~ Dar Williams
"You're Aging Well," written
and performed by Dar Williams,
1993, Honesty Room, Razor & Tie
(lyrics owned by Dar Williams)

courage to begin to lift my own veils of denial of my own aging, to take stock of the quality of my life and how I wanted to live the years ahead in midlife and now, having just turned 71, in the time I have left. The pivotal moment of crossing the threshold into my seventies is one of many on my Ageless Quest. No doubt there are more to come for me and you, too. We never stop growing and evolving across the life span. Perhaps the greatest gift of all is that Ancient Future connected me with the legacies of past generations of women and my place in creating a legacy for those to come. Ancient Future shined a light so I could learn and embrace *The Ageless Way*. She connected me to my own Agelessness and welcomed me on the Ageless Quest that has led to this book, which will illuminate *The Ageless Way* for you.

The time has come for me to share what I know and have learned about following *The Ageless Way,* about living creatively and Aging Consciously as a woman at every age, cycle, and stage, to open a dialogue with you about what you can do to embrace who you are and fully recognize what you are capable of—now more than ever. Our age is our time!

Now is the time for the new story of our age.

Now is the time for us all to walk *The Ageless Way.*

This book lights the way to live agelessly, whatever age we are. ❯

INTRODUCTION:

THE NEW STORY OF OUR AGE

We are deep into the night. From this point on all sense of time doth cease to exist. Only space and the sensory, that which we feel and experience becomes the manifestation of all the cosmic waves of the universe. The sound poisons the brain, and pushes all barriers to the outer limits of perception, and we are in space. We are above and beyond. Come fly with me.

~Allison Steele, The Night Bird, at WNEW-FM

We all have a deep, universal longing to be Ageless. The search for the Fountain of Youth and elixirs bestowing eternal life has been recounted around the world for millennia. Our obsessions with eternal youth are captured in myths, fairy tales, contemporary film, and the dreamscapes, which are revealed to more and more of us.

Today, with the advent of modern anti-aging therapies, there is a new age that looks like no age at all. Women are feeling increasing pressure not just to look good for their age, but also to never actually age at all.

But that's the old story in new wrapping.

In *The Fountain of Age* (1993), Betty Friedan describes a crucial element of this old story: "All forms of denial of age…ultimately spring that dread trap we try to avoid. How long, and how well, can we really live by trying to pass as young?" Friedan continues to explain the problem that keeps us stuck in our second childhood vs. striking out on a new uncharted segment of life's trek into eternity: "Seeing age only as decline from youth, we make age itself the problem…and never face the real problems that keep us from evolving and leading continually useful, vital, and productive lives."

Please turn back to my preface for a fuller historic exploration of feminism in our old story, our current narrative, and in our new story being re-storied together as we traverse *The Ageless Way.*

The new story is a radical reinvention of what it means to age across our life course; it requires new imagination of what's possible. It requires transcending age, not denying it. *The Ageless Way* is the new story of our times.

To deny your age is to deny yourself," Oprah said recently. Amen to that. Conversely, admitting your age is empowering not only yourself but every woman who is made to feel less valuable because she is over forty. Or fifty. Or seventy.

~ Suzanne Braun Levine, HuffPost50

The new story of *The Ageless Way* weaves together the re-storying of Agelessness and Ageless Aging into contemporary terms. It speaks of internalizing the quality of being timeless and eternal no matter our age or stage of life, not using age to define or limit our capabilities. In chapter one, we'll be taking a deeper dive into this new story, revealing more about what it means to be Ageless vs. falling into the seduction of anti-aging (where we strive to deny age or to be no age at all).

> All of us alive today are part of writing this new story, a story in which Boomer women, now grown and even more empowered than in the 1970s, are leading the way with new vision...again.

All of us alive today are part of writing this new story, a story in which Boomer women, now grown and even more empowered than in the 1970s, are leading the way with new vision...again. Given our experience, we are able to reach across generations and share tools, resources, and ideas to radically reinvent what it means to be a woman who is always aging Agelessly as she moves across her life course. Regardless of age, we are all being called together as Friedan admonishes us, to unite and "step out into the true existential unknown of these new years of life now open to us, and to find our own terms for living it."

To shed any fear of growing older, many of us are freeing our last remaining patriarchal restraints so that we can unleash our wildest wisdom and experience our true essence, our innate potential for distinction (Signature

Greatness DNA). These epoch-shifting times are our best chance to throw off our real and metaphorical restraints, especially as we age.

I am convinced all of humanity is born with more gifts than we know. Most are born geniuses and just get de-geniused rapidly.

~ R. Buckminster Fuller

We are at a distinct moment in women's history when our sheer numbers give us unheard-of voting power and financial clout with which to reshape the conversation around growing older. We do not need to deny our age in order to live *The Ageless Way*. Rather, when it comes to our dreams and our ability to reinvent ourselves and make a difference in our world, our age is not a weakness but a strength. We now have the experience, the wisdom, and the focus on what really matters that we need to live our true potential, to reimagine our lives, and to change the world in unimaginable ways. We are the authors of a new story about an age-friendly future.

We are the authors of a new story about an age-friendly future.

Ageless Beginnings

In Feminine thinking, we hold the paradox beyond the contradictions.

~ Marion Woodman, Dancing in the Flames (1996)

Today's women are already a force for positive change and transformation. We have set the stage to reframe what it means to be an older woman going forward, for ourselves and for the younger generations who will stand on our shoulders. We can redefine our role and societal position as older women by embodying what I refer to as Ageless Wisdom and ushering in a new triumphant Ageless Story for our times—and for generations to come.

We women are storytellers. Our stories are also called "yarns"—they are the threads that hold together families, communities, and friendships, connecting generation to generation over the millennia. They mend broken hearts, inspire greatness, and comfort and soothe in troubled times. Now we have the opportunity to weave *The Ageless Way* into our life stories and into our cultural story.

In drama, the beginning of the story always defines the ending. Those of us on the Leading Edge of the 1960s were about peace, the Earth, our bodies, ourselves. Now in our eleventh hour, as the oldest among us head out of our sixties, (along with those on the cusp of the Leading Edge), we are returning to our "lost" values and aspirations for the future.

In the early 1970s, our Second Wave Feminist visionary sisters sought one another out to form consciousness-raising groups to lift our voices in unison, to value our stories, embrace "our bodies, ourselves," recognize our contributions, and give choice a chance. (The original book *Women and Their Bodies, Our Bodies, Ourselves* [1970] was an underground blockbuster compiled by the Boston Women's Health Book Collective and was renamed *Our Bodies, Ourselves* in 1973, when it was published by Simon & Schuster).

The same women who broke the rules and raised the glass ceiling now face the silver ceiling, and we want answers. We thought we were savvy, prepared for life after 40. However, now we are unsure how to move into and through our fifties, sixties, or seventies, much less our eighties and some of us into our nineties and beyond. More and more women today are online seeking out women of the same world view regardless of demographics, hoping to find answers to questions not yet asked out loud.

As long ago as 1982, John Naisbitt coined the term "high tech, low touch," forewarning us of the dangers of isolation and disconnection ahead in the Information Society afterbirth. I interpreted this term to mean that we must consciously choose to retain our humanness and connection over any technology that promises us connectivity but removes us from one another and ourselves.

It is no surprise then that in these epoch-shifting times, storytelling is on the rise again. Personal stories. Organizational stories. National and universal stories. We are seeking connection and understanding. We are searching for answers.

Yet we also want to know which questions to ask! What's the history of older women? The Herstory of our past? How far back do we need to reach to find a time when Elders were revered as wise leaders? When women lived in touch with Mother Nature and their own nature? As we move forward into the unknown, uncharted future of the Longevity Economy, can we bring forward this holistic *Ageless Way* of living into our preferred future? Can we "hold the paradox" of nature and technology, connection and individuality, time and timelessness? I believe we can, and that is what this book is about. We are the visionaries who will bring all generations to the round table, to re-story the old story and create our new Ageless Story together.

Why We Need A New Story

As soon as a woman gets to an age where she has opinions and she's vital, and she's strong, she's systematically shamed into hiding under a rock. And this is by progressive, pop-culture people. My crime is...not dying?

~ Sarah Silverman

The old story about aging and women won't willingly take its place in the past tense, nor will we easily disconnect from the generations of re-telling. To my total disbelief, it is now again being promulgated by the conservative media, (e.g., Rush Limbaugh's rants against women's rights), politicians (like Texas Governor Rick Perry vs. the valiant attempts of Texas Senator Wendy Davis's filibustering in the Texas Senate in June 2013), and most dastardly, the Supreme Court's two 2014 major rulings limiting health insurance coverage for contraception and giving protesters increased rights to demonstrate outside women's health-care centers and abortion clinics. Consider any number of recent rulings that, once again, decimated our freedom of choice on every level while perpetuating the old story about "women's place" in our current times and going forward into the future.

This narrative is seeping into the psyches of savvy voters here in the States, who are, unbeknownst to them, being lured into keeping ageism alive and well.

To my utter shock, I've heard from clients, colleagues, and even family members, that Hillary Clinton is too old to run for president in 2016. Yet, when I press for an age that is "too old," no one is able to answer me. *There is no such age.* The myth that there is has its roots in views and expectations about aging that have gone unquestioned for decades, perhaps centuries. It does not seem to be changing even as we live longer, healthier, active lives to unprecedented ages.

There's something else emerging from the shadows here. Let's get real: We've had a long history of older men presidents. So what gives?

The once accepted over-the-hill after 30 mantra is now morphing extending our expiry date to over 40. Is this a result of our multiple generations butting heads in the marketplace and workforce? Or is our young vs. old youth-oriented culture just a natural outgrowth of our fixation on our youth? Then what about all of us over 50, 60, 70 or beyond? Aren't we part of the new youthing culture?

The entire concept of there being some magic number when we're too old to lead, to pursue our greatest visions, to change the world, is a myth. We parrot it, even to ourselves, believing we're too old to try something new or to take the next big leap. We rarely think to question it, yet when we do, we find it falls apart. Ageism has no basis in reality.

Ageism has no basis in reality.

Of course with the entry of the elder Trump and Sanders into the Presidential race, Hillary Clinton's age is moot, so age is not the only issue here.

Both genders experience ageism, but for women the bigotry is especially potent. Ageism is always mixed with and strengthened by sexism. As much as many liberal progressives might like to believe that both forms of prejudice exist only in the Republican narrative, the truth is that they are embedded in society's story about aging and women, in our story. No matter our political stance, age, or gender, we have all internalized this narrative to some degree.

It's time to change the story we tell as a society and the story we tell to and about ourselves. For women, especially, the old misogynistic story about aging is a powerful weapon against us, no matter our age, stage, or cycle, a mis-story that starts when we're young, in how *we* view older women, and only builds from there, preventing us from realizing the potential for greatness that ripens in our Third and Fourth Age.

We owe it to ourselves and to generations to come to step forward visibly and be not who we should be as we age but who we can be. The Age of Greatness is in our grasp, not only as individuals but also as a nation and a planet.

In reading about, and journeying on, *The Ageless Way*, some of you may feel uncertain about the idea (or accompanying wording) simply because it is unfamiliar and takes us into the unknown. Of course, whenever there is innovation and we are on the verge of a new idea, action, or perspective (as we are doing by creating a new story for our age), it will include the emergence of some unfamiliar language ("trade lingo"), metaphors, and narratives. Initially, some of these may seem unfamiliar because we are in the process of defining the way, though, as with other pioneering efforts throughout history, the terminology will likely morph from the unknown (hence be slightly discomfiting) to become universal, even commonplace. As one example, consider terms devised and utilized for various aspects of technology over the years. Wording that was completely new at one time is now part of our culture, such as television(!), radio, fax machines, computers, the web, hashtag, apps, smartphone, emoji, Google.

As a leading GeroFuturist[SM]—a unique combination of a gerontologist, who studies adult development and aging through the life course, and a futurist, who studies the future using strategic forecasting and futurecasting—I have spent decades researching, teaching, and transforming the language and conversation around growing older. My intention at this timely juncture is to share that experience in order to illuminate the way for all of us, of all ages, to co-create a new story that is relevant for today and the future. It is a story with personal, communal, and global implications that, as with any new endeavor, will inevitably include trial and error and refinement. And we can only succeed if we do it together. It will take each of us, as a Jackie Mutcheson quote goes, to make a difference for all of us.

Your Ageless Quest

Stop talking about my age! Your age always has to be mentioned and men don't really get that for some reason. It's not like you see Joe Schmo, 37.

~ Jennifer Aniston

Wherever I show up, especially as a speaker, I'm asked the same questions that catapulted me on my own Ageless Quest in my youth. However it's phrased, it comes down to the same over arching question for everyone, no matter their generation: *"Who am I if I'm no longer young?"* This question is most often followed by exasperated pleas: "I still have so much I want to do. I want to make a positive difference while combining doing well with doing good. I want to be relevant and self-sufficient! What's next for me? And how do I get there?"

To find some new answers to what it means to be a visible older woman and to ascertain our new role in creating a future that works, I spoke with women all over the United States about their views on aging and living a full life. In particular, I interviewed women visionaries over 60 years old—I was seeking answers and guidance that I wanted to share with other women asking the same questions I was asking.

The best of these Ageless conversations with visionary women are collected in my book *Visionaries Have Wrinkles: Conversations with Wise Women Who Are Reshaping the Future* (2012). The women I interviewed not only tell it like it is, but also show us how it can be. Their voices are those of interesting, everyday women who have lived, and are living, extraordinary lives.

The women whose stories I share in *Visionaries Have Wrinkles* have been creating their legacy for those of us who follow for a very long time. Several have passed on since I first started my interviews years ago. Some are still spreading the word. These conversations and personal encounters helped me reframe what it means to live passionately, impactfully, and consciously at every age. These women gifted me with knowing the importance of re-storying a triumphant ending to our ending stories.

With this book, *The Ageless Way*, I explore more deeply the unknown, uncharted landscape of long life and being an Ageless Woman, including learning and embracing *The Ageless Way,* as well as some attributes that invite Agelessness. These can include truth-telling, a sense of freedom, deepened love and sexuality, adaptability to change, transparency, living between chaos and order, being creative and playful, wisdom seeking and keeping, presence, vibrancy, discernment, the ability to balance and wield visibility and invisibility, being triumphant in the face of challenge and hardship, and so much more. Some of these attributes coincide with the benefits of aging I will describe in chapter three. All of them (and more) are attributes found in visionaries, for to be Ageless is to be visionary and to be visionary is to be Ageless. The women I interviewed for *Visionaries Have Wrinkles* were Ageless Women. What I learned from them has only enriched and deepened the learnings of my own Ageless Quest, my own understanding of what it means to embrace *The Ageless Way*, and be ever evolving into a Visionary with Wrinkles, an Ageless Visionary.

> ...to be Ageless is visionary and to be visionary is to be Ageless.

Nevertheless, even with the discoveries I have made on my own journey, so much of what's ahead of me is still unknown territory. I find myself tracking the ages of those highlighted in the obituaries. It is noticeable that most of the ages of death fall into the 80-plus range. Our ability to extend our lives even into our one hundreds is nearly unprecedented. We don't have a rule book or even a map. We don't know how to do this thing called long life.

Since none of us knows this new territory, we will explore it together by diving into the discovery process. Going forward, we will attempt to break down our outdated assumptions and limited expectations while dismantling myths and outright lies around aging and our role as women. Together, we'll invent new rules and definitions for aging into the future. We will craft a new Ageless Story for our times, and for generations to come, one that is sure to bring about greater peace, abundance, and well-being.

Modeling the Starship Enterprise's motto: We'll boldly go where no one has gone before.

I hope that this book will add to the reservoir of knowledge and the growing interest in the emerging field of Positive Aging. Additionally, I place special attention on an emerging new developmental stage and level of psychological functioning called Conscious Aging, which is rooted in trans personal, transformational, and depth psychology, along with life span development and spirituality. Conscious Aging focuses on the intentional inner journey for adapting well to the challenges of aging, while also creating new roles for Elders in our society to mentor, nurture, and join with the generations to follow. I'm excited to welcome you on this quest to actively engage with, and help create, this new Ageless paradigm.

These themes remain the basis of my ongoing work and keep me on my path to changing the conversation around aging to one about Agelessness, and *The Ageless Way*, thus turning the old story of aging on its head. In so doing, we will be freed to co-create Aspirational Ageless Futures (Sands, 2011) we can be proud to live and leave behind (more about all of this in chapter one).

AGELESS FUTURES

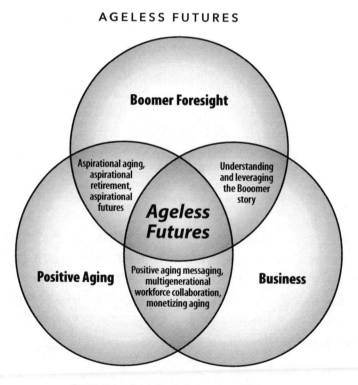

In this book, I look at some of the history—and myths—of aging in order to reorient us in relation to the past. In addition to looking at contemporary dreams and stories, including science fiction, for clues to our future as women, I track and interpret trends (for strategic forecasting and futurecasting) in an attempt to discern the quality and lasting nature of the new story of Ageless Aging and *The Ageless Way* as it emerges today.

It is Baby Boomer women (those who inspired and are now living *The Ageless Way*) who are at the forefront of catapulting all women (all people) into a new age of Agelessness as they change what it means to be an older person who matters. Though I have written this book from the vantage point of my experience as a Boomer woman, I would be remiss if I did not also keep referencing the entire 40-plus market, which includes three generations: Gen Xers; Boomers; and Matures. It will take each of us to make a difference for all of us. Once the gray ceiling is shattered, all generations, current and future, will benefit.

Recognizing the dawning of a new Agelessness moving through the collective, I look at some of the recent scientific discoveries concerning ageism, anti-aging, aging, and longevity, including new findings and theories in neuroscience that provide more in-depth understanding of how we approach aging over our life course. I also explore encore careers (Marc Freedman coined "Encore," 2007) and the growing sector of women solopreneurs, including "grannypreneurs" and others. Hopefully, new thoughts and connections will open new eyes and ears to what it means to be Ageless and to serve the future, not because of our generation or date of birth, but because of our shared aspirations for a future that matters… and that works for all of us across generations.

The more I have explored aging, women, and the future, the more I realize that the conversation about aging will never change unless we expand it. The assumptions and stereotypes about aging cannot be transcended culturally if we do not make a global, multigenerational effort to do so. We all age. Learning how to age and evolve consciously will not only benefit us as individuals; it will benefit all of humanity.

Our Ageless Quest

Those of us who grew up in the era of not trusting anyone over 30 are now well past 30 ourselves. We are the "old" ones on the edge of a new story…about to break down all historical and modern-day barriers defining us by demographics alone, especially by our chronological age and generation.

Imagine the effect we can have on the world if we no longer discount the contributions we can make after we turn 40, much less beyond midlife, but instead collectively transform ourselves to be even greater, to fully express our gifts and passions, and to lead the world into the Age of Greatness.

Instead of feeling increasingly alone, or overwhelmed, in the face of personal and global tragedy—job loss, market crashes, recession, loss of loved ones, poverty, climate change, rogue viruses, terrorism, and war—we can work together to reinvent the world as we reinvent ourselves. The more we unleash our greatness, the greater the impact we can have on the world.

This potential for greatness is within us all, in our DNA, and we can unlock it and transform ourselves at any age or stage. Accomplishing this gets much easier with each passing year, as we have the experience, wisdom, and perspective necessary for transcending the myopic stories first inherited as children (and reinforced into adulthood) from our families, our communities, and our society. As you will see in chapter one, this transcendence is part of what it means to be Ageless, to know *The Ageless Way*. Even one individual achieving it can have an enormous impact on the world.

Never forget that you are one of a kind. Never forget that if there weren't any need for you in all your uniqueness to be on this earth, you wouldn't be here in the first place. And never forget, no matter how overwhelming life's challenges and problems seem to be, that one person can make a difference in the world. In fact, it is always because of one person that all the changes that matter in the world come about. So be that one person.

~ R. Buckminster Fuller

But let's face it. A handful of individual transformations isn't enough to change the course our Earth is on, and as much as we can gain from our own transformation in the short term, it won't mean much if we do not have a world in which we can truly embrace our full potential. And living on for generations in the legacy we leave may be meaningless if our world cannot sustain those generations.

We can each individually achieve Agelessness and embrace *The Ageless Way*. However, an Ageless Future relies on a collective transformation of people at all ages and stages, and that is the ultimate goal of this book. Throughout, I discuss what it means to be Ageless, what it means to embrace *The Ageless Way,* and how these concepts apply to everything from work and business, to health and beauty, to love and loss and beyond. These are just our first steps to change the world. It is in these everyday steps, these changes in how we live and work and age, that we can begin changing the world today and modeling the Ageless Future we can have tomorrow.

Stories and myths allow us to tap into what is Ageless. In stories and myths, we tap the collective and bring forth what at first is only imagined—stories and myths are powerful, and the metaphors we live by matter.

Our personal stories are sacred. Each individual life story arc—from our birth to our death—defines our destiny. Around ancient and modern day campfires. In the consciousness raising groups (aka CR groups) of yesteryear. Sitting next to a stranger on a plane telling truths to someone whom you likely will never see again. As a participant in personal growth circles, therapy, addiction, and coaching groups. In all of these ways, and more, sharing our stories is our attempt to find meaning in our very existence, in our everyday lives, in our world and in the cosmos. Most impactful of all is finding meaning in our personal sacred stories so we can re-story the ending to be one worth living for—a triumphant life fully lived. Now that's EPIC!

To deepen our exploration in this book, I have woven in sacred teaching stories: modern and ancient myths, fairy tales, and dreams to illuminate and show us the way to our new Ageless Story for our times.

In the afterglow of completing this manuscript, I found my way to a book by mythologist and author Phil Cousineau, *Once and Future Myths*, (2001) that lay long unopened waiting for me to find the time to be gifted

Sharing our stories is our attempt to find meaning in our very existence, in our everyday lives, in our world and in the cosmos.

its treasures. I felt like I was being given communion as I read Cousineau's elegant words:

> The old storytellers knew this. They knew that every life is mythic, that each of our myths, our sacred stories, is the outpouring of deep longing for meaning, which confers purpose to our lives. To those who go beyond appearances and seek truth of their lives, everything is a symbol, everything a story, everything mythic, and the discovery of these things, back at the beginning, is an uncanny kind of coming home. This is a deep urge to seek out the lonely meaning of myth.

I invite you to join me as we step forward on our Ageless Quest (Sands, 2001). Together, we can create a whole new luminous and triumphant Ageless Story to serve as a beacon for finding our way home to *The Ageless Way* and forging new or expanded metaphors for our Aspirational Ageless Future, (Sands, 2001).

Our story isn't over.
It has just begun! ❯

STORY WATER

A story is like water
that you heat for your bath.
It takes messages between the fire
and your skin. It lets them meet,
and it cleans you!

Very few can sit down
in the middle of the fire itself
like a salamander or Abraham.
We need intermediaries.

A feeling of fullness comes,
but usually it takes some bread
to bring it.

Beauty surrounds us, but usually
we need to be walking
in a garden to know it.

The body itself is a screen
to shield and partially reveal
to light that's blazing
inside your presence.

Water, stories, the body,
all the things we do, are mediums
that hide and show what's hidden.

Study them,
and enjoy this being washed
with a secret we sometimes know,
and then not.

~ Rumi,
thirteenth-century Sufi poet

About the Ageless Way Reflections

Questions at the end of each chapter to help you find your distinct path on The Ageless Way.

Each new story or phase of life needs a creative approach to move beyond the past into a creative new hope-filled future story with the new tasks that it encompasses.

I'd like to shine a light to guide you on your quest to *The Ageless Way* by including some suggestions for getting the most out of this book. Consider my suggestions as a guide.

I've included *Reflections* at the end of each chapter to translate the substance of each chapter into portable tools for your own illumination. These *Reflections* are intended as jumping-off points for you to dig in to the chapter material as deep as you desire. I have arranged these in the general order as they arise by chapter.

Putting something in writing often solidifies new material in our minds, and allows new "ahas" to arise unimpeded. Consider writing down your answers to the *Reflections* provided at the end of each chapter instead of just scanning or reading them and moving on.

My suggestion is that you familiarize yourself with these reflective questions and exercises by doing them once through in the order they appear. However, once you've read through the book, or a particular chapter, I encourage you to use them in any sequence that suits you.

What works well is to make a copy of the *Reflections* and then spend focused time reflecting and writing down your answers. Commit to returning to these questions regularly to see how your answers change over time.

When you are ready to give your focused time to a chapter's *Reflections*, find a quiet space for reflection at a time when you won't be disturbed. You may want to settle into your favorite comfy chair or another spot that is your special chilling out, meditating, or time-out reflecting place. Relax using any process that has worked for you in the past, perhaps using a series of deep breaths and slowly relaxing and letting go wherever there is tension in your body. You'll know when you are ready to gently come back into the room. Be sure you have a pen and the list of *Reflections* you will be working on close at hand. Give yourself at least fifteen to twenty minutes at each sitting to journal your responses and insights gained. I have found that these *Reflections* will provide invaluable insights if you give yourself the gift of reserved, uninterrupted time to be with yourself.

If you have any questions or you want to share your "ahas" or stories, please send them to me directly at Karen@KarenSands.com, putting "TAW queries" in the subject line.

Thank you for joining me on the quest to *The Ageless Way.* ❯

– Karen

A Free Gift From Karen

Download a FREE COPY of *The Ageless Way Reflections Journal*
(companion workbook to *The Ageless Way*) at
KarenSands.com/the-ageless-way/workbook

Watch Karen speak about being Ageless
and welcome you to *The Ageless Way!*
KarenSands.com/ageless

They say, "I'm so glad
that you finally made it here
You thought nobody cared
but I did, I could tell
And this is your year
and it always starts here
And oh oh oh,
you're aging well

~ Dar Williams
"You're Aging Well," written and performed by Dar Williams,
1993, Honesty Room, Razor & Tie (lyrics owned by Dar Williams)

$$Chapter\ 1$$

THE AGELESS WAY

I'm tripping out on getting older…my awareness is shifting…
subtle shifts. I admit I'm holding on to my thought that "I'm fine
with aging."…BUT lately…I'm noticing now that I'm the oldest in
groups, in my circles… it's beginning to get my attention.

~Helene S., age 45

The stories we tell ourselves and one another are what inform and shape how we live and age…and how we show up in the world. It's time now to clean up our outmoded past stories and our "now" stories about what it means to age, what it means to be Ageless, and how to be firmly moving forward on our Ageless Quest to follow *The Ageless Way*.

In *Once and Future Myths*, Phil Cousineau states it this way: "Understanding of the stories at the heart of our lives that reveal—in a way nothing-else can—just how it is that we choose—our destinies." I couldn't agree more.

What Does It Mean to Be Ageless?

It's a Shift. It's a Stage. It's a Perspective. It's a Way of Being. It's a Gift.

My new favorite folktale, *The Old Woman's Hide,* of Italian origin, selected and retold by Italo Calvino (1956), shines the light on what it means to be Ageless by allowing us to "try it on for size." In so doing, we can trick the Fates as we face the challenges and reap the rewards of following *The Ageless Way* by spinning our own feminine destiny and re-storying our lives on our own terms.

The tale opens with a king, a father of three daughters, preparing to leave on a trip to a faraway fair. Being a generous and loving dad, he asks each of his girls what gift she would like for him to bring back to her. The oldest of the girls asks for a kerchief, the middle daughter asks for high-top shoes, and the youngest asks for a box of salt. The king, befuddled by his youngest and favorite daughter's request for such a large amount of salt, yet wanting nothing pretty for herself, asks the two eldest daughters why. The sisters respond on cue, "To pickle you of course, dear father."

Totally thrown by their explanation, yet believing them, he goes into a hurtful rage and tells his youngest that she must leave his castle, and curses her with poverty and misery. At the last possible moment, the king softens and realizes he can't send her out into the world unprotected and empty-handed. He commands her Elder woman nursemaid to join her on her journey and gives his princess a small bag of gold.

Never having left the protected confines of the castle before, the lovely maiden princess finds herself both confused by and afraid of the unwanted attention and sexual advances from the men they meet on their way. This is an experience many of us know all too well, whether while transitioning from pre-pubescence into adolescence, leaving our father's house (and perhaps our husband's house), or in our mature years when we find ourselves on our own in what is still a man's world.

As they wander, they come upon a grave digger who is about to dig the grave for an Elder woman who had just died at the age of 100. Since back then, even more than now, a 100-year-old woman would connote a Crone with great lived wisdom, the nursemaid protectress has an "aha" flash and asks the grave digger, "Please will you sell us this old woman soul's hide?"

After a few rounds of haggling, they agree on a price and "the grave digger picks up a knife, skins the old woman wrinkle by wrinkle, and sews her whole hide together with face, white hair, fingers, and nails." Then the nursemaid lines it with cambric and makes the girl a dress of it. Now the princess has a hide to hide within, symbolic of our own Inner Maiden archetype hidden deep within our psyche, below the surface.

Disguised as a Crone, her humor, delight, zest, and boldness rise to the surface safe from untoward advances and possible rape.

True to all our heroic myths, an unknown prince rides by. He hears the "young old" girl chattering and cavorting and is so taken by this spry, energized, and very funny old one that he asks, "How old are you, old one?" Our sassy, outspoken girl in the old skin answers with, "I'm a hundred and fifteen."

Taken aback, he questions her further. "Where did you come from?" With a smile she responds, "From my town." Not satisfied, yet amused, he asks, "Who are your parents?" Without hesitation she responds, "I'm my own mother and father." "Then what is your occupation?" the prince continues to probe. This time, when the girl in the old hide says, "Having a good time!" the prince loses his composure and bursts into a belly laugh. He has such a good time, he decides to take the old Crone home with him to keep him company and make him laugh for as long as she manages to live.

Our Hide Crone, having passed through her own crossroads, has learned to accept, to surrender her ego wants, and to accept her destiny. This deep acceptance of her destiny is what unites her Hide Crone with her hidden maiden. This new sense of freedom to stand in her own shoes, to raise her voice, brings with it a childlike energy—one of spontaneity, play, laughter, and creativity. It is the maiden (represented by the Virgin in the feminine trinity of the Virgin/Maiden, the Mother/Adult Woman, and the Crone) who is forever transforming into the maturity of the Crone all along *The Ageless Way*.

The prince's mother, the queen, calls our maiden in the old hide "Rotten Eyes," because her eyes are unreadable and look bleary from the bland coloration of the hide. The queen admonishes our Maiden-Crone saying, "Too bad you can't spin anymore with your poor vision." Our virginal Maiden-Crone responds that when she was young she was a very fine spinner, so the queen commands that she spin.

In seconds after the queen leaves, the maiden locks the door, jumps out of her old skin, and sits down to spin the flax into beautiful thread, passing the queen's test with ease.

Not believing her eyes, the queen asks Rotten Eyes to make her a blouse "so you can clothe your heart and throat chakra in beauty of your own making."

No surprise, as soon as she is alone our Maiden-Crone locks the door and pulls the hide off again. She "cut it out, (the blouse), sewed it up, and embroidered the front with the daintiest gold flowers you ever saw." As you and I know, folk and fairy tales are never to be taken literally…her embroidered golden flowers represent her own flowering and the dawn of her golden age.

But now it's not just the queen who is in doubt. Now everyone is suspicious…primarily the king's son, the prince, who spies on her the next time she locks her door. That's when the prince sees her transform from a Crone. Like any good prince, he breaks down the door and embraces the girl, demanding to know why she has been disguising herself as an old one. Our maiden spills the beans, explaining that she is the child of a king who has cursed her and disowned her.

The Crone Energy, depicted here as Hide, is strong enough to guide both men and women into the Sacred Dark Feminine of the emerging Virgin and the Crone where they can experience their own Shadow Feminine. A marriage symbolizes the integration of both aspects into wholeness.

A wedding celebration is held, and all the kings and queens far and wide are invited, including our princess Hide's father. Our princess asks that she be in charge of the preparation of her father's food, and asks that no salt be added to his food except for the roast to be served last.

To the princess' delight, after each first taste the King doesn't eat the boiled meat, nor the fish, but gobbles up the roast.

When the bride comes to reveal herself to her father, she asks him what was the matter with his meal that he took only one bite and had no more until the roast. Her father tells her that "the roast is so delicious, full of flavor, and everything else had no taste," to which she responds, "So now you see how awful food is without any salt in it?" Proudly, she tells him, "That's why I asked you to bring home a bag of salt when you went to the fair, but you believed my older sisters that I wanted to pickle you."

All ends well, of course. Her father embraces his cherished daughter and begs for her forgiveness. Her sisters don't suffer immediate death, as in other tales, but are sent away to live in poverty and misery.

The upshot of this tale is that the Ageless Feminine spins her own destiny story as she journeys along *The Ageless Way*. She embroiders her own heart of love and her outspoken voice into golden flowers representative of her Ageless golden life now coming into full flowering. She reclaims and fully embraces her true value in life by creating a taste for life on her own terms. This is *The Ageless Way*.

We don't have the luxury of trying age on for size, but we do have the gift of our Inner Maiden-Crone to own a new Ageless story of Our Age. It's time for us to journey along *The Ageless Way*.

Boomers at the Cusp

And these same Baby Boomers will spark yet another rebellion. There will be a war—an age war—like nothing we have ever seen before."

~ Dr. Bill Thomas, founder of ChangingAging.org

Because of our current age and past experiences, Boomer Ageless Aging is the portal to a new future for humanity. The challenge for our generation and for those who follow is to learn how to always live *The Ageless Way*, not just from time to time. Living and Aging Consciously doesn't always come naturally. If it did, we'd all have been doing it all this time! To achieve Agelessness in our everyday lives, despite the challenges we face personally, professionally, and globally, takes a concerted effort and commitment to inner exploration and transformation. Discovering who you really are and who you can be—and truly recognizing that these have been the same you all along—is the first step toward shifting into *The Ageless Way*.

...Boomer Ageless Aging is the portal to a new future for humanity.

For age is opportunity no less
Than youth itself, though in another dress,
And as the evening twilight fades away
The sky is filled with stars, invisible by day.

~ Final lines of Longfellow poem Morituri Salutamus

The second step, of course, is action—creating a new story of your life, of aging, and of an unlimited future from your new *Ageless Way* perspective. Then you'll be ready to rock your age at any age!

You never change things by fighting the existing reality.
To change something, build a new model that makes
the existing model obsolete.

~ R. Buckminster Fuller

A large and vital part of that new story involves the language we use to define and describe growing older. Similar to the idea of salt in the Maiden-Crone story having either a negative connotation of pickling/destroying or a positive interpretation of adding flavor and zest, it is essential to identify, redefine, and/or newly create language that shows the deliciousness and affirmative aspects of aging. As Oliver Wendell Holmes stated, "Language is the blood of the soul into which thoughts run and out of which they grow." When we change or redefine the language we use to describe growing older, we change the perception, truth, and dynamics of getting older. This is no easy feat, as integrating individual and cultural change takes effort, awareness, intention, time, and acceptance. (More on this can be found in chapter two, "Agelessness Across Generations.")

But you don't have to go it alone. More of us than ever before are ready to reshape the chaos of our lives and planet, to change what aging means for every age while transforming our lives, our businesses or careers, and our world. Together, we can usher in a new age—an Age of Greatness. We may not be able to stop time, but we can master how we use it.

We can live and lead beyond time, beyond age. We can be Ageless.

We can live and lead beyond time, beyond age. We can be Ageless.

Restoring or Re-storing

The more we participate in writing the ending of our own story, the more satisfied we are with the arc of our life.

~Carolyn Conger

Instead of solely focusing on restoring our youth or other aspects of our past, we can transcend age and time by re-storying instead—ourselves, our present, our future, our assumptions about aging, about gender, and about time itself. In some sense, this re-storying does lead to restoration—of parts of ourselves that are Ageless, that are visionary, that have held the potential for greatness since before we were born.

In parallel, re-storying humanity and the Earth also leads to restoration—of the continuity between past, present, and future. This demands a reconnection to and reimagining of the stories that have been broken by millennia of war, patriarchy, and oppression. Similarly, the sustainability of our Earth can be restored if we act now to heal the discontinuity, to connect once again with the Earth and understand that our stories are intertwined and that we have the power to create new stories, aspirational Ageless stories for our planet's future.

Re-storying humanity and the Earth also leads to restoration...

We all have stories—individual stories, family stories (immediate and ancestral), community stories, and the stories of humanity through the ages, from before antiquity to beyond the distant future. All these threads weave together into a cloth, much like that woven by the three Fates of ancient myth, the women who spun and cut the thread of birth, life, and death.

But the term "fate" is deceptive. We are not destined to be stuck in the same old, same *old*. We are not without power to shape our lives. In fact, it is when our lives unravel that we have the power, just as the mythical Fates did, to choose what to do with that thread. We can simply restore the old story, carefully following all the old patterns, only to find that the new finished product, albeit not identical to the old, is much less satisfying or useful into the next stages of life. Alternatively, we can see the threads of our unraveled past as ready material at our disposal to create new patterns that better serve our needs, our desires, and our potential.

Every story, from the individual to the planetary level, has three essential phases: past, present, and future. It's no accident that these elements are present in nearly every culture's mythology, often tied with the parallel concepts of birth, life, and death. The Fates in Greek and in Roman mythology (the Moirai and Parcae, or Fatra, respectively). The Norn in Norse Mythology. The Germanic Matres and Matrones. The Slavic Sudice. Lithuanian and Latvian variations on Laima and her sisters. The Chinese and Japanese red string of fate. Hindu concepts of dharma and karma. And more.

Re-storying humanity's mytho-poetic heroic past means re-examining our stories in a new light. Rather than living the interpretation of powerlessness inherent in being at the whim of the Fates, we can recognize the Fates in ourselves, the power to connect, shape, and alter the present and future and even, to some degree, the past. We are creating a new triumphant story for our times. We Boomer women are rewriting the end of our generational heroines' story arc to be one of triumph, for we cannot be kept down or stopped. Not ever again.

> We Boomer women are rewriting the end of our generational heroines' story arc to be one of triumph, for we cannot be kept down nor stopped. Not ever again.

Understanding the Past

Although hanging onto the stories of our past can be one of the biggest obstacles to embracing our present and creating an Ageless Future, ignoring our past is also a mistake. There's a familiar saying: "Those who don't learn from history are doomed to repeat it." The assertion is that reflecting on the experiences of those who preceded us is important for being able to avoid repeating mistakes already made or for us to glean from the victories and the hard-won lessons of those who came before.

We need the myths and stories of women through the ages because it is by way of these stories that we connect to an often unseen, otherwise unexpressed Herstory. Knowing and exploring the implications of these narratives, which draw upon the power of countless women, tell us who we have been and may still become. When we know the stories of others and ourselves, we are better able to plan and strategize for our personal and business futures. Narratives are, in essence, a way of chronicling what may be from what has been. We need to understand the stories we've lived out and the story we've been telling so that we can understand how and why we should change our present and future stories.

In our individual pasts, we can unearth our Ageless core, the identity that has been with us as far back as we can remember, despite the myriad changes we've undergone over the years. This core is rooted in who we were and what we were doing when we felt time stand still, as well as when we felt most powerful and visionary, when we were focused on what really mattered to us.

In our past we can also see our shadow selves (those hidden archetypal energetic patterns, or inner voices of our submerged personalities that we have pushed out of view earlier in our lives, or perhaps never even knew we possessed). It is essential to embrace, not repress, our shadows if we are going to transcend age and time. We need to recognize and understand our shadow selves and how our seemingly protective reaction to the shadow (that which is hidden from view) has denied us many gifts and may have harmed us and others through our unconscious actions, behaviors, or words. It can be crucial to understand that the reaction is often more damaging than the shadow itself. Recognizing and embracing the shadow is part of accepting ourselves fully, accepting reality fully, so that the present and future we shape is rooted in truth, not in wishful thinking. This acknowledgement does not mean meeting our shadow selves and throwing up our hands. It means that after we face and accept the deepest, most submerged hidden parts of ourselves, we can then begin to see how we can shape those inner forces to serve the light so we become whole.

Unless we face our past head-on, we cannot break free from our old stories, the cycles that are holding us back, keeping us stuck in a status quo that no longer works for us (if it ever did). Owning who we are in our fullness applies on multiple levels beyond the individual. The more we recognize the vast web of past stories and our place in it—in human history's failed and fatal plot lines, as well as in humanity's many moments of transcendence—the clearer we will be able to reshape our individual story in ways that simultaneously shape the story of humanity. This is important now and for the future of at least the next seven generations.

Owning and Reimagining the Present

"Oh no, I can't be a visionary with so many wrinkles!" implores a 52-year-old elegant mother of two and top branding executive. She expresses her angst over dreaming about getting old. She pleads, "Not me. I'm just getting started! But if 40 is over the hill, she wonders, what will happen to me and my dreams?"

Her lifelong pattern has been to "Achieve, achieve, achieve!" She continues, "What's really hard is realizing that I can't masquerade like a thirty-something-year-old woman anymore. I used to employ whatever it took to get what I wanted!"

Just as we can't give directions to someone without knowing her starting point, we can't decide where we're going if we don't know where we are. Understanding the stories we're currently living and telling ourselves is both an inevitable result of examining our past and a separate, often difficult effort. We are so enmeshed in our present it can be difficult to gain perspective, to see it for what it is. How much of our present is shaped by false stories we've told ourselves about what it means to age, or what it means to be a woman, or what we're capable of? How much of our present is shaped simply by the patterns and routines we've fallen into over a lifetime? We have to break down the present and take apart our assumptions before we can rebuild. We have to play the role of the Fates and unravel our lives, however uncomfortable this unraveling is, in order to move forward with a new spin, a new story, yet one that uses the same thread. That thread is Ageless.

No matter what our chronological age—30 or 70 or 101—the stories we have about aging directly affect how we age. These stories stem from within and without, especially in the youth-obsessed culture of the United States, and they clearly lead the majority of people to deny aging or, at the very least, to avoid thinking about it.

> Just as we can't give directions to someone without knowing their starting point, we can't decide where we're going if we don't know where we are.

Who wants to think about or identify with the stereotypes of the invisible, irrelevant, infirm older person, pushed aside by society, with nothing to do but retire and wait to die? For many of us, our denial or repression contributes to our tendency to overestimate that our own future will automatically be full of happiness and health. Our ingrained self-ageism doesn't mean that we don't have the potential to lead fulfilled and even blissful lives in the future, but reaching the apex of a fulfilled vital life does not happen on its own. We have to make it happen, and to do so, we have to be realistic about our present, including our aging and eventual mortality.

We have nothing to fear by facing aging head-on, because aging isn't really the problem here. The problem is the stories we tell and internalize (take on as our own from our culture, family, and media) about aging. We need to break down these stories and transcend them through the lens of Positive Aging. This growing field focuses on two aspects of aging, one I have long called Conscious Aging (growing old with deepening awareness) and its alternative of Aging Consciously (remaining grounded in the realities of aging while attaining life satisfaction). Foresight and life planning are central to achieving this continuously improving life satisfaction as we age.

When it comes to how we age positively, we have two approaches or pathways to select from. Some of us prefer to mix and match copying styles, like ordering dishes off a Chinese restaurant menu, so we can select from either alternative to create a blend that suits our temperament and risk-aversion quotient. The more commonly selected approach, which I call "Aging Consciously," others in gerontology refer to as "Successful Aging," Productive Aging," or "Vital Aging." Simply stated, this approach is about extending our receding midlife with a focus on continued or new success and lifelong productivity. Whatever we call it, I'm referring to what Harry R. Moody, educational gerontologist and author of *The Five Stages of the Soul,* describes as the adaptive approach to "maintain optimal well-being in the face of age-associated losses." One of my affiliations, the Life Planning Network, is an association of professionals dedicated to mid- and later-life success, planning, and encore career counseling. This virtually heretofore-untapped vein of gold is beginning to be mined by the savvy strategists and marketers among us. Recently, AARP (formerly the American Association of Retired Persons) has invested greatly to own this success-driven extended midlife domain. Strategically this makes a whole lot of sense for AARP to counter its longtime sole mission of political and legislative advocacy for those over age 50.

Others, like myself, choose to follow the more circuitous transcendent approach to aging, what I refer to as Conscious Aging. To this day I continue on my Ageless Quest, or my transformative, psychospiritual journey, (coalescing mind, body, and Soul), which is filled with struggle and triumph. This alternative approach is not for the faint of heart, for it takes us on a far deeper dive, into lasting transformation and continuous evolution. We are brought face to face with our mortality. This is a rich pathway wherein we experience who we truly are, and we are forced to both recognize and embrace our place in the cosmos. Unlike many, I straddle both approaches. What about you?

Conscious Aging

I will never forget the afternoon my post-graduate professor, advisor, and mentor, Harry R. Moody, Ph.D., the enormously respected educational gerontologist, invited me to lunch at his favorite little restaurant right near Hunter College's Brookdale Center for Healthy Aging in Manhattan.

It's a sunny, cool, clear, blue-sky day. I am trying to keep up with the long-legged man leading the way to his favorite local Thai restaurant. At each Don't Walk! flashing pedestrian signal we catch up on bits and pieces of what's new in the field of aging.

In the tiny congested eatery, over the fragrances of our Thai dishes, we dive right into deep talk. In a matter of moments he invites me to teach a post-graduate course on Conscious Aging. Between gulps of spicy peanut flavored noodles, not wanting to appear incredibly thrilled, I ask, "What do you have in mind for this new series?"

Looking with half-closed eyes to both sides, conspiratorially, as if to ensure that no one else is listening, he confesses, "I really don't have a firm grasp of what Conscious Aging really is. Do you?"

His question stuns me. Perhaps because I too have been struggling to bring into words the gut feeling surrounding the phrase "Conscious

Aging." Everyone I speak with immediately resonates with the term. But their quick "Yeah!" is soon followed by a question—"Huh?"

I expound on the meaning of the term as if out loud for the very first time. At times Dr. Moody disagrees and other times he seems to vaguely connect with my meandering. I hear myself saying, "It means really being in your body, not in your head…it means owning your mortality and living it. It means connecting to the transcendent…accepting where you are on the spiral of life…ahhh…Taking on the mantle of truth-teller…" None of these stuttering attempts capture the holistic response my gut knows.

As I head back alone to my downtown office, and Moody returns to campus, my mind is racing. I hear myself say to my inner audience, "And I really thought I had a handle on this! Wow! Am I tottering on the line between denial and acceptance of my own aging process?"

I live with this question every day since.

In essence, this question led to the launch of my first Conscious Aging 101 accredited course in 1993, which was a big leap of faith. Dr. Moody granted me the honor of kicking off the new Positive Aging Story to counterpoint the ingrained old story, portraying and treating aging as disease to a room full of professionals in the aging field.

Three months later, chalk in hand, I stand ready for the first class. But nobody has come into the room. Incredulous, I wonder if I am being stood up. The theme, "Conscious Aging 101" is not for the faint-hearted, but this is ridiculous! As I start to pack up, the room begins to fill. The conflicted looks on these professionals' faces, the sputtered meek apologies for being late—obviously, I am not alone in my denial.

For the final activity in one of the early sessions for women in the field of adult development and aging, on my signal, each participant opens her eyes and finds herself staring into the magnified reflection of her face in the hand mirrors I have placed before them. The twittering "oh no's" are followed by questions: "From the neck up, or neck down?" And observations like, "All these years I've been taking care of my face—moisturizing, cleansing, the whole routine. But I forgot about my neck. Nobody told me to do my neck!"

As they each examine their reflections, I ask them to notice any new details and any shifts in their attitude. Then I pop the killer questions: "Whom do you see?" followed by, "What does this bring up for you?"

> *I expected the distressed shrieks of "Oh my god, I'm turning into my mother!" as well as the intense pleasure in some as the mirror connected them to their ancestral lineage.*
>
> *As the session closes, the group notices that one woman is silent and remote, and they encourage her to speak. I reassure her that she doesn't have to. "Oh no, I want to speak," she says. She hesitates for a moment, and then says, very slowly, "I don't know who that is staring at me in the mirror. I keep trying to break the connection with this unfamiliar reflection. Yet each time I return to the mirrored image, I only see eyes and a face I do not know. What I've come to realize is that I don't know who I am as an older woman!"*

If we want to avoid falling into society's stereotype of useless, irrelevant, invisible elders as we age, we first must be fully visible to ourselves. To live our lives with meaning, as healers for our families, communities, and organizations, with passion, purpose, and possibility, we must be fully conscious of who we are and who we can reimagine ourselves to be.

As intensely as the first and second stages of life are focused on building and managing our outer world, the Third and Fourth Ages or stages are a chance for intense, impassioned exploration and discovery of our inner world (Erik Erikson's four stages are described more fully in chapter nine, "Ageless Reinvention"):

- We discover work that has meaning and adds value.

- We create real wealth and true freedom.

- We learn to see beauty in a body that's no longer youthful.

- We arrive at an emotional balance.

- We move to new levels of sexuality and sensuality.

- We discover what matters most in life.

- We reignite our passions and discern our life's purpose.

- We complete 95 percent of our life's greatest achievements in our Elder years.

Dr. Moody explains the advent of Conscious Aging this way: " 'Conscious Aging' has emerged as a social ideal at a specific moment in history, in the first decade of the twenty-first century. This historical moment reflects the convergence of two historical trends: the evolution of psychology to include humanistic, trans personal and lifespan development theory; and the widening impact of population aging in all post-industrial societies. The evolution of psychology toward a deeper view of the human person can now join with the societal transformation of institutions to create new opportunities for positive development in later life."

Robert C. Atchley, professor emeritus from Miami University and author of *Spirituality and Aging,* describes Conscious Aging as "growing old with awareness or being spiritually awake as we age, not simply being aware of our advancing years." He points out that this "involves developing and nurturing a contemplative life and engaging in service rooted in the higher levels of consciousness that a contemplative life makes available. Aging with consciousness is neither quick nor easy. It requires that we come back over and over again to our intention to be awake as we age. It requires that we practice compassionate listening and look at the world from a long-term vantage point that transcends our purely personal desires and fears."

Dr. Moody further asserts that "Conscious Aging, as an emerging cultural ideal, represents a genuinely new stage and level of psychological functioning." (You can learn more about Moody's explanation of positive development in later life by reading his Ageless Expert guest post on my Ageless Beat Blog, dated June 13, 2014, at KarenSands.com/ageless-beat-blog.)

Conscious Aging is the psycho-spiritual aspect of growing older that brings us face to face with our mortality and demands that we learn to stand in the flow of time and timelessness, to meet the deepest and highest parts of our humanness and to own our connection to the divine essence within and without. Conscious Aging is what brings us to the realization of "presence" and ushers us eventually into the role of Elders.

Aging Consciously

When I asked Elly Guggenheimer, activist-philanthropist, at age 86, "Do you talk to your children or do they ask you about your plans for your end of life?" She responded, "No, absolutely not. I never sit down and say to my children, 'Let's talk about my end-of-life planning.'" What a pity that so many of us don't have these conversations with our kids, much less our spouses or partners, long before we reach a crisis point; instead we wait until it's just too late.

Closely aligned with Conscious Aging, and of great import, is the more concretized Aging Consciously, also referred to as Successful Aging, (Rowe and Kahn), which Moody refers to as "the adaptation," characterized by ability to maintain optimal well-being in the face of age-associated losses. When we age consciously, we engage in making life and career choices to give us a leg up in aging successfully. These choices involve various levels of life satisfaction, as well as garnering the skills and awareness of what we must do to prepare for possible physical and mental changes and our eventual passing. Doing so ensures that we secure the legacy we want to leave for our loved ones and the world.

A caveat to make a clear distinction between Conscious Aging vs. Aging Consciously is supported by the work of psychologist Gisela Labouvie-Vief (2000), which is that Conscious Aging is an aspect of Jung's process of individuation as we age into our Elderhood; it is not for sissies, as it is a deep dive into our inner world of our evolving psyche, wherein we reclaim our disparate inner parts as we seek wholeness and inner integrity. For the majority of us, we will sidestep this deeper arc by choosing instead to age consciously, (or successfully), by adapting ourselves to our age-related losses and changes to achieve optimal well-being. Gerontologist Cecelia Hurwich, Ph.D., refers to this as the realization of "vital aging."

One thing I've learned from seeking answers about aging, about what it means to be Ageless and to be an older adult, and about my future, is that finding the "right" answers is not nearly as important as asking the right questions.

How many of us spent years answering questions like, "How can I climb the corporate ladder or sustain my own business? How can I make more money? What do I need to do to be successful?" And how many of us found the answers, climbed the ladder, made the money, achieved what everyone around us would call success—only to find that the answers left us feeling empty and unfulfilled? Some of us still want more of the same, but now we also want to add greater meaning, give back, make a difference, and know our life matters.

In the United States, the average age of widowhood is 55, so this time is often one of endings and beginnings, of richness, depth, connection, and loss. It is a time when we confront and embrace our own mortality. As the new Elders, we choose to simplify our existence, discarding what we want no more of and focusing our energies on what fulfills and fuels us.

We ask ourselves about:

- **Relationships:** Am I with the right person? Did I make the right choice in leaving my partner? Will I find the right person?

- **Friendships:** Whom can I trust to support me? Who will inspire me? Who will energize me? Who understands me and loves me for who I am? Whom might I want to release?

- **Money:** Do I have enough to live well through retirement? Will someone show up to rescue/take care of me? How can I make more, if it's really up to me?

- **Life quality:** Why am I spending my time with people/on things I don't care about? What must I have in my life to be satisfied? What can I give up/get out of?

- **Death/loss:** How long have I got? Will I outlive my partner? Will I outlive my children? Will I outlive my friends? How will I live without my partner/children/friends? What will my quality of life be without my…? Where will I live if my partner dies? Do I have enough money to maintain my quality of life if I'm alone?

- **Retirement:** What will I do? Where will I live? How do I want to spend my later years? Will I be healthy? Will I be alone?

- **Health:** Will I be healthy enough to enjoy my elder years? Can I afford to be well cared for if I'm not well? Will I become caretaker to my partner or parents? Will I become a burden on my partner or children?

- **Leadership/leaving a legacy:** How can I make a difference? How can I improve the world for future generations…for my children and theirs?

At this point you might be saying to yourself, "Yes, I am definitely thinking through all these questions, so I guess I'm on the right track. Now how do I accelerate the process?"

These questions are all part of the time you spend examining your past, present, and future stories and, to some degree, this formative period cannot be rushed. Finding the path to self-actualization and fulfillment involves understanding who you are and what you want, and that's easier said than done. Yet, having helped hundreds of people through this transition over the last forty years, I can assure you that if you focus on living consciously, you will emerge with a much deeper understanding of how much power you have to reimagine your story once you've fully recognized it for what it is, the dark and the light. When you learn how to enjoy your unique journey through this exciting stage of life, you'll never yearn to be 20 again, as 50-plus is far more fun.

> As life begins to seem more limited and precious, we realize that there is no longer time to waste on the nonessentials or on what others think of us.

An important part of coming to peace with aging is fully living who we are and who we are meant to be. As life begins to seem more limited and precious, we realize that there is no longer time to waste on the nonessentials or on what others think of us. Now it is time to make a real difference and to discover and live our purpose here on Earth. Living on both planes, the transcendence of Conscious Aging and the reality of Aging Consciously, is what it means to live Agelessly.

Creating an Aspirational Ageless Future

Once we understand the stories of our past and present, especially the stories we tell about aging, we can create a new story around aging—for ourselves, our society, our world—for generations to come. We can live both fully in the present, in what really matters, and in the future tense, living the future we want to have, modeling the new story of aging, all while remaining grounded in the realities of our times, our lives, and our life stages.

Just as we can embrace new roles as the Fates of our own lives, we can reconnect with and step into the role of oracle (a person or agency of the gods in classic antiquity who interfaced with the gods to receive wise counsel, prophetic predictions or precognition of the future), thereby reimagining the mythical prophets of old in the context of today. The oracles of ancient Greece were believed to connect Earth and heaven, grounded yet transcendent. Oracles from cultures throughout the world also shared this connection, such as in Tibet, where the oracle was the medium between the natural and spiritual realms.

Ultimately, the ability to embrace both Conscious Aging and Aging Consciously is our modern-day mirror of the abilities of the oracles. We can't predict the future—no one can—but we can use our understanding of the past and present to create realistic scenarios—stories—for alternative possible futures. The secret to prophecy is to recognize that, to some degree, all prophecies are self-fulfilling. We can continue to live our old, limited stories about aging and in this way create a self-fulfilling prophecy in which some of our worst fears about aging come true. Or we can choose to change the story and, therefore, the prophecies we fulfill. We can create an Aspirational Ageless Future for ourselves and the world, one that is grounded in reality but that transcends the self-imposed limitations we've inherited from our culture's old stories, limitations we've internalized often to the point that we don't even notice they are there.

On a societal and global level, we can be a part of a much larger prophecy by leading all generations toward a new global story around not just aging but also social, economic, and environmental justice and sustainability. The word "oracle" is rooted in the Latin verb meaning "to speak." The time has come, for women especially, to step out of the shadows and speak their truth, to be seen and heard, to show by example what humanity is capable of at every age and stage.

Nonetheless, our stories are not all about our grandest visions for the world. They further encompass our internal journeys, the stories we tell ourselves in the quiet reflective spaces within. In ancient Greece, the oracles were in such high demand that they were not consulted for everyday concerns. For this purpose, people turned to seers, the prophets who guided individuals by interpreting signs in birds, bones, and reflective surfaces. Opening ourselves to signs and taking time to reflect are crucial everyday actions we can take, not only to reimagine our stories from inside out but also to keep them grounded in reality. This is a daily process, not a one-time act. Staying in tune with change and with ourselves requires periods of reflection and making adjustments based on these changes and what we see in our reflection. Such a process is necessary to create an Aspirational Ageless Future that resonates on every level of who we are and who we can be.

The Ageless Way

Legends say that hummingbirds float free of time,
carrying our hopes for love, joy and celebration. Hummingbirds
open our eyes to the wonder of the world and inspire us to open our
hearts to loved ones and friends. Like a hummingbird, we aspire to
hover and to savor each moment as it passes, embrace all that life
has to offer and to celebrate the joy of everyday.
The hummingbird's delicate grace reminds us that life is rich,
beauty is everywhere, every personal connection has meaning and
that laughter is life's sweetest creation.

~ Papyrus

Being able to see the big global picture but also take the time to rest among the flowers and enjoy the intricate, beautiful detail of everyday life—that is essential to *The Ageless Way*. Through the combination of Conscious Aging and Aging Consciously, we can transcend time and see aging and life for what they really are, precious gifts.

The Ageless Way is not a linear path. It is not a means to an end. It is both the end in itself and unending. *The Ageless Way* exists between time and timelessness, between chaos and order, between the spiritual plane and reality in all its brutal beauty. We do not find *The Ageless Way* so much as we remember it, become conscious of it, an old friend who has always been there for us, at our core, in our DNA, passed on from generation to generation. It is the light that makes the shadow possible and the shadow that gives the light meaning.

The Ageless Way is the story that changes with every retelling yet is eternal in its truths. What will that Ageless Story be for you? ❯

CHAPTER I ~ *The Ageless Way Reflections*

The questions and exercises below are to help you find your distinct path on The Ageless Way. Turn to page 28 for more about The Ageless Way Reflections.

1. What would you do if you had no limits based on age? On gender? On money? On location? Or if you had no limits on your past story and you could direct what is done?

2. Meditate on the word "aging" for a few minutes, and then write down a list of descriptive words you associate with aging.

   Now do the same with the word "Ageless" and create a list of the descriptive words you would use to categorize someone as being Ageless or embodying Agelessness.

   Compare your list with a list that came out of recent workshops on page page 353.

   The descriptors we attach to the concept of aging, many of them stereotypically negative, restrictive, or diminishing, inform the stories we currently tell ourselves and each other about becoming older. Those stories shape our choices, hence the ways in which we live our lives and whether we hold back or are true to ourselves, as we grow older. On the other hand, the attributes we associate with the concept of Agelessness are the foundation for the new story of *The Ageless Way*. Consider taking a few more minutes to select your two top attributes of Agelessness and write three ways each of them currently shows up in your life, personally and/or professionally. Then ponder more ways in which you will make these attributes a priority in your life and work.

3. Select the top three most meaningful myths, folklore, or fairy tales for you. Express for yourself in a few sentences why each is important to you. In what ways do (or have) these myths, tales, and stories play(ed) out in your life, career or business? Are there any aspects you'd want to change or integrate anew?

4. Reflect on your old personal story to locate aspects you may want to change or look at from a different perspective, re-story. Then ask

yourself what is your aging story now? How much of this story is inherited or imposed by others in some way? Now that you have a liberating opportunity to reshape and re-story, what do you want your new aging story to be?

5. Prioritize setting aside fifteen to twenty minutes each day to reflect on your old story and the new story you want to create. Put it on your calendar as an appointment that you can't miss. Perhaps journal after you meditate on these ideas or before you start your day. One approach is to take one of each of the attributes of Agelessness that resonates with you. For each week, or month (or whatever time feels right), consider that attribute for your daily reflection and ponder how it shows up (or doesn't) in your everyday life.

6. Have you taken care of the basics of Aging Consciously by either preparing or updating documents for your older years and eventual passing? Have you broached these topics with your loved ones? If not, what are you waiting for?

7. If you are choosing to embody Conscious Aging in your life, how will you do this? How will you be or become more of a Visionary with Wrinkles today and into the future? Consider creating a running journal entry so you can come back to it each week or month to select which of the attributes of Agelessness you can incorporate daily. This can be as simple as asking yourself each day what and who has meaning for you right now and how you can demonstrate this.

Chapter 2

AGELESSNESS ACROSS GENERATIONS

We should be hopeful that the struggle we do does bring change.
And I am hopeful that we do achieve our goals.
But we need to work together. History is neither sent from
the sky nor does it get made up by itself. It is we who make history.
It is we who become the history. So let us make history,
bring change, by becoming the change.

~ Malala Yousafzai,
Youngest-ever Nobel Peace Prize recipient

L iving *The Ageless Way* is not limited to midlife and beyond, the years
when we become more acutely aware of our aging. By definition,
Agelessness applies to all ages because it focuses on who we are as
individuals, not who we *should* be at a particular age.

Ageism affects all generations. Merriam-Webster defines ageism as
"prejudice or discrimination on the basis of a person's age," which, for
me, means the same for a 30-year-old as it does for an 80-year-old. No
age group is immune to age stereotypes and the resulting snap judgments
about who they are, what they are doing, and what they are capable of.
Sometimes, these stereotypes are so internalized that we judge ourselves
by them. Often, especially in the workplace, we use them to dismiss one
another. Rather than talking over a problem and coming to a collaborative
solution, it's all too easy to throw up our hands and pin the problem on the
other person (or ourselves) being too young or being too old, something
we can't do anything about, so we don't even try. If we took age out of the
equation (or in other words, if we saw each other as Ageless), we'd be able
to focus on who we are as individuals, on the common ground we share,

on the true root and reasons for our differences, and how to manage and even leverage them together.

Sexism and ageism have many parallels. Both rely on artificial limitations that hurt everyone. Both are deeply rooted in our culture and society. Both require changes at every level: individual, community, societal, global. Gender roles and expectations limit and hurt women and men. Ageism limits and hurts all ages, even if the form it takes changes over our lifetimes. And just as feminism (as defined by Wikipedia, "Feminism is a collection of movements and ideologies aimed at defining, establishing, and defending equal political, economic, cultural, and social rights for women), helps both genders by working to abolish gender-based limitations as well as inequalities that harm us all, Agelessness helps all ages by removing the age-based limitations that hurt all ages, dividing us and holding us back from our true potential to be great—together.

We need to engage young people to change the conversation about the future of aging. With advances in genomics and longevity science, they have the prospect of even longer lives, and a personal stake in ensuring that those lives are healthy, productive and purposeful.

~Paul Irving, chairman of the Milken Institute Center for the Future of Aging and distinguished scholar in residence at the University of Southern California Davis School of Gerontology

Changing the Story of Aging

One of the most important tasks we have together, all generations, is to change the story we tell one another and ourselves about aging. Too often, the story is assumed to be important only to people over 40 (and even then, only to those who choose to think about the topic in our age-denial society). It's easy to forget that a transformation of how we view aging—indeed, in how we age, period—can occur only if our conversations on the topic are multigenerational. In fact, the only way we can transform the world for ourselves, and for at least the next seven generations, is if we recognize the need for multiple overlapping conversations about the past, present, and future story of what age and growing older really means.

THE POWER OF MULTIPLE CONVERSATIONS ON AGING

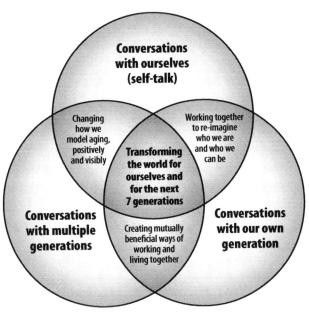

Conversations with ourselves (self-talk)

Changing how we model aging, positively and visibly

Working together to re-imagine who we are and who we can be

Transforming the world for ourselves and for the next 7 generations

Conversations with multiple generations

Creating mutually beneficial ways of working and living together

Conversations with our own generation

©2012 Karen Sands/Sands & Associates, LLC

For many of us, the way we talk to ourselves about what it means to age is the starting point for change. To look ahead and see opportunity instead of a life winding down; to see beauty in its complicated, rich nuance instead of only as a superficial societal judgment; to adjust to the present and future changes in our lives, our bodies, our energy, our work, with an eye toward making the next stage our most visionary yet. These are just a few of the steps we need to take within ourselves so that we can embody them and, as a byproduct, naturally extend them to others. Through this conversation, we can engage with younger generations in ways that model and mentor the ripe possibilities they too have ahead of them. Further, the process of learning and manifesting change can teach us how to open our minds to learning from those we mentor as well as those we emulate.

...the only way we can transform the world for ourselves, and for at least the next seven generations, is if we recognize the need for multiple overlapping conversations about the past, present, and future story of what age really means.

Changing the conversation we have with ourselves also informs the conversations about aging that we have with others in our generational cohorts who are at the same tipping point in their lives as we are and want a present and a future story that's different from what was modeled by previous generations. This applies, as well, for those under 40, dismissed as too young to have wisdom or enough skill sets to be taken seriously, as well as for those over 50, who face increasing invisibility, irrelevance, and a winding down from participation in work, communities, and the world. The good news is that the more we change how we see ourselves, the more we can band together with others in the same boat and row ourselves to a new shore, a new future, immigrants to a new land of long life where, no matter our age or stage, we are valued for what we can bring to the table. Most especially, for the over-50 crowd, the older we are the more we have to offer because we are closer to realizing our greatest vision yet.

At the same time, we can't people this land with only one or two generations. The conversation about aging needs to move beyond self-talk and beyond the lips of those going through the same stage of life. It needs to go beyond simply modeling what it's like to be a strong, visionary leader in our fifties, sixties, and beyond. All generations need to work together to find the common ground that binds us, such as everyone's need for more flexible work-life arrangements. Everyone has the need for communities that nurture and sustain us at every age and stage.

> All generations need to work together to find the common ground that binds us...

The conversation is not just about Baby Boomers (*born 1943-1967) and the younger generations either, the Gen Xers (born 1965 to early 1980s) and the Millennials, also labeled Gen Y's (born early 1980s to early 2000s). Lest we not forget those just arriving on the scene, Generation Z is the cohort of people born after the Millennial generation starting approximately from the mid-2000s to the present day. One important connection, for Boomer women in particular, is with the generation of Matures (born before 1943) those women who are in their seventies, eighties, and beyond right now (many were part of the early First Wave Feminist movement and/or early champions of the Second Wave of the 1960s and 1970s) and were the first to transition from work to "retirement" and to benefit from our increasing longevity.

How are they making this transition? What can we learn from those who are happy and healthy in their seventies and beyond?

Ultimately, when all three conversations overlap, we go beyond changing ourselves, beyond reinventing all stages of life, and beyond creating new ways of working and living and being able to capitalize on the unique strengths of every age. When all three conversations come together, when our visionary voices harmonize, we will do nothing short of transforming the world in ways we can't even imagine doing alone, to a magnitude that will ripple out in lasting ways for generations to come.

> One of the most important tasks we have together, all generations, is to change the story we tell one another and ourselves about aging.

Who Defines Us?

The conversation you have with yourself and others in your generation will be ongoing and multifaceted, but an excellent starting point is to consider these questions: What does your future story of aging look like? When you think about getting older, how do you define what that means for you? Do you ever see yourself as being "elderly"? Do you envision yourself when you hear the words "senior citizen"? (And let's face it, that's probably the most ridiculous of the terms out there, considering we don't have "junior citizens" or anything of the sort.)

Perhaps we should drop the label "senior" or redefine it. Clearly this term has helped to embed ageist stereotypes into our societal psyche. It used to be, as David Wolfe, author of the pioneering books *Serving the Ageless Market* (1990) and *Ageless Marketing* (2003), wrote, "*Senior* is not an inherently negative term…Being a senior used to connote a superior standing in every context but aging."

Sure, many don't mind enjoying the "senior" discounts. And for those who do retire—fully or partially—the advantages of having more free time, fewer demands, and less stress overall are additional perks.

But of course we don't have to wait until we retire to create this kind of lifestyle. We don't have to retire at all.

In fact, many characteristics of the stereotypical senior citizen don't really have much to do with age at all. Or at least they don't have to be related to age, even if we as a society have somewhat arbitrarily decided they do. These characteristics can include retirement, volunteer work, adapting our lifestyle to physical changes, having more control over our time and environment. *All of these are choices we might make at any age.*

So if we strip away other people's definitions of what it means to age, what it means to be over 30, 40, 50, 60, 70, 80, 90, 100…where does that leave us? How do we define ourselves as protagonists in our own aging story?

We all have different comfort levels with various terms. Some shy away from "elderly" but don't mind being seen as an "Elder." Some don't mind being called "older" but feel uncomfortable being called simply "old." Yet another person might get fed up with euphemisms and actually demand to be called "old," dammit!

I've always relished the term "Crone," the idea of taking back its original meaning of wise old woman. Some, including those who have chosen not to have children, prefer to be seen as grandmother. In ancient times, the Crone was valued and revered as a wise and prophetic goddess in her own right. Traced back to pre-history, societies that are thought to have been the first "partnerships" between women and men lasted for about 20,000 years. Then as Riane Eisler describes in her underground classic, *The Chalice and the Blade* (1988), these early societies "veered off on 'a bloody 5,000-year detour' of male domination." Along with these partnership societies, the Crone and all images of the positive feminine were devalued, leaving only the Divine Feminine (e.g., Mother Mary) as the preferred universal Mother image to survive intact into our modern day.

Fortunately, today's twenty-first century women are resuscitating the whole panoply of feminine archetypal goddesses, like those we have buried way below our consciousness carrying the powerful energy of the Black Madonna, the flip side of Mother Mary (e.g., Mary Magdalene, Sophia, Kali Ma, Kuan Yin, and more), so that we can reclaim our fullness by embodying the whole range of our womanhood.

I'll tell you a secret. Every time I write—for my blog, for a workshop or keynote, for a book or article—I have to stop yet again and consider this issue: What do we call ourselves? Elders? Do I avoid the word "old" or use it unabashedly? Do I refer to us as aging or stick to euphemisms or numbers, like post-50? Maybe the over-sixties? But what about including

40-plus? Boomers…and older? Matures? How do we distinguish between the early and late Boomers, who are as different as Led Zeppelin is from the Beatles? At what point do generational labels lose their usefulness?

It's tricky, this act of labeling, and even trickier when we try to define a larger group of people who may or may not have anything in common besides their similarity in age, if even that.

That thinking brings me back to the only person any of us can ever truly and accurately define: ourselves. Yet this is the one person we so often let others define for us. We plan to retire roughly when we're supposed to. We see ourselves as less and less attractive according to the dictates of Society (with a capital S). And heaven forbid we start any long-term venture—a business, a campaign, an ongoing artistic endeavor—beyond "retirement age."

Fortunately, fewer and fewer people are allowing themselves to be defined by these expectations. More Baby Boomers, for example, are starting new businesses than any other generation today, and women are at the forefront of this movement. The Kauffman Index of Entrepreneurial Activity reports that Boomer start-ups increased from 18.7 percent to 23.4 percent between 2003 and 2013. According to the American Economic Journal, one out of every ten United States women is starting or running her own business. More people are realizing that they don't want to (or perhaps can't) retire, and regardless of the circumstances, they are exploring new ways of working and of making the future work.

Once again, we're back to that place where the old definitions no longer automatically apply. For many of us, this shift away from outmoded definitions means that how we define ourselves in our forties, fifties, sixties, seventies, eighties, and beyond is not a whole lot different than how we would define ourselves in our twenties and thirties—based on our interests, our values, our plans for the future, our relationships, our capacity to love, to give, to create. The only differences are that now we have more experience and more wisdom, and that now our bodies are changing in new ways that we must incorporate into our plans for the future. But even these vary from individual to individual, and age to age.

So, when you strip away who you're supposed to be, how do you define who you are? In your entry in the World Dictionary of People, are you a

Who are you, really? What is your "Now" Story? Do you know what your "Future" Story is?

noun? An adjective? A verb? Do you have multiple meanings depending on context? Who are you, really? What is your "Now" Story? Do you know what your "Future" Story is?

Seeking the answer to this question and not just accepting it but *embracing* it is key to the process of becoming Ageless and integrating *The Ageless Way.*

That's only part of it, however. Who *we* are—as a generation and across generations—is also a necessary question to answer together if we are going to create a world in which we change the cultural story around aging, where all ages and stages can find that Ageless self and create an environment where that self can thrive.

Working Together

Perhaps the most important topics for a multigenerational conversation revolve around the future of the planet and the workplace. In the latter, we see the generational stereotypes played out, such as Boomers being resistant to change and technologically inept, and younger generations having no discipline and spending all their time texting. Added to these caricatures are the post-recession fears fueled by media claims that Baby Boomers are stealing jobs away from younger generations by not retiring or the (bizarrely contradictory) claim that Generation X and Millennials will be unfairly supporting the large Boomer generation, even though Boomers who do retire spent their lives already paying into Social Security and Medicare.

Despite media fear-mongering about Baby Boomers working longer, studies consistently show that more Boomers in the workforce does not increase unemployment among younger generations. In fact, the opposite is seen to be true. A 2012 study by Boston College's Center for Retirement Research found that those who work past retirement age are also consuming more, which creates more demand for products and services and, therefore, more job creation. Baby Boomers also tend to have specialized jobs for which younger generations are not yet qualified. Having people in the workforce with this specialized experience, if anything, provides a way to speed up the careers of their younger colleagues, who have the opportunity to learn from hands-on mentorship and the wisdom and experience of the older generations.

Unfortunately, studies also show that ageism is a barrier to this kind of collaborative learning. A study by the Association for Talent Development found not only that all generations stereotype one another but also that this stereotyping leads to unaddressed tension and conflict that saps productivity by as much as 12 percent! Perhaps most interesting were the similarities among the stereotypical characteristics each generation applied to the others. For example, younger generations would refer to older colleagues as lazy because they are old, and older generations would refer to younger colleagues as lazy because they are young. All generations tended to make judgments about behavior based on age and then, because age was seen as an unsolvable part of the equation, the behavior itself was never discussed. Co-workers simply continued to work together with this tension among them that they felt incapable of addressing solely because they all mistakenly attributed behaviors to age-based stereotypes. (Talk about chasing one's "tale"…)

Of course, there is more going on here beyond the ageism, particularly the tendency to leap to a judgment (e.g., lazy) about a behavior instead of finding out what is really behind the behavior. Any conversation among people, across generations or within the same generation, has to start with focusing on the facts of the situation, not an interpretation of those facts, especially negative assumptions that are likely to shut down the conversation before it starts. If we are going into a situation with the assumption that behaviors are related to age rather than to individual traits and circumstances, then we are more likely to assume that a solution won't be found because we can't change someone's age. In this scenario, we are more likely to skip right to the judgment because we know we won't be having a conversation about the facts and what to do about them. Take the age biases out of the situation and we are far more likely to be willing and capable of reserving judgment until we talk it over.

As someone who works with trends, especially those related to particular generations, I can understand the difficulty of navigating the gray area between generational tendencies and stereotypes. The key is to understand that trends for a group apply only when discussing the group as a whole.

When dealing with individuals, you have to take them on their own terms, not assume they follow the patterns of the group.

The learning styles methodology and approach in education has some useful applications for the workplace. Within a group of students all the same age, we find vast differences in how they approach learning. Some need visual input to fully understand a concept, while others learn and work best with the written word. Others learn and express themselves best by talking with others face to face. These are just a few of the styles of learning that apply, but you can see how they might affect workplace habits.

The workplace is a place of learning and application of that learning. Habits that may seem incomprehensible to you could very well be rooted in how another person learns best. Understanding this concept can lead to better communication as well as solutions that enable everyone to do her best work.

For example, if you learn best by talking with others, it can be difficult to understand why your co-worker sends emails about everything, even small issues that could more easily (to you) be taken care of in a quick conversation. When you both look at this situation from the perspective of learning styles, you'll both be less likely to insist on your own preferred mode of communicating and will, perhaps, come up with a compromise, such as email followed by periodic conversations to check understanding.

If you lead a multigenerational workplace or are a solopreneur working with people of multiple generations, I highly recommend a proactive approach. Read up on learning styles and Howard Gardner's multiple intelligences theory, and try to incorporate various options and strengths in your regular communication and output. This approach can be exceptionally useful as a way for people to occasionally try out styles that aren't their strongest. As long as they feel safe to explore and make mistakes doing something in a way that's not as comfortable, they will surprise you with new insights and perspectives that wouldn't have come out if they'd continued thinking inside the box.

Conversely, leading with your strengths and enabling others to lead with theirs will create an environment in which everyone feels valued and has the opportunity to experience success. This experience motivates us all to continue striving for more success, most notably when we feel valued as

The workplace is a place of learning and application of that learning. Habits that may seem incomprehensible to you could very well be rooted in how another person learns best.

part of a team. Consider taking the time as a group to try StrengthsFinder, the book or the online tool (www.strengthsfinder.com).

Another important step is to focus on common values shared among colleagues of multiple generations. Having conversations about values and aspirational visions—for one's self, the company, the community, and even the world—and keeping these commonalities front and center can motivate everyone to celebrate and leverage diversity (in age, gender, race, ethnicity, religion, etc.) in service of collaboration toward common values, goals, and visions.

The coming of age of 86 million Millennials who will be entering the workforce by 2020 has spurred a recent spate of attention to making the workplace ready for these new entries into a three-generational workforce and to predetermine what Millennials are looking for in future employers, as association members, and as event and conference attendees. But a recent study by commercial real estate services and investment firm CBRE debunks our accepted myths about the difference in generations' workplace preferences. CBRE findings have discovered that the attributes typically associated with what Millennials want are important for all generations. In fact, the CBRE survey found that there is little difference among the three working generations—Millennials, Generation X, and Baby Boomers—in how they want their workplaces to incorporate variety, choice, access, and transparency.

A study released by LinkedIn, the Relationships @Work, sheds light on the importance of relationships in the workforce—46 percent of all professionals report that friendships with colleagues make them happier at work. The key takeaway is that creating a work culture that resonates across generations, roles, and personalities is a key factor in building a successful environment and driving career and organizational success. As a result of this study, LinkedIn is fostering a worldwide conversation across generations by using #workbff to share "selfies" with colleagues.

This discussion is just one example of why multiple generations need to be involved in changing the story around aging, in developing an Ageless perspective through our conversations. Only when we achieve an Ageless perspective will we be able to move forward on the other conversations we need to have, not only to collaborate in the workplace but also in our personal lives, our communities, and across the globe. The sooner we all learn to understand and work with diversity of all kinds on its own terms rather than seeing it as something to fix or as a source of frustration, the sooner we can transcend the ordinary requirements of our jobs, businesses, and personal lives and achieve the extraordinary—the visionary—together.

The Future of Intergenerational Collaboration

There was a time when the older you were, the more respect you garnered, but this was also a time of disrespect to youth, when children (and women) were supposed to be seen and not heard. Then in the 1960s and 1970s, the Baby Boomers turned this notion on its head, and the mantra flipped to not trusting anyone over 30.

Now, with Baby Boomers clearly over 30 themselves, we are poised on the brink of another transformation in perspective. However, that transformation doesn't have to be a return to the past. We are at a time when we can choose mutual respect and intergenerational cooperation. A time when everyone can be seen and heard and valued.

> We are at a time when we can choose mutual respect and intergenerational cooperation.

This form of cooperation isn't in and of itself new. We've always relied on it to varying degrees, although I think it is safe to say that today, people younger and older than ever before are now a regular part of any form of intergenerational effort. We've always had child prodigies as well as remarkable achievers late in life, but only in modern times are we actively bringing the very young and the very old into the conversation. In science and technology, health care and longevity, business, politics, and art, events such as science fairs, internships, and online presentations put the very young in touch with real-world opportunities. Now, the same exposure to new information and educational opportunities is coming true for the other end of the age continuum. More businesses and governments are discovering this heretofore hidden gold mine as they gear up to re-envision the aging population as vital, active, productive workers, leaders, and innovators for decades to come.

I'm glad to share that, after decades in absentia, higher education is now paying attention to the emerging 50-plus generation by eagerly serving the "third stage of education" (read more about this in chapter seven, "Gray Is the New Green").

The lines we have carefully drawn between age groups are blurring.

A recent article in The New York Times's "Booming" section speaks to the value of intergenerational partnerships: "(These partnerships) defy the persistent stereotype about younger and older people battling over jobs in the still-shaky economy. When these multigenerational ventures succeed, it is often because of the different sets of skills and perspectives that an older and younger person can bring to solving problems." Across the globe, more and more meet-up venues, online communities (e.g., the interest groups on LinkedIn, Google Hangouts, and more) are forming, bringing together young entrepreneurs with experienced leaders, accomplished innovators, entrepreneurs, potential investors, and mentors. Our Millennial generation, as are our Elders, are concerned, deeply, about what the twenty-first century will be like for them…and for all of us.

Many of the Boomers' kids (labeled "Millennials" or "Gen Ys") are purpose-driven and demand life-work balance. While they want to work, and many seek to make money, most are good with making just enough to be comfortable. There's a caveat: As long as their thirst and driving passion makes a difference. Gen Ys want to have fun and be with the people who matter most, but what moves them out into their world is solving the problems that plague our Mother Earth and humanity. They'll do it faster and smarter than ever before with advancing technology at their backs. What's telling about the twenty-first century is that our youngest young and oldest olds are in this together and are beginning to know that in a tangible way. Harnessing this intergenerational force field will happen only if we come together.

The clincher paragraph quotes Nancy Henkin, executive director of Temple University's Intergenerational Center, questioning how this kind of working and thinking can be applied in ways that even go beyond a specific venture or project. "How do you build communities that are welcoming for people of all ages, and how do you engage people of all ages in a collective effort to make the community a good place for growing up and growing older?" My sentiments exactly. I also resonate with Henkin's idea that "Instead of a senior and a youth center, why not a vibrant community center where people come together and intentionally foster trust, empathy, and interaction?"

Technology is no longer a symbol of the great divide between the generations. People over 50 have become the fastest-growing group of social media users, increasing their presence on Facebook by 84 percent between 2009 and 2011. In fact, women over 65 increased their presence on Twitter by a whopping 96 percent during that time.

Some media experts and self-proclaimed journalists say that this spells the demise of these media as the younger generations pull out, not wanting "their news feed cluttered up with their parents' news," but this prediction ignores two key trends: (1) social media is evolving to be so individualized that no one can clutter your news feed but yourself—you choose entirely what and whom you wish to see; and (2) social media, and society as a whole, is becoming more interest based, with other factors, such as age, being irrelevant.

Just as AutoCAD software can't tell the difference between the 70-year-old architect and the 20-year-old engineer using it to draft buildings of the future, the 95-year-old lab tech and the 10-year-old who discovered a molecule aren't going to leave a beloved chemistry Facebook group because of the other's age.

It's the chemistry that matters.

No transformation is inevitable, however. I see the signs of this trend developing, such as the egalitarian digital future laid out in Dan Abelow's book *Imagine a New Future: Creating Greatness for All,* but life and society can change on a dime. I believe this trend is worth developing and that it's time we reach out across generations and work together based on common interests and visions for the future. A future that has a place for all of us is one with fewer artificial barriers, such as those based on age, gender, race, and class stereotypes, and more genuine connections.

It's the chemistry that matters.

Again, it's the chemistry that matters. Together, we can discover more than "just" a new molecule. We can discover, we can create, new worlds.

Together we can change the story around aging and model the new *Ageless Way.* ❯❯

CHAPTER 2 ~ *The Ageless Way Reflections*

The questions and exercises below are to help you find your distinct path on The Ageless Way. Turn to page 28 for more about The Ageless Way Reflections.

1. How do you define yourself? Where (or from whom) do those definitions come from? When I was a kid, my dad always called me "Dizzy." For a long time I confused that word with "ditzy." Not such a good replacement word for a young girl with visual learning disabilities. It wasn't until after my dad passed in my early twenties that I learned he was on the bench for the Brooklyn Dodgers. The newspaper clippings I discovered described my long-legged dad as "Dizzy" Fish. Clearly the way we self-identify is impactful on every part of our lives and our world as we move through it.

   There are other more commonly used descriptors you can use to get started. Are any of these yours? Big Guy, Li'l Woman, Husband, or Wife, Dad or Mom. Shy or bold, maybe too loud. Leader. Executive or employee. Entrepreneur. Baby Boomer or Gen Xers. Self-starter or follower. Old or young. Over the hill. Invisible. You get the idea…

   Next, reflect on the ways you have described yourself over time. How have they changed? Was there a particular event or interaction that inspired the change?

2. How would you define the ideal Ageless you? What's stopping you from embodying that definition? Here's a suggestion if you are hesitant to get going. Once you are in a reflective state, think of someone you consider the epitome of being Ageless and who embraces *The Ageless Way.* If possible, bring the image of this person clearly into your mind's eye. Note all the ways you describe this person as a model of Agelessness and the ways she embraces *The Ageless Way.* When you return to your journal, capture what you've noted and any insights you've realized.

To ripple this conversation out further, consider bringing the topic of how we all define ourselves and one another, and share those thoughts with family members (a good dinner conversation!), your workgroup or your book group, during a friends' night out...or start a new online conversation group.

3. What stereotypes do you have about other generations? What stereotypes do you have about your own? Any ideas on why or how you came to think this way? How much of your view of colleagues, friends, family, and even yourself, is filtered through the lens of these stereotypes? What impact is this thinking having on your key relationships at work, home, in the community, and even how you vote?

4. At work, or in your community, start a conversation group that bridges generations to brainstorm solutions to a pressing problem that is meaningful to all invited. Make it fun, relaxed, and inspiring so everyone learns to feel safe and free to contribute. Start small so the group can gel. (An example of a fun start-up exercise to "break the ice" can be to have each person share three things about herself, one of which is not true. Then have everyone guess which claim is the untruth.) Be sure to chunk down the problem into small bites for starters. You can do this anywhere, including such locales as an office, a local teen center, or a town hall.

Chapter 3

POSITIVE AGING

All my feelings about the release of human possibilities, all of my convictions about renewal, are offended by the widely shared cultural assumption that life levels off in one's 40s and 50s and heads downhill, so that by 65 you are scrap heap material.

~ John Gardner

Positive Aging is the latest meme for describing new approaches to life post-40, approaches that focus on changing the story about aging to encompass the reality that the years ahead of us hold more potential, not less, for meaningful work and business, making a difference, and living lives of significance, value, and visibility.

I am wholeheartedly on board with this movement and what it represents for women, especially, for we often bear the brunt of the negative aging stereotypes. Culturally, women are still judged based on our appearance, at every age, and many of us internalize this equation of appearance = value. This internalization makes aging particularly difficult, as our appearance naturally begins to become less and less in line with our cultural youth-driven standards of beauty.

And this is one area where I feel we need to be vigilant about not reinforcing these damaging stereotypes under the guise of "staying positive."

Harvard's Daniel Gilbert wrote in *Stumbling on Happiness* that we tend to underestimate the bad and way overestimate our happiness, especially when projecting our future. He goes on to explain the many psychological illusions that tend to distort our perception of happiness.

I surely am an example of this stumbling around seeking happiness. I never see what happens to me as tragic. And I've surely had my share of challenging times. I always find the silver lining, the nearly invisible gold thread, and some positive rationale as to what my takeaway is going to be.

Women tend to be really adept at taking on this Pollyanna view. The good news is that it means our psychological immune system is working at optimal levels. The not-so-good news is that we tend to go into positiva mode and not see reality for what it is. Instead, we keep the falsely positive story going and stay in denial, much like Helene quoted in chapter one, who kept telling herself she was just fine with her own aging until the reality set in that she was now the oldest woman in her circles. This is true for all of us who repeat gleefully, without thinking, that 50 is the new 40, 70 is the new 60, and 80 is the new 70. Just another form of age denial. I assure you that 50 is the new 50, 60 the new 60, and 70 and 80 respectively the new 70 and 80. We age chronologically, but inwardly we feel fifteen years younger. When folks exclaim, "You can't possibly be seventy-one!" I respond with a smile, "Yes, this is what seventy-one looks like!"

Denial of aging comes in many guises.

Denial of aging comes in many guises from (literally and figuratively) buying into the idea that we're beautiful only if we look young to not saying our age for fear that we'll be discounted. The problem is that the more we perpetuate this narrative, the more we reinforce the idea that at a certain age we should be discounted. What if more of us proudly proclaimed our ages? What if we women spoke openly about menopause, including all the not-so-comfy body changes and symptomology? Would we make a dent in the stereotype that life ends at 40 or 50?

Women and men deny aging in multiple other ways. Numerous studies have found far too many people underestimating their likely future needs, from finances and health to the kind of home and community they will need to age comfortably and actively. For many, there's undoubtedly a sense of everything working itself out. After all, we're already much healthier and more active than the generations before us were at our age. Who's to say this trend won't continue? Advances in medicine may keep pace with us as we age. Cosmetic advances, from surgery to products, will continue. We are able (and many of us eager) to continue working long past the usual retirement age, so we don't need to prepare financially for retirement the way our parents did.

And there's some truth in all of this. The most effective deception, particularly self-deception, always has a kernel of truth. Even the impression that aging is fundamentally positive leads to an optimistic outlook on aging that is itself deceptive, for at the root of this approach there is something we want to avoid. This something is all the negative associations and assumptions we have about aging and what they mean to grow older. In many minds, aging conjures images of nursing homes or being sequestered from the world in a retirement community, shut-ins relying on others to drive them or to run basic errands, boredom, loneliness, invisibility, and irrelevance. It's tempting to live for the moment rather than depress ourselves with facing any of this isolation sooner than we must.

Until, however, we face the realities of aging and prepare for various alternative futures, we won't recognize how much choice we really have in how we age. The worst-case aging scenarios do not have to be true for us, but too many of the scenarios could come true if we wait to deal with them until we have to.

What's more, if we don't start thinking and planning now for the possible futures ahead of us, we will also miss out on discovering the Aspirational Ageless Future that it is in our power to create, the chance to see the many positive aspects of aging and to discover the Ageless core within our aging bodies that can lead us to the greatest accomplishments of our lives, to a legacy that will live on in the generations to follow. We'll miss the opportunity to examine the story we are in right now and decide that we wish to tell a different story with our lives, our work, and our legacy.

Our attempts to focus on the positive by ignoring or even denying what we see as negative, ironically, only make us and our society less open to Positive Aging in general. This focus is in part from a lack of role models showing what is possible at any age, but, even more important, this is from too few people speaking out about their needs and desires as they age because they don't want to call attention to the fact that they are aging—not even to themselves.

> **Until we face the realities of aging... we won't recognize how much choice we really have in how we age.**

It is only when we shed the denial and look at the future realistically that we have the opportunity to ensure the best possible future not only for ourselves but also for our families, our communities, and our world. We have the chance to see where our needs and desires intersect with those of other generations so that our solutions are truly age-friendly. We can see an age-friendly emphasis already in universal design in homes, a design that is beautiful and functional for families with young kids as much as it is for aging bodies. City design that enables us to get around easily and independently, such as improved and accessible public transportation, is not only good for all ages but for our Earth as well. Flexible work arrangements suit your colleagues with families or those who are caretakers as much as they suit you. These are just a few examples of how truly age-friendly solutions are those that work for all ages and stages. Imagine how much more we could do together if more of us were more visible and vocal about aging and what it means for us.

It's time to embrace reality and who we really are, including our age. We are the visionaries we've been waiting for—because of our age, not in spite of it.

> We are the visionaries we've been waiting for–because of our age, not in spite of it.

Aging Benefits

"As you get older, step into your grace.
Step into it. You can't be 27 and be a queen."

~Tori Amos

Optimism that's rooted in denial is not authentic optimism. It's a thin veneer over the things we do not wish to think about or face, and this veneer is easily cracked by reminders of what we are trying so hard to avoid.

Because we all tend to default to denial, Positive Aging must be rooted in authenticity, a genuine grasp of the upsides and downsides of aging and of yourself, as well as a conscious choice to discard what is not true for you and to embrace both what is true and what is possible.

The disease view of aging in modern society is decidedly negative, to the point where many of us dread the future and expect the worst, if we allow ourselves to think about it at all. In this context, it can be difficult for some to imagine that aging has any benefits, much less having the potential to be the most incredible time of our lives.

Others are on the cusp of recognizing some of these benefits while still mourning the losses that come with age. Still others are reveling in this stage of life, wishing they could go back in time to tell their younger selves to reach this perspective on aging and life much sooner.

We are all individuals, however, and even two people who are the same age are not necessarily at the same stage in life, and certainly not in the same circumstances. Some of the benefits of aging even show up in some people at a very young age, and in others, they never do. For example, some young people are wiser than their years, and some people spend a lifetime without ever attaining wisdom.

Since defining young and old by their birthdates is fallacious, the concept of Agelessness applies to all generations. These benefits are really the attributes of the visionary, and we all have that visionary inside us, encoded in our Signature Greatness DNA. The benefits of aging are the characteristics of the Ageless Visionary. It's never too soon to cultivate the characteristics that enable us to reach our full potential, to achieve greatness and true fulfillment in our lives, our work, and our world. What's more important, though, is that it's never too late.

> The benefits of aging are the characteristics of the Ageless Visionary.

Some of the benefits described in the next several pages may ring true for you now, while others will take some time to develop. Some may not be important to you, and that's okay too! There is not just one way, nor a single combination that unlocks the Ageless Treasure. What I hope, however, is that you recognize yourself in these pages, even if it's a glimpse of your future self, of the person you've always known you could be. Aging has the unique potential to bring out this person, this Ageless Visionary.

When and how this happens is up to you and the story of aging and your life that you decide to create.

Here are some benefits of Positive Aging.

Optimism

Contrary to the popular image of aging being a source of dread and anxiety, three-quarters of people over 60 in a 2012 National Council on Aging survey said they expect their lives to stay the same or get better over the next five to ten years. This result might at first be read as a "nowhere to go but up" attitude, but two-thirds said that the past year had been normal or better for them.

Some analysts attribute this optimism in part to the Great Recession—the general economic decline of the previous decade—not having quite the same effect on these generations, which include the Leading Edge of the Baby Boom and their parents. Many of us over 50 managed to sell our homes before the market plummeted (those who aren't aging in place), and many were able to retire with their full pensions, again before the economic downturn gouged retirement plans across the nation.

Had Baby Boomers been polled as a whole, however, the results might have been quite different. The younger Boomers are more likely to still be working and more likely to have been hit harder by the recession. They, and the generations that follow, face a very different Social Security and Medicare system, yet the same, or potentially higher, medical and long-term care costs. Those still working are faced with significantly pared-down retirement plans (such as no matching contributions) and are likely to continue working long past traditional retirement age.

But *having* to work past retirement age just happens to coincide with people *wanting* to do so. One reason for optimism about aging (for all ages) is that we are living longer and healthier lives with each passing year. The entire concept of a retirement age is rather pointless these days, when retirement is no longer desirable for many and age has nothing to do with it.

In fact, many of the gloomier predictions about our future, and especially about the future for people over 50, tie in with opportunities to reimagine our lives and work in ways that not only counter potential problems of the future but use them as a springboard for making our midlife into Elderhood the most meaningful, productive years yet. But we have to start making the necessary changes now.

If we look at some of the most common challenges we face, we can see how solving them is a by product of simply creating the life and work we want in the coming decades. For example, the possibility of Social Security dwindling in the future is offset by more and more people continuing to work and delaying Social Security payments. The longer a person waits to start receiving Social Security, the higher the payments will be, every month, for life.

Working past traditional retirement age is an opportunity to seek work we enjoy, work that has meaning, work that enables us to make a profit and a difference. It doesn't have to mean a life sentence in a career that stifles us. Why not choose work you want to do rather than working because you have to?

We also have it in our power to affect the future of medicine and health care. We just have to act now. Speak up to your representatives not only about health care but also about funding and education in science and technology—the keys to treatments, and even cures, for the most expensive medical problems we potentially face as we age.

Furthermore, we can be active in building and reinventing our communities to support us at every age and stage, minimizing our expenses and our fears about continuing to live independently into our eighties, nineties, and beyond.

Perhaps most important is to realize that all the opportunities we have to change the story of how and where we live and work, and how we manage our health and our finances, are opportunities we share with all generations, not just our own. Mutually beneficial communities, health care that doesn't bankrupt us, medical advances, flexible work arrangements…all these and more are just as important to people under 50 as they are to the 50-plus population, just for different reasons. Our shared values, desires, and vision for the future are why it is crucial for us to consider all aging-related issues as part of a conversation we have with multiple generations, not just our own.

We all have reasons to be optimistic about our future now. Together, we can create a future that lives up to that optimism.

We all have reasons to be optimistic about our future now.

Less Regret

Contrary to
popular belief,
regret is more
the domain of
the young.

Contrary to popular belief, regret is more the domain of the young. In general, as we gain wisdom and experience in life, we learn to let go of what we don't control and focus on what matters most to us—and regrets of the past simply don't matter.

This attitude of letting go has been confirmed by multiple studies. Stefanie Brassen, of the University Medical Center Hamburg–Eppendorf in Germany, and her research team, found that feelings of regret tend to decrease as we age unless we suffer with depression. In fact, the researchers found differences in brain scans in the different groups, suggesting that this change is hard wired, solidified with time. These findings, published in Science, only confirmed earlier research, such as that done by Carsten Wrosch and colleagues at Concordia University's Centre for Research in Human Development (CRHD) and a 2010 study in the Proceedings of the National Academy of Sciences.

I wonder if this change has anything to do with the high success rate of start-ups founded by people over 55? I also wonder what role it plays in the increasing number of Boomer women starting their own businesses? Obviously, many factors are at play, but I'm curious if this tendency to worry less about the past doesn't play a role in the willingness to take risks (vs. being risky) and the motivation to follow through on our visions. The Global Entrepreneurship Monitor found that Americans between ages 55 and 64 were more confident in their entrepreneurial success and were less afraid of failure than other age groups. Donna Kelley, associate professor of entrepreneurship at Babson College, found in her research that "Women entrepreneurs show a substantial boost in well-being as their businesses mature, demonstrating the personal return on investment that comes with venturing into entrepreneurship."

Regret is often seen as a reminder to avoid making the same mistakes again, but how well does that work, really? How often do people go through life doing the exact opposite—repeating the same mistakes over and over again? And how motivated are people who dwell on the past, on beating themselves up? Often this focus on the past leads instead to a sense of futility.

Why take risks only to end up failing again? It's almost as though regrets about the past become regrets about a future that hasn't even happened yet.

And it's worth noting that the people in these studies continued to learn from mistakes and had emotional reactions to them. They simply didn't dwell on these mistakes or what could have been.

It's no accident that people with depression were the exception to the pattern of having fewer regrets with age. This aspect only underscores the idea that regret is not a motivator. As many of the researchers note, these findings point to the possibility of teaching tools for letting go and focusing on the here and now as a way to ease depression (e.g., take time out, practice yoga, listen to music, meditate, get a massage, exercise, learn how to step out and take a big-picture view of your situation, journal, learn expressive arts, go to a museum or gallery, eat well, limit alcohol and caffeine, get enough sleep, laugh and love a whole lot).

Keep in mind that these study results reflect a range, with the changes in overall well-being and the loss of regret happening over the span of decades, after 50 and most prominently after 65. My point is that by knowing about our probable future psyches and brain chemistry, we can more consciously and confidently avoid giving our fear of regret (and of failure) so much weight in decisions about the future.

We can move forward boldly based on where we want to go, not where we've been.

Truth-Telling

As we age, we tend to worry less and less about what other people think. We speak up about what matters to us, when it matters—in both the words we choose and the actions we take. This forthrightness, in turn, requires standing in our own shoes and walking our talk—in other words, being a truth-teller, a characteristic that can definitely show up in some people at any age, particularly Ageless Visionaries.

Sometimes, the truth we tell is brutal. People don't want to hear it, and often there's backlash.

With every major social movement in the history of the world, we've seen backlash when visionaries have spoken the truth–abolition, civil rights, women's rights...the list goes on. But once that truth is out there, it cannot be put back in its cage.

With every major social movement in the history of the world, we've seen backlash when visionaries have spoken the truth—abolition, civil rights, women's rights...the list goes on. But once that truth is out there, it cannot be put back in its cage. It has a way of unlocking the truth from more and more people until it reaches a critical mass leading to profound transformation—such as the end of slavery and major strides in equality for all races, for same-sex couples, and for women.

The saying is true: The truth will set you free. That's only part of the story, though. The truth will set others free as well.

Eleanor Roosevelt acted her truth by not only supporting women's organizations, but also by holding weekly press conferences that were for women journalists only, forcing media organizations to add female reporters to their staff. Rosa Parks acted her truth when she refused to sit at the back of the bus. Sherron Watkins, Enron vice president, acted her truth when she called out Kenneth Lay on the company's fraudulent accounting. Retired Army Lt. Gen. Claudia J. Kennedy, the highest-ranking female officer, acted her truth when she spoke out about sexual harassment in the United States military. This list could go on and on.

Truth-telling isn't just about speaking out on big issues. It's about embodying our truth, big and small. It starts with being honest with ourselves, with who we really are, inside and out, and then stepping into that truth, ultimately leading and inspiring change in our world.

Every day is your moment of truth.

Truth-telling is definitely one characteristic of aging that can be the most freeing, yet the most difficult to embrace. We can generally agree that telling the truth is the right thing to do in most situations. Yet often we hold back, saying what we think others want to hear, or simply refraining from expressing an opinion or idea when we suspect it won't be well received.

Of course, not all opinions should be shared, especially when they would have no possible positive effect. We don't need to volunteer our opinion of a relative's cooking or a co-worker's fashion choices, for example.

But when the truth could lead to positive change—such as more efficient and effective business practices, more meaningful communication in a relationship, or even social changes that rely on speaking out against injustice—we don't do anyone any favors by withholding the truth or saying something different from what we really think.

One of the barriers to telling the truth is societal. Many of us, chiefly women, are taught to be polite, that we are responsible for other people's feelings. Truth-telling might upset the status quo, and we will be responsible for the chaos, real or imagined, that will ensue.

We fear the consequences, which are unfortunately often very real. Women who are direct and truthful in the corporate world or in politics are often labeled as bitches. Women and men who are willing to tell brutal truths often encounter defensive reactions and, sometimes, downright hostility. On top of these consequences, when we are nearing retirement age or fearing outplacement we don't want to make waves.

Too often, however, we don't tell our truths because we imagine the worst. Even if telling the truth could, in fact, build trust and transparency and free others to tell their truths, we are too afraid.

Sometimes, we don't tell the truth because we lack the communication skills to do so in a way that focuses on solutions, not problems, eliciting feedback and fostering collaboration instead of competition. When this is the case, we do experience negative reactions, which only seem to provide evidence that we should be more careful about telling the truth in the future when, actually, they are evidence that we simply need to approach our truth-telling more skillfully.

And sometimes, of course, no matter how carefully we communicate, and no matter how much being a truth-teller is an expected part of who we are, we still face consequences. In some cultures where truth-telling is not the norm, or where politics make truth-telling risky (such as in many longtime groupings, corporations, academia, and other hierarchal organizations and institutions), putting ourselves out there might not always have the intended effect, at least not immediately.

My rule of thumb is to "tell it like it is for you," that is, how you see things solely from your perspective. Most importantly, sharing how you want things to be, or how things need to change, can shift the dynamics in a flash. Consider using a simple-sounding phrase like, "The way I feel when you don't take out the garbage is…" or stating what impact the other person's actions or words have on you, from your perspective. It is best to come from an objective witness viewpoint reporting back the facts.

It is important to take total responsibility for your thoughts and actions and stay honest, rather than placing blame. But should your truth-telling fall on deaf ears or if those receiving your truth-telling are in denial or they themselves are at cause, then you may have to make some hard choices (e.g., you can choose to go head to head, stand your ground, ask a trusted third party to mediate, or decide it's just not worth your time and energy to be in a win-lose conversation).

Remember, there are always two or more involved, so that means all parties are responsible for their own responses and/or reactions in every interaction gone astray. It's up to each person to keep checking in with their Self frequently to be sure that they are awake and aware of their own motivations and truth. Continue refocusing in the present tense as often as you can so that what you share is true for you. It's paramount that you take responsibility only, but fully, for your part in your interactions. You can't be responsible for anyone else's mistruths or misjudgments. This is a lesson hard earned over the years that means letting go of the belief that I am or you are responsible for someone else's beliefs, actions, and reactions.

Over the years, while leading and facilitating groups (coaching, consciousness raising, women's circles, team building, organizational system change, and more), I've seen the fundamentals of Group Dynamics 101 play out before my eyes. Heads up: The ugly side of group dynamics shows up most often when entering into a group with longtime established cultural mores and bonding and/or when bringing together turf-protecting silos within organizations. Truth-telling is the only way group consciousness will evolve. Each of us has to be willing to stand up and tell the truth. In facilitated groupings, the facilitator-leader takes the place of "witness" and will call the group to task when group dynamics go awry or when someone is out of line and the group needs to be brought back to center. Long-standing studies in group dynamics show that when group bonds have formed they can be formidable.

In fact, when someone challenges the old way, the existing members tend to close ranks, even if the longtime member is the perpetrator or is dysfunctional. The newbie truth-teller has only a few choices: either

> **Truth telling is the only way group consciousness will evolve.**

succumb to the accepted rule of law of the existing group and shut up forevermore or pursue the truth and run the risk of being considered an interloper, outsider, or outlier, who might get devoured or pushed out. If you decide to stay, then your choices are to duke it out; try to reason for a higher truth or find a mutually agreeable solution; take a break or "time out" to temporarily disengage from the conflict and get some space and fresh perspective; or simply recognize that this person, group, or system is toxic/dysfunctional, it's too dangerous to stay, and that the risk outweighs any benefits of remaining.

If the group refuses to review the situation or make any change and things remain stuck and destructive, this comes at the expense of everyone involved and is inherently troubling and divisive. In the case of leaderless groupings, the problem is that no one steps forward to truth-tell or to call out bullying. Instead, the members close ranks around the bully who holds the group's shadow material. For a leaderless group to keep its integrity, every member has to be willing to hold everyone to the same truth-telling mandate.

Needless to say I, like all of us, have experienced and witnessed conflicts. Fortunately, my life experiences have honed my innate gift to "see" and recognize patterns and key players in a dynamic, as well as to forecast potential conflicts and probable outcomes. I've found that it's critical to know when to stand up and be counted by telling it like it is while accepting the inherent risks of rupturing a relationship or a system's dynamics, much as any whistleblower does. But in so doing, veteran truth-tellers also have to recognize when to call it quits so they can walk away before being devoured by the shadow powers who perpetuate the untruths and dysfunction. Truth-tellers also have to know when it's in the best interest of all concerned to be the one who walks away from conflict and its potential (overt and covert) backlash that may arise when the veil of denial is lifted, untruths called out, and collusion revealed. The role of truth-teller is never easy, but it's necessary if we are to evolve from what's so to what can be.

For instance, a very prominent midlife woman scientist client of mine called me recently for a consultation on how to effectively approach a challenging, abusive client. Her long-distance, high-fee client behaved erratically by one day complimenting her, the next berating her, and then threatening to hold back on past-due invoices. Although both of these professionals shared a vision for the future of the work at hand, it was becoming clear that the dynamics were off the chart, pushing them closer to the brink of breaking their contract. But the high fees and hopes for being paid back invoices, kept my scientist consultant on the edge of the abyss, unable to take action on her own behalf while raging inside. The only possible answer was to encourage her to take matters into her own hands by requesting a one-to-one truth-telling conversation. Like so many of us today, this was even harder to imagine at first since the only means of communication was virtual rather than an in-person visit, since her client was thousands of miles away in another country.

To ready her for this confrontation, we role played over and over again until she had removed all her hesitation, excuses for her client's behavior, and deleted any hint of her taking responsibility for the breakdown and disconnect. Instead, my client addressed her cantankerous client by expressing her truth about what she believed to be *not okay,* and doing so moved both of them to an open, deeper dialogue about the root causes of their breakdown in communications and erratic dynamics. Surprisingly to both of them, new information arose that clarified misunderstandings and misconceptions. As I prompted her to do, they agreed on monthly Skype face-to-face conversations and agenda setting, as well as weekly updates. As a result of this outreach, all past invoices have been paid to date, and both of them welcome their ongoing monthly virtual meetings.

There is no expectation on my part or hers that this client will change his ways permanently, for as the old adage goes, "A tiger doesn't change its stripes." The same is true for ingrained aggressive and erratic behavior of abusive power holders if not dealt with directly on an ongoing basis. In time, it may behoove my client to drop this challenging client and replace him with new high-paying clients who are positive and appreciative, and pay on time.

The most important takeaway is that my client has now learned how to stand in her own shoes and speak her truth, no matter how intimidating the other person is. This will hold her in good stead for the rest of her consulting career and will carry over into all her interactions, personal and professional.

As we age, it can get easier to look beyond the immediate situation to the bigger picture. The more of us who tell the truth, the more we create an environment where truth-telling is valued, where others feel comfortable stepping up and doing the same.

Sometimes telling the truth isn't about standing up for a cause or speaking up against unethical or immoral behavior. Sometimes telling the truth means owning our mistakes, taking responsibility for our actions. Telling the truth is often noble even when the actions we own are far from it.

But of course telling the truth often has consequences, and lying or evading the truth all too often does not. The latter is so in part because, as a patriarchal culture, especially in Corporate America and politics, too many people equate admitting mistakes with weakness.

In actuality, truth-telling takes strength and courage, especially when we have to acknowledge our own imperfections. Truth-telling also strengthens our relationships, our communication, our trustworthiness, our leadership, and our ability to solve problems. We can't solve a problem without acknowledging the part we play in it, without acknowledging that a problem even exists.

> We can't solve a problem without acknowledging the part we play in it, without acknowledging that a problem even exists.

From killer tidal waves to ISIS and Boko Haram wanting to pull us back into the Dark Ages, we find ourselves in shock that our rights as women, perhaps even more so as we age, are being eroded before our eyes. Our very survival and how we thrive at all ages now depends on how skillfully we ride the curve of change together and speak out, our public truth-telling. Malala Yousafzai, Elizabeth Warren, Analisa Balares, and Ruth Bader Ginsberg come to mind as examples of women across generations who are emerging as inspirational examples of courageous truth-tellers in the worst of circumstances challenging the status quo in our times. Examples of women emerging as inspirational examples of courageous truth-tellers continues to abound. Perhaps you, your daughter, or your granddaughter are (or will be) one of these women?

Recent climate change gatherings and protests are forcing us to tell the truth to one another, young and old, publicly, even with risks attached (like jail time, for one). Around the world, people are dialoguing and finding ways to turn our global conversations around before it's too late to stop continued planetary destruction. Our Earth and humanity's survival depend on the outcome of our intergenerational truth-telling conversations and high-integrity collaboration. A welcome blessing is that in hearing and speaking with one another, instead of at one another, we'll form deep abiding win-win, even loving, relationships in all domains of our lives.

Here in the States, I'm hearing more and more lately about circles of women forming at a fairly significant increasing rate. These groupings are forming networks that crisscross the United States and, no doubt, the Earth. If we're really smart and conscious, we can stay ahead of the curve. Some are spiritually based, others forming around our life experiences, still others for activist or philanthropic reasons.

All of these newly emerging circles I'm hearing about once again are about women coming together, much like we Second Wave Feminists did in the early 1970s. Back then we came together to form consciousness raising groups, better known then as "CR" groups, and to change the conversation around what it means to be female in America...and around the world.

In the 1970s we women were all about speaking out and being heard in whatever role(s) we filled in our personal and professional lives. All of us came together to make change happen. We were afraid to take such bold chances. At minimum we were hesitant. We hadn't a clue how the circle was going to work or if it was going to be our "thing." We had to trust the process while allowing transformation to occur, even if not at our desired pace.

Today these circles are even more evolved. They are filled with women who have been doing their own personal growth for a long time, are now seeking an even deeper awakening and greater leadership roles, and are willing to fully step into their own shoes so to speak. Gaining or already attaining personal and professional mastery, these women are well funded and ready to make change happen.

One example of a large and growing gathering of women making a difference around the globe, which meets in Manhattan each autumn, is Womensphere Summit, the realized outgrowth of Analisa Balares's Womensphere Foundation and conference.

Just like in my youth, the men are coming too. You can track this shift from 100 percent women in attendance to now a growing percentage of men showing up at educational venues like the well-respected Kripalu Yoga Center in Great Barrington, Massachusetts, and the Omega Institute in Rhinebeck, New York.

Never doubt that a small group of thoughtful committed citizens can change the world: indeed it's the only thing that ever has.

~ Margaret Mead

There are also growing movements afoot to transition our communities into sustainable oases to serve our towns, villages, and neighborhoods, even urban ones. If you are interested in more information, please check out Transition.org.

For the foreseeable future, even as Millennials age, our demand for affordable housing is going to keep going through the roof, yet supply is limited, much of it shoddy, and certainly not age friendly. The only way to go forward as we build anew and retrofit existing communities, enclaves, and cities, is to go age friendly, as in designed for all ages. Equally important is to stay in touch with our inner world, telling the truth as fast as we can while we stay firmly grounded in reality.

An aspect of telling the truth requires that we are honest with ourselves first and foremost. What most of us are not so good at is defining boundaries and game rules from the get-go so no one loses. Rather, we create win-win situations and exchanges. A not-to-be-forgotten basic rule of thumb: When the excrement hits the fan, go for truth-telling without blame placing. I'm not promising it will be easy, but nothing else in life is easy at first, especially when it matters the most.

Being able to embrace our whole inner world is crucial to being a truth-teller. The ability and willingness to tell the truth, even when it hurts us—especially when it hurts us—is the most empowering possible benefit of aging, and the one that can unleash our potential to be truly great

...when the excrement hits the fan, go for truth telling without blame placing.

individually and together. We can make a difference in the lives of other humans on this planet only by owning the fact that we too are human.

Discernment

Being a truth-teller goes hand in hand with another ability we are more likely to develop with age: discernment. Being able to go below the surface and see beyond what's obvious, distinguishing differences among options, reading character and motives, and, most important, discerning patterns (consciously or not) that organize everything, individually or collectively—all are crucial to seeing what the truth really is.

We are all shaped by our experiences in our personal lives and in our careers or businesses, and these go a long way toward helping us grow, improve, and take calculated risks. Our experiences can help us discern the truth of a situation or a person. Our past successes, and especially our failures, can help us see past the obvious, going beyond the information at our disposal to see how it connects, what it really means, and what is likely to happen if we take action A, B, or C—or no action at all. In fact, a recent study in Topics in Cognitive Science found that declines in such attributes as short-term memory over time are matched by increases in pattern recognition and our ability to notice the nuances in a situation or in information. This change is in part because we simply have more information in our brains, accumulated over a lifetime. It takes longer to sort through it all, but all that information increases our ability to discern important patterns and subtle differences.

These experiences and cognitive changes may explain why entrepreneurs over 50 are twice as likely to be successful when starting a business compared with those under 50. For all of us, discernment often requires stepping out of our experiences, for they can narrow how we view the world. Often, our experiences keep us stuck in a rut because we don't see new ways of looking at situations or people. Although discernment tends to develop more in the aging brain, it is a skill that we can learn and develop consciously at any age.

You can start practicing this skill on your own by reviewing past decisions to see what you missed and by consciously asking questions about what really matters to you, what's worth your time, and what matters only because you think it should. Stepping back and looking at the big picture (the god's-eye view or view from the universe) can help you to see which part of you is experiencing a particular situation. What you are experiencing may not really be what's there, or it may not be the whole truth.

Often, we need to seek an outside perspective to help us see past our own blind spots and to challenge our assumptions about what the truth really is. Skilled facilitators can take you to a big-picture view so that you can move away from your experience and access those parts of you that can make conscious decisions rather than knee-jerk reactions. Trusted family and friends can also give us perspective if we are open to hearing the answers, although this can go only so far, for we tend to share a group blind spot along with long-ago ingrained patterns with those close to us.

In business, outside sources are essential to discerning the truth. Without focus groups, surveys, social media analyses, and other ways of asking for feedback, we'd be far more likely to assume our customers want what we want, which is often a mistake. Take, for example, the Ameriprise ads that attempted to connect with Baby Boomers by playing to nostalgia. The Ameriprise commercials, featuring the now-deceased iconic Boomer Dennis Hopper, star of the beloved iconic movie *Easy Rider,* concentrated on the theme that dreams don't retire and Boomers need to have an advisor. These ads all failed because, as David Wolfe pointed out, "They try to connect with where Boomers were, not where they are."

No matter how accomplished we are or how much experience we have under our belts, we all need guidance at some point in our lives—in fact, throughout our lives, most notably during transitions. The only thing that is constant in this universe is discontinuous change. We can't make a difference in our lives, our work, or our world if we cling to the same mind-set, even if that mind-set brought us success in the past.

> No matter how accomplished we are or how much experience we have under our belts, we all need guidance at some point in our lives.

Wisdom

We who are old know that age is more than a disability.
It is an intense and varied experience, almost beyond our capacity
at times, but something to be carried high. If it is a long defeat,
it is also a victory, meaningful for the initiates of time,
if not for those who have come less far.

~ Florida Scott-Maxwell, *The Measure of My Days*

One of the most obvious attributes associated with aging—yet the most elusive to define—is wisdom. We usually know it when we see it, but what is wisdom, exactly?

Wisdom is, in a sense, a composite of many different characteristics—profound knowledge, conscious awareness, intuition, foresight, patience, the ability to see the big picture, experience, openness, and empathy—but even then, wisdom is greater than the sum of its parts, just as the use of wisdom has a greater impact beyond the self.

These characteristics alone do not confer wisdom, although developing them can lead us toward it. To do so requires going beyond the surface. Knowledge alone, for example, is not enough, although having much knowledge is often mistaken for having wisdom.

Knowledge itself has many layers that go beyond simply understanding facts. Profound knowledge, which can help lead to wisdom, includes strategic knowledge (which often goes hand in hand with experience and foresight), understanding change and variation, knowledge about context and relationships and about the multiple, often subtle consequences of our choices. Profound knowledge leads to embracing transformation and to knowing, both crucial aspects of wisdom.

Wisdom is often associated with age and experience, and this association isn't entirely false. With years of experience living and working and relating to others, our intuition and foresight are honed, and our ability to see the big picture is usually strengthened simply from having a larger picture of experiences in our past to draw from. This idea is supported by the research I mentioned earlier about the cognitive changes that occur in the aging brain. But we all know that not everyone over a particular age is wise, and most of us have encountered remarkable wisdom in a young person. We may have an edge as we age when it comes to developing wisdom, but it's no guarantee. Other factors are in play.

As my mentor Dr. W. Edwards Deming (1900-1993), the godfather of the Continuous Quality Improvement movement and a leading thought leader and renowned management consultant in Total Quality Management, said, "The past does not always determine the future." Deming went on to share with me that "just because you did well at something before doesn't mean you will in the future, and just because something worked in the past doesn't mean it will going forward. We can't predict the future from the past." This is so because there will always be unexpected discontinuous change. Seemingly more frequent "black swan events" (high-impact, unpredictable events) disrupt what was, and dismantle what appeared solid. Our increasing ability to recognize patterns as we age can therefore be a detriment if we cling to these patterns as truth. We need to also develop the other characteristics of wisdom that enable us to be adaptable, to see and embrace all facets of ourselves and the world with a sense of our place in the grand scheme of things, to recognize that our significance lies not in being the center of the universe but in joining with others to center the universe, our world, and ourselves for generations to come.

In fact, other research on wisdom has shown that those who demonstrate it, who are most fulfilled and able to respond wisely to the challenges of aging, are more focused on others than on themselves. They are more self-aware, with a combination of empathy and humility that I call "humanility." Being humble is to be free from false pride and arrogance. It does not mean lacking confidence or being falsely self-deprecating. Humanility rests on a clear sense of the truth of what we don't know and how much we still have to learn, while owning the knowledge and the inner knowing that we do have, and respecting our earned wisdom.

Humility paired with compassion and empathy, an understanding of how we are all interconnected in the flow of life, nature, the universe, results in humanility. This enables us to see what the world needs while being acutely aware of how our unique talents, knowledge, and knowing can meet those needs, as well as what we still need to learn.

Humanility is key in a visionary leader of any age. As business expert and researcher Jim Collins found in his research of companies who have managed sustainable success, "The most powerfully transformative executives possess a paradoxical mixture of personal humility and professional will." Making a difference in this world requires collaboration, leaders with vision who can help the people they lead and serve to bring out their visionary voices as they move toward meaningful, sustainable success—as individuals, as a team, and as planet Earth.

This attribute is essential for all of us, not just those at the helm, for ultimately we are all leaders of ourselves and we are all part of various teams and networks of people at work, in our families, in our communities, both online and in person. Even the solopreneur with no employees does not live and work in isolation. Humanility can help us get in touch on a deeper level with everyone we are connected to, from our colleagues and clients to our family and friends. These deeper connections, particularly intergenerational connections, are the path to reinventing our world story together and with the wisdom it takes to do so sustainably.

When we can meld earned wisdom with constantly evolving profound knowledge about chaos, complexity, and transition, about Starship Earth and one another as visionary cohabitants navigating into the future, we can create our preferred aspirational futures. We can open the gateway to greater creativity, innovation, and resiliency to sustain all that matters most—in our personal lives, our professional endeavors, and as a stewards of today's tomorrows.

A wise person tends to be optimistic about these tomorrows, although whether this optimism is the result of wisdom or a necessary factor in developing wisdom is interesting to ponder. For example, wisdom enables us to face uncertainties and chaos with confidence that we will be able to solve the problems before us, even if it takes us a while (and no small amount of patience and sometimes hardship) to do so. Wisdom also enables us to

> Humanility is key in a visionary leader of any age.

distinguish between the problems we can and should solve (e.g., a leaky roof or relationship) and those we need to let go, (e.g., anything that drains you, including an abusive loved one).

We are moving into an era of increasingly available information at our fingertips, yet as a nation and as a planet we are clearly not using this information wisely. Three major reasons for our underutilization and unwise use of this new data are the overwhelming speed and volume of information and the fact that few of us regularly take time to reflect (a necessary habit of the wise). As a result, our environment and our social and political landscapes are paying the price. At an alarming rate we are experiencing cybercrime, invasion of our privacy, and the unauthorized capture of confidential data from corporations. Not as obvious to most of us is that we are as yet unable to control or decipher this bombardment of information so that we can make savvy choices based on in-the-moment updated metadata while retaining confidentiality and security.

Yet we are at the threshold of having more of our population than ever before in the position to seek and develop wisdom while also having the health and longevity to put this wisdom to use in the world, to model the profound difference we can make. We are also at a tipping point in the human race, in the age of humanity, when we are finally ready to evolve, to mature into a people that prizes wisdom at all ages, an Age of Greatness for our Earth that parallels the Age of Greatness within each of us. This future is far from inevitable, but never before has it been so within our reach. Will you reach for it?

The Power of Invisibility

*And then not expecting it, you become middle-aged
and anonymous. No one notices you. You achieve
a wonderful freedom. It is a positive thing.
You can move about, unnoticed and invisible.*

~ Doris Lessing

One of the biggest fears we have about aging is of becoming invisible, irrelevant to the world. Women, who are valued for their appearance first and foremost in our society, tend to feel this diminishment more acutely than men as they age. The negative side of being invisible is clear to most of us. The world no longer seems to notice or care about us or what we have to say—if it ever did in the first place. We seem to lose our voice because no one is listening. Sometimes we don't even use our voice because we don't believe we'll be heard, so why bother? Being invisible contributes to the vexing problem of low self-esteem, robbing women of the confidence they need to stand up and make a difference.

But there is a positive side to being invisible, as Doris Lessing captures so eloquently: "And then not expecting it, you become middle-aged and anonymous. No one notices you. You achieve a wonderful freedom. It is a positive thing. You can move about, unnoticed and invisible." Lessing had it right that there is a power to being able to work behind the scenes and make change without worrying about our own egos. We have the ability to go with the flow of nature, of life, and the profound opportunity to influence others to make earth-shattering changes without anyone even realizing we are doing so.

Jim Collins studied 1,435 top companies and found that only eleven companies managed sustained growth. At the helm of each company was a leader with a clear vision for the future of the company and how it conducted its business, paired with humility, working quietly behind the scenes to shape the organization, and to realize its shared vision. This is but one example of the power of invisibility—if we learn to understand, embrace, and leverage it.

This concept is not new. In fact, it's ancient, found, among other places, in Taoist wisdom. As Lao-Tzu wrote of the invisible power of a leader: "When actions are performed without unnecessary speech, people say, 'We did it!' "

David Straker describes this principle further: "In Tao, a leader is sage and invisible. With touch so light, sensitivity so sharply honed, the leader seems to do nothing special, yet somehow they achieve their goals." The wisdom is ancient but not prevalent in our patriarchal military-industrial society in which only visible leaders are valued. Therefore, the ego constantly disrupts the natural flow and inhibits transformation and the collaboration required to make changes that benefit all of us, not just a few.

The inner masculine aspect is dominant in some women, as well as in most men, making invisibility undesirable and all but impossible. War, environmental destruction, social and economic injustice—all lie at the feet of a society in which the desires of the ego supersede what is right and what is necessary for the world to survive and thrive.

But women have the opportunity to harness their dominant inner feminine aspect, to go with the flow, making changes and collaborating with others in ways that go unnoticed by a society so focused on the visible, on the ego. When we fly under the radar of the good old boys' network, we can make significant, sustainable changes without anyone standing in our way.

Thus, women must step forward today and act on our power to make a difference—through our votes, our purchases, our leadership, our vision, and, yes, our success. Striving for meaningful, sustainable, and profitable success is necessary if we are to have the resources and power to lead significant change—at any age and for all ages.

The challenge is to balance the invisible and the visible, to know when we need to work behind the scenes and when we need to speak up and be heard—be present. We need to learn how to marry our invisible power with our visible, visionary leadership. We need to lead the way toward women being a powerful presence for change without losing the invisibility required to effect that change.

I suggest we start by recognizing the power of invisibility in the first place and understanding that to be invisible doesn't mean to be inadequate or without value or voice—just the opposite. Invisibility is inherently powerful. By understanding and learning how to use this power, we will begin to see more clearly the times when stepping out of the shadows will make the biggest difference in our lives, our work, and our world—and when remaining in the shadows is the only way to shine a light on a future that matters, to all of us. Sen. Elizabeth Warren is one woman who comes to mind as an example of balancing the invisible and the visible as she works both in the open and behind the scenes, traversing the edges and subtly making change happen. Whether moving forward, often with pushback

The challenge is to balance the invisible and the visible...

from others (such as the powerhouses of Wall Street), or being seemingly out of play while, in fact, actively cultivating connections and being engaged on all levels with the work at hand, Warren has mastered flowing with the Taoist's wu wei. She uses subtle invisibility to bring truth to the fore, while knowing when to stand up to the bullies who want to take her down. Warren has attained and owns a truth-teller's presence. The senator also knows when and how to use the power of invisibility and is not afraid of stepping out as a truth-teller and change agent when at a crossroads where her actions greatly impact, and even determine, the future. Warren is a genius at making the choices that open up possibilities.

As for the best leaders,
the people do not notice their existence...
The second best leaders, people honour and praise...
The next best leaders, people fear...
The next, people hate...
When the best leaders' work is done the people say,
"we did it ourselves."

~ Lao-Tzu

Presence and Luminosity

The phenomenon of growing increasingly invisible as we age, and using that invisibility to empower us and others to be change agents, is related deeply to another attribute that increases with age—and especially when coupled with wisdom—presence.

The invisible power to fly under the radar and quietly lead change is a part of the ineffable presence Ageless Visionaries carry in their everyday lives.

Have you ever been around someone who draws people to them, who seems to emanate a strong sense of who she is and what she is about? No matter what she is doing, from socializing at a party to simply riding in an elevator, she has presence, and she is fully present in the moment, moving between time and timelessness.

Odds are this someone has been you at different points in your life when you've felt clarity about the big picture and your purpose on this Earth. During these times, you've made your deepest connections with others, drawing out who they really are and what matters to them, feeling in sync with one another and with your vision. Your Inner Visionary voice was wide awake and you were not only listening, but you were also physically, viscerally resonating with that inner voice. You embodied your Soul's purpose, your reason for being here at this time in our Herstory, the greatness encoded in your DNA. You had presence.

Imagine recapturing that feeling. Imagine having that presence every-where you go, knowing exactly what your vision is—whether it be a vision for yourself, your family, your community, your world, or all of the above. Imagine easily conveying it in every encounter, inspiring others to awaken their own Ageless Visionary voices. Imagine finding ways to align your visions in ways that lead to breakthroughs, profound shifts, and innovative ideas for taking action to transform your life and change the world—individually, through your work or in the services your business provides, and so on.

If you can imagine it, you can achieve it.
If you can dream it, you can become it.

~ William Arthur Ward

When we resonate with our Inner Visionary voice in everything we do, our presence is palpable yet effortless. We are in the zone, going with the flow, yet able to move that flow in subtle directions simply by proceeding through it toward our clear vision. The flow moves with us, and the people around us shift as well, often imperceptibly, for we are all interconnected. The more others get into their zone, moving with the natural flow of nature and life, the more they too will be able to gently shift the flow toward their vision.

When we resonate with our *Inner Visionary* voice in everything we do, our presence is palpable yet effortless.

As more and more of us awaken our Inner Visionary voice, these gentle shifts in flow become a tidal wave of change.

Science is discovering the power of invisibility and presence in quantum mechanics. According to Heisenberg's Uncertainty Principle, the act of observing changes what is being observed. We do not need to be the bulls in the china shop to effect real change. Several small, subtle changes—many of them carried out through collaboration—can make a monumental difference in our lives, our work, and our world.

The word "presence" itself hints at multiple meanings. Within the word phonetically is both *essence* and *sense*. Presence is about getting to the core of your essence; discovering what really matters to you; and stripping away the mental, emotional, and physical clutter in your life to get at what you really are. Interestingly, the origin of presence is "being at hand," and the word can also mean "exists unseen, like a ghostly presence."

When you have this clarity of focus, you will find that your senses also sharpen. Without the clutter of our mistaken, self-limiting beliefs, our preconceptions, our commitments of time and energy to things that just don't matter to us, we clear the way for our senses to perceive what is truth—a necessary element of that other aging benefit we've discussed, truth-telling.

When our senses are sharpened with presence, we even gain the ability to "pre-sense," as first described by Peter Senge, to be so in tune with others, with the world, with the natural flow of things that we begin to expand our senses into the future, like the oracles of ancient Greece. We sense the possible futures so that we can create our preferred aspirational future, the trends that we can use as tools in this creation, and the ripple effects of our possible actions.

As you focus on how to use invisibility to empower you to make change, I recommend that you also take the time to reflect and make conscious choices about what really matters to you. If you start clearing away the clutter from your life today, the boulders in the stream interrupting your flow, you will be that much more empowered to change your world tomorrow.

As with the other possible benefits of aging, presence is one that we can develop at any age. However, the fact that presence becomes simpler

> Presence is about getting to the core of your essence.

with each passing year does not necessarily make it easy. It's not something that you simply attain and then forget about. Many of us have embodied presence before, but we all have to work to renew and sustain it. We all teeter off center and temporarily fall out of sync, especially in uncertain, challenging times.

Even when we know that responding is the best course, we all fall back into reacting—to emergencies, upsets, losses. Our presence can slip away when rush mode is our default. Going all out, giving all we've got to what matters most, can throw us out of whack. Whatever the reason for our disconnect, we need to take the time to get back in touch with ourselves, to reawaken our Ageless core, our Inner Visionary, and once again embody her voice.

But how do you go about doing this? The answer isn't simply a matter of doing A and getting B. In fact, the answers aren't nearly as important as the questions.

Some of the first questions you must ask yourself are these:

- What matters most to me?

- What does the world need?

- And where do they intersect?

It is at the intersection of your Soul's purpose and what the world needs that you will find your vision, or refine it with renewed clarity and focus.

Of course, there are many other questions you must ask yourself, some of them questions we all need to ask and some of them questions that are specific to you. Most of us need professional guides to get us outside our own heads and repeating patterns to figure out what these questions are. But for now, let's keep it simple. Put the above questions out there, but—and this is important—don't rush just yet to answer them. Let possible answers flow through your mind, your Soul, your body, but resist the urge to grab one just to satisfy that part of you that needs to have the answer, that needs certainty. Right now, uncertainty is where you need to live if you are to find a true vision instead of just another goal disguised as a vision.

To discover your vision and move into the expansive field of possibilities, embracing myriad alternative future scenarios and finding your aspirational

> Our presence can slip away when rush mode is our default.

future story, you need to stop that voice in your head that wants to tell you all the answers. All too often that voice is so loud we don't even hear our Inner Visionary when she speaks. Now is the time to simply listen. Listen and wait for inner voices and outer symbols and messengers.

These messengers come in all sorts of guises if we are open to the message. Sometimes it's a conversation with a total stranger on a plane who refers you to an article or, as happened to me, introduces you to an organizational guru you hadn't heard of before (an experience that led me to opportunities I would not otherwise have known). Other times, it's a book that falls unexpectedly off a shelf demanding to be read at that time. Sometimes a message of great meaning comes in a sleep dream, or in an awake dream state, just waiting for you to take action on its message. For me, my messengers have come in unexpected ways in "appearances," apparitions, and visitations.

Some messengers can easily be blown off as happenstance, unless you've learned to pay attention to your internal bodily truth-verifiers as I have learned to do. Mine are rather obvious as I'll get teary eyed, feel heat similar to hot flashes rise from my chest upward, and feel an internal vibrating throughout my body. So at this point it's hard for me not to recognize a new messenger. Recently I attended a restorative yoga class as a rank beginner. The teacher turned out to be the owner of the yoga center. When the class ended and the other participants left, the owner and I chatted. Unbeknownst to my new yoga teacher, I had been yearning to find a women's circle of experienced seekers and teachers. Just as we were about to say good night, this woman, almost as an afterthought, asked me if I'd consider joining a women's circle she belongs to, since they are open for one more woman to join. I easily could have blown this invitation off, as I knew nothing about her non-yoga related circle, but I knew in a split second, by my bodily truth-verifiers going bonkers, that this woman was a messenger opening a new door for me to enter.

Although you don't control what they are or when they show up, you can start now preparing yourself to recognize them and to listen to what they have to say. Being in the presence of others who are in touch with their own Ageless core is perhaps the most powerful way to awaken your own.

Being in the presence of others who are in touch with their own Ageless core is the most powerful way to awaken your own.

Someone who can guide you through meditation, in-body experiences, Shaktipat, guided imagery, or the expressive arts is invaluable at this stage.

Even without a guide, you can create conduits for this inner voice and outer symbols and messengers: meditation, music, being in nature and connecting with something bigger than yourself, writing…trying something new in and of itself can shake up your perspective and open you to new ideas. Try asking your inner dream-maker to bring forth your Inner Visionary voice, or something you need to know at this time, and keep a dream journal to record the messages you receive.

Regardless of how you go about it, don't give in to the temptation to rush or skip this step. In fact, this isn't even a step so much as it is an ongoing process, an undercurrent to keep you in touch with your inner world and open to messengers even after you've started grounding your vision in the outer world. When you are truly listening, your presence will speak volumes.

> When you are truly listening, your presence will speak volumes.

This process is holistic, bringing together your body, Soul, and mind in alignment, creating synchronicity, or what I call "coHERency." Our ability to be in sync with our deep feminine knowing and aligned with our values can bring us to a state of coherence like none other. Presence is itself visceral. It isn't a head-trip but a physical embodiment of your Soulspeak. Even the visionary within resides in your body, connecting Soul with its vessel. When you start hearing that inner voice and seeing messengers and symbols all around you, don't be surprised if you feel the truth of what you're receiving deep in your belly. There's a reason for the saying "I feel it in my gut."

That's the archetypal inner feminine rising within you, the intuitive wisdom that your Ageless Visionary voice embodies. Women and men have this aspect, but in women it's closer to the surface and often easier to access. But the archetypal inner masculine plays a role in this process as well, supporting the inner feminine for women. For men it's the opposite in their archetypal inner world, with the inner masculine taking the lead. As you work on asking the right questions and opening your Soul and body to the answers, to that visionary voice, you can take the next step and start opening up your mind, gathering the knowledge that will feed the insight you gain.

Begin doing your homework, the research in the outer world that your inner world needs to process for you to ultimately make your vision reality. (You can find out more in my blog www.KarenSands.com/ageless-beat-blog.) If you are focusing on your career or business, research the market, emerging trends, new business models and best practices, technology, visionary leaders and companies, and gaps in what the world needs that business has yet to fulfill, or fulfill adequately.

Dr. Katy Fike, (mentioned in chapter six, "Women Shaping the New Story of Our Age," and chapter seven, "Gray Is the New Green") has found an innovative way to bridge the digital divide in the 50+ marketplace by combining technology and caring when she founded Tech Savvy Daughter, a blog she edits that is dedicated to helping older adults "use technology like their children and grandchildren do."

If you are focusing on reinventing retirement, research what others are doing and where, flexible arrangements with companies or nonprofits that enable you to focus your energy and time the way you want, or encore entrepreneurial opportunities that would enable you to fulfill your Soul's purpose and make a difference while still making a profit. One of the newest trends is for older adults to do internships to test new directions and scenarios before making the leap.

If you are seeking to make changes in your personal life—a move, a renewed focus on relationships, more travel, or more time and energy devoted to new or neglected meaningful pursuits—research places, social opportunities, logistics, and personal growth resources. For all of the above and more, consider what skills you will need to learn and develop to make the most of whatever opportunities you will eventually pursue.

Now is not the time to draw definite conclusions or make decisions. Not just yet. The purpose of this information gathering is to give your visionary something to work with and to fine-tune the messages and interpret the symbols you receive to hone in on your Ageless vision. Continue the inner work of asking questions and developing conduits for your Inner Visionary voice. By consciously getting your inner feminine and inner masculine to work together, you are on the path to creating a future that works—for yourself, your community, and your world.

Creativity

Another benefit to aging that many are unaware of is both an increase and a shift in our creativity, our ability to innovate. Studies, such as by the Kauffman Foundation and Northwestern's Kellogg School of Management, consistently show that innovation increases with age, despite the popular examples of young entrepreneurs Steve Jobs, Mark Zuckerberg, and Bill Gates. These men are notable largely because they are counter to the norm, which is vast numbers of innovators in midlife and beyond working away in companies, science, academia, and more.

Tom Agan wrote about this phenomenon for The New York Times, where he raised excellent points about changes companies should make—for example, to reward retention rather than set their sights on short-term profits with younger employees who cost them less.

He notes that a key to innovation is also the ten to twenty years after the initial discovery, when development and further study of the applications determine how much the innovation takes off. Nobel Prize winners, for example, usually win the prize a good twenty years after the initial discovery, when the world has had a chance to learn about and recognize just how game-changing the discovery was.

As I've mentioned, studies show that the most successful companies are started by entrepreneurs over 55 years old, including tech start-ups. And our present and past stories are full of examples of accomplishments, always fueled by innovative thinking, of people in their forties and beyond.

- Dorothy Fuldheim became the first woman in the United States with her own news show in her forties, and she invented a new format for television news: weaving commentary and interviews into her news summary.

- Ben Franklin invented the lightning rod at 44, discovered electricity at 46, co-drafted the Declaration of Independence at 70, and later invented bifocals.

- Arianna Huffington was 55 when she launched The Huffington Post, and 63 when she held the inaugural Third Metric conference, which led to the successful counterpart section of the Post.

- Willa Cather published her first novel at 40, won the Pulitzer Prize at 50 and, after a period of personal despair in her early fifties, bounced back to write what scholars and critics agree were her greatest works.

- Henry Ford introduced the Model T at 45.

- Frank Lloyd Wright built Fallingwater, a masterpiece of architecture, at 68.

- Jane Addams, suffragist, was a preeminent founder of American sociology as well as founder of Hull House in Chicago, a center for sociological research. Addams, who was also a founding member of the ACLU and charter member of the NAACP, published her first book when she was 50, foresaw World War I and, at 55, started the Women's Peace Party and the International Congress of Women in an attempt to avert it. In 1931, at the age of 71, she received the Nobel Peace Prize.

- Silicon Valley pioneer and serial entrepreneur Sandy Kurtzig started the software company Kenandy in her sixties, receiving $10.5 million in early funding.

And this list is only a small fraction of the examples I could name.

A recent IBM study found that CEOs worldwide believe creativity to be the number one attribute a leader must possess, above even integrity and vision. Outside the corporate world, this attribute is even more clearly a necessity: Creating or radically reinventing your business, your retirement, your relationships—your world—all require creativity.

I've had many clients tell me they are just not creative people, thinking the term describes only artistic people, but this couldn't be further from the truth. We all have creativity inside us, just as we all have an Inner Visionary voice. Seeing alternative futures and selecting and going for your preferred aspirational future, seeing other possibilities for your lives, your work, and your world, require creativity, and new storytelling. Creating paths to these possibilities requires innovation every step of the way. Problem solving is in and of itself a profoundly creative act.

Problem solving is in and of itself a profoundly creative act.

That is one of the reasons creativity increases as we age. We have more experiences to draw from when solving problems and a wider network of people to collaborate with and seek advice from. We are often more able to focus our creative efforts on what really matters, having reached a point in our lives when we no longer want to expend limited energy and time with anything, or anyone, that isn't truly meaningful to us. The procreative energy we once required for other important parts of our lives, such as having and raising children, can often be channeled into the creativity required for new pursuits.

Creativity is in all of us. We simply need to learn how to tap it and develop it. In that sense, creativity can be seen as a skill. So what can you do to start developing this skill? The ways to inspire your creative self, or kick-start an idle creative process, are truly limited only by your imagination, but here are a few tried-and-true methods:

Follow your own interests, regardless of whether others tell you they are impractical, a waste of time, or irrelevant. Bridgette Shannon, of Corning, would have never helped develop the honeycomb material for catalytic converters that neutralizes toxic exhaust compounds if she had listened to others telling her not to bother with taking chemistry in school, a class she found to be an inspiring source of creativity. And if Steve Jobs hadn't followed his interest in calligraphy, he never would have reimagined typefaces for the personal computer.

Play. Make time in your life and in your work to simply play. Reshma Shetty, co-founder of Ginkgo BioWorks, and her colleagues have a LEGO model of a DNA helix in their office. Throughout the day, they play with the model, which fuels their creativity in biological engineering, such as customizing genes in bacteria to create a fuel—or even to smell like a banana.

Redefine "creativity." Debra Sandler, chief health and wellbeing officer of Mars, recalled, "When I was younger, I thought, I'm not an artist. I'm not creative. But I've discovered my creativity is that I can tell what might move consumers." Her creativity included the reimagining of Mars brands, such as the M&M's pretzel chocolate candies that boosted sales even in the midst of the Great Recession.

> Creativity is in all of us. We simply need to learn how to tap it and develop it.

Reimagine past interests. Michelle Khine loved Shrinky Dinks as a child. In her research at the University of California, when they didn't have the equipment to make tiny chips for experiments and medical diagnostics, she reached back into her childhood and reimagined her beloved toy, using Shrinky Dinks to create molds for the chips, a remarkably affordable solution to creating micro devices that became the basis for the company she co-founded, Shrink Nanotechnologies.

Seek out novelty. Even if you already have outlets for expressing and inspiring your creativity, you can boost your innovative thinking by trying new things, especially something you'd never ordinarily try. Similarly, seek out new groups of people to broaden your perspective and inspire new ways of thinking. Here are some possibilities: Consider delving into mindfulness, taking a restorative yoga class, meditating, joining a drumming circle, exploring expressive arts, or just trying something outside of your norm to trigger a new shift and open up your thinking.

Feed your brain, body, and Soul. Creativity requires fuel and raw materials to do its work. Read more, get out more, and get involved in the world around you, but also give your body and Soul time to rest and reflect—go for a walk in nature, meditate, start a journal, do art, play music, dance…make more time to get together with friends for no purpose other than to talk or sit in silence together…or hang out with your kids or, like me, your grandkids, to re-engage with your childlike innocence, curiosity, joy, and creativity.

> The beauty of creativity is that it tends to take on a life of its own, fueling itself and leading you toward unexpected realizations and profound shifts in direction.

Perhaps most important, don't just read about creativity and then do nothing to fuel that fire. Commit to trying at least one thing on this list today, and another tomorrow, and so on. The beauty of creativity is that it tends to take on a life of its own, fueling itself and leading you toward unexpected realizations and profound shifts in direction. All you need to do today is provide that first spark.

Looking Forward

Neurologist and author Oliver Sacks wrote an op-ed piece for The New York Times about his upcoming eightieth birthday, "The Joy of Old Age. (No Kidding)." I highly recommend that you read it in its entirety.

His closing resonated with me in particular:

> "My father, who lived to 94, often said that the 80s had been one of the most enjoyable decades of his life. He felt, as I begin to feel, not a shrinking but an enlargement of mental life and perspective. One has had a long experience of life, not only one's own life, but others', too. One has seen triumphs and tragedies, booms and busts, revolutions and wars, great achievements and deep ambiguities, too. One has seen grand theories rise, only to be toppled by stubborn facts. One is more conscious of transience and, perhaps, of beauty. At 80, one can take a long view and have a vivid, lived sense of history not possible at an earlier age. I can imagine, feel in my bones, what a century is like, which I could not do when I was 40 or 60. I do not think of old age as an ever-grimmer time that one must somehow endure and make the best of, but as a time of leisure and freedom, freed from the factitious urgencies of earlier days, free to explore whatever I wish, and to bind the thoughts and feelings of a lifetime together. I am looking forward to being 80."

This is Positive Aging. This is what it means to be Ageless. It doesn't mean denying age or pretending to be something we're not. It doesn't mean being this perfectly confident person who is doing and being everything she wants to do and be. Earlier in the article, for example, Sacks comments on feeling as though he should be completing his life.

But this feeling doesn't stop him from feeling complete in his life.

Being Ageless means, in part, developing this ability to step outside our lives, to step outside time, and see the world and life as it really is. To go beyond simple knowledge and take that step into knowing. To feel in our bones what time really is and to appreciate both the transience and the beauty that is Ageless.

It also means stepping inside ourselves, to curate our lived experiences, thoughts, feelings, and wisdom, to learn and constantly refine what really matters most to us so that what we add to this collection from here on out can be nothing short of masterpieces, even in the simplest of acts and quietest of moments.

I love Madeleine L'Engle's optimistic words describing her view of Positive Aging, "The great thing about getting older is that you don't lose all the other ages you've been."

Time is just a page number. It's not the story itself.

Welcome to *The Ageless Way*. ❯

CHAPTER 3 ~ *The Ageless Way Reflections*

The questions and exercises below are to help you find your distinct path on The Ageless Way. Turn to page 28 for more about The Ageless Way Reflections.

1. What current and future realities of aging are you most concerned about?

    a. Write each one down, and then brainstorm what you can do now to adapt and prepare.

    b. Which of these solutions have components that are age-friendly and would be beneficial for other generations?

2. Most of the wise women I've interviewed put having a community of mixed ages as the top "must-have" as we age. Do you have this now? If not, how can you create this for yourself going forward?

    Another gem I learned from those visionaries was that no matter how small you downsize, even more so in an urban area, always have a small, easy-to-tend garden so you have your own outdoor space and can connect with nature. As you make your plans for your changing home base over the years, be sure to remember this advice. If you don't like to garden, even one pre-potted plant is still significant.

    I have a client who is very ill and in preparation for her eventual passing. We have worked together to make her remaining time as stress free as possible. She has created a spiral notebook with everything anyone needs to know if she needs to go to the hospital or hospice, as well as instructions on how to close up her affairs. It's hard enough losing someone you love, and no one wants to struggle with wondering what you might have wanted.

3. What benefits of Positive Aging do you see already in existence in your life or in the lives of others?

    a. Combine your list of benefits with the benefits I've highlighted in chapter three, Positive Aging, (e.g., optimism, less regret, truth-telling, discernment, wisdom, the power of invisibility, presence & luminosity, and creativity.)

b. Go down the list mentioned in "a" above and note how you are currently exhibiting these benefits or attributes (truth-telling, creativity, playfulness, etc.) in your life and work.

c. Next, choose the top five benefits you desire to embody.

d. Then make what I call a "T-chart." All this means is to draw on your paper or screen a large "T," but be sure to make the top horizontal line go across the entire page. Create two evenly sized columns so there is one column on each side of the middle vertical line. Place the heading of "Positive Aging Benefits" on the left side of the "T" with a heading of "Benefit Rankings" on the right side of the "T." Voilà! You have a "T" chart.

e. Scan the top five benefits from "c" above, which you desire to embody. Then, without hesitation, rate yourself on how well you've mastered and incorporated each benefit of Positive Aging in your current life and work. Do this exercise for each of the listed benefits, using a rating scale of minus five to plus five or, if you prefer, rate them from plus one to plus five, five always being the highest score. Ponder your rating and why you gave it that number.

f. Next, for any benefit with less than a five, write down three things you can do now to bring the rating score up to a five.

4. What are some benefits of aging, such as invisibility, that could be viewed through an empowering lens or different perspective? What do these benefits look like in your life through that different lens?

a. Start crystallizing your vision by journaling your responses to the following questions: What matters most to me? What does the world need? And, most importantly, where do they intersect?

AGELESS WOMEN

But I feel like I'm just getting started. What's the point of
increasing our longevity if we can't contribute and be valued?

~ Elly Guggenheimer, at age 84

The Ageless Quest

In many ways, the Ageless story for women is the story of a quest, with tasks to complete, fears to conquer, and puzzles to solve within our psyche. One of my favorite analogs for this quest is the Russian story of Baba Yaga and Vasilisa, particularly the insights into the story that Clarissa Pinkola Estés provides in her book *Women Who Run with the Wolves*.

Both Estés and I see the story as a tale of initiation into the power of intuition passed on from one generation of women to the next. The tasks revolve around a young girl, Vasilisa, learning the ways of the wild Crone Baba Yaga, a fearsome wise woman in the guise of a witch who presides over life, death, and rebirth, much like goddesses throughout time and across cultures. Some seek her out because of her wisdom, even though most who do so are killed and eaten.

The story begins with Vasilisa losing her mother, the safe and protected life she knew. By letting her mother go, just as we let go of the safe and familiar, she takes the first step toward developing her own independent sense of self. But the mother leaves her a doll to protect her, which Estés describes as a talisman of her inner spirit, a reminder of her inner power.

In the Ageless Quest, this moment carries additional layers of meaning. For all that our mothers may have passed down to us, most of us don't feel

Well I know a woman
with a collection of sticks
She could fight back the
hundreds of voices she heard
She could poke at the greed,
she could fend off her need
And with anger she found she
could pound every word

~ Dar Williams
"You're Aging Well," written and
performed by Dar Williams, 1993,
Honesty Room, Razor & Tie (lyrics
owned by Dar Williams)

109

we really learned how to be an older woman from our mothers, at least not the kind of older woman we want to be. This may not be true for you. Perhaps your mom is already embracing *The Ageless Way*. If she is, then consider yourself an evolved ancestral version now standing on your mom's shoulders lighting the way for matrilineal generations to come.

The stories our mothers lived or live can be the stories we dread living ourselves, feeding our denial of aging because we don't realize that our mothers' stories do not have to be our own. We are not only without the safety net of the mother in our psyche—as well as, for many of us, in reality—but we are often without the talisman to guide us toward *The Ageless Way*. We have to create our own.

The next part of the story is similar to that of Cinderella, complete with wicked stepmother and stepsisters who are jealous of Vasilisa and attempt to break her down by making her constantly work. Finally, the step family sends her to Baba Yaga to get rid of her once and for all, under the pretext that she needs to get a light to ignite the hearth fires from the witch.

Estés describes the stepmother and stepsisters as representing women's shadow selves, the parts of us that are like the step family, and the struggle between who we are expected to be and who we really are. The doll protecting her from the family, and in her journey through the dark woods, represents the inner knowing we can rely on to navigate the unseen and the unforeseen.

> Our inner knowing is the talisman we've created for ourselves over years of experience.

For those of us on the Ageless Quest, this is a task we have completed before in our lives. Now we face it anew as we attempt to discern who we are when we're no longer young. For us, our inner knowing is the talisman we've created for ourselves over years of experience. Instead of following the visible path of those who've gone before us into midlife and beyond, we instead strike out into the dark of the unknown in our Ageless Quest.

On her journey, Vasilisa witnesses three horsemen, white, red, and black, and the changes in time of day that accompany them. The colors represent the three stages of a woman's life: white, the virginal innocence of youth; red, the menses of adult womanhood; and the black of the wise Crone, the midwife of the feminine mysteries, who can cross over and integrate the dark and the light, the known and the unknown, time and timelessness.

Vasilisa finally reaches the hut of Baba Yaga, which is surrounded by a fence made of bone with skulls atop the fence posts, skulls with fiery red eyes. She must face the fearsome Crone. Estés describes this moment as learning to confront the power in others and in ourselves, to face life and death, creation and destruction. On the Ageless Quest, this is the moment when we need to recognize the power we have as older women, and the source of that power, to combat the myth that aging necessarily means growing increasingly powerless and irrelevant. This is also the moment when we face our future selves in the Crone before us. On the Ageless Quest, we are both Vasilisa and Baba Yaga, both the young girl and the woman older than time itself, both life and death. We learn to embrace both and to balance seeming opposites on the fulcrum of our Ageless core.

Baba Yaga gives the girl tasks to complete, hoping that Vasilisa will fail so that she can cook and eat her. In addition to cleaning the house and the yard, doing the laundry, and cooking, Vasilisa is to separate good corn from rotten corn (or good wheat from bad wheat, depending on the story). On the second day, she has to separate poppy seeds from soil. Both days, with the help of her doll, she is able to complete the tasks, so a disappointed Baba Yaga cannot eat her.

These tasks represent adapting to the wild womanpowers, inner purifications and clearing the psyche. Even the wild woman needs to periodically unclutter her mind. The cooking fire is both passion and the means to feed Baba Yaga or die. The separating tasks are about learning discernment.

These tasks parallel some of the benefits of aging I described in chapter three, all critical tasks and skills we need to acquire to become Visionaries with Wrinkles. If our birth mothers did not teach us, the Elder wise women Crones among us will shine the light so that we can see the way. Discernment, creativity, and so forth tend to come more easily with each passing year, but there are no guarantees. The process of simplifying, sifting and sorting, clearing our life of all but what really matters to us, is necessary for us to be able to incorporate the Ageless flow consistently in our lives. Feeding the wild woman inside, the Ageless Crone, is necessary to be truly alive. We are the New Story Crones, the wise women with wrinkles, mentoring our Inner Girl and the younger women who will follow us on/ in *The Ageless Way*.

> Even the wild woman needs to periodically unclutter her mind.

Finally, Baba Yaga tells the girl that she is allowed to ask her questions, but to remember that knowing too much will make her old too soon. Baba Yaga is the archetypal truth-teller and will answer any question truthfully—although she might kill you after you get your answer! Vasilisa asks about the red, white, and black horsemen and learns that they are the Crone's servants, the sun, the dawn, and the night. She then decides not to ask anything more. Baba Yaga then gives her the light to ignite a fire in the hearth that she needs to bring home—one of the fiery-eyed skulls from her fence. Guided by the light of the skull, Vasilisa returns to her stepfamily who have been unable to keep a fire lit since she left. She gives them the light they asked for, the skull, and it burns them to cinders, leaving her free.

Among Estés's interpretations are that we do not need to push for knowledge, that the knowing will come with time. Vasilisa is given the ancestral knowledge carried in the skulls of the dead, a new power that initiates her into a "matrilineal legacy of knowing."

As both the girl and the Crone, and everything in between, on the Ageless Quest we can both bestow and receive the power of inner knowing. We can seek out the knowing of the women who have gone ahead of us. We can add to that knowing on our own before passing it on to the generations that follow if we are brave enough to go on the quest in the first place, to face death, to embrace and own our inner Crone, and to accomplish the tasks ahead to prepare us for *The Ageless Way*. That way, we may realize our own Ageless Future, and be better poised to leave an Ageless legacy.

> We can both bestow and receive the power of inner knowing.

Embracing the Crone

One is not born a woman, one becomes one.

~ Simone de Beauvoir

When we tap into the chthonic, or subterranean, vein of transformative energy within each of us, our inner Baba Yaga, it allows us to stand in our full presence, speaking out as the truth-telling visionaries we've been waiting for. We are then able to fulfill our destiny as wisdom messengers, visionary leaders, and educators for the twenty-first century and beyond.

We are entering the Age of Greatness. Our Inner Visionary is calling us to act as we become more and more conscious of our claim to our birthright of greatness as women leading the way, shaping our preferred, aspirational future.

For those of you reading who may recoil from this emerging archetypal Feminine force of nature, the original meaning of Crone was a "feisty or mischievous woman" who stood up to the patriarchy who ran the show in the fourteenth century.

It's no accident that the Fates, the oracles, the seers, and so many powerful women of ancient times were often described as Crones. The Crone is not the withered old woman, the hag that patriarchal society has portrayed her to be. She is older than those definitions. She reaches back in history to claim a lost female identity that views older women in a positive light.

Mythologically defined, she is the "wise one—the Crone," the one who knows. She is also personified in myth by Hecate, Medusa, and Kali Ma, who carry the darker mysteries, and La Lobe, Kuan Yin, and Sophia, representing the mother of all. Whatever persona the Crone embodies, she is our midwife into life, death, and rebirth mysteries. She is both the creator and the destroyer of life.

This archetypal motif, which is showing up in dreams and art, is symbolic of the force that will turn the tide from destruction to re-construction of Mother Earth and the resurrection of our Souls. Out of the chaos, new potential will rise from the ashes of what no longer works.

Wherever the Crone is called, she creates transformation amid ambiguity and chaos. Crones are passionate change agents, innovators, activists, teachers, healers, visionaries, and prophets.

> Crones are passionate change agents.

Crones are the ultimate truth-tellers as well. They are authentic and transparent, in touch with the difference between fact and truth. You'll know you've found a true Crone if she is completely present—totally being herself.

She is vulnerable yet she owns her power, and she values her own experience and knowing. Women who carry this archetypal energy will

113

spend much of their time between two dimensions—inward on the psychic plane and outward in the world of everyday concerns. Their point of view is both/and, not either/or. Moving between time and timelessness, they live in the moment and have the wisdom to get ready for the future.

In my interview with her for *Visionaries Have Wrinkles*, Carolyn Conger, Ph.D., a visionary for visionaries, speaks to the quality of those who carry this energy: "There is a lot of strength and sturdiness in Crone energy. No matter how frail the body might appear, there's an energetic there that is absolutely connected to life, and is dedicated to life. This dedication brings women new strength. As I have aged, I have to be careful sometimes because my inner Crone comes across too strong and bold in my knowing."

Conger goes on to compare how those of us in the United States vs. other countries value the Wise Woman Crone: "In this country, there is the fascination with youth and a need to identify with it. Here we fight the Crone energy. In other countries, like the Far East, Bali, Indonesia, and South America, the Crone is respected. In Mexico, for instance, she is a woman who has attained the age of Cronedom and has strength, beauty, and wisdom—and everybody knows it. The Mexican Crone is dripping jewelry from her ears, neck, and arms. She wears a fine shawl, and she has a cane that is carved. At family gatherings, she has her chair, and everyone offers her the best of everything first; not because she's an old lady but because she has earned that honor."

Cronehood is a summation of Feminine life experience.

Cronehood is not limited by chronological age, but is rather a summation of feminine life experience. Cronehood is not limited by gender, either. Men who fully realize the Sacred Feminine within can achieve the wisdom, presence, and consciousness of the Crone.

The onset of midlife accelerates the emergence of this aspect of womanhood to awaken. Menopause may be the initiatory bridge into "Crone Time." But it is in our sixties and seventies that she turns up the heat.

Like puberty, before we got our periods, and now as we leave midlife, we are again moving into uncharted territory. As young pubescent girls, the prize was becoming a highly desired woman. But the prize of becoming a wise woman Elder has not yet been embraced.

In our forties, fifties, sixties, seventies, and beyond, we have the ability to come into our fullness. Something's shifting in the deep bedrock of our Souls—it's the Crone rising. This potent archetypal energy force will not come to all of us as we age, but those to whom she reveals herself are being asked to speak their truth like never before. You'll know it if it happens. For me, my Dream Maker brought images of the Elder Sacred Dark Feminine Crone dressed in telltale black shrouds beckoning me to follow her. She appeared both during sleep and in my daytime reveries. In these numinous visitations she shared messages of what was to come and my role in illuminating *The Ageless Way.*

The Crones are the culmination of greatness. They are the future of aging. Through the full expression of their passions, their presence, their truth, they will lead us all into a new consciousness, and they will embody and model *The Ageless Way.*

Taking Care

I can bring home the bacon, fry it up in a pan, and never, ever let you forget you're a man!

~ Enjoli perfume advertisement, (1980)

Serving others is such an integral part of so many women's lives. If there is one aspect of being post-40, post-50 that we all share in one way or another, it is the concern about care—caring for our parents, our spouses, our grandchildren, our children. Many of you can probably check off several of the above as immediate areas of concern, especially if you are a member of the sandwich generation, those caring for aging parents while still helping your children get on their feet in a slowly recovering economy.

Women continue to find themselves in caretaking roles even as more and more of us are also working full time. The physical, emotional, and financial strain inevitably takes its toll. Yet the one person who seems to be left off the list for care is the one person who is most crucial to everyone's needs being met—you.

This is not news to you, I'm sure. Yes, yes, you know you must replenish yourself so that you have something left to give, but who has time? And on the one hand, you know that you have to make time, even a little, or you will simply wipe yourself out and not be there for anyone. Yet, even knowing this, you push forward. That superwoman ethos we first imposed on ourselves as working mothers, able to do it all, has not gone away.

Our nests may be empty, but we still feel responsible for everyone's well being. We are "younger" and healthier than people our age were a generation ago. We're thinking about starting a business more often than we're thinking of retiring from one. Yet we know that we won't live forever, and we can't deny that our energy is not the same as it once was. It's shifting, yet our lifestyles are not necessarily shifting with it.

I'm not talking about recognizing that we really do need to retire. Just the opposite, actually. Too often we get stuck in either/or thinking, that we either keep going at the same pace and in the same way as we have always done or we throw in the towel and retire to some cookie-cutter senior complex in the desert. But those aren't the only choices. Those really aren't choices at all, frankly.

When I say that our energy is shifting, I mean just that. It is simply moving within us, changing form, no longer the energy of all-nighters to meet a deadline or the kind that fuels caring nonstop for small children. But it is still there, and it is even more powerful than ever before. Especially at menopause and beyond, the energy heats up in us creatively. We can easily miss this, however, if we are focused only on trying to make use of the physical energy we think we need to accomplish everything we want to and need to in our lives.

...it is crucial to find time to care for yourself

This is why it is crucial to find time to care for yourself, to tend the fire of your inner Baba Yaga and feed her in yourself. Not only do you need to restore yourself physically and emotionally, but you also need to learn how to get in touch with this creative fire so that you can use it to shift gears and rebalance, to determine what you need to do now to start that business, for example, so that it nurtures you and fits best with who you are and who you will be with each passing year. If you are feeling stuck in a cycle of work and caregiving, these moments to pause and reflect, to express yourself and tap into your inner wisdom, are necessary if you are going to get unstuck and find solutions that go beyond quick fixes.

Believe it or not, taking time for yourself now will free your time in the future, making it possible for you to not only rise above the day to day but to give more to others and to the world in ways that don't drain you but sustain you. Take the time—make the time—today.

Now let's get ready to rock our age! Come along with me. ❯❯

*You don't get to choose how you're going to die. Or when.
But you can decide how you're going to live now.*

~ Joan Baez

CHAPTER 4 ~ *The Ageless Way Reflections*

The questions and exercises below are to help you find your distinct path on The Ageless Way. Turn to page 28 for more about The Ageless Way Reflections.

1. Consider the older women you have known in your lifetime. What story(ies) have they told with their lives about what it means to age? What story(ies) have they told with their words about what it means to age?

2. Has anyone you know embodied characteristics of the Ageless Woman you aspire to be? If yes, what are those characteristics and how have they shown up in that person's life? If no, close your eyes and envision the ideal older woman, the Ageless Woman you aspire to be. What is she like? What attributes does she have? How does she interact with other generations? What does she tell herself? Now imagine this same woman ten, twenty, thirty years younger. What is the same and what is different? Why are these differences there? What would you like to tell her from your current vantage point?

3. Where are you on the Ageless Quest? Are you in the beginning stages of recognizing you are on your own like Vasilisa? The sifting, sorting, and clearing stage? Or do you identify more with Baba Yaga than with Vasilisa and consider yourself one who has done that work and is holding the light and guiding others to find their way?

4. In what ways are you feeding or nurturing your inner Vasilisa and Baba Yaga? How are these choices different from before, and how do you envision them changing (as they inevitably will…) at various future stages?

Chapter 5

AGELESS ATTRACTION

Beauty and femininity are ageless and can't be contrived, and glamour, although the manufacturers won't like this, cannot be manufactured. Not real glamour; it's based on femininity.

~ Marilyn Monroe

Mirror, Mirror

As I lift my head from the sink to dry off the early morning cold splash of water, I am once again caught by the "unmade" face in the mirror. It is so easy to turn away and not notice…easy to see what I want to see, the perpetually 30-something face peering back at me. This morning I do stop, go eye to eye with this vaguely familiar stranger—and notice the changes in facial lines, the dropping jawline, the eyes now like watery tide pools pulling me down into my inner world. The longer I look, the stronger the urge to turn away. I resist, knowing how much this reflection has to teach.

These lifelines suggesting so many mini-deaths…so many losses…Father, Mother, dear, dear girlfriends in their prime…youthful marriage and divorce, years of painful separation from my children, cherished dreams never to be realized. The familiarity of my long-rejected resemblance to my mother, and her mother before her, engulfs me. My eyes fill for my maternal ancestors' unexpressed Souls, while a bittersweet smile spreads on my reflected face for their gift of life to me. I am reminded that I too am a keeper of their painfully earned wisdom. The weight of this responsibility is palpable. At a cellular level, I feel a resonance with both the past and the future. An awareness floods—my image, too, will someday reflect back to my daughter and her daughters.

*Why is it that as we grow older and stronger
The road signs point us adrift and make us afraid
Saying, 'You never can win'
'Watch your back,'
'Where's your husband?'
I don't like the signs that the signmakers made*

~ Dar Williams
"You're Aging Well," written and performed by Dar Williams, 1993, Honesty Room, Razor & Tie
(lyrics owned by Dar Williams)

I call a dear friend to share the morning's encounter. As I relate my story, she responds in agreement with all the yeahs and mmhmms in all the right places. She even gets right before the bathroom mirror with me, saying, "This morning I noticed that who I see in the mirror looks older than I feel! It's quite a discrepancy. And when I started to put on my makeup, I could hear the cosmetic industries' advice to 'just apply the shadow on the two areas of your lids.' Well, it just doesn't work anymore! My lids have fallen. There are no two areas left!" We laugh like comrades going through some secret rite of passage.

For many of us, the inner reflective quest begins with a more literal encounter with reflection. Looking in the mirror and seeing those first fine lines, then the deepening of those lines into wrinkles, along with the sagging and other changes in my aging body, was never easy. The person I saw in the mirror didn't match how I felt inside. That isn't me. And if that isn't me, who am I?

Who am I if I'm no longer young?

Just as we are both Vasilisa and Baba Yaga, we are both Snow White and the queen. When the mirror stops telling us what it has told us for so many years, the first impulse is often to cast away the reminder of our youth, our Snow White. This impulse helps us to feed our denial of aging for just a little bit longer, a denial that the anti-aging industry feeds with the old myth that youth and beauty are synonymous. It's long past time we do away with that harmful story and create a new story of Ageless Beauty.

The issue with anti-aging isn't that women don't or shouldn't want to enhance their beauty or that these products aren't useful and desirable. The issue is that being *anti*-age is being anti-self, denying a part of ourselves that ironically could be the *key* to finding the sleeping Ageless Beauty within.

The anti-aging promise does away with Snow White, the reminder of our aging, so that we focus solely on the mirror and not on whom we are inside. Anti-aging offers us a reprieve from having to face the question of who we are at this age.

Yet, answering the question for ourselves can be the most meaningful, liberating, and life-affirming step we ever take. It can lead us to fulfilling our purpose on this planet Earth, to awakening our Inner Visionary and creating the legacy we were always meant to create but couldn't until we'd reached this point where experience, wisdom, and the search for meaning all coalesced. But we can't create this future if we are focused on living in the past or as characters in the damaging beauty fairy tale we've all been raised to believe.

We can embrace Snow White in ourselves, to see beauty in us or in the mirror. We don't have to be anti-aging—or anti-self—to find and enhance our beauty at every age and stage.

The less time and energy we spend distracted by the promise of holding on to our youth, the more we can focus our time and energy on what really matters to us, to the people we love, to the world. The more we make the effort to find actual meaningful beauty in ourselves, in who we are now, the closer we get to fulfilling our greatest vision yet.

After all, how clear and grand can our vision be if we don't even see ourselves in the mirror clearly?

Ageless Beauty

Older women, once considered wise goddesses,
are often portrayed as bitter, sexless hags.
Wrinkles on a man? Rugged, distinguished.
Wrinkles on a woman? Horrifying.

~ Beth Howard

Studies show that 84 percent of women feel misunderstood by marketers who are out of touch with what real women want and need, how they see themselves, and how they want to see themselves.

Many women certainly do want to look more youthful, but this desire is not the end-all, be-all of how we define ourselves and what beauty means.

Julia Roberts at age 47 is still a superstar beauty. Recently, Roberts spilled the beans about her decision to take a big career risk: "By Hollywood standards, I guess I've already taken a big risk in not having a facelift, but I've told Lancôme that I want to be an ageing model—so they have to keep me for at least five more years until I'm over 50."

I personally strive more for vibrant, luminous Agelessness, rather than completely erasing all my markers of aging and the hard-earned years of wisdom and experience they represent. We are individuals, and we live in reality. Showing us an unattainable and obviously unrealistic image of how we should look to be beautiful ignores how beautiful women already are, ignores that true beauty embraces the whole woman across the life course.

Our skin, our wrinkles, our hair, gray or colored, our glow, our health, our spirituality, our intelligence, our hard-earned wisdom and accomplishments, our *stories* are three-dimensional and individual. Ageless Beauty is about embracing and enhancing who we are, not being shown an impossible and outdated standard of who we should be.

> Ageless Beauty is about embracing and enhancing who we are, not being shown an impossible and outdated standard of who we should be.

Oprah Winfrey captures my sentiments in her magazine, O, (May 2011): "We live in a youth-obsessed culture that is constantly trying to tell us that if we are not young, and we're not glowing, and we're not hot, that we don't matter. I refuse to let a system or a culture or a distorted view of reality tell me that I don't matter. I know that only by owning who and what you are can you start to step into the fullness of life. Every year should be teaching us all something valuable. Whether you get the lesson is really up to you."

It may well be a matter of surety that comes with maturity. The UK Daily Mail, for instance, reported that those aged 65 and over feel the most confident in their appearance (81 percent), compared with youngsters aged between 16 to 24 (70 percent). Only six in ten Brits (60 percent) aged between 45 and 54 said they feel most confident in their appearance.

New research by UK beauty product company L'Oreal shows we feel younger than our actual age. L'Oreal's study discovered that over half (53 percent) of British people claim to feel more youthful than they are, while a third (34 percent) feel as much as ten years younger. It seems men feel more positive about their looks in their later years (21 percent), compared with just 16 percent of women. Meanwhile, 70 percent of men feel "very confident" in their appearance, compared with just 58 percent of women.

The L'Oreal Confidence Index reveals confidence in our looks goes through ups and downs as we age. Beauty may also be more than skin deep, with 65 percent believing their physical appearance affects their overall confidence. For women, appearance plays the most significant role in confidence, with 70 percent saying it is one of the areas that most affects them.

Marketers, and society as a whole, need to understand that we no longer wish to be told that aging is something we need to be against (if we ever wished this). We don't want to be "youthenized." Anti-aging products and therapies are making record profits, $8 billion and counting! This means only that women continue to seek ways to enhance their beauty—*despite* the advertising focus on aging as a negative process, not because of it. The ageism in these ads, unfortunately, parallels the ageism in our judgment of ourselves and older women in general, both in equating youth with beauty and in assuming that wanting to be beautiful means being superficially obsessed with youth. We can transcend this ageism in the marketplace and in our minds by recognizing that age doesn't need to have anything to do with it. Agelessness—of body, mind, and Soul—and age-friendly—marketing, products, communities—are the next (r)evolution in our conversation about aging, for all ages and stages.

Transcending ageism does not mean that women do not want products and therapies that enhance our beauty or slow the aging process. What it means is that on their own they are not enough. We also want to feel beautiful and Ageless inside and out. We want products that are not "anti" who we are but that encompass who we can be, holistically.

We want a new story about beauty that recognizes how Ageless Beauty truly is. Elisabeth Kübler-Ross captures the true essence of what Ageless Beauty—and beauty itself—is all about: "The most beautiful people we have known are those who have known defeat, known suffering, known struggle, known loss, and have found their way out of the depths. These persons have an appreciation, a sensitivity, and an understanding of life that fills them with compassion, gentleness, and a deep loving concern. Beautiful people do not just happen."

We are seeing the shift already in more strong Ageless Women owning their place on the silver screen: Meryl Streep took on the complex character of Violet in *August: Osage County* (2014), a self-described truth-teller who

> Marketers, and society as a whole, need to understand that we no longer wish to be told that aging is something we need to be against.

at one point monologues about how women all get less attractive with age, asserting, "Men…can still be sexy while they grow older, while women grow old and ugly." She is an ironic character considering that the actress herself is a quintessential Ageless Beauty. Thankfully there's a shift going on as expressed in the 2014 film *My Old Lady* with 79-year-old Maggie Smith, 66-year-old Kevin Kline, and 54-year-old Kristin Scott Thomas. When Kline responds to Scott Thomas's "I'm not beautiful…I'm nearly old," he tells her, "A perfect flower is nearly old."

For years there has been a lack of older female leads in Hollywood, and most big-budget high-profile films have been male-oriented. Breaking the mold, 2013 through 2016 have been great years for women over 40 in Hollywood and for women of all ages in advertising.

We are all-too-gradually seeing more strong Ageless Women in leadership positions. However, the numbers of women at the helm of their own businesses are increasing at a rapid rate. Some companies we'd least expect are recognizing the need for multigenerational "legacy" marketing, such as Cover Girl, with 55-year-old Ellen DeGeneres as its new spokeswoman. American Apparel's new lingerie model is a beautiful 62-year-old, Jacky O'Shaughnessy, and its campaign slogan is phenomenal: "Sexy has no expiration date." Marc Jacobs and NARS are also starting to use more models in their fifties and sixties (more on this in chapter seven, "Gray Is the New Green").

A 2014 mind-blowing, heart-wrenching video interview with the once unknown, newly discovered O'Shaughnessy captures the way our pervasive inner shame berates us as not enough…never thin enough, never beautiful enough, never young enough. In the "What's Underneath Project" video, O'Shaughnessy, an elegant, stunning model, conveys her life story while removing clothing from her body one piece at a time until she is nearly naked, dressed only in her lingerie. What is so shattering about this interview is that the story she shares, despite her being a gorgeous professional actress and model, conveys how much of her life she has spent feeling not good enough, not attractive enough, not thin enough, not enough…As O'Shaughnessy so magnificently unveils in her disrobing and disturbing interview, we've interjected and made patriarchal sourced rating criteria of our outer beauty into our own yardstick by which to measure what it means to be beautiful

> We've interjected and made patriarchal sourced rating criteria of our outer beauty into our own yardstick.

at every age and stage. (You can watch the "What's Underneath Project" video interview at www.youtube.com/watch?v=mBZQpsXUsfw.)

Susan Sarandon warms my heart with her thoughts on Ageless Beauty in V Magazine (Winter 2010/22): "I wouldn't want to be 20 now. I know so much more and I'm much more comfortable in my skin, saggy as it is. … When I hear young girls complaining about superficial things…(I think) You're at the peak of your physical beauty right now! Just enjoy it and stop worrying about your thighs being too big. …If you're upset with how you look at 25, life's going to be tough."

Since this story is already changing on the silver screen, in ads targeting women, among women, and around the kitchen table, it's high time it took place around the boardroom table in companies marketing to women, as well as those who should start serving the 40-plus market of savvy, accomplished peri- and post-menopausal women.

The story appears to be morphing as older Hollywood screen actresses are now giving Millennial women a run for their money! These older women actors espouse the new beauty secret that maturity is hot! Dame Helen Mirren claims that getting naked in front of the camera has gotten easier as she's gotten older. She is emphatic in her claims that wrinkly, full-on nudity is liberating—not humiliating.

A new fashion trend is to go gray! The young and famous Lady Gaga and Kelly Osbourne are sporting faux-gray dos, inspiring other women to do the same. No surprise, now the beauty mavens of Chanel and Dior are showing models with every shade of gray. Perhaps we should be careful what we ask for, though. Are we now going to diminish ourselves if we don't go gray? Whatever hair color we choose, it's now, albeit slowly, getting cooler to be of a "certain age."

So let the reprogramming on aging and women's beauty begin.

We can take back beauty. We can change the story. We can redefine it for ourselves and for generations of women to come. We can make beauty Ageless.

Ageless Women are strong, multifaceted, unique, and real. They control the largest percentage of purchasing power in this country. Ageless Women are the future. Businesses that do not recognize and respect who we really

> We can take back beauty. We can change the story. We can make beauty Ageless.

are, what we want, and how we deserve to be served, will soon be a thing of the past, aged out!

Taking Back Beauty

Sharon Stone has been in the media everywhere, from Shape magazine to an interview on Oprah Prime to The Huffington Post, saying she doesn't want to be an Ageless Beauty, and claiming that it is an unreal idea. At age 56, she was quoted as saying "I don't think ageless beauty exists. …I think it's just a catch phrase. And so I think that's absurd. …I'd rather be my best at my present age, inside and out."

She then goes on to explain: "We have to have internal health and internal wellness. …And I think that's physical health, mental health, spiritual health. I think it's a sense of ethics. It's everything. If you want to keep yourself together, it's all things."

In other words, she describes many of the key components of Ageless Beauty: a rich, multifaceted holistic beauty that embraces the whole woman across the life span.

At a glance, my disagreement about Ageless Beauty may seem to be a minor issue of how we define terms, because I think we're on the same page as far as what really matters about who we are as post-40 women. But when it comes to beauty, how we define terms is at the crux of the issue.

I love another ironic quote by Stone: "This idea that being youthful is the only thing that's beautiful or attractive simply isn't true. I don't want to be an 'ageless beauty.' I want to be a woman who is the best I can be at my age." Stone's wonderful quote sends a mixed message as it is placed in an age-denying juxtaposition alongside her airbrushed, ageless photo.

Who *owns* the term "beauty" is at the crux of the issue.

For far too long, beauty has been defined by society, not by women themselves. Even in standing up against traditional societal expectations, Stone is implicitly accepting the definition of beauty as solely focused on a woman's appearance, the fairy tale of beauty that we have all internalized.

Women of all ages struggle with self-image and body image, largely because of the unattainable standard we see held before us in the media. Far too often, however, the choices we're given are either to try to live up to this standard or to reject it wholesale. In reality, rejecting the desire to feel beautiful is not as easy as it may seem, so women are caught between two impossibilities.

Accepting or rejecting superficial notions of beauty only legitimizes the superficial definition in the first place. Either choice limits us and who we can be.

I propose that we go further and redefine what beauty really means, a beauty that is as Ageless as the core of who we are, that embraces our creativity, our intelligence, our hard-earned wisdom, and so much more, and how these characteristics manifest on the inside and out—our Signature Greatness DNA shining through to the outside.

Apparently my favorite adolescent beauty queen, Sophia Loren, and I agree when she says, "There is a Fountain of Youth; it is your mind, your talents, the creativity you bring to your life and the lives of people you love. When you learn to tap this source you will have truly defeated age."

Instead of choosing between two negative options, I propose we choose the positive, truly empowering third option of creating and being vocal (including bringing our financial clout, buying, and voting power to sway product makers, movie makers, service providers, and legislatures) about the beauty we want to see modeled around us, the beauty we simultaneously aspire to and appreciate as already existing and evolving within us with each passing year.

At age 41, Cameron Diaz, a dazzler at any age, has come to terms with getting older as she shares with People magazine, "I can't help that other people may be uncomfortable with that, but that's not my responsibility to make them feel okay with the fact that I'm getting older. I'm okay with it. I like it."

"There's no such thing as anti-aging," she says. "There's no such thing as turning back the hands of time, and it makes me crazy that we live in a society where that's sold to women—that we're supposed to believe that if we're getting older, we've failed somehow, that we have failed by not staying young."

There's nothing wrong with wanting to feel beautiful. In fact, there's no shame in being a woman, at any age or stage. We don't need to add that to our already-long list of ways we unnecessarily berate ourselves. What's wrong is how we define what beautiful is, the damaging narrative we've inherited, a narrative we can refuse to live and pass on to the next generations of women.

Perhaps Coco Chanel always knew this to be true when she told us all, "You can be gorgeous at thirty, charming at forty, and irresistible for the rest of your life."

The Next Sexual (R)evolution

After loss of Identity, the most potent modern terror, is loss of sexuality, or, as Descartes didn't say, 'I fuck therefore I am.'

~ Jeanette Winterson, *Art & Lies: A Piece for Three Voices and a Bawd*

One of the most prevalent American stereotypes about aging is that we become sexless beings. This stereotype is akin to the invisibility we feel, experience, or fear as we face the years ahead of us.

Recently I roared with laughter from episode to episode as I binge-watched the first year's reruns of "Frankie and Grace," played by Jane Fonda and Lily Tomlin, respectively. One scene where these two recently divorced older women, who are desperately breaking their self-imposed rules of abstinence, go to a local market to purchase the forbidden cigarettes—only to find themselves totally disregarded by the young male clerk who doesn't appear to "see" them no matter their efforts to gain his attention. In total shock, Frankie and Grace watch from a position of invisibility as this same clerk leaps to attention when a far younger cutie comes to the counter to check out. This scene captures the utter invisibility and lack of sex appeal we older women (and men) are forced to experience on a daily basis. Another scene makes me adore Fonda (who to this day remains slim and trim) even more, when she flaps her unexpected "grandma upper arms" as if to say, "F**k off, this is me, so get lost!" Bravo to these women and to Netflix for bringing all of us into a new conversation about the everyday realities of women growing older with respectful humor.

Why does it seem that French and other European women are "allowed" to be sexy as they age, while older American women get pushed aside? Elle magazine's answer is, "Typically in French cinema, sexuality and sex appeal are viewed as an intrinsic quality within women, which evolves with age but doesn't fade." Not true in America. Here it's a big deal to have beauty and seduction as core to the characters our older actresses portray.

This invisible sexuality is particularly ironic with Leading Edge Boomers, the generation that brought the first sexual revolution. Are we prepared to start the next one? To spark not just a revolution but also an evolution in how we embrace our sexuality at every age and stage? Are we prepared to write the new story of Ageless Sexuality for ourselves and generations of women to follow?

The Inuit have a story about Skeleton Woman, a woman who was cast into the ocean by her father. Over time, the flesh fell from her bones until all that was left was her skeleton. She lay there at the bottom of the sea until a fisherman got his hook caught in her rib cage. Upon reeling her in, he became frightened and rowed back to shore as quickly as possible, not realizing that she was tangled up in his line. Every time he looked back, the Skeleton Woman seemed to be chasing him, in the water and then upon land, as he took his rod and reel with him in his race toward the safety of his snow house.

He had of course dragged her in with him, but now as he looked at her, a pile of bones in a heap, he began untangling her, speaking to her softly, and then wrapping her in furs to keep her warm and fell asleep. As he slept, a tear slid down his cheek. Skeleton Woman slaked her thirst on the single tear, which provided a river's worth of water. She then pulled his heart out of his chest and began drumming on it, chanting "Flesh, flesh, flesh," and as she did so, her body began to fill out with flesh. She sang her body back, then sang the fisherman's clothes off and lay down next to him, returning his heart to his chest.

In so many ways, this story resonates with the invisible sexuality of older women, cast aside in our society's story about sex and sexual attraction, skeletons without womanly flesh. The idea of women as sexual beings beyond midlife is a taboo subject that we run from just as the fisherman runs from the Skeleton Woman, and our sexuality and sexual attraction are just as inextricably tied up with who we are as in the fisherman's line. Once unearthed from the deep, there is no running from the Skeleton Woman. As menopause turns up the heat, we have the power to nourish ourselves, our sexual vitality. Our sexuality does not depend on a man, is not defined by a man. He sleeps in the tale as she recreates her own flesh, as she restores herself and re-stories her sexuality. She has the power to choose to lie down with him.

If we can listen to our inner Crone's voice, truly hear our ancestral Herstory, we have the power to re-story our own sexuality and attraction, to discard the myths of the sexless older woman that have been handed down to us. Not only do current generations have a very different mind-set toward sex than past generations—we are also living longer, healthier lives than ever before. Our vital and vibrant extended longevity puts us in the unique position to redefine what it means to be sexual beings and to change the way the world sees and limits sexuality.

Can we grow older "disgracefully"? I share this story shared with me of a woman in her late fifties to illustrate our potential sexuality and sexual desires, if we so choose.

My bathroom has a wall-to-wall mirror. Could I bear to see my aging body at full frontality every time I had a bath? Should I compromise by bathing in the dark or should I face the reality of the bumps, sagging lines and overripe flesh that was the physical part of me? It would be hard to acknowledge this ageing body daily as it deteriorated in the years ahead, but I was resigned to accepting that this was my lot. Not a pretty sight. Poor but mine own.

Imagine the shock to my system just a few years later faced by the gazing eyes of a man 21 years my junior, as I bathed. Earlier in the evening he had asked me if he could sleep with me. His desire had startled but delighted me and when I said yes I had not thought through the implications of his examination of my body. When the bathroom door opened, I was doubly exposed—both to the mirror which threatened me with cruel honesty and to him. I gasped with embarrassment, instinctively drew my arms in against my breasts and shivered nervously. But he knelt down at my side and gently pried my arms open, looked at me with delight, smiled and began to stroke me gently. No part of my body escaped his hands. Slowly I began to relax, to pulsate with excitement and to begin to experience my most sensual time for many years. …This was no toy-boy experience but an episode of learning, rejuvenation and confirmation of me as a woman with sexual desires, no matter how I choose to satisfy them.

~"The Mirror by Shirley"
About Time: Growing Old Disgracefully by Irma Kurtz, 2010

Our sexual health is an important part of our holistic health—physical, emotional, mental, and spiritual. The forms our sexuality takes are far more varied than our society and media portray, and this is true at every age. Our sexuality and our sexual attraction are as unique as our personality, differing from person to person and even differing within an individual at various ages and stages and circumstances.

But sexuality is itself Ageless, an ever-present part of who we are as human beings, one of the many forms of our post-procreative years' creative energy and our bodily expression.

Here's what Gloria Steinem has to say about romance, sex, and sexual attraction as she moved from midlife into her older years, "For me as an individual, aging has also brought freedom from romance; freedom from the ways in which your hormones distort your judgment and make you do things that aren't right for you. When I was younger, there was a part of my brain back here that was always thinking about sex. I might not have always been tending to it, but every time I turned around, it would be there. Sometimes it took over, sometimes I forgot about it, but it was there. It's not there anymore! It's funny—it's like you have an entire part of your brain that's free for other things. Going through menopause makes the difference. If someone would have told me this at forty-five, not only would I not have believed it, I wouldn't have wanted to believe it. All I can tell you is: it's wonderful. It doesn't mean you don't enjoy having sex when it happens, just that you don't think about it when it doesn't. It was wonderful before—I'm not knocking it—although I do think I confused sex with friendship, love, affection, and aerobics all in one. I could have substituted aerobics for some of it. It isn't that I regret the past, but it's equally wonderful now in a different way. To young women I can only say, 'Don't worry about it!' "

To deny this essential expression of our deepest capacity for intimacy, (in-to-me-see), in ourselves or in others is to deny an important part of our humanity.

We don't lose our sexuality as we age; it just shifts.

My long-held belief is that we don't lose our sexuality as we age; it just shifts. Yes, we let go of our procreativity as we move into menopause, but we do not lose either our creativity or sexual juiciness. Erica Jong, the author of the enormously popular 1973 novel *Fear of Flying*, shares this belief, as evidenced in her statement, "The greatest Feminists have also been the greatest lovers. I'm thinking not only of Mary Wollstonecraft and her daughter Mary Shelley, but of Anais Nin, Edna St. Vincent Millay, and of course Sappho. You cannot divide creative juices from human juices. And as long as juicy women are equated with bad women, we will err on the side of being bad."

It's long past time that we begin demanding a change in our portrayal in media and advertising, as well as in the multigenerational conversations we have. This demand can take the form of choosing to use our significant spending power with companies that recognize our full humanity, including our sexuality and our innate sexual attraction.

It can also take the form of speaking out about our sexual health concerns, just as we do about other aspects of our health. Some are standard concerns related to perimenopausal symptomology like dry everything, (e.g., vaginal dryness, flaky skin), logeyness or brain fog, widening at the hips, and watching our breasts and ass head downward followed by our upper underarms. Others are more individual concerns, such as frequency and desire for sexual relations, etc. We deserve to have these concerns taken seriously in medicine and in society, for women as well as men, addressing the real needs and desires we have, not just the oversimplified male-focused needs that can be addressed with a pill. For too long, our bodies have been secondary characters to the male protagonists, plot devices in a story told by a patriarchal culture.

But our sexuality is more than that. We are more than that.

My Second Wave Feminist cohorts catalyzed and drove the late 1960s into the 1970s women's movement. (Please turn to my preface for a fuller historic exploration of feminism—telling our old story to provide some context for the new story being re-storied together as we traverse *The Ageless Way*.)

Part of this movement involved throwing off the medical nomenclature of earlier times that had co-opted us, robbing us of a place at the table even for control of our own bodies. The nomenclature included female hysteria, which was an all-too-common medical diagnosis for women who exhibited a wide array of symptoms, including faintness, nervousness, sexual desire, insomnia, fluid retention, heaviness in the abdomen, muscle spasm, short-ness of breath, irritability, loss of appetite for food or sex, and "a tendency to cause trouble." In persistent cases, women were sent to asylums where many had involuntary hysterectomies to correct the "hysteria." But this wasn't all. There were the degrading references, including "the inferior member," "weak, frail, impatient, feeble, and foolish," "in her greatest perfection woman was created to be subject to man" and "all women are commanded to serve, to be in humility and subjection."

Women's concerns were trivialized and our healthy emotions stigmatized with the label "hysterical." Then came Freud. We were treated accordingly to remove the dangerous craziness, emotionality, independence, and so forth that were apparently signs of that horrible disease of simply being female. (See Betty Friedan's classic *The Feminine Mystique*.)

Miriam Hawley and Judy Norsigian, among others, gave us permission to trust our own knowing and smarts, woman to woman, by creating a cooperative manual that was on every Boomer woman's bookshelf, *Our Bodies, Ourselves*. Kind of our own Wikipedia of women's health and wellness.

We began to see the changes and differences in our bodies, like different sizes or shapes of our genitals and breasts. Even our orgasms or lack thereof, attributes once classified in terms of disease and dysfunction, were actually part of the natural cycle and beautiful variation in the female body. The same is true for female aging.

Pioneers like sex educator and therapist Betty Dodson, Ph.D., one of the visionary women I interviewed for my book *Visionaries Have Wrinkles*,

> Women's concerns were trivialized and our healthy emotions stigmatized

began to fearlessly explore women's sexuality in art, films, and women's groups (work she continues today at dodsonandross.com).

Fast-forward forty years, and I am at a conference listening to a middle-aged man discuss research done for Big Pharma into sexual dysfunction in younger Baby Boomer women.

He reports, "Most women are too embarrassed to talk about vaginal dryness. They suffer in pain for years." It blows me away to find that women still don't talk about these issues, even with one another. I am less surprised to hear that they don't speak with their physicians either, and that when some do it's around two years after the onset.

Worse: 93 percent of the women report a significant effect on their lives, yet they continue to have painful sex…as often as once a week.

Hearing this man reveal such private details about the sacred space of women's bodies brought a wave of déjà vu. I viscerally felt a trespass as yet another women's health issue was trivialized as a dysfunction, as another path of women's life cycles was co-opted and made into a pathology. The natural changes of aging were being discussed as though we were robotic Stepford Wives who had to get fixed, oiled up for our men. Just so Pharma can market and sell a new product.

Which came first, the solution or the research?

And who says it's a dysfunction anyway? Menopause occurs for a reason. Why is it so shameful, so scary, for us to talk about our changing bodies? Why aren't women talking with one another? Why do we suffer in silence?

Menopause occurs for a reason.

Pharma is always ready to fill the void with fear disguised as hope within the same old clichéd story of women being valuable only for their use to men: *Don't lose your man to someone who doesn't have this symptomology. You can eradicate this. You can stay young, ready, and able, desirable, rather than old and useless.*

Something is terribly wrong here. Did we Second Wave Feminists fail after all?

Haven't I heard this story before?

An even older story comes to mind. Perhaps you've heard some version of it. In Greek mythology, the warrior-goddess Artemis is bathing in her sacred lake, hidden in privacy amid lush forest. Actaeon, in the forest on a hunt with his dogs, spies the goddess, vulnerable and unclothed. He is captivated by her beauty.

When Artemis catches him spying on her, she warns him never to speak again or he'll be turned into a stag. Foolishly, he calls out to his hunting party and transforms immediately into a stag. His own hunting dogs tear him to shreds.

A woman's feminine psyche, her sacred temples, are still fair game in a patriarchal culture. No, it's not okay to spy, even under cover of the hunt for women's health information. No, men shouldn't speak for us about our most intimate concerns. But men are just as stuck in the patriarchy as we are, in the way things have always been done.

Many are just savvy businessmen in a culture still so infused with centuries of patriarchy that the sexism is almost on autopilot. They equate it with profit. After all, they can see the magazine headlines and book topics just as we can—how to keep your man, drive him crazy, and keep him satisfied at all costs. Anti-aging is the name of the new money-making game, a game still rigged so that even if women sometimes "win," the men always do.

At least superficially. In truth, the only winners in this game are the businesses exploiting it.

Women today are stepping into their own power in many ways. On so many topics, we are using our own voices, speaking up. Yet we are still being co-opted and not just in the health arena. Have you noticed, for example, how many personal growth and transformative venues for and about women, online and off, are owned or promoted by men, even moderated and directed by men?

As women, we need to step up and own our conversations, our Herstory telling. Women and men both benefit from this action. As we can see in many arenas, such as business, when women are speaking up and leading, the results benefit the companies, the shareholders, and the world.

What if we women reimagined a new ending that truly serves our womanhood vs. solely refilling big business's deep pockets at our expense? What if we took control of the story of our bodies, ourselves? What if

> **A woman's feminine psyche, her sacred temples, are still fair game in a patriarchal culture.**

we could change that story, and the world, simply by taking one radical step—talking to one another? Sharing the truth of our past and present stories and our aspirational stories for the future?

What I find particularly interesting is all the conflicting information about our sex lives that we get from studies. Contrast the negative results above with the findings in a 2012 American Journal of Medicine study that women are increasingly satisfied with sex as they age, both women having sex and those who are not. Perhaps most promising was that for a *majority* of the women, median age 67, orgasm and arousal were frequent, with the highest frequency among the oldest and the youngest surveyed.

So what do we make of these extremes, the women reporting painful sex and those reporting increased sexual satisfaction with age? I have no doubt that there is this variation among women, but why? Again, if women talked more with one another, more freely about sex and sexual attraction, if we stopped making ourselves sexually invisible, we could learn so much. Are the satisfied women masturbating more? Are they and their partners more accepting of their changing bodies and desires? Is there better communication? Less stress? Are satisfied women more in tune with their own bodies and what turns them on? All of these factors and more are so important to explore as we age, to take back control of our own sexuality and what it means to us, to free ourselves from the expectations and limitations of a society that defines and values our bodies only in the way they serve others.

Bottom line: I believe that Aging Beauty is hot and sexy! Elle magazine captures my own philosophy when we are reminded "that we each have to believe we are an object of desire throughout our lives, but don't pretend you are forever 25. Mademoiselle Chanel told us that 'fashion fades but style is eternal.'" Why not, then, say the same about youth and sex appeal?

Who Are We if We're No Longer Young?

I am convinced that most people do not grow up....We marry and dare to have children and call that growing up. I think what we do is mostly grow old. We carry accumulation of years in our bodies, and on our faces, but generally our real selves, the children inside, are innocent and shy as magnolias.

~ Maya Angelou
Letter to My Daughter, October 2009

This question resonates beyond what we see in the mirror. Our identities are also changing, or seem to be. Having it all used to be the ultimate definition of success, especially after the women's liberation movement of the 1960s and 1970s. We can have careers or our own businesses, raise our families (even on our own), manage our households, take care of our bodies and brains, bat our eyelashes, join associations and clubs, volunteer, pursue hobbies, travel…

But for many of us, this compulsive goal to have it all at any cost has led to burnout, less time to appreciate anything we're doing, health issues, and a loss of identity once the kids are grown or we get laid off, change careers, or retire.

Who are we if we're not busy all the time, achieving, achieving, achieving? What's left if we are invisible?

Who are we if we're no longer young?

Gloria Steinem shares her own revelations on what it means to her if we are no longer young, "I didn't really begin to feel my aging until I was fifty, because I didn't have the markers of the passage of time like children or illness to remind me. …Actually, after fifty, aging can become an exciting new period; it is another country. Just as it's exciting to be an adolescent after having been a child, or to be a young adult after having been an adolescent. I like it. It's another stage of life after you're finished with this crazy female

Who are we
if we are no
longer young?

role. …Mostly it's a feeling of freedom to do what you want to do instead of what you have to do. For me, it's the belated ability to occasionally ask, 'What do I want to do?' As opposed to, 'What needs doing?' Hopefully, that's something women will always ask themselves in the future, but for many of us—especially those who were trained to be 1950s women—it takes a lot of unlearning…."

We are not and have never been an age nor a role we play—a wife, a lover, a mother, a volunteer, a job title. We are more than an arbitrary number, more than meets our own eye in the mirror, more than the sum of our parts. We are not our past, our present, or our future. We are all of those and more.

Every change in our lives, even the positive, is in some way a loss. Every negative change is in some way a gain. These changes have swirled around us like electrons and protons, in a never-ending dance of energy, interacting with the energy of others, colliding, spinning, coming apart, and recombining. Through our lives, our form has changed, our energy has changed, but our nucleus, our Signature Greatness DNA, the core of who we are, has remained—neither young nor old, it just is.

The transitions in our lives, even those that are traumatic, throw what really matters into sharp relief. We have the opportunity amid the chaos to be still and pay attention, to truly show up in life.

Showing up is, in part, being present in the moment to possibility, to our own inner voice, the Ageless Visionary inside that knows exactly how to make a difference if we just listen. That voice is our talisman, like Vasilisa's doll, our guide through the dark forest and the tasks we have ahead of us.

Showing up also means living fully, spending our time being present to what matters most to us so that the genuine opportunities for greatness don't get ignored when they appear while we're busy doing other things.

Choosing what not to show up for is just as important, especially the more you need to manage your shifting energy levels. The best way to know when to show up and when not to is to be really clear what your criteria are for living your greatness and leading others to theirs. Sort the rotten corn from the good, the seeds from the soil. If you know for sure that something will not support your criteria, then it makes sense not to show up. When we act in accordance with our core values and aspirational visions, both synergy and synchronicity take over.

Really showing up, giving up our preconceptions, means fully trusting the process. Even when we show up for something (or someone) and it appears we failed, we must continue to follow the process to its completion so that new outcomes will be revealed. Unexpected doors open, obstacles melt, and detours lead us to possibilities we never imagined.

It's pretty simple. If you show up—as who you really are—the unexpected also shows up. Not only does that allow miracles to happen, but it also gives you the ability to create them. ≫

CHAPTER 5 ~ *The Ageless Way Reflections*

The questions and exercises below are to help you find your distinct path on The Ageless Way. Turn to page 28 for more about The Ageless Way Reflections.

1. Spend some time in front of the mirror really looking at yourself. Who do you see in the mirror? Who else do you see? Your mother? Your grandmother? An aunt? (Or, for men, your father, grandfather, uncle?) What aspects do you see reflected on the outside? What aspects don't you see? Doing this exercise can bring up many emotions, memories, and "ahas." Please notice feelings and emotions without judgment and consider what arises for you, adding those thoughts to your journal. If needed, take a step away, get a cup of tea, breathe deeply, or do something to healthfully nurture yourself.

2. What makes you feel beautiful? What aspects of your outer beauty do you love the most? What do you want to enhance or soften? What about your inner beauty shines through on the outside, such as your humor, your warmth?

3. Who are your Ageless Beauty role models? What is it about these people that makes them someone you aspire to be more like? Which of their attributes are you incorporating now? Which need your attention now? Now ask the same questions, but about older Ageless Beauty role models you aspire to be more like. Is there a difference in your responses?

4. What is your sexual story? How has it changed throughout your life? What do you believe about the role of sexuality as you age? What story do you want to create for your body and your sexuality in the coming decades?

Chapter 6

WOMEN SHAPING THE NEW STORY OF OUR AGE

*If we all do our part, I am convinced that future historians
will one day look back on our time as the dawn of
'The Women's Century'—a century that is more open, more hopeful,
and more prosperous than any that has come before.*

~ Muhtar Kent
Chairman of the board and chief executive officer The Coca-Cola Company

*Crossing the threshold into the main ballroom, my awareness floods
with the realization that I am entering a new dimension of my life. The
energy in the room crackles with the recommitment to making a difference
for, by, and with other women!*

*Moving toward the podium to greet my colleague, Barbara DeBaptiste,
chairwoman of the Commission on the Status of Women, I am struck by
her enormous presence. She engages my woman-spirit with her embodiment of the archetypal Black Madonna—strength and vulnerability all
in one, pulled to her like iron filings to a U-shaped magnet. She embraces
me with her magnanimous grin. In a flash of awareness, I recognize that
she is a reflection of me—of all of us—a powerful energetic aspect it is
now time to unbridle.*

*The topics haven't changed over the years since the "revolution"
began—women's health care, starting businesses, financial planning,
workplace equality—but the content and the audience have. The attendees
no longer are predominantly young and naïve middle-class heterosexual
white women in their twenties and thirties. Now the rooms are filled
with a large percentage of midlife women of all colors, sexual preference,*

and economic strata—all women who have ventured out into the harsh realities far from our old coffee klatches around the proverbial kitchen table. Unlike the raging fervor of the earlier years of the movement, now there is a deeper resolve and greater understanding of what we are striving for—for one another and generations to come.

Closing the conference, Marcia Ann Gillespie, then editor of Ms. magazine, asks us all, "How's your life different from your mother's?" As I reflect on the question, she asks us to step up to the challenge once more—"Be the best kind of woman…truthful, bold and willing to take chances."

Stoking those long quiet embers of passionate activism, her Crone-like closing words, "It's in your hands!" ignites coals that had begun to cool down and die out.

> **My woman's story is a Baby Boomer women's story. We can't be kept down. We are humanity's portal to The Ageless Way.**

My woman's story is a Baby Boomer women's story. We can't be kept down. We are humanity's portal to *The Ageless Way*. Like Vasilisa, we women are being called to light the way to a new triumphant story for our times.

In many ways our new story is the next chapter of the evolving story of feminism. We are the keepers of the flame, it is our turn to share the light, the wisdom, so others too can walk through the portal.

Our Prime-Time Story

Women's stories are rife with a "Mission Impossible" theme. We've overcome and moved on and into seats of economic power. The game has changed for us since the 1970s. With a heightened onslaught on our rights of choice and parity around the world, women post-40 in particular, are shining the light and showing up in every grayed-out nook and cranny, demanding change. We are now the largest numbers of adult women ever on the Earth at the same time, just in time to muck up the works of the old game rules that made us out of date, over the hill. What's different from the 1970s is that now we have the power in voting booths, at the register, and we are fast becoming the drivers of our Longevity Economy. Remember, they can't keep us down. Next we will find our wrinkles have parity around the kitchen table, the bedroom, and the boardroom table.

> **Our Ageless Future doesn't stop with Baby Boomers! It starts with Boomer women!**

Our Ageless Future doesn't stop with Baby Boomers! It starts with Boomer women! Our role in pushing the edge of the envelope to expose and eradicate embedded fundamental ageism is making positive change happen. We are here to stay until we turn the aging paradigm inside out.

This may come as a shocker to some of you, but we are *all* aging. Denial seems to be rampant across younger generations, and certainly across most sectors. A real wake-up call is that in 2015 the first Generation Xers turned 50!

Boomer women, whether Leading Edge or later born, are ready to rock right over any limitations put in our path because of our age. We are paving the way for all generations to follow. Yet out in the "real world" of commerce and politics, and most everything, story has it that only Baby Boomers get old!

Our next paradigm to flip in our favor? Boomer women are reinventing aging for everyone! The implications are enormous. We women of a "certain age" are the ones who in droves are changing the landscape of the Longevity Economy. We are poised to rock our age for the ages.

We are poised to rock our age for the ages.

Our Greatest Challenges

The most pervasive and challenging obstacle for many women is low self-esteem. For some of us, aging provides a new perspective on what really matters, which helps us to ease up on ourselves over what doesn't matter. We may grieve the losses of youth (and perhaps health), the empty nest, and for some, the status or the activity of work we no longer do. At the same time, there's often a freedom from having to worry about relying on our appearance, being the perfect mother and partner, and the stresses of our jobs. For others, some or all of these stresses do not disappear, or do so only incompletely. For still other women, the feelings of invisibility and irrelevance simply replace past reasons for feeling like we're not good enough.

The irony of accomplishment is that often those who are the most successful are those who do not fully recognize their worth. They are constantly proving themselves to the trio of archetypal inner voices inside—the inner perfectionist, the inner critic, and the inner pusher—that criticize and tell them they aren't good enough…that they simply aren't enough, period. These voices are like our own personal spiteful stepmother and stepsisters from the tale of Vasilisa and other fairy tales across cultures.

The successes we achieve never satisfy these inner voices, and the fear of failure (which this trio contends is an ever-present risk), keeps us from taking chances that could lead us beyond mere success toward realizing a greater vision for our future. These inner voices are often at the root of our past and present stories, telling us a distorted narrative that we believe to be true, that we believe to be our own.

Fear of failure keeps us from taking chances.

We all must further contend with the Inner Patriarch (women and men), embedded deep within through societal and cultural programming and messaging. This inner voice, like a stealth bomber, flies under the radar. We often don't recognize it's even there (constraining men and boys, but markedly ruthless and unrelenting in women and girls), telling us we are less than, we are limited—always falling short in some way as a professional, a mother, a wife, a daughter, a father, a husband, and a son.

Those who, on the surface, appear to be successful often live in constant fear of being "found out" for whom they really are (what I call the "Sham Syndrome"). Given this sense of dread, they don't sell themselves professionally, may turn down promotions because they feel they aren't ready, or they don't assertively and confidently seek funding and customers for their own business—if they even take the chance on starting that business in the first place.

These inner voices bellow, "You won't be taken seriously. You can't do this. Don't make waves!" For women at midlife and beyond, some of the voices of aging can get particularly nasty, starting with what I call the "Dragon of Aging": "It's too late for you. You're not credible unless you are young and beguiling! Haven't you got that yet?" These inner voices berate us for the changes in our bodies—our appearance, our energy, our health—and "remind" us that we are no longer relevant, that we are a burden, or that we shouldn't bother speaking up because no one will take an "old woman" seriously. Add to this the inner voice I call "Beat the Clock Syndrome," the one reminding us that we have only so much time left, throwing us into a panic to check off our bucket list, to accomplish something meaningful, to *matter* before it's too late.

Shaming and guilting us, these archetypal inner voices hit every nerve we have, plunging us into self-doubt. Early on, we believe we can't be successful without abandoning our families. We aren't strong enough, smart enough, savvy enough for that promotion. Or we're just not ready. Then before we know it, there's a new inner voice telling us it's too late. (You can read more on this topic in my interview with Sidra Stone in *Visionaries Have Wrinkles*, 2012.)

Virginia M. Rometty, chief executive at IBM, remembers how, early in her career, she was offered a position she didn't feel she was ready for, so she told the recruiter she needed to think about it.

That night, her husband asked her, "Do you think a man would have ever answered that question that way?"

At Fortune magazine's Most Powerful Women Summit, Rometty says, "What it taught me was you have to be very confident, even though you're so self-critical inside about what it is you may or may not know. And that, to me, leads to taking risks."

For many women, the complex dance of high expectations for what we should achieve and low expectations for what we are actually capable of leaves us trapped in a rut, a never-ending vicious cycle of striving for success that leaves us unfulfilled and dissatisfied. As long as these inner voices—the patriarch, the critic, the perfectionist, and the pusher (all always present in the shadows or running the show), now along with the devouring Inner Dragon of Midlife (Sands, 1992)—team up, the more positive Voices of Aging have a hard time being heard, so our Inner Ageless Visionary voice gets drowned out. This cycle is bound to continue.

The solutions are as complex as the problem, of course. Many of us realize that when dealing with low self-esteem in ourselves or in others, praise alone just doesn't cut it. A person being led by low self-esteem "knows better" about herself and doesn't believe the praise, or doesn't feel that what she's being praised for is good enough or makes up for her other many faults. Making a point to recognize a person's good qualities and choices, in specifics (vague "good jobs" do more harm than good), is absolutely worth doing, don't get me wrong. But it's not enough.

In fact, I can't offer a quick fix here. This deep-seated issue requires multiple approaches and often ongoing expert guidance, particularly to uncover the inner patriarch and perform a "destructive restore" so that the Inner Visionary can harness and transform this powerful force to work

Beating yourself
up for not being
good enough
does not work.

with the whole range of other inner voices. But I can offer two ideas to guide you toward recognizing this challenge and committing to facing it.

The first is to understand fully that beating yourself up for not being good enough does not work. Many of us continue doing this to ourselves based on the mistaken notion that "tough love" of this sort will actually produce results, but obviously, if you still feel you are never good enough, the approach simply isn't working. In other words, you will never satisfy your inner critic, perfectionist, pusher, or patriarch by solely listening to those voices.

Second, recognize that these inner voices aren't going to just disappear. We don't want these inner voices to disappear completely. Rather, you can aim to tame them so you become the CEO of your inner psyche and your outer world. They are a part of your panoply of sub-personalities, or inner voices, some of which reside in the shadow or hidden parts of our psyche. That doesn't mean that they get to narrate your story. Instead of focusing on what to do about those voices, focus on helping your Ageless Visionary voice speak out. Let that voice be the narrator, the protagonist in the story you are creating from here on out, the guiding light your inner Baba Yaga provides. The louder that voice is, the more likely it is to drown out all others. The more all of us listen to our Ageless Visionary, the more inspired we will be to rise above mere success and strive to create a future story that matters to us and that makes a difference in our lives, our work, our world. The more we follow where our Inner Visionary voice leads, the more we will experience what it feels like to be happy, fulfilled, and living our purpose—the more we will understand that we all have the potential for realizing our Signature Greatness DNA.

From this state of being, of strength, questions of whether we are good enough are no longer even worth our time to contemplate.

Stop waiting until you are perfect before you seize an opportunity—or better yet, create one. Start from where you are and take the leap, learning as you go.

Stop listening to the inner voice that tells you you're selfish or indeed crass if you care about money, or that there's just not enough to go around, that you can't be successful without being a bitch or a whore. Or, most

146

insidious because it's so ingrained, that you are just not good enough and never will be because you are a woman—worse yet, an older woman!

These inner voices seep into the words we use in our thoughts, speech, and writing, and those words become a self-fulfilling prophecy: *Women are never successful in this field. It's just too hard to balance everything in my life. I can't make a living and do something meaningful. It's just not realistic. My business idea can't succeed in this economy. It's too late for me to change, to start a business, to take any risks.*

Michael Port, author of *Book Yourself Solid* and speaker for entrepreneurs, has an excellent blog post on this idea. One of his examples is spot-on when it comes to success: "If you generalize that, 'All rich people are snobs,' how are you going to see yourself as a wealthy person so that you can improve your professional and financial status?"

Right now, especially, with the top one percent being considered synonymous with unethical, greedy, and criminal, it's difficult for us to strive toward the wealth we need to make our visions a reality and to feel that our futures are financially secure. Of course, some, and maybe even many, of the one percent are unethical and even criminal, but certainly not all. The more successful you are, the more resources and power you have to make a difference. It's how you choose to use your money, and how you choose to earn it, that is important. Having money itself is not evil. If you'd like to learn more on the topic of Soul and money, then check out my evergreen article entitled *Soul & Money: Can We Get It (& Them) Together?*

We need to start being more careful about the words we choose, particularly when speaking to ourselves. We need to consciously embrace the inner patriarch for its gifts and protection, thus giving our Inner Visionary center stage. Similarly, when we fully embrace and own all our Voices of Aging, the voice of our Inner Visionary is exalted, not derailed. The visionary tells us, "Take your attention off other people. Keep focused on your goal. Stay true to your mission. Everyone's vision is worth the same! You know what you are doing. Go for it!"

Replace: "Women are never successful in this field."

With: "We need more women in this field to reinvigorate it and improve it. The field needs *me*."

> We need to start being more careful about the words we choose, particularly when speaking to ourselves.

Replace: "It's just too hard to balance everything in my life."

With: "I can choose what matters most to me, delegate what I can, and not waste time and energy on other things, especially living up to other people's expectations."

Replace: "I can't make a living and do something meaningful."

With: "The world craves people (and businesses) who live and work according to their values, highly creative and innovative self-starters who can make a real difference. Consumers will pay for it, now more than ever."

Replace: "My business idea can't succeed in this economy or in the time I have left."

With: "How can I make my business idea succeed in this economy and be adaptable to any possible changing needs as I age?"

Perhaps most important, replace "It's too late for you. You're not credible unless you are young and beguiling!" with "My experience, my talents and intelligence, and my unique perspective make the timing perfect for me to act now. I know how to focus on what really matters. *All great visionaries have wrinkles.*"

Start paying attention to your words and languaging today and make a conscious effort to change them, for words are at the root of your story, now and in the future. I have pointed out some of the more common and powerful inner voices here, but multiple different voices tell our stories, and many of them make unreliable narrators! I discovered and concretized the Voices of Aging in my own exploration and research to develop a model for transforming our conversations, as well as the stories we tell about aging. I am indebted to Dr. Sidra Stone (another interviewee in *Visionaries Have Wrinkles*, 2012) who, with her husband, Dr. Hal Stone, pioneered the Voice Dialogue model of our inner sub-personalities, or "voices" within our psyche, which provided a foundation for my understanding of the inner panoply of voices or selves that reside in our psyche and drive our choices. I highly recommend their website for more information and guidance (Voice Dialogue International.com, http://voicedialogueinternational.com).

A female client of mine, now 56, returned to work with me because she found her successful career that we launched years before had now become stalled, perhaps even derailed. My client had been promoted and rated highly for years as she moved from one position to the next to become a highly paid officer of the company. That is, until now. If you've been through the "squeeze 'em out" push as you headed over the hill after turning 50, (or you've been observing this trend in your own workplace), you know how being pushed aside, ignored, even ridiculed can be so demoralizing, as it cuts deep into an already-diminishing confidence, even when we are performing a yeoman's job producing stellar results. As you'd expect, I advised my client to keep a dossier of any shreds of abuse and misuse of power toward her on the job. Of course, we worked on alternative scenarios both within and without her company, and even in and outside her industry, both near and far. Nevertheless, it was critical to keep her on track and producing. This was a perfect situation in which to apply my morphed version of the Voice Dialogue model.

My office is set up so that when I facilitate clients in a Voice Dialogue session they can move freely from one sub-personality energetic to another as they physically move around the room from chair to chair, stand, or move back and forth around the room. As my client described her distressful work situation, I invited her to move to a seated position where her broken spirit, or currently diminished self, might be willing to reveal itself. As she moved into this position, it was as if she aged decades, weighted down with low self-esteem and hopelessness. She even described her revealed self as very, very old, "a shrinking violet" shrouded in a black cloud that was filling up the room and shadowing her every move. After we spent some time conversing from the vantage point of this diminished broken self, another inner voice demanded attention. Moving my client to another position, this voice bellowed, "Whom do you think you are kidding?" Her inner patriarch's voice adamantly insisted, "It's all over, she's toast! Wake up, sweetheart, you are over fifty! You are just too old!" Clearly this patriarchal voice's languaging was eroding my client's confidence and had become her own negative languaging.

I invited my client to move to another standing position, this time away from her seated "shrinking violet" self. When she found a comfortable standing place, I asked her to close her eyes and to recall or remember a time when she felt on top of her game, and then I worked with her to "call in" or "dial in" (like on a thermostat) the energetic feeling of being in that moment. Her whole demeanor and physical stature changed from the slumping, diminished, aged self to a vibrant woman in her mid-fifties with an enormous force field around her. There was no stopping her! When I asked her name, "Fuchsia" answered, and she had quite a bit of great advice on my client's current career dilemma. Needless to say, this process is ongoing, but the good news is that now, whether virtually or in person, my client is retraining herself to "call-in" her powerhouse Fuchsia self when she is in the office and confronted by her abusive boss. As a result, her boss is backing off and my client is now off and running interviewing and wowing her potential new employers and colleagues in a way she didn't know she had in her.

This modality is not off the wall, nor is this a party game, but a sophisticated model and system of discovery that allows us to get acquainted with each of our many inner selves, or sub-personalities. It is always striking to me that each of our inner selves has its own patterning of behaviors, feelings, and thinking…in most cases, my clients have discovered different speaking voices, energetics, colorations and opinions, associated with each of their sub-personalities. All have much to tell us. The Stones categorized these inner selves into Primary and Disowned selves. The Primary selves make up who we are in the world, or our persona. Our disowned selves may be totally hidden from our conscious awareness yet hold great gifts for us that will complete our wholeness.

Financial Confidence and Women

A close second to self-esteem as a problem for many women is financial confidence, also tied into women's difficulties getting access to money and investment capital for our businesses.

A recent Prudential study ("Financial Experience & Behaviors Among Women") found that more than half of the women in the study were the primary breadwinners in their households. The reasons for this finding are varied—the economic crisis, divorce, women choosing to marry later (or not at all).

Particularly interesting are the differences in how women and men view their financial situations—22 percent of women and 37 percent of men feel "well prepared" to make decisions about their finances. Much of the gap in confidence between men and women can easily be explained by history.

Before the Second Wave Feminist movement of the 1970s, women couldn't even get their own credit cards or bank accounts. The first women's bank was a big deal when it opened, but even that had a man at the helm and proved to be a failure. Men have more personal experience as the primary earners as well as more role models of other men in the same position. Many women today were raised by women who did not work outside the home, much less serve as the family's primary source of income, and of course, even today, women still earn less than men for the same jobs. According to the White House, full-time working women earn 77 percent of what their male counterparts earn. The Pew Research Center, based on hourly earnings of both full- and part-time workers, estimates women earn 84 percent of what men earn. Pew further reports that for young women the wage gap is smaller—at 93 percent—meaning they caught up to their same-aged male counterparts at the end of January 2014. Although the estimated sixteen-cent pay gap today has narrowed from thirty-six cents in 1980, it's still not okay to not have full parity. If this history isn't an obvious reason to have less confidence about making financial decisions, I don't know what is!

This history affects the skills, confidence, and unspoken attitudes about money that have been passed on to us from generations of women before—in other words, the cultural story shared about money. This history also means, however, that we can make a huge difference in the world by breaking this pattern and creating a new story for ourselves and the generations of women to follow us. Once again, I am reminded of the Ageless Quest, with Vasilisa dependent on a father who cannot help her. She has to change her story, seek the discernment, wisdom, and guiding light she needs from Baba Yaga, a wise woman Crone, a Visionary with Wrinkles.

This guiding light might come from expert guidance in managing your finances. I suggest that you seek financial advisors with experience and perspectives that are aligned with women's concerns and priorities. I suggest you start by asking your contacts, as well as Googling advisors in your area who have a specialty in working with women. For those already over 50, ask how they serve the needs of Baby Boomers and Mature women. Make sure you check out their online reviews before proceeding. In the Prudential study, women and men tended to list the same top three priorities, but in a different order. Women listed them in this order:

1. Not become a financial burden to loved ones

2. Maintain lifestyle in retirement

3. Make sure not to outlive savings

Men listed lifestyle first, followed by not outliving savings, and ending with not becoming a financial burden to loved ones. The study additionally showed that women's financial worries rest primarily on the household, meeting expenses, and avoiding or overcoming debt.

Whether you seek financial advice from a person, a website, or another source, the advice will suit you best if you look for an emphasis on ensuring that your needs are met, both current and future. However, I recommend that you take a good hard look at your beliefs surrounding money, the story you tell yourself, for these differing priorities and concerns also reflect an ingrained tendency in many women to see themselves as greedy, selfish, crass (or all three) if they focus on their wants and not just their needs. But we do not need to choose between fulfilling our needs and our wants, or between doing well and doing good. These are not either/or concepts. They are both/and.

> I recommend that you take a good hard look at your beliefs surrounding money.

In making financial decisions and in seeking financial advice, consider first those decisions that will meet both needs and wants. Meeting these needs and wants could happen simultaneously or in an overlapping way, such as focusing first on immediate needs but ensuring that the wants can then be met, as well, in the near future.

> The more successful you are, the more resources you have to help others.

Even more important, consider those decisions that will not only help you do good for your loved ones, your community, your world, but that will simultaneously help you to do well financially. The more successful you are, the more resources you have to help others. In fact, if you can intertwine your success with helping others, you will not only feel confident about the financial future for yourself and your family, but you can also join the visionaries who are creating a rock-solid future for the world.

Women and the Story of the Future

The ongoing trend of women leaving the corporate world to start their own businesses is no surprise considering that the glass ceiling is still unbreakable (and compounded by the newly revealed silver ceiling) in many companies throughout Corporate America, as demonstrated by a few statistics from a 2013 Catalyst report, "U.S. Women in Business":

- Percentage of women in the U.S. labor force: 46.9 percent

- Percentage of women in management, professional, and related occupations: 51.4 percent

- Percentage of female Fortune 500 corporate officers: 14.3 percent

- Percentage of female Fortune 500 board seats: 16.6 percent

- Percentage of female Fortune 500 top earners: 8.1 percent

- Percentage of female Fortune 500 CEOs: 4.2 percent

Many women, especially women over 40, who have spent their working lives climbing the corporate ladder are faced with the difficult choice between leaving to start their own businesses or staying with their company and striving to be one of the exceptions, perhaps fighting to change the system from the inside. Examples of such notable women include Virginia M. Rometty at IBM, Anne Mulcahy at Xerox, Indra Nooyi at PepsiCo, Peggy Foran at Pfizer, and Sarah Teslik at Apache Corporation. These Ageless Visionary Leaders guided their companies to sign the Aspen Principles by which companies, investors, and corporate governance professionals agreed to commit to long-term value creation over short-term profits.

This is our present story, but what does the future story look like? Will we collectively force the hand of Corporate America to recognize that transformation begins with visionary leaders who understand how to do good while doing well? Are we on the verge of seeing the collapse of the old patriarchal culture, and if so, will we also see fragments of that silvered glass ceiling among the debris?

Some observers would say only time will tell, but that view discounts the power we have to change our own future, to create a new story for the future of women. Time may tell us what has worked, and what hasn't, in the past. (For a fascinating and timely look at the past and present of corporations, I highly recommend the award-winning, once underground film *The Corporation*.) Time may tell us when we are repeating history, and what we can learn from how we have reacted or responded to epochal change in the past—conservative and restrictive, wild and revolutionary, consciously evolutionary, or downright radically transformative.

Time doesn't have a voice. We do.

But time doesn't tell us everything. Time doesn't have a voice. We do. We can't predict the future, yet we can lead the way toward creating Aspirational Ageless Future scenarios that transform the world as we know it. We are truly modern-day oracles, with one significant difference. We do not speak only through men, who go out in the world and "interpret" our words and then act on them. Modern-day oracles speak with their own voices, their Ageless Visionary voices. Modern-day oracles take action.

Whether career professionals, new or seasoned entrepreneurs, or solo-preneurs, we cannot afford to ignore the opportunity we have right now to step up amid the chaos and lead the way to a greater future—not just for women, but for the world. Protesting is powerful, but it's not enough. We can't just decry the problem. We have to step in with solutions. Katy Fike is an example of a new breed of entrepreneurs bringing technology to solve the issues still faced by caregivers and elderly individuals across the country. Read more about Fike in chapters three and seven.

I encourage you to come up with your own solutions to everyday problems you see around you that really set your ire on fire. To kick-start your beyond-the-box thinking on solution-finding, here are a few places to start: Create a cross-generational think tank to solve local community problems; at work, (profit or nonprofit) start an initiative that connects the disparate organizational "silos" or cross-functional teams (e.g., sales vs. service) to brainstorm about products/services, processes, and policies; take on leadership roles; run for office; start a Transition.org chapter in your community to lower the carbon footprint, etc.

Now is the time to listen to that visionary voice inside you.

Now is the time to listen to that visionary voice inside you. No doubt the world chaos has stirred her. The world is literally crying out for creative disruption of the status quo, for new ideas to change business so that it reflects our values, honors our responsibility to one another and to our

Mother Earth, and capitalizes and strengthens the interconnected global society we have become.

Women Mean Business...
Boomer Women Mean Big Business

For more than thirty years, women have been starting businesses at about double the rate of men. For many, this was the result of hitting the glass ceiling or discovering that they didn't want the long hours and unbalanced lives, dysfunctional corporate culture, and work that didn't give them a feeling of significance, of doing what really mattered to them.

Although men were most affected by job loss in the Great Recession, during the recovery, while men were gaining jobs, women were actually losing them by the hundreds of thousands. Even women at the top aren't safe: Yahoo CEO Carol Bartz, fired, criticized for characteristics that no one would bat an eye at in a man; Wall Street maven Sallie Krawcheck, known for her integrity and directness, first "restructured" out of Merrill Lynch, then fired from Bank of America, where she had headed the Global Wealth and Investment Management division.

These women had managed to rise above the glass ceiling only to have it shatter beneath their feet. For other women, this ceiling has gotten impossibly low and very gray.

Predicting where these facts are leading us is a no-brainer—the number of women-owned businesses will likely increase at an even faster pace. Add to this group the people hitting the silver ceiling (according to the Bureau of Labor Statistics, between 2009 and 2012, 3.5 million more people over 55 remained in the workforce, and by 2022, 82 percent will be women), coupled with the ageism and sexism alive and well in United States organizations (evidenced by the pay gap, dearth of women in leadership, and much more), and we can see that the future for many post-40 women especially, will be in entrepreneurship, particularly serving other post-40 women.

Boomer women mean BIG business. This is the big story of the future, a story we've already begun to create.

Boomer women mean BIG business. This is the big story of the future, a story we've already begun to create.

According to the Center for Women's Business Research, "If U.S.-based women-owned businesses were their own country, they would have the 5th largest GDP in the world, trailing closely behind Germany and ahead of countries including France, United Kingdom and Italy."

Think about the impact we can have on the world simply by following our own lead, standing in our own shoes, and building our businesses and/ or contributing to our employers, our communities, and our families on the visionary voice we all have inside us. Now is the time to leverage change to our advantage, to reinvent ourselves and our world through innovative and conscious businesses that hit the Triple Bottom Line: People, Planet, Profit.

THE TRIPLE BOTTOM LINE

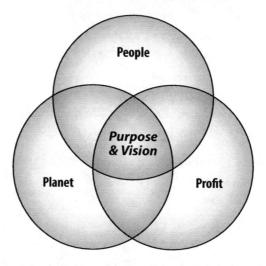

We are already creating a story for the world in which we can work how we want, when we want, and most important, why we want. Not only are more and more people starting businesses that make money and a difference in the world, but more and more consumers are choosing to patronize these businesses over those that don't combine profit with purpose. (Check out chapter seven, "Gray Is the New Green" and chapter eight, "The Longevity Economy," for more information about these trends.)

How Being Successful Can Save the Planet

When it comes down to it, even with the inequality in the workplace I just described, women are increasing their power all over the world, and the world is profiting from it. A recent McKinsey survey showed an increase in profits in emerging markets for 34 percent of companies who'd made empowering women a priority. According to Catalyst, companies with women board members outperform those with all-male boards by 42 to 66 percent in terms of returns on sales, equity, and invested capital. In developing countries, women reinvest 90 percent of their income in their families and communities (men, only 30 to 40 percent).

As Jessica Bennett writes in Newsweek: "Between 1997 and 2002, female-led firms grew by nearly 20 percent, while overall firms grew by just seven percent; by 2005, women represented more than a third of people involved in entrepreneurial activity, and the number of women-owned firms continues to grow at twice the rate of all U.S. firms. Indeed, it's not a leap to say that female entrepreneurship may help revive the fortunes of the middle class in the developed world."

Despite all the growth in women-owned businesses we only account for 30 percent of all United States businesses, and we receive only four percent of all federal procurement dollars.

Yet Candida Brush, a professor of entrepreneurship for over thirty years, blogged for the Wall Street Journal sharing the same experiences I have had when asking undergrads, MBAs, and entrepreneurs to name a successful entrepreneur…it takes several names before a woman is mentioned.

> …women are increasing their power all over the world, and the world is profiting from it.

The Downside of Entrepreneurship

Most recently, the lack of gender parity was unearthed in a study by a U.S. Senate committee that exposed a large gender imbalance in entrepreneurship, with women lagging behind men in many of the areas crucial for business success.

Supporting the U.S. Senate's committee findings, Forbes recently reported that, in the United States, new male entrepreneurs launch their businesses with a median start-up balance of $30,000, compared with only $8,000 for women entrepreneurs.

This inequality for women entrepreneurs' median start-up balance is clearly linked to the scarcity of venture capital funding. Women have surely made progress, but we need a whole lot more when it comes to venture capital funding. Per the recently released Diana Project study, which is the first comprehensive study of venture capital investments in female entrepreneurs, the findings bear this out. The results, although positive, are unsettling and clearly a barrier to women's entrepreneurial success. We must reverse them.

- In 1999, businesses with women on the executive team got fewer than five percent of all venture capital investments, followed by an increase to nine percent in 2011, and a rise to more than 15 percent in 2013!

- More than 97 percent of venture-funded businesses have male CEOs.

- Health and medical firms get most of the funding.

- The total number of women partners in venture funding firms dropped from a measly 10 percent in 1999 to a disgraceful six percent today.

- Yet venture funding companies with at least one woman partner on the investment team are twice as likely to invest in female entrepreneurs or companies with women on their management team.

Despite believing in the positives of women-owned and -led businesses, I'd be remiss to not share the downside of entrepreneurship. Bottom line… it is not a piece of cake. Rather, it's a walk on the wild side. Sometimes being an entrepreneur is unbearably challenging. Like Sisyphus, entrepreneurs just keep on keepin' on, trudging up the mountain, failing, trying once again, failing, and then up goes that darn rock again. Then, unlike Sisyphus, if the gods are with them, sooner or later they succeed—only to have to try over and over again. Yet I wouldn't trade in my entrepreneurial life. My lifelong career has been a mix of entrepreneurship, intrapreneurship, and then back again into an entrepreneurial mode. Now, with that said, let's look at the upside.

The Upside of Women Entrepreneurship

The good news is that this new light being shined on the barriers to women's entrepreneurship, at least in the United States, is making the situation improve. Professor Brush also sees a shift as students now more readily name Oprah Winfrey, Melinda Gates, Arianna Huffington, Tory Burch, or Sara Blakely among known successful entrepreneurs. Bottom line, women entrepreneurs are still relegated to second-tier importance, yet they are majority owners in an estimated 10 million businesses, and as reported by the Small Business Association (SBA), 36 percent of all businesses in the United States.

And there's more good news. Women are launching more businesses than ever before at a rate of 1,288 per day as reported by American Express. It has been estimated that women-owned businesses have risen since 1997 by 68 percent.

In fact women entrepreneurs in the United States have the highest rate of entrepreneurial activity of all developed countries surveyed; one out of ten was starting or running a new business as reported in 2013 by U.S. Global Entrepreneurship Monitor (GEM). Susan Duffy blogged for the Wall Street Journal noting that since 1997 woman-led companies have outperformed all but the largest publicly traded companies based on growth rate, employment, and revenues. Good for us!

A report commissioned by Dell Inc. titled "Forget the Glass Ceiling: Build Your Business Without One" identified four ways women bring value, and our values, to the new emerging entrepreneurial marketplace. To paraphrase, these four ways are the following:

1. Social responsibility is embedded in our DNA.

2. Our giving and volunteering benefit all businesses, as well as our own.

3. Women help other women achieve and succeed.

4. For women, business is about more than making profits… it's about making a difference.

"It's an empowering feeling when you generate enough money where you can do what you love & have extra for those causes you are also passionate about.

~ Sandra Yancey, founder and CEO of eWomenNetwork.com

We are proving our worth, according to an ongoing study by Emory University, which has discovered that women-founded start-ups are "20% more likely to have generated revenue" than their male-founded start-ups. American women account for 80 percent of consumer spending, according to Competitive Edge Magazine and EPM's Marketing to Women. Women over 50 control $19 trillion and own more than three-fourths of U.S. financial wealth (MassMutual Financial Group).

Regarding female entrepreneurship, there's even more good news! The results of the Gender-GEDI Index, ranking how various countries do at fostering a favorable environment for female entrepreneurs, were announced at Dell's 2014 Women Entrepreneur network conference. The index gave the United States a score of 83 (out of 100), followed by Australia (score of 80), Sweden (score of 73), and a tie between Germany and France (score of 67).

Women of Color Entrepreneurship

While the impact of Women of Color entrepreneurs is undeniable, a 2012 study by the Association of American University Women found that African American women made 64 percent, Latina women made 53 percent, Asian women made 87 percent, and white women made 78 percent of their white male counterparts' wages for the same positions. The Center for American Progress reports that black female entrepreneurs are making significant gains. For instance, in 2014, African American women opened businesses at six times the rate of the general population. According to the center's study, businesses owned by black women are the fastest growing segment of female-owned businesses. From 1997 to 2013, the number of businesses owned by African American women skyrocketed by 258 percent. African American women also hold the largest share of businesses owned by minority women at 13 percent. In fact, women of color are the majority owners of close to one-third of all women-owned firms in the nation. But why are so many women of color turning to entrepreneurship? It's really the same reason as it is for all women, only to a greater degree for women of color. These women turn to entrepreneurship because of a lack of advancement, limited access to mentors, the gender wage gap, and of course being excluded from elite networks. We, therefore, are in the midst of a longer-term trend for women to leave the workplace due to so many obstacles for advancement in traditional corporate culture, which limit all women and force us to find new alternatives.

Empower all women, and you recharge the world. Empower Boomer Women, and there's no stopping us; we will crack the silvered glass ceiling. Creating a climate of success for women is smart business—and not just for consumer-products companies. Today, it's smart business for every company and every country. In the years ahead, women's economic participation and entrepreneurial growth will drive the world's economy. It's no longer a matter of if but of "to what heights."

Prior to hearing Sandra Yancey, founder and CEO of eWomenNetwork, Inc. (eWN), speak for the first time at a Success Summit hosted by Anne Garland, Director of eWN's Connecticut chapter, I had been ruminating on the "right" women to invite to write the forewords for *The Ageless Way.* I was clear before that evening that the women I was seeking must be powerful representations of evolving Ageless women who have radically reinvented themselves and empowered other women to do the same—those who authentically, vulnerably, and powerfully are living *The Ageless Way.* When I heard Yancey speak, I had hot flashes of deep recognition that she is one of these women.

As within the pages of *The Ageless Way,* Yancey espouses the values of being true to your heart, showing up, being open to profound transformation, lifting other women as you climb, and finding your tribe. Yancey's motto for eWN says it all: "Give first—share always.")

This is the dawn of "the Women's Century"—a century that is more open, more hopeful, and more prosperous than any that has come before.

Backlash Rears Its Ugly Head…Again

By all accounts, women are stepping into their power and profiting more than ever before. Yet, at the same time, women are losing jobs as men gain them in the "recovery." Fewer than 20 percent of executives are female, and more executives are losing their jobs as Wall Street prunes away all but the old boys' club.

Most disturbing, the renewed onslaught against women's right to health services and freedom of choice is on the rise, as demonstrated in the personhood initiatives being put on ballots around the country by the right-to-life proponents. These legislative attempts are meant to redefine at what point life begins (upon conception? in utero at twenty weeks or six months?). If made law, these initiatives will shatter the definition of "person" and "child" in states' criminal codes, opening the door to more intrusive legislation making contraception murder and intrauterine devices and birth control pills into murder weapons, and women in control of their family planning into murderous women. If this isn't enough to bring all of us to our feet and to the voting booths, then add to these initiatives the increasing threats of the abhorrent treatment of women as objects as shown by reports of serial sexual harassment in business, academia, politics, and the military.

As reported by Global Research.org, one in five women report being a victim of sexual assault while studying at America's colleges and universities today. Another study determined that one in four college women have survived rape or attempted rape since age 14. A current trend estimates that one in three women will be sexually assaulted during her life.

As a result of this escalating trend, President Obama renewed a call to action to uncover and eradicate this epidemic. Based on the new report by the White House Council on Women and Girls, nearly 22 million American women and 1.6 million men have been raped in their lifetimes.

The Associated Press also reported that President Obama has directed the Pentagon to better prevent and respond to the crime within its ranks or face further reforms. White House officials say they want to set the example by turning around the sexual assault problem in the military.

How can these two extreme opposite trends be growing side by side? And more importantly, what can we do about it?

What we are seeing is a backlash. The more women gain power and successfully fight for equality in practice, the more the patriarchy goes to extremes to push us back down. The "old women are inherently less than" and "women belong at home" misogynist stories about women are deeply embedded in our society. The protagonists in these stories, the ones who profit from women remaining two dimensional and dependent, can see that their stories are falling apart, that women and enlightened men are waking up (like those in the film *The Matrix*), and refusing to act out their parts in an imaginary world that sucks out their life force.

What we need to do, every last one of us, is to start using our power to continue to create a new story for women, but first we have to acknowledge and embrace that we are powerful. The evidence is there. We control more and more wealth. We are the keys to success in this new world of technology and socially driven business. Yet, as individuals, too many of us are still products of a society in which women who speak up are dismissed as bitches or too loud to be listened to, in which our achievements are still looked at as great "for a woman" or the product of tokenism. We doubt our abilities, our achievements, and ourselves. Many of us still try to please everyone—except ourselves.

> We have to acknowledge and embrace that we are powerful.

This demeaning has to stop. We need to recognize that doing what is right for us can go together with what is right for the world. We need to band together, with other women and enlightened men, and use our voices, leverage our power, and courageously demand change. Even more, we need to recognize that it is fully in our power to step in and create change. Our companies can reinvest in our communities. They can stand for social and environmental justice. The more successful we are, the more of a difference we can make. That's why we need to start (or continue) letting our Ageless Visionary voice narrate our aspirational future stories and unapologetically strive to be successful in a "whole" new way. The Earth is counting on us.

> The more successful we are, the more of a difference we can make.

The Future Is in Her Hands

Based on all these current and likely trends, I believe that women, particularly women in their forties and post-50, are poised to reshape the future for all of us. The leadership skills of the future are in our Signature

Greatness DNA—more and more businesses are recognizing that profit goes together with collaborative, values-based leadership and flexible win-win employee arrangements that arise from the Feminine emerging in all of us. In a very short time, there will be a huge shortage (think millions) of knowledge-based workers, and women, who outnumber men in institutions of higher education (particularly in earning advanced degrees), will be the ones who step up to fill these roles.

Fem power is here at last! Women now have a significant edge over men when it comes to higher education. We are earning most of the associate, bachelor's, master's, and doctorate degrees. USAtoday.com reported that for every 100 degrees men received in 2013, women got a whopping 140!

The new career and business opportunities in serving the growing population of post-40 women and men are staggering. The sky's the limit in what you can create in various aging-related fields, in product design and development, in technology, in simply knowing how to reach out to your cohorts with your shared story. Now is the time to review our skills, training, and education and prepare ourselves for this part of our Ageless Quest—going back to school, apprenticing ourselves, or whatever we need to do to be ready.

President Obama's emphasis on higher education calls to mind President Kennedy's push for science funding and education in the midst of the space race, which quickly led the United States to the top in science, technology, engineering, and mathematics (STEM). Today, we have even more power in our hands to collaborate and share ideas (such as TED.com does so brilliantly with their TED Talks and other offerings), and women and girls in particular are in a unique position to level the playing field on that last frontier, with more encouragement than ever to go into STEM fields. That three young women took the top three prizes in the first international Google Science Fair 2011, a young woman won the grand prize in 2012 and in 2013, twelve of the eighteen finalists were young women (as were two of the four award winners) is prophetic of what's in store.

My colleague Fran Pastore, who has been at the forefront of the entrepreneurial trend, is also optimistic about the future of women entrepreneurship, stating that "While the women's movement of the 1960s was marked by ardent feminism, more than a half century later a new wave of empower-ment for women is being epitomized by an explosion of entrepreneurship. We are not just having a movement anymore, we are living in the moment."

The future looks bright, but it won't necessarily stay that way if we aren't lighting the way, as both Vasilisa carrying the light before us and Baba Yaga passing that light on to other women via Vasilisa. Two women who have opened the way for other women are Mary Furlong in technology, innovative entrepreneurship, and aging and, more recently, Sandra Yancey in advocating for women's entrepreneurship, which is why I am so thankful to have Sandra write the foreword to *The Ageless Way*. More about Furlong in chapter seven, "Gray Is the New Green," and in chapter eight, "The Longevity Economy" and about Yancey earlier in this chapter.

It's easy to fall into complacency, to wait it out. I was one of many women who fought hard for women's rights and equality in the 1970s, never thinking we'd see anything like the backlash against women we're seeing today. And even the promise of STEM is not a given, with budget cutbacks threatening STEM education, the one area with the most potential to pull us out of this economic pit we're in, as individuals and as a nation.

None of us, no matter our generation, should take our hard-earned rights for granted. Things change, as demonstrated by events such as elec-tions and the resulting shifts in leadership. At this juncture, for example, there are some leaders or potential leaders who are intent on shearing back women and minority rights (as well as basic voting rights), which have been in place for years, if not decades. Is that what those who stay home from the polls want to be the outcome of their message? Regardless of your views, or who is in power, it is central to *The Ageless Way* to get out and make your voice heard with your vote. Those who do not vote out of feelings of disillusionment, impotency, and/or to send a message to the White House and the U.S. Congress…be careful what you wish for…the message will be received, but perhaps not as you intended.

Right now, the future is on our side as women, only if we stay awake and alert. Only if we act. Now is the time to awaken (or reawaken) the visionary within you, to create a vision for your personal and professional future and entrepreneurial venture that intersects with what the world needs.

> The future looks bright, but it won't necessarily stay that way if we aren't lighting the way…

> None of us, no matter our generation, should take our hard-earned rights for granted.

It is equally important for those of us who work inside our homes and our family caregivers to create a new story as well, one that acknowledges and elevates the value of all of our contributions to society. I get riled up every time I review my Social Security income calculation statement. To my continued consternation, all of our years as stay-at-home moms, wives, and caretakers is totally devalued by the powers that be who do not consider it appropriate for our non-payroll years to be included in the calculation of Social Security benefits. In fact, should our spouses pass on before us, the idea that their benefits to do not default to us automatically helps to force all too many older women to fall below the poverty level or, at minimum (when we are most vulnerable), find ourselves no longer able to sustain our quality of life.

The more of us who speak out and act now, the more our visionary voices will resonate together and tear down what no longer serves anyone in order to rebuild a future that works—for everyone. (Read more about an exciting new business model emerging for women in chapter seven, "Gray Is the New Green.")

A Multigenerational Legacy

Mattel recently came out with Entrepreneur Barbie, which at first blush seems like an excellent step forward for women. It recognizes the rise in women business owners, especially solopreneurs. This model seems like one of the steps forward Barbie has taken over the years, away from stereotyped occupations for women and closer to the "you can be anything you want to be" model we all want for girls.

But the Barbie itself, with her perfect but sexless body in her pink dress and stilettos, is more limiting than empowering. She still embodies the stereotypical woman more than she represents the diversity of women entrepreneurs. In fact, if anything, this group of women is the least likely to be putting on stilettos for work. These entrepreneurs likely dress comfortably in their home office, and they are likely to be 50-plus, an age when the pain of impractical shoes is not worth the dubious benefit of trying to look sexy for men. Women entrepreneurs are far less likely to be wearing or doing anything just to please men. After all, these women are the boss, the ones who empowered themselves to take the risk on their own ideas and abilities.

Beyond the problems with this particular Barbie is another galling issue. As in advertising and other media, older women are absent from Barbie's life. Where is Barbie's mother? Grandmother? Aunt? One of the latest Barbies has a dog, Taffy, that comes complete with poop and scoop. I kid you not. Mattel creates poop but not once a woman in her thirties or older.

The point, of course, is not that we should have high expectations for Barbie, a doll that has always limited women and girls based on gender roles that are decades old (and never accurate). Barbie is, however, an interesting barometer of our times. Rather than buying Barbies, we need to consciously put our dollars toward toys and dolls that reflect the actual lives and experiences of women (both as we are and as we are capable of becoming with age and experience). By the time Mattel catches up to the realities of women's lives and the strides we've been making for decades, we will be even further enlightened and in more power positions, especially as entrepreneurs. Sadly, despite these years of growth and empowerment, the marketing strategies and methodologies of best-selling items and brands like Barbie show that there is still a long way to go for such progress to become the cultural norm.

Of course, Barbie is just a recent incarnation of the Ideal Woman story. The details change, but the core narrative of judging women against a standard that limits them and boxes in their potential is a recurring story throughout history. In Victorian times, the Barbie story was the "Angel in the House," a poem by a man extolling the virtues of his wife in such a way as to set up both an impossible standard for the "ideal woman" as well as a definition of women that, like Barbie, rested on her role in relation (and subservient) to a man. We can go even further, back to Helen of Troy (the mythological daughter of Zeus, considered to be the most beautiful in the world, whose abduction caused the Trojan War), both an idealized woman and a scapegoat plot point in the lives of men. The details change, but the story remains the same.

We have the awareness and the power to break this story cycle once and for all by creating and living a new story, one in which women of all ages and stages show the power and diversity within them to the point where the old story no longer resonates with anyone's reality.

Making the Barbie story obsolete is a side effect of what we're doing as women to lead the way for generations to follow, not to mention the work we can do together, all generations, to collaborate on the legacy today's girls will leave for their grandchildren and great-grandchildren. Simply the act of stepping into your own shoes—running shoes, oxfords, or platforms—speaking up and being visible, reaching out for your vision, is itself a step forward for all generations, a part of the greater legacy we are forging together.

You Are Not Alone

If you think you're too small to make a difference, you've never been in bed with a mosquito.

~ Anita Roddick, founder of the Body Shop

Wherever you are on the Ageless continuum, whatever experiences you are having as you age, remember that you are not alone. We can share in the collective wisdom, empathy, and solutions of other women who are going through the same experience, as well as those who have blazed the trail ahead of us, our inner Baba Yagas. Don't wait to build a network, in person and online, of women in your tribe, those in the same life stage as you or across generations, for support, empowerment, advice, and laughs. Start now to consciously build communities of multiple generations in the various circles of your life. Forming community is crucial as we age and experience the inevitable losses of friends and family members in our generation and in the generation ahead. Seek out a women's group of mixed ages, a book club or a special interest group like a knitting circle, study group, or an advocacy group focused on topics that matter the most to you. If you're an established business owner or an aspiring entrepreneur, seek out community. One great fast-growing community to check out is eWomenNetwork.com, which loves to say, "None of us makes it alone." If you can't find a group that suits you, start your own. Whatever you choose to pursue, make sure it meets consistently.

If you don't yet know about my European colleague Margaret Manning's site, www.Sixtyandme.com, and her blog, Boomerly, do yourself a favor and check it out. I recently heard about the website, www.70candles.com, run by Ellen Cole (71) and Jane Giddan (72), as a place for women around 70 (approaching it or past it) to share their experiences, their hopes and fears and insights—their stories. I'd like to share with you the three common factors in the lives of those most happy with who they are at 70 and beyond.

Acceptance: Women who accept who they are, age and all, are far more likely to feel happy and fulfilled. This is a challenge for Boomer women, who are from a generation obsessed with youth. But to accept whom you are instead of longing for the past is an essential step—at every age, really—toward finding happiness in the moment.

This acceptance doesn't mean resigned to who you are. It means celebrating the wisdom, experience, and freedom of being an older woman—even reveling in being an old lady, or being one of my favorite terms, a wise Visionary Crone. Take back the original meaning of the term, which was not a witch or a hag but a wise and powerful woman living beyond age (age didn't confine or define her) and helping others at the various crossroads of life.

Connection: Without exception, the happiest women are those with a strong social network. As we age, we lose people—friends, spouses, colleagues. This inevitable loss makes it even more crucial for us to create and strengthen our connections with other people, of all generations, as much as possible. Also key is to connect with other women in your generation so that you can share experiences, hopes, and fears, with people you know will get you completely, and so you can see all that is possible by mentoring and supporting one another into the later, new stages of life.

Action: The idea of "retiring" is an antiquated concept. And this is not just the view of Baby Boomers heading into the traditional retirement age in an economy that won't allow many to retire. The generation ahead has already discovered the secret that, regardless of the economy, true fulfillment in your sixties, seventies, and beyond comes from continuing to live,

> Women that accept who they are, age and all, are far more likely to feel happy and fulfilled.

to be active. This fulfillment doesn't necessarily mean working a full-time job. It can mean part-time work, consulting, community activism and volunteering, or starting a business on your own terms. It can and should be adapted to who you are specifically, not who you are supposed to be. But whatever "it" is for you, keep doing it!

Above all, account for lag time in your hopes, expectations, and plans. Every seed we plant needs time to grow. Don't give up too soon, and be savvy about what you will do in the meantime, before you see a difference in the world or in your bank account. I'm always reminding myself when there's a lull that I'm meant to use the time to reflect, reimagine, and write, write, write. Keep the big picture in mind while living fully in the moment. That is the challenge and the reward of being a visionary. Remember that this journey started for us decades ago. Lag time is an important concept as we wend our way toward our destiny, our story ending. We are not in control of the timing, but we are most definitely responsible for showing up until the timing finds us.

In our roles as guides for the generations coming after us, let's not slip back into the stereotype of being valuable only in what we can pass on. We are also valuable in who we are and what we can create today—just as we always have been.

We are not done. We are just getting started. We are Visionaries with Wrinkles! ❯❯

We are not done. We are just getting started. We are Visionaries with Wrinkles!

CHAPTER 6 ~ *The Ageless Way Reflections*

The questions and exercises below are to help you find your distinct path on The Ageless Way. Turn to page 28 for more about The Ageless Way Reflections.

1. Take a few minutes to assess and list all of the things/people/situations around you that promote your being "average" or "less than." Next, do the same for all the things/people/situations around you that promote your fully embodying your Signature Greatness DNA. Do you notice how you feel in your body when you respond? Is there a difference in your bodily response when you write about what drains you vs. what enlivens you? Please journal what each evokes in a word or image or thought.

2. What ways can you raise and enhance your sense of worth, your self-esteem? When have you felt most respected? Journal about when you were last at the top of your game and what that felt like.

3. What ageism have you experienced or witnessed in the workplace? Did anyone identify it publicly, or was it accepted or swept "under the rug?" How would you handle that same situation today? What would an age-friendly and women-friendly workplace look like? What can you do to create this?

4. What would your Entrepreneur Barbie look like? What other Barbies are missing that would reflect the positive reality and preferred future for all ages? Do you have an idea for another children's toy that does or would encourage Agelessness?

5. What is one thing you can do in the next month to "accept, connect, and act" in ways that will ensure your own Agelessness and life satisfaction so you can empower others in the same way?

6. Be sure to take some time to be in silence so you can access your own Inner Visionary voice. Keep your journal at hand and write or draw in it as words or images arise.

Chapter 7

GRAY IS THE NEW GREEN

The problem is that as people have matured and markets have evolved, marketing has not. ...Clearly marketers have to change a great deal to adjust to this new world order.

~ David Wolfe

Without a doubt, the most massive transformation we're undergoing as a nation (and around the globe) is catalyzed by the "change-every-thing-in-its-path" Gray Force Field of Baby Boomers (born 1943-1967), approaching or past traditional retirement age. Boomers control more than 75 percent of our nation's wealth, and they are spending that wealth, outpacing other generations in nearly every buying category. Even if Boomers work less, we're still talking about a starting point of $2.4 trillion in annual income. Combine this with the fact that women alone control 85 percent of consumer spending, and that they outlive men by about five or six years (according to Scientific American, there are six women to every four men by age 85), and the conclusion is clear: Women mean business.

Women mean business. ... Boomer Women mean BIG BUSINESS.

But that's not all. Boomer Women mean BIG BUSINESS. Just look at these statistics:

- United States women over 50 control $19 trillion.

- Women over 50 control more than three-quarters of U.S. financial wealth.

- People over 50 are 43 percent of U.S. adults and 27 percent of the total U.S. population.

- Women are 20 percent of U.S. adults.

- Seventy-five million-plus U.S. women over the age of 50 are working outside the home.

- Between 1997 and 2013, the number of U.S. woman-owned businesses grew by 59 percent, vs. 41 percent for all new businesses in the United States; a rate almost one and a half times the average.

Ageless Women are where it's at!

Ageless Women are where it's at!

Everyone from solopreneurs to large corporations needs to recognize that this market is essential to staying in business in the future, or even in the present. Especially important is that Ageless Women themselves are in a unique position to serve this market just as they are in this market to be served. In other words, gray is the new green!

As author David Wolfe observed, "I believe companies are largely ignoring the largest and richest customer group in history for three reasons. First, stereotypical beliefs about older customers paint them as resistant to change, so why bother. Second, there is widespread uneasiness about how to market to older customers, so let's spare ourselves the pain of failure. Third, people under 40, who are not in the same mental space as members of the new adult marketplace majority, dominate marketing processes. They relate most comfortably to customers of their own ages or younger."

Yet, the economy, business, and the workplace are all undergoing glacial change from the status quo, despite a combination of massive upheavals and a constant media focus on the aging Boomer population. Throughout history, chaos and major shifts have always been accompanied by renewed attempts to hold on for dear life to the (false) security of How Things Have Always Been Done. There is an ongoing conflict between the stories of our past and the stories of our future, and the battlefield between them is inevitably our present story.

The Truth about Our Future

Knowing full well that the maturing Boomer generation was about to turn aging on its head, in the late 1980s I set out to sound the clarion call of gray is the new green. For years wherever I showed up I provocatively asked, "Are you leaving money on the table by ignoring the Baby Boomer boom?" I continue to ask this question today.

My message continues to be, "Here's how to stay in sync with the generation that keeps you in business." I present to professional and corporate marketers, strategists, and entrepreneurs (experienced and newbies) across many sectors. I attempt to wake up those who have the most to gain or lose in market share and reach if they close their eyes to the 40-plus market potential. I warn them that they best get on board fast, because their ability to monetize going forward will be based on their willingness to serve this enormous force field of new Boomer demand in the workplace, the U.S. marketplace, and around the globe.

I continue to travel the country to present one of my signature talks, "Visionaries Have Wrinkles: Serving the Generation Who Will Change the World…Again" to my fellow futurists, academicians, coaches, consultants, gerontologists, and all manner of professionals from marketers and service-providers to product companies, those in financial services, and from large to small businesses, including solopreneurs.

A small percentage of marketers "get" what is coming, so they are leaping ahead to own segments of this market. Others, studies reveal, may be undervaluing a key demographic and losing a changing game.

Most businesses are still trying to figure out what Baby Boomers want, and Boomers are still trying to figure out what they want. The Gray Tsunami is heading to Madison Avenue and Main Street, USA.

No matter your industry or field, those who recognize the new rules of the game will reap the benefits and gobble up market share. For starters, the new rules are customer-centric, not product-centered, as has been the case for eons. At least until Millennials turn 40, youth no longer rules! But "PrimeTime Women" do! More on this later in this chapter.

Let's get back to the here and now stats that should blow your socks off! Based on a briefing paper prepared by Oxford Economics for AARP, it is estimated that "a 106 million-plus market is expected to grow by over 30% in the next 20 years." If you snooze, you lose. Any entrepreneur or service professional who ignores the enormous power of the Big Gray already on our threshold might as well kiss her business goodbye. To anyone not

Are you sure you want to leave money on the table by ignoring this 40-plus market?

paying attention, I must ask, are you sure you want to leave money on the table by ignoring this 40-plus market?

If you are not already serving or planning to serve the 40-plus market, you are not only missing out financially—you are missing out on the chance to align what matters with an audience that is consciously choosing companies that are making a difference as well as a profit.

The aftermath of the Great Recession can seem like the worst possible time to focus your business on your values, but the opposite is true. Boomers are an indication of how your clients are changing. Living your values and focusing on what matters in your business is not only what you need; it's what the world needs—and it's what the world is willing to pay for.

Businesses that want to tap into this trend must shift their focus from value to values, from the bottom line to the Triple Bottom Line: People, Planet, Profit.

Just consider how this trend is likely to play out. People and businesses that find a way to combine a larger visionary purpose with their business model will be the most profitable. More people and businesses will follow their lead until visionary business practices become the norm. Not riding this trend now not only means missing out on a larger market, more money, and greater impact—it could make your ideas and your business ultimately obsolete.

Boomer women over 50 grew up watching prime-time TV and now are emerging as the hottest market to serve. Some of us, like myself, fall into the "Boomer Classic" grouping of those who were born and grew up in the 1940s and 1950s. The oldest Boomers, referred to as Leading Edge Boomers, are heading into their seventies. The next wave, the Later Edge Boomers, were born and grew up in the 1960s and 1970s.

There's a lot of talk in marketing and advertising circles these days about splitting up these two groupings. Why is this distinction between Leading Edge Boomers vs. later-born Boomers important to know?

In some important ways these two groupings are vastly different based on their formative adolescent experiences. I learned this early on when my then-graphics designer, a classic Leading Edge Boomer, when reviewing my website plans declared, "I don't like being lumped in with my younger

Boomer sisters. I love them, but they were not 'sistas.' I was a flower child, I wanted to save and change the world. I was/am about peace, love and rock 'n' roll. My sisters were the "Me" generation, all about getting more, not into the world around them. We are no way the same generation!"

I'm all for inclusivity, but it's important in crafting our marketing and branding messages to recognize the disparity between Leading Edge Boomers and their younger Boomer counterparts, labeled as Later Edge Boomers (aka, the Me Generation, Generation Jones, and Trailing-Edge Boomers). What is critical to glean is that all Baby Boomers have suffered and come through a tragic reversal of our youthful idealized "we-can-all-have-it-all" Boomer story. We went from "life is good" to tragedies within each decade to now having the dream's downfall be additionally triggered by unforeseen events outside our control (like natural disasters, the long Great Recession, a world taken over by extremists—terrorism, cyber crime) and our Mother Earth fighting for the planet's life as we know it. We now need to re-story the Boomer story.

> Baby Boomers have suffered and come through a tragic reversal of our youthful idealized "we-can-all-have-it-all" Boomer story.

Leading-Edge women Baby Boomers (born between 1943 and 1955) moved through adolescence and into adulthood in a drastically different time of chaos and tragedy that scarred our youthful aspirations for the future. Seventy-eight days after the assassination of JFK, the Beatles arrived on the American scene. Then we lost Martin Luther King Jr. We were in deep mourning, but we grew up with rock 'n' roll. We came of age during the Vietnam War era and experienced the draft. We grew up in a time of cultural rule changing and intense social upheaval. Dylan and the Beatles gave us hope, stoked our revolutionary dreams again. We had transistor radios back then. Remember them? What about black-and-white TVs? I couldn't wait to see the next episode of *Zorro, Bat Masterson* and most memorable of all, *The Twilight Zone*. I still can hear Rod Serling guiding us behind the outer curtain of time and space into another plane of existence. Scary and addicting. My folks loved Ed Sullivan, and we all loved *I Love Lucy* and *The Honeymooners*. My younger sister was the epitome of Boomer youth. She was into political unrest, anti-war protests and riots, social experimentation, sexual freedom, drug experimentation, and everything associated with the Woodstock culture. We all shared the awe of the first moon walk and the Civil Rights and the Second Wave Feminist movements of the 1970s.

The Later Edge Boomers (born between 1956 and 1964) bypassed much of that Leading-Edge rocky youth. Per a good description of Boomers on Wikipedia, their defining experiences were "the Cold War, Vietnam War, Watergate and Nixon's resignation, lowered drinking age in many states 1970-1976, the oil embargo, raging inflation, gasoline shortages, Jimmy Carter's imposition of registration for the draft, Ronald Reagan and Live Aid." Their music was a blend of rock, pop, disco, some punk and funk. My sister loved watching *The Brady Bunch* and *Happy Days*. Birth control was taken for granted, as were graduate school and plentiful career opportunities.

Caveat to share. Women born in the mid-1950s found themselves in the midst of these two coming-of-age cohort groups (seemingly polar opposites on the generational range and spectrum). Are you one of these women? I bet you also remember where you were when JFK was assassinated. Did you play the Beatles at recess and listen to Dylan on the radio? Even though you were too young to participate fully, these events and people were formative for you, too.

Wikipedia goes on to list the key characteristics of Leading-Edge Baby Boomers as experimental, individualists, free-spirited, and social cause oriented. On the other hand, these are the characteristics listed for the Later-Edge Boomers: less optimistic, distrustful of government, and generally cynical. Again descriptive of extremes. Back to extreme characterization and categorization. Mixed in are those who find themselves psychologically and behaviorally profiled in the wrong end of the generation. Remember, these are generalized descriptive profiles based on data profiling. If I missed you in my attempt to share some defining distinctions within the enormous Baby Boomer generation, please let me know by email so that we together can keep redefining to be inclusive. (Please send to Karen@KarenSands. com and put "TAW" in the subject line.)

We've moved from burning with passion for change, to burning up with impotent rage and then being burned out.

Now all of our assumptions about how the world works were in disarray. But it wasn't supposed to be this way—even for the "one percent!" Now the whole range of Baby Boomers have incomplete, or unfinished stories. We've moved from burning with passion for change, to burning up with impotent rage and then being burned out. Many Boomers who once thought being a Boomer was awesome now think the 1960s failed. Many of us have broken hearts and weary Souls after realizing that the tragic reversal that befell us is so much bigger than we are. We thought we'd be coasting right about now. Instead, we have been in shock and awe in the face of the enormity of devastating loss all around us. People have lost their savings. Planned pensions have evaporated. Our homes have been taken from us or we have lost our equity. Rampant but hard-to-diagnose PTSD plagues us after learning we really are not completely in charge of our story. OMG, we are not masters of our selves after all. What a cosmic death has been visited on Baby Boomers who were pioneers in self-actualization and intent on a cosmic connection. We lost our *whole* Boomer story; we are still in a survival mode with uncertainly our constant shadow. What a mess!

In David Wolfe's 2003 book, *Ageless Marketing,* he writes of the fall out from our Boomer tumble from grace: "Uncertainty reigns, but this much is certain: To regain a steady hand on the directions of our work, our society, and perhaps our own lives, we must unlearn a host of old rules and learn many new ones. There is no more daunting task we face than to adapt to the idea that much of what we thought we knew is wrong." But isn't older age all about living in grace, being transcendent, and winding down to the good life? Post our tragic fall, we now seek warmth around the campfire flames, rather than the ravaging rage and hopeless despair that has been ever present during the Great Recession of the twenty-first century and into the years following.

Turns out everything before now was just a dress rehearsal. We've lived through tragic reversal of fortunes to learn what really, truly matters. This is the same for both ends of the Boomer demographic. We are still re-evaluating, reimagining, reintegrating, and going through values-based reinvention. What carries us forward is that we are re-storying and reclaiming our tomorrows based on our values and what matters most.

There are a couple more wrinkles in the Boomer women's story. We've had two cognitive jolts that change everything for us going forward! We've never had this many women living healthy and long lives, nor have we experienced post-menopausal brain before, much less in these numbers.

I have long called the symptomatic changes that come with "The Change" a "Trick of the Feminine." Perimenopausal symptoms like brain fog, hot flashes, mood swings, and vibrant dreamtime force us to "pause" so we can go deeper into examining our lives to date, reclaiming parts of

Boomer women have had two cognitive jolts that change everything for us going forward!

ourselves long ago left behind and tossing those that no longer work for us. These biochemical hormonal shifts foster deep cellular and psychic openings that form new pathways to access our deeper truths and embrace the wild, wise energy of the archetypal Inner Crone.

No small wonder that this menopausal-induced shift into our inner psyche coincides with a tendency to create a renewed orientation to our right brain as our primary orientation, with our left brain moving into a support function. This inward shift brings with it an increased ability to access both our metaphorical right brain processing and intuitive Feminine knowing. No wonder Jungians have long referred to the right-brain processing function being associated with the Inner Feminine, our psyche, our Soul, whereas the left-brain analytical, goal-focused processing function is associated with the Inner Masculine, our mind, our spirit.

Considering that the average age of the onset of menopause is 51, I am always in wonderment that "The Change" occurs as we women developmentally and chronologically move into the midpoint of our midlife course (more on the topic of Menopause in chapter nine, "Ageless Reinvention," and chapter thirteen, "Ageless Futures").

For three hundred years or so, women were kept as barefoot girls and then impregnated young women with short life spans. Now, with elongating lifespans and the advent of new findings in neuroscience, women are just beginning to discover and tap into potent post-menopausal brains in numbers never known before. In my view, this rising of women and the Inner Feminine (divine and sacred dark) happening is not coincidental; it is synchronistic, which leads me to believe that we older women will bring new intuitive foresight and imagination, and a vast number of new possibilities, to the forefront. We can radically reframe the stories we tell ourselves about aging, as well as confront modern-day global issues like hunger, climate change, barbaric terrorism, deadly plagues, rising misogyny, oppression, and more.

Post-40 women will become the source and resource of most of the new evolutionary visionary thinking and whole-brain wisdom leadership skills for our re-storied times. This will neither replace nor displace the Inner Masculine, nor the men in our lives. Rather, we will partner with our menfolk to usher in a new Feminine era where what matters most, for everyone, drives our future.

Now, as we enter our middle and later years, we are retrieving interrupted and unfinished stories to reshape our new story endings. We are returning to our first and earlier chapters to rewrite a new Aspirational Ageless Future, while creating new legacies that matter far into future generations.

Word to the Wise

What worked in the past to garner our Boomer women's attention and gain loyalty won't work today. We don't have time to waste, so skip the B.S. Only straight-up transparency and authentic outreach will make a dent. The only way through to our pocketbooks is story telling based on our core values and valuing our personal stories as meaningful.

Businesses that target boomers will need to ask deeper questions. …Businesses that understand dream fulfillment, lifestage marketing, and the desire of baby boomers to make a difference will lead the pack.

~ Mary Furlong, *Turning Silver into Gold*

Too Big to Fail

I can attest to those stories about "too big to fail" companies that are so mired in *what was* and *what worked* in the past that they totally miss the opportunity that is coming down the pike…it's already here.

My all-time favorite women business writer, Harvard Professor Rosabeth Moss Kanter, described and categorized these same behemoths in her 1990 book, *When Giants Learn to Dance*. I was still considered a "new breed" intrapreneur in the financial services industry when I first read Kanter's book in which she disrobes the dysfunctional nature of financial services in particular. Kanter's astute commentary still applies to all forms of business entities and institutions, especially when it comes to the lack of foresight and the next-to-nil fleet-footed adaptation skills required to best serve this Ageless Women demographic. The financial services industry today is still mired in outmoded ways of doing business (e.g., applying dated product-driven and transaction-centered approaches vs. providing a customer-centric relational approach, which is spot-on for this demographic).

> **The financial services industry today is still mired in outmoded ways of doing business.**

The Hudson Institute, a prestigious think tank in Washington, D.C., describes future prospects and significant workforce changes projected over the next several decades in both of its highly respected comprehensive reports; Workforce 2000 and Workforce 2020. A key takeaway from both reports is that this unprecedented "PrimeTime" demographic shift will rear its head in the world soon, if it hasn't already. This disruptive shift will be a game changer no matter how it first emerges on your workforce radar. Some telltale signs are already showing up: your firm's dwindling number of Boomer knowledge workers, gaps in workforce skills, or the stagnation of many of your current pre-retirees who are choosing not to make waves. It may be seen in the increasing number of women leaving after working their tails off for years only to be treated as invisible after 40, or beyond their expiry date after 50. However this shift manifests, a shake-up is under way. Are you prepared or asleep at the helm?

• When Baby Boomers Say Sayonara

Don't minimize a sudden exodus of Baby Boomers by thinking this mass departure will solely impact consumer products. Instead, consider its impact on every field and industry, as all will be affected. I was in total shock a few years ago when I heard from top scientists and management leadership futurist colleagues of mine in the National Aeronautics and Space Administration (aka NASA) that the majority of the agency's scientists, astronauts, and leadership are over age 50. After years of passionate dedication to the mission of NASA, due to cutbacks imposed on them, these professionals have been deflated and demoralized. In response, most are taking early retirement (or at least considering it), saying that they are done, "over and out," because they were too old for such shenanigans. This mass departure will bring with it a great loss to NASA, and to the world, given that their hard-earned knowledge goes right out the door with them.

An article in Networkworld.com woke me up by highlighting another sector implosion caused by departing Boomer knowledge workers, which is about to happen across all industries with an in-house IT organization or dedicated contracted IT department. Are you counting on Boomers to put off retiring and stick around? Counting on Baby Boomers to "hang in there" is bad planning when it comes to your IT workforce development and succession initiatives. Just ponder this for a moment. Think what would happen if all the Boomers on your team decide to leave at the same time. Wouldn't it be better to limit your exposure to brain drain directly caused by your knowledge workers retiring or changing employers?

It's important to raise the veils of denial around the conflicting stories we are told about our aging workforce and the places in which we work. A shocking, but important, denial eradicator is a study by KPMG based in the Netherlands (it is one of the largest professional service companies in the world and one of the Big Four auditors), wherein executives and HR directors were surveyed about their attitudes regarding managing older staff. When asked if there is a "silent tipping point" at which employees are "perceived to be less valuable or attractive to the organization," two-thirds of HR chiefs said there was an "over-the-hill tipping point." Almost one-half of HR directors said this tipping point occurs at 50 years old and more than one-third said at age 60. So there it is. Over the Hill is universally age 50! However, without a doubt, Baby Boomers at the helm of companies, government, and institutions across all sectors, are pushing the benchmark further along the age continuum. Whatever the moving target age is today for a pink slip, the silver ceiling is hovering over all our heads. Leading-Edge Gen Xers are moving closer and closer to the current expiry date. Does this mean Over the Hill will move to age 60 by the time Gen Xers head into their sixties?

Women in droves are bypassing not only the glass ceiling, but now the silvered glass ceiling as well. Our impact doesn't stop in the workplace. Instead, we are making change happen faster and faster...like a fast-engulfing wildfire—right into retail dressing rooms, online shopping, cosmetic

> Women in droves are bypassing not only the glass ceiling, but now the silvered ceiling as well.

counters, who and what we watch on the silver screen, and most of all, in all our coffers and spreadsheets!

Yet, giant corporations, like elephants, don't know how to dance. In fact, most of these giants, as well as the "little guys," are leaving trillions on the table, as they turn a blind eye to what's going to rock their boat... maybe even sink it.

Times They Are a-Changing

A new story is emerging written by marketers and product makers.

A new story is emerging, written by those marketers and product makers who recognize that it is worthwhile to get beyond the rampant malevolent ageism in corporate marketing and product development decision making. A finding in a Nielsen study projects that by 2017 Baby Boomers will control 70 percent of the country's disposable income. No surprise that only the most nimble entrepreneurs and avant-garde among us are taking the lead. The "good old boys" at the helm of the big elephant behemoths will pay the price of sticking solely with the youth market. Clearly they still haven't learned to dance decades after Kanter's call to action.

Mary Furlong, whom I refer to as the "grand dame" of the business of aging, has for decades been sounding the clarion call bringing business leaders, innovators, and investors together to capitalize on new business and investment opportunities in the longevity marketplace.

From the start in 2007, when I first read her book *Turning Silver into Gold,* and later when I learned about her annual winter What's Next Boomer Business Summit and then attended as a luncheon author-blogger table host, it was clear that there are many parallels in our respective visions for entrepreneurs in the business of aging and for the global community of women 40+. But that's not all she's up to. Furlong also offers her annual summer event, the Silicon Valley Boomer Venture Summit for entrepreneurial talent and investors. On top of all her accomplishments, Furlong is also the dean's executive professor of entrepreneurship at the Leavey School of Business at Santa Clara University and founder of SeniorNet (1986), Third Age Media (1996), and her current incarnation, Mary Furlong and Associates (2002).

Bottom line: I am inspired by Furlong because she both epitomizes an Ageless woman, and represents a true Visionary with Wrinkles. In her current leadership role at the helm of Mary Furlong and Associates (MFA), she continues to elevate the business of aging and foster innovation and entrepreneurship. You can find out more at www.maryfurlong.com.

I'd be remiss to not mention Lori Bitter, one of the new breed of women visionary leaders in the business of aging. Formerly she was president of J. Walter Thompson's Boomer division, JWT BOOM, and led client services for Age Wave Impact. Recently named to Entrepreneur magazine's 100 to Watch List, Bitter provides strategic consulting, research, and product development for companies seeking to engage with mature consumers at The Business of Aging. She also serves as publisher of GRAND—the digital magazine for grandparents. Her book, *The Grandparent Economy* (2015), is a must-read.

The Silver Screen Leads the Way

In the past, there have been fewer roles available for women over 45, except for a smattering of niche films. Word has it that Hollywood studios value men's work over women's, most definitely as they age. Older women are breaking the silver screen's once-impregnable silver ceiling with 80 percent of 2014's female Oscar nominees older than 50, including many of our favorite stars like Judi Dench (then 79) in *Philomena*, Meryl Streep (then 64) in *August: Osage County*, Emma Thompson (then 55) in *Saving Mr. Banks*, Sandra Bullock (then 50) in *Gravity*, and June Squibb (then 84) in *Nebraska*. In response to winning her first Oscar in her role as Jasmine in *Blue Jasmine* (after six previous Oscar nominations), Cate Blanchett (then 39) stated in her acceptance speech that "women's movies are no longer niche movies. Older women have powered their way into the mainstream, dominating cinemas' screens, winning awards, garnering box-office receipts, and showing the Millennials how it's done: Combine a triple threat of wisdom, talent, and patience to hone your craft."

Another new blockbuster film, *Elsa & Fred,* is appearing on the silver screen, demonstrating Hollywood's current shift in focus from producing films solely for the youth market to now offering films by and for the mature

Older women have powered their way into the mainstream.

majority market. This thrills me to no end. The grand dame of America's cinema, Shirley MacLaine (80 and counting), has returned to center stage as the character Elsa. Bravo both to MacLaine and to the director, Michael Radford, who uses MacLaine's character to explore the polarities of a woman's ownership of her real chronological age vs. how she feels inwardly. This is truth-telling onscreen, which I've always admired in all of MacLaine's performances. Now MacLaine will shake us up and portray what research already bears out, that for most of us we still "see" ourselves at around age 40 whether we are in our sixties, our seventies and beyond.

For me, Kim Cattrall, who played Samantha on *Sex and the City,* tells it like it is now that she is newly turned on to finding a forum to speak to the Baby Boomer generation. Why is she so turned on? She says, "Because I feel that we are the biggest generation out there, and nobody (except PBS) is really addressing us as far as entertainment." She adds, "I want to speak about this generation in my work. I am interested in making programming for actresses and stories of women in their sixties. I'm just shocked that there isn't more programming for us out there. The biggest generation that ever was is completely ignored and I want to do something about that." Kim, if you are reading this book, please know that I'm here ready and raring to go, so give me a call anytime! So many older actresses are now inspiring audiences to change the dialogue about aging.

Forward-Leaning Fashion and Beauty Product Companies at the Head of the Runway

Ageism in advertising is also becoming old hat! New research shows women over the age of 50 are the highest increasing-spending demographic when it comes to fashion and beauty. Spending on clothes and accessories is increasing in the over-50 market and falling in the under-50 market.

UK's High Street fashion retailers are mirroring a quiet but fast expanding evolution in which the 50-plus women that High Street abandoned years ago are now being wooed and reclaimed for good reason: This demographic group is accounting for 41 percent of retail sales, along with an impressive 90 percent of the UK's retailers experiencing their fastest growth from this same age group. Confirming that this trend is here to stay, University of Kent's Professor Julia Twigg, author of *Fashion and Age*, says, "Women over 75 are now shopping as frequently as those in their teens and twenties were in the Sixties." Twigg goes on to say, "Now, the lives of those in their sixties are not immensely different from those in their forties." In fact, "The over-fifties are not a funny little niche to be pandered to, but a market every bit as stylish, active and alert as their daughters—and with more disposable income."

Other smart American marketers and product makers are following suit by paying attention to a Boombox survey in which almost 60 percent of Boomer women responded that they can't relate to most beauty ads and 80 percent shared that they don't aspire to look like models in those ads. Women aren't holding back any punches when they tell Boombox the real core truth: "We'd like to see more 'real people' and more 'people of our age.' " American Apparel and Marc Jacobs, both major fashion labels, as well as NARS, a cutting-edge beauty products company, and L'Oreal are jumping on the Ageless Beauty bandwagon. Breaking the age barrier, Marc Jacobs has hired 65-year-old actress Jessica Lange as the face of its new beauty campaign, NARS has chosen 68-year-old actress Charlotte Rampling as its lead, and L'Oreal has a Boomer favorite, Diane Keaton (69) as its new celebrity portrayal of *real* beauty. But that's not all. At age 69, Oscar winner Helen Mirren is the newest addition to L'Oreal's roster of stars, taking a natural approach to aging and portraying Ageless Beauty. In her own words, Mirren says, "I hope I can inspire other women towards greater confidence by making the most of their natural good looks. We are all worth it!" As I highlight in more detail in chapter five, "Ageless Attraction," 63-year-old, newly found model, Jacky O'Shaughnessy, has been chosen as American Apparel's newest lingerie model instead of its usual 20-something model, proving with its new tagline that "sexy has no expiration date." All marketers and product companies can follow suit by morphing into an age-friendly, Ageless Beauty model that will both sustain their brands' leadership in the anti-aging women's market and expand market opportunities in the multi-generational legacy market as they reach across generations to mothers, daughters, and granddaughters, as well as sisters, aunts, and nieces.

Over-the-Top Ageism in Marketing and Advertising

Baby Boomer women represent the first generation in history to take full charge of their lives...at every stage.

~ Marti Barletta

Marti Barletta aptly coined Baby Boomers and Matures "PrimeTime Women." We grew up watching more television than younger viewers today. Yet a large number of older women tune out ads. I know I do. According to findings by GlynnDevins Advertising, older adults surveyed do not believe ads portray them as "people to be respected." That response should come as no surprise when scanning current advertising spots that either portray the post-50 demographic as moronic and past tense, or out of commission due to a variety of age-related "dysfunctions." Not exactly a positive depiction of older adults.

According to a Nielsen study on the state of advertising buys and the dollars spent on the post-50 market, it appears that media buyers and marketers have turned a blind eye to the over-50 demographic. The majority of media buyers and marketers consider post-50 adults worthy of only five percent or less of their advertising and marketing dollars.

The measly five percent allocated and the out-of-touch-with-reality cut-off age of 49 is no surprise, really. Advertising and marketing companies, consultancies, and internal departments are notorious for being youth-driven not only in their campaigns, but also in their hiring, promotion, and retention practices, with employee value decreasing as employees move into their mid-thirties. The Bureau of Labor Statistics (BLS) states that the median age of advertising employees is 39.3; that's approximately three years younger than all workers they studied.

But what really hurts are the ad campaigns that make us want to rage and stop buying the products associated with the in-bad-taste, over-the-top, blatant ageism. I am appalled by the recent spate of Esurance ads in which older women are depicted as old bags and dumber than dumb. The reverse mortgage ads with Fred Thompson, the former senator from Tennessee, bring instant credibility (and incredulity!) while he speaks about the benefits of his sponsor's product. What I find so distasteful is that while Thompson continues to espouse the benefits to us, the camera pans to a couple who are not using their house value to cover their lifestyle as they age, looking harried and sad as they paint their peeling white picket fence. Then, from this downer depiction, the camera pans to a different smiling, chipper, relaxed couple surrounded by their bright-colored flower garden. Give me a break. We may be over 50, or 90, but we aren't stupid. This portrayal is insulting, almost as much as the Esurance ads! The worst offenders these days are the misogynist and ageist ads by Geico and VW. Both have ads putting down older women and mothers! Both depicting us as ding-bats, losers or raucous self-centered older women.

Then there are the Sandals escape luxury vacation ads that speak volumes about whom they are trying to reach. What about Viagra and Cialis? For the longest time, we've been besieged in the Cialis ads by a man and woman ending up in separate four-footed tubs placed on a beach. I don't think I can easily get in and out of one of those tubs, much less look sexy doing so. Have you ever noticed that the model couples look like they shouldn't be having erectile dysfunction issues, since they all look younger than their early fifties? The newest spot now goes right to clean porn with a lovely blonde Aussie or English woman dressed in a Marilyn Monroe–like sensual beach-dress, lying down with a beguiling deep-throated plea that you men just must get over your erectile dysfunction, and when you do, look what will happen for you! Voilà! She's all yours, fellas! Okay, fan the guys' egos, get them aroused, but promises, promises.

Financial Services Still Can't Find Their Dancing Shoes

Last but not least are my long-ago colleagues in financial services who are still trailing the marketplace when it comes to women, most definitely Boomer women. From what I can tell and am told, nothing has changed much in this industry for decades. Making matters worse today, the Financial Planning Association found that 88 percent of consumers indicated that they would not seek services from a broker if they knew the broker was not required to act in their best interests. Sad but true, industry research supports my contention that the primary challenge for this industry is that 91 percent of women feel misunderstood by advisors. It's only up from here, but nobody's paying attention. To my amazement, Metropolitan Life dismantled and closed the doors of its treasured MetLife Mature Market Institute, which had been under the respected leadership of Sandra Timmermann. The institute was revered by anyone seeking up-to-date, relevant research. Has AARP's rebranding pushed such a high-quality research resource out of business? Or perhaps the Mature Market Institute just didn't fit with MetLife's mission any longer in these and future times? Why else would MetLife have closed its doors? Once again I ask, "Where are your dancing shoes?"

(If you would like more information on how you can be a rock solid advisor, and how best to serve the over-40 women's market, let me know by email, Karen@KarenSands.com.) There's hope on the horizon.

Old School Male-Dominated Industries Taking a Peek

Even the auto industry is catching on. The 50-plus demographic is again having an enormous impact on American auto sales. Over the last three years, this buying age cohort contributed a startling 84 percent of the $1.5 million increase in sales.

Believe it or not, Walmart is launching a new circular designation label announcing when the company behind a product (any items from lingerie to hummus) is women-owned. Watch out, gluten-free, fair-trade, or made in America. Walmart is putting its money where its mouth is by pledging to source $20 billion of goods from "Women Owned Businesses" (WOB) in the United States by 2016. For other reasons, Walmart is not a favorite employer or retailer for me, yet they are super-savvy market strategists.

Swiffer, another cutting-edge advertiser, is so savvy it is appealing across generations. Every time I see the Swiffer ads, they make me laugh and feel warm inside. The most popular Swiffer spot is when we are invited into the Valley Stream home of a couple in their nineties, Lee and Morty Kaufman, who, with the magic of their first Swiffer, discover how much dirt and dust has been left behind from using traditional dusting and cleaning tools like brooms, mops, and even vacuums. (I'm always amazed. I still show my husband when I get a big Swiffer load!) I read the other day that Elizabeth Ming, the spokeswoman for Swiffer, confirmed my take that this spot resonates with Americans of all ages—because many consumers aspire to have a similar loving, enduring relationship. What a plug for Ageless Marketing!

You'd think other retailers would be following suit in droves, right? Yet, this trend of investing in post-50s is not only lower in the United States, but also in many other countries. So what gives?

The truth is, we are back to the conundrum of sometimes opposing pulls between profit and mission again. If you want to pay your bills and have a life, then profits win every time. Just keep an eye on the marketplace and you'll observe product designers, marketers, and service providers waking up and moving into this new story of *The Ageless Way*, albeit ever so slowly.

Higher Education Steps Up to the Plate

It's crucial for all industries and fields to reach out to the 50-plus demographic; some of the most savvy are doing so. Higher education is no exception. Both Professor Rosabeth Moss Kanter at Harvard and a spanking-new initiative at Stanford University are trawling for a new kind of student seeking to reinvent the next stage after midlife. Stanford openly espouses that it wants to attract proven leaders with twenty to thirty years of work experience on the hunt to reinvent their futures.

University and advanced adult education and professional development programs are the future. No doubt a proliferation of new higher education programs modeled off of the Harvard and Stanford programs will emerge over the next decades.

> University and advanced adult education and professional development programs are the future.

Twenty-First Century Boomtime Careers

I've been known to get rather passionate when I speak about the paucity of career changers and younger generations enrolled or even interested

Are you leaving money on the table and growing opportunities in the dust?

in the field of aging. Both are leaving money on the table and growing opportunities in the dust.

I want to rant and rave that the aging field is not all about changing bedpans. Don't get me wrong; personal care for the frail elderly and disabled is a critical task for one of the fastest growing careers today as a health care worker.

Rather, what I'm so excited about are the enormous possibilities for meaningful work in serving the maturing 40-plus market, and those succeeding generations who will soon be 40-plussers themselves. That's why in this chapter I'm compelled to include the trend information relating to new careers in aging.

Yet we continue to read and hear from the media that Millennials have no opportunities before them, or that Boomers and Millennials will continue to fight for job positions. Give me a break! There are so many untapped career opportunities in the aging field (and its tangential fields) that no one needs to be out of work! That is, not if they are trained and skilled, especially those with a long career history.

Just take a look at the numbers: The United States Census Bureau and Civic Ventures project reports that by 2030, Americans age 55 and older will number 107.6 million, 31 percent of the population. Those over 65 will account for 20 percent of the total population. The Nielsen study reports that by 2017 Baby Boomers will control 70 percent of America's disposable income. This is a market to be reckoned with, so it's best to get on the new millennium job growth curve in the field of aging sooner rather than later. Otherwise, you may miss an incredible opportunity of these times for your career, your business, or your organization.

Please be advised that everything in the field of aging is morphing rapidly, creating an exciting plethora of emerging opportunities in a variety of specialty roles and services. Not only because of the swelling ranks of the over-50s, but because the field of aging is evolving at warp speed. It's not just bedpans anymore.

My goal here is to make sure you stay with me and not get turned off to this meaningful, high-impact field as your possible "what's next" or as your new marketplace to increase your market share. So I'm going to ask you to stay with me while I share an overview of the aging field's history right up to today…and tomorrow.

As I write, there is a great deal of healthy Creative Destruction going on in the aging field. The new "older adult" demographic of Leading-Edge Boomers is wreaking havoc on the longtime preferred and universally accepted disease model of aging that has long been the underpinning of the field.

I'm a rabid fan of transforming the language, symbolism, and narrative around aging. Our languaging, especially around hot-button topics, reveals what's not being said out loud or what is still unconscious and informs how we perceive or imagine things to be. So let's start off with the languaging, including commonly accepted definitions and how they are integrally entwined with the history of the aging field.

The Basics: A Language and History Overview

My previous pejorative references to bedpans equating to the essence of the aging services field is a perfect example of how negative symbolism in the current narrative around careers in aging has a significantly pessimistic impact on the future of the aging field. We need a more enticing symbolism and depiction of the field of possibilities now emerging for younger generations, as well as for Baby Boomers seeking Third and Fourth Age recareering or new start-up ventures.

The more common notions people have about the field of aging are rooted in geriatrics, which is built on the disease model. Geriatrics is solely about comprehensive health care of older adults, with a focus on the study of illness and diseases of later life. For as long as I can remember, working with older adults fell into the realm of health care only.

Gerontology is the antithesis of the disease model, as it is the study of the process of aging and adult development, (emotional, psychological, spiritual and physical) across the life course and the societal implications of the impact of an aging population. Since the field of gerontology is multidisciplinary, it is a catch-all for many professionals like myself who are known as professional gerontologists. Many of us have other fields of expertise that enhance what we bring to the field and the 40-plus market.

Gerontology is the antithesis of the disease model.

There are no limits to the creative integration of a variety of disciplines that are possible now in serving the enormous and fast-moving older adult market.

Only recently, the field of possibilities began expanding as never before. The "change-everything-in-our path" Boomer demographic is creating an insatiable market need for innovation in the development and delivery of new services and products as it heads into older and Elder adulthood. Leading-Edge Boomers are paving the way for all who follow by demanding to remain productive, independent, and active wherever they live and work. This is heaven-sent to social entrepreneurs seeking new avenues to make a difference and add to the Triple Bottom Line of People, Planet, and Profit.

Historically, academic programs in gerontology modeled the narrow worldview of geriatrics with the disease and illness model deeply embedded in the curriculum.

In 1994, when I received my post-graduate certification in Adult Development and Aging at Hunter College's Brookdale Center of Aging under the auspices of Rose Dobrof and my mentor Professor Harry R. Moody (aka Rick), our curriculum and course resources were almost all based on the geriatric disease model of aging. I almost quit the program several times because I was so done with the old paradigm. At that time, there were neither master's degrees nor Ph.D.s in gerontology being offered in the tri-state metro area, so this was my only choice. Clearly the cosmos was watching out for me as Moody offered me the opportunity to teach the first *Conscious Aging 101* course at a university level—a precursor of the new Positive Aging genre now growing by leaps and bounds here in the United States and around the world.

Back then, author-consultants with expertise in the 40-plus market were hard to find, many relatively unknown working on the edge of the mainstream. Emerging as new thought leaders but still in the shadows of mainstream were my mentors, teachers, and colleagues. Among them were breakthrough marketer, author, and creator of *Ageless Marketing*, David Wolfe (who turned how we market to older adults inside-out) and Ken Dychtwald, author of *Age Wave* and founder of his corporate consultancy of the same name, who was, to my knowledge, the first to get Fortune 500 companies to consider the elderly as a market for consumer products and services.

I know about what was happening back then because I was one of the few visionaries sounding the clarion call to serve the emerging and burgeoning 40-plus market. Unlike the others, I also had bottom-line responsibility for producing breakthrough results and increased market share in a variety of ventures serving the emerging 40-plus market in financial services. My leadership role in securing my company's market position as the one-stop provider for retirement products and planning services propelled me into an unexpected role as the resident futurist studying the Graying of America and the world. I am forever grateful for this fortuitous opportunity to hone my skills and knowledge base as a futurist and gerontologist. Any extra time I had, I spent studying the future of women and aging, along with entrepreneurship in America for the twenty-first century.

Conscious Aging Bursts onto the Scene

Paralleling the new breed of Ageless marketing geniuses and joining these new thought leaders in the aging field were the groundbreakers in the human potential and consciousness movement. In the early 1990s, these visionaries and groundbreakers started a new movement with a vision they eloquently and improvisationally enunciated as Conscious Aging.

In 1992, the Omega Institute in Rhinebeck hosted a two-day conference in Manhattan entitled "Conscious Aging." I was one of the 1,500 attendees who found ourselves in seventh heaven finding new community while rubbing shoulders with idols like Maggie Kuhn (who in 1970 founded the Gray Panthers), Robert Atchley (a pioneer in the Conscious Aging field and author of *Social Forces and Aging,* now in its 10th edition), sharing the birthing of a new paradigm with Jungian author, teacher, and my beloved mentor, Marion Woodman, joined by spiritual leaders and authors, Ram Dass and Rabbi Zalman Schachter-Shalomi…and, of course, my deeply valued Harry (Rick) Moody still sounding the call and supporting others to keep the Positive Aging flame lit. There are other trailblazers I've met along the way, like pioneering radio show host and author of many books on caregiving, Connie Goldman, and professor-author Wendy Lustbader. I'm sure I've forgotten a few, but check these folks out so you can get a handle on what's really going on in the field of aging.

We all left the Omega conference on a high. We were carrying the message Atchley, chair of the Department of Gerontology at Naropa University in Boulder, Colorado, captured so well when he described the essence of Conscious Aging as "our intention to be awake (conscious) as we age." As a whole, those of us in attendance committed ourselves to the view that later life (I see midlife as the portal) is, at core, about our inner spiritual growth and hopefully our enlightened contribution to humanity no matter our age, cycle, or stage.

In 1994, there were a couple more of these inspiring events, but as outspoken Atchley decries, convening conferences is a bottom-line business, so profits won out over mission, leaving the Conscious Aging community to be nomadic, splintered for a long time.

Positive Aging Eclipses Conscious Aging

Approximately a decade ago, a new conference convened, reconfiguring our community around the concept of Positive Aging. The first of its kind, the Positive Aging Conference was hosted at Eckerd College, St. Petersburg, Florida, in 2007. The second conference migrated to the University of Minnesota's Center for Spirituality and Healing, then back to Eckerd for the third conference. In 2010, the conference moved west to Los Angeles, California, under the esteemed hosting of the Fielding Graduate University's Institute for Social Innovation, where the next three sterling conferences were held. Upcoming hosts are the Society of Certified Senior Advisors and Fielding University. Fortunately, this conference will continue to reach more of us as it moves to different hosts, bringing us together to sound the clarion call for Positive Aging.

What's Next for Positive Aging?

Perhaps Atchley is spot-on when he concludes that "if we seek a wider audience, we experience commercial pressures from promoters and publishers to make our efforts fit within their models." I'm all for monetizing our visions, but as of yet we have not found a successful formula for convening this cutting-edge community of professionals together. I'm holding on to the vision that our niche professional community will rally and come together again. The Positive Aging story is incomplete as we again splinter into myriad smaller gatherings, some online and some off.

No matter what happens around how or when we convene again, I'm thrilled to be part of a growing generation of new thought leaders in the field of aging who are ushering in a new Positive Aging paradigm. This new paradigm is breaking up what was, and in it's place it is birthing an organic, unlimited holistic view of the life course and of our unlimited, as yet untapped, human potential available to us as we age.

New scenarios are developing around the concept of Positive Aging. This new perspective on aging is driving a growing interest in measuring, tracking and evaluating the behavior and real and perceived needs the the forty-plus demographic. At the same time, 40-plussers are also directly impacting innovation for all ages in a variety of fronts, i.e., from products and services needed, to new delivery solutions, workforce development, encore careers, and new start-ups.

Why You Need to Know about Educational Gerontology

A longtime respected name in the field attended my "Visionaries Have Wrinkles" talk at the 2014 Positive Aging Conference. Afterward, she came up to introduce herself. While chatting and exchanging tales about the field and how we arrived on this career path, she described herself as an "educational gerontologist." I had not heard that term before in my advanced training programs, so I asked her what the term means as a career. I got a hearty laugh as she told me, "Karen, you too are an educational gerontologist." I just didn't know there's a name for what I have been doing my entire adult career!

When I got back to my hotel room, I Googled "educational geron-tology." What I found is that David A. Peterson in 1976 introduced the definition of educational gerontology, which I'll paraphrase as the study and practice of instructional activities for and about the aged and aging. For me, it was enlightening to find an umbrella for what I do within the

> The Positive Aging story is incomplete.

aging field, which as Ronald H. Sherron and D. Barry Lumsden (in their 1990 third edition textbook, *Introduction to Educational Gerontology*), state "to prevent premature decline, to facilitate meaningful roles, and to encourage psychological growth." In translation, they describe what I do, and what educational gerontology is about, "designed as a positive approach to helping people better understand and assist themselves." I was thrilled to read that Howard McClusky, 1971, shaped the definition that resonates with me as a "positive domain" in which the potential of the individual is accepted and developed in order to ensure continuing growth throughout the life span. For years I've struggled with how to define what my work in the field of aging is. I need look no longer!

AGE RUSH: CRISIS AND OPPORTUNITY

Now for the challenges facing the aging field.

Educational Gerontology

Much like the underfunded Positive Aging and Conscious Aging conferences of the past, my research has uncovered that many of the academic gerontology programs at universities and colleges around the United States are also experiencing dwindling enrollment and difficulties in contributing to their institutions' balance sheets. The downswing in registration and enrollment are putting these programs on notice, and some may end up on the chopping block as no longer viable.

How the Great Recession Affected Higher Education

Let's start with a look at how the Great Recession impacted higher education in general. Harvard's Jeffrey Brown and Caroline Hoxby, eds., in their 2013 revised paper, "How the Great Recession Affected Higher Education," conclude that the Great Recession had far-reaching effects on both the supply and demand sides of higher education. Based on the analysis of the Integrated Postsecondary Education Data System (IPEDS), an annual survey of colleges (2014), it appears that college enrollment and attendance levels increased during the Great Recession, "especially in the states most affected by the recession. Part-time enrollment increased while full-time enrollment declined, and the gains in attendance were concentrated among students of color. In addition, the authors share that "The tuition revenue collected per student also grew, while grants did not offset the increase in cost and student loans increased." The authors referenced the study by Dellas and Sakellaris (2003) in which they concluded, "college enrollment decisions are countercyclical with the business cycle."

Conundrum: Something Is Not Quite Right

So if enrollment tends to rise in poor economic times, why is it that enrollment and attendance in gerontology programs is on the decline…or, as has been suggested to me, why is it that some programs have prospered while others are declining?

According to a review article on the survival of small college gerontology programs, Drs. Ronald Lucchino and K. Della Ferguson, the director and assistant director, respectively, for what was then the Institute of Gerontology of Syracuse University, conclude that small colleges are "currently undergoing a squeeze between a decline in students and a reduction in federal support." The authors claim these downward changes translate directly into "reduced resources to support academic programs and community initiatives."

Could it be my bedpan analogy again? Methinks gerontology careers and, by default, educational gerontology, have a branding image problem. Clearly there's a language barrier. Even the name of the field causes folks' eyes to glaze over, to defer to the youth market. More difficult to dismantle is our shared deeply ingrained image of what aging is and how we envision it. For most, it's of no interest, or just not relevant.

There's more. It comes back to profit over mission. Are we as a nation and global economies willing to risk the elimination or curtailment of gerontology programs at all levels, from certifications to doctorates? Doing so would mean that serving the growing population of people over 40 would no longer be a vital part of our higher education programming.

That's nuts in my book! The current and continuing record growth of employment opportunities for graduates with gerontological training brought on by the "graying of America," and the "graying of the globe" is where it's at for employment growth. The increasing demand for new and upgraded services, as well as product and delivery systems built around a techno-savvy older consumer, is growing rapidly, benefitting all of us now and when we are 40-plus.

Labor force projections indicate that large numbers of additional professional personnel will be needed to serve this tidal wave of older people, especially women service providers and entrepreneurs. I'm not referring to only health care or bedpan changing, but myriad career and entrepreneurial opportunities in related fields and industries where gerontological knowledge is greatly valued and sought after. Examples of opportunities include cutting-edge age-friendly technology and devices, home design and architecture, smart electronics, adult education, and many emerging services catering to the unique needs of 40-plussers as well as addressing the universal needs of all consumers.

Here are some things you may not yet know about. The current number of health care providers and social workers trained in gerontology is totally inadequate, and there's not a doubt in my mind that the demand is going to increase more quickly than we can train and hire new professionals. From my survey of curricula, faculty expertise, and program and university resources available across the United States, it's clear to me that most programs do not have sufficient up-to-date content nor educational resources required to keep demanding Boomers and fast-learning Millennials matriculating, much less entering the aging field. What a missed opportunity all around!

The first Gen Xers turned 50 in 2015.

By no means is the Boomer bubble going to become a blip in time. Fifty-plusser Boomtime is here to stay—with the forty-plusser boontime along side. Wake-up call: The first Gen Xers turned 50 in 2015.

Please don't be myopic or hesitate because you don't want to make waves. There's a humongous "happening" now that will continue to expand opportunities for older and younger students to acquire or upgrade their gerontological knowledge and skills so they, and we, have an enviable advantage as a wage earner, top honcho at the helm, savvy investor, innovative business owner and/or consumer. This is a long-lasting next Gold Rush. Now is the time to educate and up-skill, so you are in demand. No matter what your ideal work or give back role is, this "gray is the new green" field of possibilities will impact you both directly and indirectly. Why not make it yours? (You can read more about this in chapter eight, "The Longevity Economy.")

Our higher educational institutions must cater to careers in aging, as well as offer adult learning and continuing lifelong education. Demand is so high that more and more gerontology certificate programs are showing up at the undergraduate level. Then there is the range of gerontology degrees available at various colleges and universities (e.g., associate, bachelor's, master's, and more recently Ph.D. degrees). Add to this list an assortment of professional certifications like Certified Senior Advisor, Certified Age-Friendly or Aging-in-Place Specialist, Business and Aging Specialist, Certified Financial Planner, and on and on. These certifications are becoming standard fare faster and faster to fill the exploding need. At the same time, professional certifications and credentialing are becoming more mainstream, gaining in popularity with students of all ages and acceptance by industry and consumers. These new professional certifications are popping up all over, giving educational institutions new competition.

Bottom Line

There is an unprecedented opportunity rising to the top of every industry's consumer landscape. To be successful in the anti-aging, luxury-brand women's market today, a company must address the specific needs, buying patterns, and attitudes of Boomer women who account for 95 percent of the purchase decisions for their households.

Modern-Day Story Conflicts and You

For those going through life stage shifts, particularly at midlife and beyond, these greater societal shifts and story conflicts run parallel to the transitions and upheaval in our personal and professional lives. The chaos and uncertainty is coming from all sides, and it's tempting to hang on for dear life to anything stable and certain we can find, even if doing so means remaining in an unfulfilling career or toxic work environment, such as what former BBC presenter, Miriam O'Reilly (53) experienced. O'Reilly was one of four female presenters, all in their forties or fifties, who were dropped from the 23-year-old show. Not only did she leave…she filed an age-discrimination and victimization suit and won.

> **These are the times when we have more opportunities, not fewer, to transform our work, our world, and ourselves.**

These are the times when we have more opportunities, not fewer, to transform our work, our world, and ourselves.

A fast-moving wave of a diverse cross-section of us is leaving behind the hallowed halls of large corporations, institutions, and organizations. No matter how you leave one chapter to the next, the *no-exit* terror of those *no-return* revolving doors as you make your way out are anxiety-producing, even frightening, especially in chaotic times. We are in the midst of a page-turner. We are witnessing, and are morphing into, lean and mean new start-ups. Clearly our feminine entrepreneurial spirit is rising.

The new breed of entrepreneurs is primarily women, remarkably powerful, savvy, experienced Boomer women—most of us social entrepreneurs going for the Triple Bottom Line: People, Planet, and Profit. We are well connected and ready to rock. We can maximize our capabilities, get greater reach and scope, to serve exiting and emerging markets. To me, the most exciting of these are women-to-women networks of women serving one another. Perfect for Baby Boomers and the younger generations moving forward.

BBC News reports that among United States encore entrepreneurs, women are actually more prevalent than men. Babson College, a Boston-area business school with a highly regarded entrepreneurial program, reported in 2010 that 10 percent of U.S. women aged between 55 and 64 had taken steps to start their own businesses, compared with 7.5 percent of men. By 2030, it is expected that at least 18 percent of the U.S. population will be 65 or older. That's at a rate of ten thousand people turning 65 every day in the United States alone.

Now is the time of small business and solopreneurship. For others, it's perhaps time for reinvigorating and evolving existing businesses or taking careers full steam ahead. The old story is being rewritten by significant advancements and shifts in technology, financing, and corporate culture, which are rippling out to make more and more of us reinvent our businesses and ourselves.

The human brain naturally seeks patterns and order, especially in chaos. The bigger the problems we need to solve, the bigger the innovations we create. When the world around us is orderly and certain, we tend to think inside that same box that is serving us so well. But when the world around us is falling apart and that box has been torn to shreds, we have no choice but to think outside it, creating new connections by drawing together seemingly disparate ideas from the chaotic whirlwind that surrounds us. This is the idea behind Bucky Fuller's concept of "emergence through emergency," that most times it takes an emergency, such as on the scale of climate change, for our best selves to emerge collectively and act in innovative ways. In the 1960s the emergencies included the assassinations of JFK and MLK, the Vietnam War protests, civil rights marches, and the Second Wave Feminist movement. Now the emergencies are squeezing out the middle class, causing potential planetary demise, allowing big business to gain a stranglehold on politics, triggering barbaric international terrorism, exposing stateside police brutality, and more.

There is a reason mythology tends to personify destruction and creation in one being, such as in the Hindu goddess Kali and the Buddhist goddess Kuan Yin, and the Egyptian goddess Isis. The two ideas go hand in hand. Where there is destruction, there is a powerful drive to create something new. Sometimes, creation requires destruction—destroying the habits and limited ways of thinking that stand in the way of forging new paths, for example. Now, we refer to this phenomenon as "Creative Destruction." More often, innovation relies on selective destruction, getting rid of what no longer serves us without losing what does. Just as our Mother Earth depends more and more on recycling and creating something new by reworking the old, transformation that leads to sustainable success and innovation often depends on new combinations.

Now, more than ever, you have the opportunity to go beyond temporary solutions and quick fixes toward sustainable game-changing ideas that could alter your life, your work, and the world in ways only you can imagine. The future belongs to those who are starting those transformations now, who are reshaping or shaping the world and creating their own place in it. For example, take the new smartphones with bigger screens and adjustable fonts. They are perfect for enabling the enormous audience of over-40s

> The human brain naturally seeks patterns and order, especially in chaos.

> Where there is destruction, there is a powerful drive to create something new.

who are beginning to feel the vision pinch to stay connected. Or consider Eyebobs, the high-fashion mid-priced reading magnifiers that are pretty and utilitarian. Just perfect for the 40-plus women's market. I recently came across another example when I met with a Millennial female founder of an online start-up built on an amalgamation of several business models and platforms. For her, it all started as she headed for an important high-fashion business event overseas. The suddenly cold and wet weather of her destination country put her in a quandary as her travel wardrobe was unsuitable for the inclement weather. She was forced to buy an expensive high-fashion coat, which she'd rarely use again. Frustrated, she was determined to come up with a solution for women on the go to avoid having to spend a fortune on such emergency, infrequently worn, or one-time outfits. Now, this fashion diva is growing her win-win exchange platform whereby a combination of high fashion, recycling, and consignment short-term rentals is available online. The takeaway from this story is that opportunity is all around us, if we just look with non-judgmental beginner's eyes.

A Future That Works

The future belongs to those who are starting those transformations now.

If you can't afford to make a huge leap now—starting or reinvigorating your own business, changing or reinventing your career, transforming your organization—you can, and should, start doing the legwork now so that, when the opportunity presents itself, you'll be on firm footing to make that leap with confidence, without hesitation.

Staying on top of trends can help you lead change with your ideas, instead of being swept along by it uncontrollably. As I describe in chapter one, we can all step into the role of modern-day oracles, connecting the realities of the present story with probable futures. We can then see which of those preferred futures we aspire to and begin to make steps to create our own self-fulfilling prophecies.

The trends you analyze will depend somewhat on your personal and professional interests, experiences, goals, and vision. For most of us, however, having an idea of where the world of work is likely to go is crucial to creating a future that integrates what matters most to us and how we want to spend our time with what the world wants and needs. We need to know what story we are currently in and what stories are possible if we are going to create our ideal aspirational story. In other words, knowing something about the likely future of work will help us to create a future that works—for all of us.

Each and every one of us can tease out a through line within our stories that intersects with an emerging trend or trends, as I have over and over again as a serial entrepreneur. The same is true to the max with Katy Fike (mentioned in chapter three, "Positive Aging," and in chapter six, "Women Shaping the New Story of Our Age.") In her own words, Fike, formerly an investment banker with Lehman Brothers, shares what propelled her into the field of aging, caring, and technology as a youngster: "I was just seven years old when my ninety-year-old grandmother moved in with my family after breaking her hip. I witnessed firsthand many of the issues still faced by caregivers and elderly individuals across the country." As a result, Fike is now the founder and CEO of INNOVATE50 Consulting LLC and co-founder of Aging2.0, a global innovation network.

Consider these trends:

- The United States Department of Labor estimates that the number of information-technology jobs is expected to grow at more than twice the overall job-growth rate. These jobs include knowledge work, an area that has been growing explosively for years now, such as jobs related to software, problem solving and strategy, communications and networks, and various careers in math and science.

- Health care, education—anything related to the enormous gray market—are expected to continue being reliable areas of job growth, especially as the large generation of Baby Boomers continues to age. By 2022, the estimated job growth in personal care and home health workers is expected to be up to 50 percent of the current market. Health care and age-friendly home modification will grow exponentially.

- The business world is finally realizing that it can save money by offering leadership, team, and individual executive coaching, and by promoting work-life balance, flexible work arrangements, and collaborative business models. For example, telecommuting can save businesses real estate and payroll costs. Reduced hours, unpaid sabbaticals, lateral employee movements (such as from one department to another) without any of this sidelining employee career growth are more cost-effective than laying off employees and having to start from scratch as the economy improves.

- Baby Boomers and succeeding generations will be working past traditional retirement age (at least nine years, according to T. Rowe Price), some for financial reasons and others because they simply have no desire to retire. The flexible arrangements mentioned above will come into play, such as more job sharing, even at senior levels, as well as more Boomers filling the need for knowledge workers as strategists, consultants, and coaches—not to mention as entrepreneurs.

- Companies will be hiring more and more women in all positions, including senior management. Women executives and board members tend to lead to higher returns, and the cost-saving measures described above have their roots in the collaborative management style and emphasis on work-life balance introduced in many businesses by female leadership. The coming gap between college graduates and the need for college-educated workers will be filled primarily by women, who earn more college and advanced degrees than men do.

- Women already control 85 percent of consumer spending in the United States. They are the present and future market for businesses worldwide. Boomer women in particular have spending clout. Businesses who ignore this market of Ageless Women and continue to portray us in ways that are not relevant to our preferred futures do so at significant risk of losing a huge market share.

- Boomers and Millennials in general are choosing to spend their money based on their values, such as purchasing from green companies.

- The aging field is growing at a rapid pace as more and more people require aging-related services, mainly women, simply because they tend to outlive men. Now more than ever, women can make a dent in this growing market, no matter which field or career path leads them to serving one another and themselves. I foresee and relish a model of "women-to-women" businesses emerging to serve the needs and desires of the enormous 40-plus market, especially women serving other women and being paid well to do so.

Whatever your vision for the future, these trends can help you determine the shape of it. First, consider the story you are currently telling yourself about your work, your ideal customers or clients, your future. How do these trends change that story?

As an entrepreneur, consider what these facts and probable events tell you about what you have to offer, what your audience needs and wants, your options for hiring and outsourcing, and how you can create a business model that combines purpose and profit for sustainable success that also makes a difference in the world.

As a leader in your organization, you have the opportunity to create win-win situations for the company and the people you lead by being among the first to make changes that lead to more profit, happier and more productive employees, greater loyalty among your customers, and improved products and services for the market of today and of the future, all while increasing your bottom line.

As a professional looking to change careers or to transform how you work—because you are approaching retirement age or wanting to devote more time and energy to what really matters—these trends can show you many scenarios and their relative risks and benefits, as well as spark your own reimagining of your personal and professional life. When you have the alternative stories laid out and grounded in reality, you can better see which narrative you wish to create with your tomorrows. In other words, you can change your story when you are happy with the probable ending.

Don't be afraid to think outside the statistical box, either. Sure, you could look at the aging Boomer population and think about the need for more senior living communities and nursing homes, or you could look at what this community needs and wants and strike out in a novel direction that offers an alternative to these kinds of places or that recognizes how this generation is likely to turn stereotypes about aging on their head. For example, there is an emerging interest in creating communal intergenerational living situations based on shared values rather than grouping Elders together regardless of whether they have anything in common besides their age (see chapter eleven, "Ageless Homes and Communities").

Of course, looking at trends is only one small part of an overall strategy for reinventing your future. But this is an action you can start taking today, even if you feel trapped in your current situation. You may not feel in control of your present, yet your future is entirely in your hands. The new green is your opportunity to monetize the future by applying an Aspirational Ageless Approach to "PrimeTime Women." ❯

CHAPTER 7 ~ *The Ageless Way Reflections*

The questions and exercises below are to help you find your distinct path on The Ageless Way. Turn to page 28 for more about The Ageless Way Reflections.

1. Take each of the trends mentioned in this chapter (also read more in chapter eight, "The Longevity Economy") and write down how each affects you now. How might each trend affect you in the future? What can you do to leverage the trends in your professional life, existing business, by volunteering, or in a new start-up?

2. Here are a few trigger questions to apply to each trend to get you started thinking way outside the box:

   a. How might this trend influence your current customers?

   b. How might this trend influence your core business?

   c. How does this trend impact your current and future workforce and workplace?

   d. How might this trend attract new customers?

   e. What are your two closest competitors doing about this trend?

   f. Are there other trends co-evolving with this one?

   g. How fast is this trend developing and what might accelerate it or slow it down?

   h. How is your business reaching and serving the 40-plus market?

   i. If you are planning to leave your job or sell your business, have you formulated an exit strategy?

   j. What is your business doing to change with the needs of 40-plus existing and potential customers? What about your current colleagues and employees?

   k. How are you getting your organization or your one-woman show ready for the prime-time Boomer women challenge and turning it into a humongous opportunity? What can you start now to leverage the 40-plus trend?

l. What and who needs to change so you and your business or organization can leverage this prime-time Boomer women trend?

m. What is your vision and intended outcome relative to each trend?

3. What are the three top challenges you face or your most pressing questions you have about serving the 40-plus market and, more specifically, in serving "PrimeTime Women?" Please contact me if you would like to discuss this further. Send your email to Karen@ Karen Sands.com, with "TAW Challenges" in the subject line.

Chapter 8

THE LONGEVITY ECONOMY

I won't step aside.
We are not going to play dead 'cause we are a "certain age."

~ Cher, 2014

What Is The Longevity Economy?

Before we move on, I want to respond to a query I'm often asked: "Why do you prefer to focus on the forty-plus segment versus solely focusing on fifty-plus, especially Baby Boomers?" My response is much the same as David Wolfe's on this topic, as he describes the future of the Ageless Market: "Markets over forty will grow at a far faster clip than markets under forty."

This changes everything. Marketing and sales become all about serving the Ageless Market, principally Ageless Women.

As you are well aware now, the 50-plus demographic is an unstoppable powerful force for change, which is impacting the United States economy, as well as most other economies, and will for generations to come.

The group of "oldies but goodies" now 50-plus are expected to represent 54 percent of the over-25 population by 2032. With thirty more years now added to expected lifespans, this group is morphing everything in its path as it moves from an elongated productive midlife into a later and later onset of old old age. A briefing paper prepared for AARP by Oxford Economics states that this force of older people in the United States alone is composed of 106 million people responsible for at least $7.1 trillion in annual economic activity—a figure that is expected to reach well over $13.5 trillion in real terms by 2032.

It is important to note that the Longevity Economy isn't just defined by demographics. This term also applies to the total of all economic activity related to serving the needs of the post-40s in the United States, as well as the products and services this same demographic purchases directly and the continued economics their spending engenders.

Echoing my own take on the Longevity Economy, the briefing report concludes that this is not a passing phenomenon. Long after we 40-plussers are past tense, longer and longer life spans will result in continuously occurring large post-40 populations.

I want to share another striking and telling statistic from the briefing paper that nails the import and impact of this new economic trend "The over-50 population controls almost 80% of U.S. aggregate net worth; the average wealth of households headed by people over 50 is almost three times the size of those headed by people aged 25 to 50."

The Effect of Longevity on Our Future Economy

We know that living longer, healthier lives, coupled with the sheer numbers of the aging Boomer population, presents us all with a financial challenge. How do we make our money last as long as we do?

Sound financial planning is an obvious answer. It's also an ideal-world answer. In the real world, the aftereffects of the Great Recession, the costs of caring for parents and children, and the denial of the eventual effects of aging on our health are just a few factors that can make financial planning insufficient to secure the future.

For many, the solution is to work past traditional retirement age, some by necessity but many others out of a desire to keep working. Individuals and companies are catching on to the idea of flexible working options, particularly those that allow telecommuting, job sharing, and shorter workweeks. These are benefits not just for Boomers but for the younger working generations as well.

Most age-friendly ideas for the workplace (and indeed for our homes and communities) are beneficial to all ages and stages. The sooner organizations and governments recognize this growing customer demand (and the more we emphasize it), the more prosperous and secure we will all be, in the workplace and as a nation.

In fact, longevity has been shown to have a positive effect on the economy. This is indeed the new story of our times. A 2005 study, "The Value of Health and Longevity," by Robert Topel and Kevin Murphy, of the University of Chicago Booth School of Business, demonstrates massive economic benefit to living longer and healthier than in the past:

> *Over the 20th century, cumulative gains in life expectancy were worth over $1.2 million per person for both men and women. Between 1970 and 2000 increased longevity added about $3.2 trillion per year to national wealth, an uncounted value equal to about half of average annual GDP over the period. Reduced mortality from heart disease alone has increased the value of life by about $1.5 trillion per year since 1970. The potential gains from future innovations in health care are also extremely large. Even a modest 1 percent reduction in cancer mortality would be worth nearly $500 billion.*

Therein lies the paradox: Longevity is undeniably good for the economy as a whole, while presenting economic challenges for the individual. How do we bring the economic benefits to the individual?

This question is crucial not only for Baby Boomers but also for future generations, especially the massive (80 million-plus) Millennial generation. We need more than short-term fixes. We need lasting changes in the workplace as well as changes in how we—at the individual, organizational, and governmental level—ensure a financial safety net that is adequate for the longer lives many of us will have. The Longevity Economy is the new story for our future, but it's up to us to shape that story for our families, the world, and ourselves.

Retiring Retirement

One of the first steps we need to take is to re-evaluate retirement, especially as a default assumption at an arbitrary age. This seemingly picked-out-of-a-hat age demarcation hit home for me particularly when I was reading an article about retirement age, and how it has changed and is changing. All I could think was, "What difference does it make?"

Why do we even have a "retirement age"?

Why do we even have a "retirement age"? Maybe in the past, a particular age could be associated with a time when people were physically and mentally ill-equipped to continue working, so this age provided them with some guarantee of health care and continued income (although I would argue that this arbitrary age was never accurate and perhaps contributed to a dangerous myth that kept people from fulfilling their true potential beyond midlife).

Do you wonder why we have a mandatory retirement age? Right out of the United States rule book of federal legislation, "mandatory retirement," also known as "enforced retirement," is the set age at which people who hold certain jobs or offices are required by industry custom or by law to leave their employment, or retire. Typically, mandatory retirement is justified by the argument that certain occupations are either too dangerous (military personnel) or require high levels of physical and mental skill (air-traffic controllers, airline pilots). Most mandatory retirement decisions rely on the notion that a worker's productivity declines significantly after age 65, or now age 70, and the mandatory retirement is the employer's way to avoid reduced productivity. Of course nowadays, an employer can no longer force retirement or otherwise discriminate on the basis of age against an individual because he or she is 70 or older.

But today, we know that people are living longer, healthier, more active lives across the board. You've heard that 60 is the new 40 (and 70 the new 50, 80 the new 60, etc.). This isn't just a marketing slogan. We all look around at our friends, our families, ourselves, and we know this is superficially true. Yet I would argue that the deeper truth is that 60 is the new 60. Who we are inside has earned every year of our existence. Why downplay even a single year that has shaped who we are?

No matter which way you look at it, it doesn't make any sense to be quibbling about a few years here and there in a person's sixties. What kind of sense does it make to be thinking about a retirement age for someone who is functionally in her forties yet with the experience and wisdom of her full sixty years? Or conversely?

And when you really start thinking about what "retirement age" means, what kind of sense does it make, period?

The only valuable purpose I can see for having this demarcation at all is to be sure everyone in our society is taken care of when they are not as equipped to care for themselves. Isn't this an ideal for people of any age? If health or disability interferes with a person's ability to provide for him or herself, does it really matter whether the person is 65 or 25?

So that leaves Social Security, which we've all been paying into. Yes, it does make sense for this fund to be available as we age because it is true that at some point we will be less able to work as much as before (even if we keep working). It is true that the longer we live, the more likely part of our income will go increasingly toward health-related expenses. But what on earth does this reality have to do with retirement?

I'm not talking about denying age. Just the opposite. I'm talking about looking at the realities of aging for what they really are, and this includes what they are not. The old stories about aging are simply not true for us. Aging does not equal retiring. It does not mean we step back and sit on our rocking chairs while the younger folks take over. We may want or need to work less, or to have more flexible working arrangements, but think about that: Don't we all need that at every age?

A young parent who needs to be able to work from home or work more flexible hours and a 70-year-old who needs the same arrangement are functionally equivalent. A 40-year-old who wants to "retire early," meaning she wants to stop working for someone else and pursue her own interests, be they travel or entrepreneurship or both, is no different from an 80-year-old who wants the same thing.

"Retirement age" and similar phrases, in other words, lump together a bunch of characteristics and needs and wants that really don't have much to do with age at all. People of any age may wish to "retire"—even for just a phase of life, before returning or starting a new career. People of any age may need flexibility and help because of a health- or disability-related crisis or ongoing situation. People of any age may wish to never retire in any sense of the word, not even at 90 or 100. They want to keep working and creating and leading. They simply need to make adaptations in these

> The old stories about aging are simply not true for us. Aging does not equal retiring.

pursuits that take into account the realities of their lives—just as we all need to do, at every age.

- What if organizations, academia, families, and local and national government start looking at the needs and wants of society on an individual basis rather than lumping us by age?

- What if flexible work arrangements become the norm—for whoever wants or needs them?

- What if lifelong learning is implemented and sponsored in every nook and cranny of society—for all ages?

- What if we seek ways for those with health and disability issues (their own, their parents', their children's, their spouse's) to adapt their lives without worry, without having to give up entirely on the idea of doing what they want to do in life and giving back to society through their work, their creations, their leadership?

I believe strongly that these are all key elements to the new story of our times. This Aspirational Ageless Future may sound utopian, but it is actually a pragmatic approach to economic growth, national well-being, investment in the future, and innovation that could save us all and the planet (not to mention individual happiness). The approach is pragmatic in that it is based on doing away with stereotypes about aging, myths that keep huge numbers of people from contributing to society in unimaginable ways simply because they've hit an arbitrary number. The approach is pragmatic because it means implementing policies based on reality.

The reality is, there is no such thing as a retirement age.

The reality is, there is no such thing as a retirement age. I doubt there ever was. We've reached the end of that old story. It's time for a new story, one created by each of us that eliminates the need for a mandatory retirement age. To do so will in turn expand a new Ageless story for all of us.

Another wrinkle for women to consider when it comes to retiring is that if you are expecting to retire to have more time to spend with your friends, think again. Today.com caught my attention with an article entitled "Women Working Longer Will Change the Face of an Aging Workforce." Apparently, if we are looking forward to retiring to have more time with friends, we are in for a shock. The article referred to a study by BLS Data, in which BLS found that the share of older women remaining in the workforce has increased sharply over the past twenty years (interestingly much more quickly than for men). BLS is projecting that women will account for 82 percent of the over-55 workforce by 2022.

The Multigenerational Workplace

All over the media we hear constant discussion about the possible growing rift between the generations as younger people are (or simply feel they are) being edged out of the workforce or promotions by the over-55 crowd. Many people in all generations take for granted as fact that every person who chooses not to retire is essentially taking a job from a younger person. I discussed this myth a bit in chapter two, "Agelessness Across Generations" but knowing it's a myth doesn't necessarily heal the anxieties overnight, especially to those who are still unemployed or underemployed. We need a new story to replace the old.

We know that, for the most part, experienced workers are filling positions that younger workers are not qualified for, simply because the younger workers haven't had the time to build the necessary skills, experience, and specialized knowledge. On the other hand, there certainly is a growing trend in hiring people over 60 for retail and similar jobs because of the perception that they will be more responsible than a younger employee. Even if they require a higher wage, the savings in training costs alone, a problem plaguing high-turnover service jobs, can be worth it. Therefore, even though the idea of older people taking jobs from younger people is as a whole not true, there are exceptions that are very real and consequential to some. We have to address the full picture if we are going to close the generational rift, however much of it is a media-manufactured story.

Focusing on ways to get more people to retire, under the belief that this will free up jobs for subsequent generations, is a mistake. Even if it were realistic, which it's not (as I note above—eschewing retirement is a trend that will only continue to grow), increasing the numbers of people receiving retirement benefits would offset the possible gains in youth employment.

Here's a show-stopper U.S. Department of Labor statistic that shocks me and might do the same for you: As recently as 2015, most members of the American workforce will be in their twenties. Sarah Sladek, CEO of XYZ University, a Minnesota-based consulting company, says it like it is: "Many companies—even industries—are in danger of 'aging out' because they haven't been able to appeal to younger generations."

So what can we do about this situation, particularly about the possibility of increasing conflict and distance among generations over perceived and real job competition? Instead of futile attempts to restore a status quo that no longer works, we can take this relatively new energy, both the negative and the positive, and re-story our present and our preferred future. Together, all generations can eliminate the generational divide, increase productivity and, thereby, we can create a new story for a future that works for all of us.

Primarily, we need to communicate with one another about it. This step seems obvious, but how often do the generations really talk about this situation? It tends to get talked about through politicians and the media rather than in collaborative, hands-on, deliberately multigenerational conversations. The World Café model (www.theworldcafe.com) is a particularly effective way of holding productive and meaningful conversations among people with seemingly disparate perspectives in any setting—businesses, homes, schools, and communities.

However we hold these conversations, they are crucial not only to get our fears and perceptions out in the open, but also to clear up the misconceptions that can lead us all to make decisions based on incorrect information or assumptions.

Second, we need to explore alternative scenarios and solutions together based on the probable and the preferred future, not the past. Now is the time to create a new story together, an aspirational future story for all of us. Yes, Social Security was an effective solution to many problems that stemmed from the Great Depression (the devastating global economic crisis that began approximately with the stock market crash in October 1929 and continued through most of the 1930s), and it continues to be a necessary element in our economy, but pursuing ways to once again push millions of post-65 people out of the workforce is not going to work. Being 65 today is not even close to what it was in that era.

Third, we should look at generational partnerships, such as job sharing/ mentorship arrangements, that enable two people to be employed instead of one, enable training costs and salary to combine, stretching a company's dollar and quickening the pace at which younger employees can gain the skills, knowledge, and some of the experience they need to be more valuable to that company and the marketplace. These arrangements could work with a shifting percentage of time, starting with the mentor working three-quarters of the job, then gradually decreasing to one-half, then one-quarter, with an ultimate shift into mentoring another employee or into a consultant arrangement.

Which brings me to my fourth and final point. We need to encourage people over 60 (and in fact over 40 and 50) to remain employed by starting their own businesses. These could be less complex solopreneur home offices or larger operations that would not only remove the competition for the same job between two generations but would also generate employment.

Encore entrepreneurs, those of us over 50, are on the rise. In fact, AARP notes that folks ages 55 to 64 between 1996 through 2012 have a higher rate of new business start-ups than those ages 20 to 34.

Ken and Maddy Dychtwald of *Age Wave* fame, both authors, consultants and top-notch speakers, have long been preaching the gospel to corporate moguls and their boards about meeting the needs of our aging populace. Marc Freedman, author and founding inspiration for Encore.org, asks his audiences (as I do), "What are people in their fifties, sixties, and seventies going to do with the next thirty years of their lives?" This same question is where I started from, too, but what's at stake now is much larger…it's hard to grasp the enormity of these questions until we acknowledge that not only does this apply to almost 80 million Baby Boomers here in the United States, (the Leading Edge of which are already into their sixties and heading toward 70), but in the years to come the numbers of Millennials will overshadow those of the Boomers. It blows me away whenever I stop to ponder the enormous impact each of the generations now here on the Earth have and will have on shaping the future. For as each upcoming generation ages, these questions will be re-asked again and again…long after most of us reading this book are gone.

Ageless Workplaces

The new reality is that our employees and leaders will be working until we die. A report by the British trends consultancy The Future Laboratory, supports my view that in time more and more employees will want to age in place, but in the workplace. Let's face the facts. It's not just Baby Boomers who have another good twenty to thirty years of being productive and adding value; our current 40-somethings have the option of working at least another thirty to forty years more if they choose to do so. The Future Laboratory's findings point to a growing trend in which most of us will continue to work into old age; thus, our workplaces will morph into a new form, an Ageless Workplace! Clearly it's time to retread forced retirement into voluntary "returnment."

The future of the marketplace (and the world) lies in the rapidly growing values-based business model. People are now spending their money consciously, choosing to buy from companies that are making a difference in the world over those that aren't. More often than not, these are small, women-led businesses, the emerging new "Boomer Women Mean Business" story. Increasing numbers of these Boomer-led enterprises are supported by Ageless Women of all ages.

The Boomer Values Realignment Study adds great insight into the new Boomer generational priorities and shifting mind-set. Baby Boomers have come full circle. Well, almost. The Boomer Values Realignment Study recently showed that the Boomer reaction to the economic downturn and other national and global crises has been to focus more on relationships. The authors of the study refer to this as "a big shift from consumerism to relationships" as Boomers turn inward and focus more on what really matters. But this isn't an "I don't care too much for money" attitude by any means. The study also showed that Boomers care enough about money to bargain hunt and develop more thrifty spending habits. What's more, the renewed focus on meaning has affected *where* they spend their money—Baby Boomers are more likely to purchase from companies that are in line with their own values, as well as companies that will enhance their relationships with family and friends. For example, as the study shows the following:

- Ninety percent want their home to be an enticing gathering place for family and friends.

- Eighty-six percent desire a vacation connecting them with family and friends.

- Eighty-five percent are interested in a home with a smaller carbon footprint and lower operating costs.

- Eighty-three percent believe companies need to focus more on long-term growth than on short-term profits.

What do these numbers mean for businesses, especially entrepreneurs? Baby Boomers, on the whole, have $2.1 trillion in annual buying power, according to the MetLife Mature Market Institute, under the brilliant leadership of Sandra Timmerman. Many Boomers have no intention of retiring anytime soon, or they are planning retirement on their own terms with a flexible schedule and the ability to pursue what matters most to them, including building businesses based on their values (encore careers). Odds are, you are (or will be) one of them.

The shift toward a focus on relationships couldn't be more perfectly timed, as technology has changed the marketplace to be dependent on multiple networks connecting people around the world in almost infinite ways. Not only that, the market is savvy. People want more than just a connection, even with people they will never meet in person. They expect that connection to be genuine.

In the aftermath of the Great Recession, it can seem like the worst possible time to focus your business on your values, on the quality of your relationships with your clients rather than on the quantity. But the opposite is true. Baby Boomers are an indication of how your clients are changing. Living your values and focusing on what matters in your business is not only what you need, but it's what the world needs—and it's what the world is willing to pay for.

News flash: As Baby Boomers' needs change, so will the employment picture, and the very services and products available to serve the emerging needs of this generation…and all future 40-plussers.

At the same time that the Longevity Economy is demanding a new business model to serve consumers, a new model is being demanded in the workplace. People, organizations, and governments need to focus on encouraging experienced professionals and executives, especially women, to start intrapreneurial and entrepreneurial businesses with a strong focus on the Triple Bottom Line—People, Planet, Profit. In this way, we can solve, or at least ameliorate, multiple societal problems simultaneously through the specific social missions of these companies. No doubt the formation of more start-ups focusing on the Triple Bottom Line will have a significant positive effect on the job market, offering a way for all generations to make a living and a difference, and to secure their future and that of the world for generations to come.

The Future of Multigenerational Leadership

Despite the clear trend of Baby Boomers working longer, and some not planning to retire at all, the media, academia, and research firms are still discussing the question, "What will companies do when Baby Boomers step down?" The latest attempt to answer this is found in a report by researchers at Cass Business School at City University London, "After the Baby Boomers: The Next Generation of Leadership."

Their findings are interesting, particularly in the distinctions drawn between the Boomers and Generation X and Y (Millennials), but once again, I have to call into question the premise the entire study is based on—the assumption that Boomers will simply step down from leadership. I believe this premise is false. This is not to say that the younger generations won't be stepping into leadership positions more and more, but that the shift will be gradual, with generations working together. This is a future story for us, but it's being reported as a present story, and doing so only contributes to the disconnect and discord between generations.

Many of the findings of this study are still worth a look, however, even if we dispense with the assumption that we're facing a nice, neat "X in/Boomers out" scenario. The characterization of the X and Millennial generations as being much more ethnically diverse and insistent on work-life balance—for all genders—is just as easily a characterization of business trends as a whole. It's simple: Businesses not actively preparing for and welcoming these trends toward diversity, gender equality, and balance will be left behind by those who are. This is the *real* story of the marketplace now and in the future.

The *real* story is rapidly becoming a happening, but not because these trends are growing as Baby Boomers leave. On the contrary, these trends are growing as Boomers incorporate them into their own core values. Even those of us post-50 who once took part in the now-outdated definitions of success—making money, reaching the executive suite or corner office, achieving, achieving, achieving—have long realized that this kind of success is empty on its own.

Those few Baby Boomers who were still pursuing the "success at all costs" methodology are now facing a future where work-life balance is not a luxury but a necessity.

In other words, no matter how we get there, and no matter what generation we are in, diversity and work-life balance are the keys to futures that work for all of us. Whether we want that balance because we're starting a family or because we want time to visit our established families, the outcome is the same logistically. Work locations and hours must be increasingly flexible for everyone, without penalizing anyone for taking advantage of this flexibility.

> ...diversity and work-life balance are the keys to futures that work for all of us.

The multigenerational businesses that will thrive will have Baby Boomers mentoring the upcoming generations and will provide a clear path for employees who wish to work less, but not retire, to move more and more into consulting and specialized niches. Boomers will need to develop their own succession plan, as well and clarify their what's-next game plan as they begin transitioning, whenever and however that looks (semi-retirement, full retirement, never retirement, encore careers, etc.).

The future is not a zero-sum game or one in which one generation has to lose while the other wins. When we look closely at what all generations want as employees, entrepreneurs, and leaders, we can see that behind the differences are the same aspirational visions and sustainable solutions.

What's interesting is that for all the media hype pitting the generations against one another, more and more members of all generations—X,

Millennials, early and late Boomers, and Matures—are becoming more vocal about putting aside the generational stereotypes and looking at the common ground.

The question then becomes not whether these generations will work well together but how, and what changes we are likely to see in the future of business as a result of the changing, more age-diverse face of tomorrow's workforce, from professionals to executives to the growing number of entrepreneurs. What aspirational future story will we create together?

A recent panel called "Don't Generalize My Generation," sponsored by Deutsch NY, raised many interesting answers to this question on topics ranging from work styles to telecommuting. Here I'd like to focus on one area that I think has important implications for all aspects of how—and why—we do business: leadership.

The traditional business model is hierarchical and, at its extreme, this top-down model has meant that those lower in the hierarchy simply "follow orders" based on what the leadership passes down. We all know that this has been changing for decades. The hierarchy is still the most common structure, but more and more businesses recognize the need to cultivate a shared vision, a sense of the big picture and where every person within the organization fits in that picture. I see this as a flattening of the pyramid, not doing away with it entirely.

We are at a remarkable transition point where many among the younger generations expect leadership to be essentially crowd-sourced, a concept that at first blush might seem foreign to their older colleagues. But is it?

> It is important that all generations have a shared vision.

It is important that all generations have a shared vision. As Boomers age, the need to focus on what really matters most to them becomes increasingly important. Ultimately, for all generations, true leadership is the vision itself, a purpose that everyone can feel genuinely invested in—not only those working toward that vision as a part of the business but also those the businesses serve. It's a story we co-create and step into together. The trend I'm seeing is from businesses being client-centric, to employee-centric, to *human*-centric, focusing on the humanity of everyone the business touches.

Businesses led by a strong shared story do not rely on holding on for dear life to the same people as leaders, or the same type of people who have always led in our past stories. Story-led businesses can weather changes that result from retirement, job-sharing arrangements, people transitioning from full time to part time, and similar changes in the fluidity of how people manage their careers and their own transitions (be they related to aging, starting a family, or simply wanting to pursue multiple intersecting paths to self-actualization and professional fulfillment).

This fluidity is only going to increase in the future, and it has as much to do with the changing priorities of the older generation as it does with the new expectations and preferences of the younger—and every age and stage in between.

The future story of leadership is not only multigenerational, it is collaborative and, above all, visionary. Those who recognize and nourish this trend, as well as the visionary purpose within all of us, will not only survive but also thrive with their roots in generational common ground.

> The future story of leadership is multigenerational, collaborative andabove all, visionary.

The Age-Friendly Workplace

Any good story has to include a well-developed setting, and our new story for the future is no different. The term "age-friendly" refers not only to environments and technology that are tailored to the aging population, but also to those that meet the needs of multiple people at all ages and stages of life. One of the key reasons for us to have intergenerational conversations is to determine where our needs and desires intersect and to develop ideas that will meet those needs and desires for as many people as possible.

Some of the most compelling age-friendly ideas for the workplace fall under the umbrella of flexible work arrangements. Long thought of as a concept that caters primarily to women with children, flex work is increasingly being recognized as an ideal way to also serve the needs of those who wish to work beyond retirement age. Not only that, but new research from Catalyst shows that the only companies able to consistently attract and retain top talent, regardless of gender, age, or life stage, are those offering some form of flexible work arrangements.

Further, the research shows that the costs of implementing such a program are offset by savings in operational costs—by more than $10,000 a year per person telecommuting part time.

Telecommuting has become synonymous with flexible work arrangements in many minds, but the former term encompasses many possibilities. Even companies with hourly employees whose work must be done onsite, such as manufacturing work, can benefit employees—and their own bottom line—with various flex options:

- Compressed schedules

- Flexible start and end times

- Job sharing and/or shift trading

- Voluntary overtime (those who want the extra money can work the overtime, and those who don't aren't compelled to)

- Employee-designed schedules

- Sabbatical programs

- Unpaid time off

- Half-day options

- Assignment variety based on availability and skill, not seniority

- Flexible space onsite for employees to use to meet in support groups (such as for people caring for elderly parents, working parents, etc.) or for personal computer use during breaks on long shifts.

What works best—for company and employee—depends on many factors. People have different work styles and preferences, and some tasks are best accomplished in particular ways or at particular times and locations.

Collaboration between the business and employees is key to uncovering what is most important to everyone and why and to determine how employee needs and those of the company can both be met. A regular process for review is essential to adjust what isn't working as well as to meet the changing needs of the organization, its talent, and its customers.

Ultimately, "Continuous Improvement" is about focusing on results and outputs rather than on micromanaging people. The belief that the latter is necessary to the former is contrary to the data. After voluntarily leaving my corporate perch in the late 1980s, I was blessed to synchronistically find myself studying with and under the tutelage of my deeply admired teacher, mentor, and friend, Dr. W. Edwards Deming. He encouraged me to take an even bigger systems' view to identify which outliers or special causes in any process might be producing defects in the outputs or derailing the process, as well as identifying those excelling in producing outputs and innovation within Six Sigma of perfection. ("Six Sigma" is lots of things depending on how it is applied, but in short it is a metric, as well as a rigorous and disciplined methodology, that aids in quality improvement and overall quality management.)

There is an old Chinese saying that I'll paraphrase: "When the fish stinks, it stinks from the top!" Deming knew this saying to be true, and he went on to prove it to be so in his many real-time international and national corporate client stories, in his Continuous Improvement studies, and so much more detailed in his many notable books, articles, and talks. In his own words (that say it all), "The worker is not the problem. The problem is at the top! Management!" Dr. Deming expanded this statement even further by adding, "95% of all the problems and failures in business are system failures; it has nothing to do with the individual manager or worker and only 5% are people driven." He ardently believed that 95 percent of these same problems in business are caused by management because they create and are responsible to manage the system. Only the leader can change the system. So if the workers or employees screw up, it's most certainly not their fault! Sadly, Deming was also spot-on when he declared, "A poor system will win every time over a good employee."

> "When the fish stinks it stinks from the top!"

The most important thing I learned from Deming is his theory that system correction must come from the top down (vs. blaming workers) if its to make a difference, a sustainable lasting improvement. In fact, he stated in his book *Out of the Crisis* that the most important strategic action to take is to continuously improve the system and its processes to realize sustainable, ongoing process improvement and high-quality results.

I was very fortunate to study with and be mentored by Dr. Deming, especially since by the time I met him he was firmly committed to trans- formation and the importance of his lifelong body of work codified by his later life's *System of Profound Knowledge*, (SoPK). This system is an incredibly effective theory of management, applicable no matter the size of an organization or its mission. That is, if you or your organization seek to transform and create a thriving organization with win-win as your foundational objective, follow Deming's system of knowledge model.

Dr. Deming's legacy is saved for eternity within the W. Edwards Deming Institute he founded in 1993. In the institute's own descriptive mission statement, "The Deming Institute is bringing the teachings of Dr. W. Edwards Deming to a new generation, for a rapidly evolving new world. We believe in inspiring individuals and organizations to make a difference, think differently, ask better questions and seek new knowledge."

> Intrinsic rewards achieve far gareater innovation, and ever-increasing quality, productivity, and outputs.

He believed and demonstrated in his world-famous "Red Bead Experiment" (an exercise wherein executives play both the part of the worker and management), the truism that intrinsic rewards achieve far greater motivation, innovation, and ever-increasing quality, productivity, and outputs. Yes, we are in more disruptive times now, and rapid response to change demands innovation and creativity, which seems the antithesis of Deming's insistence to reduce variability in our systems and processes. To be sure, he never suggested that innovative outliers should be thwarted; rather, he encouraged innovation with continuous quality improvement (CQI) built in to the very underpinnings of every system and process. Indeed, Deming never suggested that a system is foolproof. Quite the opposite, he took the view that any existing system is satisfactory for accomplishing the work of today, but he also insisted that we must constantly improve our systems and processes to prepare to address the problems of tomorrow as well as the problems of today. I had the grand pleasure of reading his drafts for his *Out of the Crisis*, which is a Total Quality Management bible for the rest of us. If Deming's fourteen points are followed to a tee, then long-term success is ensured.

Survival is optional. No one has to change.

~W. Edwards Deming

Dr. Deming's over two hundred published writings, including papers, articles and books, are not a quick read, nor for the dilettante. A good starting point is to avail yourself of the many resources available through The W. Edwards Deming Institute online (www.Deming.org).

If Deming were alive today, he'd be a raving fan of age-friendly workplaces.

We can all work toward creating age-friendly workplaces by bringing these ideas, and the facts behind them, to the attention of our employers, especially if we wish or need to stay until we transition into retirement, a new career, or entrepreneurship. If you own or manage a business or organization, you are in a perfect position for guiding your employees to create an age-friendly workplace together.

As more and more employers recognize the need to capitalize on their experienced workforce in order to retain them, we should see an increasing emphasis on flexible work arrangements—part-time work, consulting, and job sharing, just to name a few. This, in turn, will provide more visible options for Baby Boomers to consider beyond the false dichotomy of retiring or not retiring.

Forward-thinking companies have already begun this shift, but far too many are not looking past their own noses to prepare for the coming wave of Baby Boomers making pivotal choices about how to design their lives and their stories around work. For many businesses, the planning for a changing workforce won't happen until the sheer numbers of Boomers on the precipice of leaving reach a critical mass, or until multiple generations start working together to make these changes happen. Waiting is a huge mistake for these businesses, of course, yet this lack of foresight does not have to extend to the rest of us.

We all have the opportunity, no matter our age or stage, to design our futures starting today, to create an aspirational future story for our work lives. You don't have to wait for your company to provide options for you. Now is the time to develop your own game plan, to think BIG about the next stage of your life, and to then create your own options to make that big vision happen.

This manifestation may mean going to your employer and laying out your plans and what you need from them to make those plans happen in ways that are advantageous for both of you. Or this may mean laying out a succession and exit strategy that takes you into your own business, your chance to combine passion, profit, and purpose, to make a living and a difference while enjoying more flexibility to work where and when you want.

Parents of young children and 70-year-olds alike can find work or create businesses that are flexible in hours and location (among myriad other factors), to work with their realities and their desire to focus on what matters most. Organizations that do not recognize the need to customize the work world for every employee will find that their employees will do it themselves, especially in midlife and beyond. These companies will not only lose the experience and wisdom of their post-50 staff, teams, and leaders, but they are likely to lose money to many of them as former employees become entrepreneurial competition.

Boomerpreneurs and Solopreneurs

A significant number of the many people who plan to continue working past retirement age are or will be entrepreneurs. This fact is part of the present story for Boomers, and all signs point to it being integral to the future Boomer story. According to the Kauffman Foundation, people ages 55 to 64 consistently start more new businesses than those in any other age group, and this reality has been true for about a decade. We also know from this foundation that people over 55 are the most likely to be successful with their business start-ups. The Sloan Center on Aging & Work estimates that about 38 percent of small business owners (including solo companies) are age 60 or older.

Even more interesting is that in a recent Civic Ventures survey of 45- to 70-year-olds, about 25 percent indicated an interest in being entrepreneurs, and more than half of them wanted their venture to address a social issue.

The years ahead may be the era of the Boomerpreneur and solopreneur, as we collectively reinvent work after 40 and turn stereotypes about aging and retirement on their head, re-storying what it means to live and work at any age. Not only will more and more people age 40 and beyond be looking to start or grow their own businesses, or continue leading their organizations, they will also represent the largest market segment for these

> A significant number of the many people who plan to continue working past retirement age are or will be entrepreneurs.

businesses, which is one of the reasons it makes so much sense to start off thinking about solutions for your own needs and problems. Necessity may be the mother of invention, but in the twenty-first century, the grandmother of invention is reinvention—of yourself, your future, your business, your world, and your story.

In fact, the 40-plus market is perfect for a new encore entrepreneurial start-up, the opportunity to change ageism into age-friendly while making a profit. Boomer women are at the forefront of this movement. An increasing number of women are rising to executive and board positions (though still not even close to the number of men). According to the National Association of Women Business Owners, more women are running successful businesses, generating $1.3 trillion in annual sales and showing net increases in employment, growth that can only be matched by large publicly traded corporations. With this increasing rise in women's power, there has been a backlash in American society and in the workplace, and older women bear the brunt of it. Women of all ages witness repeated cycles of ageism and related firings under the guise of "poor performance" that have nothing to do with measurable performance and everything to do with measurable age. Women, and men too, see their older colleagues being pushed aside, diminished, and ostracized by frightened colleagues who fear they might catch the firing bug if they stay connected. Rather than staying in repressive, stultifying positions with a silver ceiling looming and poor performance reviews on the horizon as they head toward 50 and beyond, regardless of actual performance, women are standing in their own shoes and starting their own businesses, particularly as solopreneurs. And many of them are savvy enough to recognize the most important market out there: women just like them.

> Women of all ages witness repeated cycles of ageism.

Starting or Reinventing a Business after 40

Whether you are thinking about starting a business or are already running your own company, the next steps are similar. Even those already in business must frequently reassess how their business is doing, and not just financially. You might be considering how to add more meaning to your business and work life, how to combine what you are already doing with ways to make a bigger difference in the world.

Regardless of your situation, your first step is to consider what kind of business you want to create, evolve, or reinvent. The new story for your business needs an outline. Scan and ponder the ten questions that follow. You can consider these questions more fully when you take time to focus on the Reflections at the end of this chapter.

1. Do you want to continue in your current field or try something new? If new, is it related to your existing skill set or industry, or will you need further education and training before you can open your doors? If in your current field, are you in love with what you do, or are you choosing this field because it's familiar? Choose something that you are genuinely, passionately interested in, that you are already drawn to read about, talk about, and learn about at every opportunity. If you are planning to reinvent an existing business, you need to go beyond what you've done in the past—beyond good service to extraordinary service, beyond meeting expectations to exceeding them and offering a lot more value-added services or products. How does this look in terms of what you could offer, and how does that compare to what you do already?

2. How will your business address what matters most to you? In what ways do you want your business to also address what matters most to your family, your community, the world? Will it meet the Triple Bottom Line: People, Planet, Profit? Where do your talents and passions intersect with what the world needs now and what it will need in the future?

3. Do you want to sell products, provide services, consult, or some combination?

4. Do you want to go totally virtual with your business or a combination? Which option suits your lifestyle choices?

5. Do you want to be a solopreneur or do you want to be an employer?

6. If starting a new business, what kind of time and money are you willing and able to invest in the first three years (the average lag time between starting a business and breaking even)? If reinventing

your business, what time and money are you willing and able to invest to revitalize and revamp what you're already doing?

7. What is the income potential for your business? Will it be enough to meet your needs? Will it be enough to meet your desires? Make an appointment with an accountant and business growth expert who has experience with entrepreneurs to get a realistic assessment of your business costs and potential.

8. What kind of competition is out there? How are they doing, particularly since the recession? How will you do things differently to stand out, avoid the competition's mistakes, and capitalize on trends so that you are ahead of change?

9. What does the day-to-day operation look like to you realistically? What do you want the day-to-day operation to look like?

   • Consider how lifestyle-compatible your business is. If you live near the top of a mountain, a business that requires a lot of in-person contact or travel will be tricky without easy and affordable transportation. If you need regular human interaction, don't create a business model that chains you to your computer all day. If you want to sustain your business indefinitely, doing the work you love into your nineties or beyond, design your business to weather any physical changes you might encounter down the road. Consider how much freedom and flexibility you want—to travel, spend time with family and friends, do volunteer work, or just relax whenever you need to.

   • Consider what everyday tasks you enjoy, which ones you find mundane but doable, and which ones you loathe. Will you have a balance? Will you be able to delegate the latter? Or will the day-to-day requirements of your business idea likely damper the passion you have for the business? Will you have enough variety or enough routine to suit your personality, needs, and preferences?

10. How tech savvy are you now, and how tech savvy will you need to be to run your business successfully? What technology is required for the business itself? What technology is required for marketing,

accounting, sales, distribution, etc.? What new technologies can keep your business on the edge of change? Even the most experienced, savvy professionals will need to be on a continuous technological learning curve to keep up with the changing marketplace. If you don't have the interest or time to learn new technology, can you afford to get technical help as needed? If you are planning a business that you can run for the next thirty, forty, or fifty years, consider now what technology can enable you to do that, including what you would need to keep your business running virtually.

The future of business, and of our world, lies in the hands of those who are taking steps right now to reimagine the marketplace, the workplace, and the small business in ways that intersect with where we are headed as well as where we want to head globally—sustainability, cooperative business models, flexibility in our work and our lives, and the ability to pursue what is meaningful to us in everything we do, at every age.

Time Is Money

At this point, you may know that you want to start a business but still feel unsure about exactly what kind of business. You may only vaguely know that you want to do something purposeful, but you aren't sure if this means volunteering, work, or some combination, or what exactly you would be doing.

If you have not yet decided on what you want to do, consider the opportunities inherent in our most precious resource—time.

For all the timesaving technology we gain each year, we somehow seem to have less and less time available to us. Busy working parents don't have as much time to volunteer in schools or spend as much time with their children as they'd like. Even kids don't have as much time for free play with all their activities, sports, and school-related commitments. In an increasingly urban society, some kids have the time for free play but no safe spaces to do so, and their parents don't have time to take them to safe spaces.

Many areas of traditional volunteer work, such as visiting with the sick and infirm, feeding the homeless, helping to care for animals in shelters, and so forth, are lacking in volunteers because people simply do not have the time.

One answer, of course, is to simply step up and be a volunteer. But consider looking at this from a different perspective. How can you or your business save people time in ways that specifically allow them to have more meaningful time? With their children? Their parents? Volunteering themselves? In essence, ask what plot holes there are in the present story of your community? Where are the gaps that need attention? How can you fill them and give new direction not only to the story of others but also your own?

If you run (or plan to run) a business with employees, designing flexible work schedules could be a part of how you set up your workforce. Using job sharing, flexible hours, work-at-home days, and so forth will enable your employees to balance their lives by being able to choose the options that work best for them. Or your business could be the meaningful work that you (with or without employees) want the time to do.

If you are still with a company, planning your own eventual exit, now is the time to research and develop alternate preferred scenarios that could serve you, your colleagues, and the business, such as a consultant relationship or part-time substitute situation that enables everyone to take "meaning days," along with the traditional vacation time and sick time.

Any business that brings extended families and communities together to help one another out and save time is bound to hit a ready market. What if busy parents only worried about cooking dinner once or twice a week? How about a service that brings young kids to meet with parents over lunch near or at their work?

How about a program for companies to buy into that sends groups of employees to volunteer with their families in the name of the company?

The possibilities are endless—as are the potential profits—when you consider what is truly meaningful to you and to others. Contrary to the trope about the later years of life, time really is on our side.

Grannypreneurs

Along the same lines as focusing on providing ways for others to strengthen relationships, another avenue to consider is accommodating the changing needs of grandparents. When thinking about the needs of Baby Boomers and Matures, whether as members of these groups or as those who serve them (or both!), products and services for children may not even be on our radar. Yet grandparents and even later-life parents are spending more time and money on children than ever before.

A recent MetLife survey found that grandparents are spending an average of $8,661 annually on grandchildren, a number likely to increase as younger Boomers become grandparents. Consider this number in light of the Boomer Values Realignment Survey that found "a big shift from consumerism to relationships" in Boomer focus.

If you already run a business, targeting your existing products and services to Baby Boomers and Matures is only part of the picture. Transcending the status quo by focusing on ways to help grandparents spend more quality time strengthening their relationships with their grandchildren and children has visionary potential for you and for the people you serve.

If you are a grandparent and an entrepreneur (or just thinking about starting your own business), this trend provides you with an opportunity to look at your own needs and desires and align them with what others in your tribe are seeking.

UK research supporting the positive trajectory for Boomerpreneurs, and most definitely grannypreneurs (which most likely reflects U.S. study results as well), has revealed that modern-day "grand-trepreneurs" are the over-sixties real boomerang generation. A quarter of these retirement-age adults working into later life run their own business, with 21 percent opening their doors while in their sixties. The conclusion drawn by the reporter is that these over-60 entrepreneurs show that there is a trend to "unretire" or to never retire.

Just as Baby Boomers are changing the way we all age, they are likely to redefine the role grandparents have played in the past. By anticipating the needs of this reimagining—especially by drawing on your own needs and

> Modern day "grand-trepreneurs" are the over-sixties real boomerang generation.

desires for the present and future—you can create a sustainable business and lifestyle in which what matters most to you in life is integral to making a living. Grannypreneurs just might be the sleeper story of the future!

Boomerpreneurs and Technology

One of the most pervasive myths about Baby Boomers is that we are technology Luddites. As with any generational stereotype, there are certainly individuals that fit this bill, but as a whole, Boomers are the fastest-growing group of technology users, not to mention the generation that invented much of the technology that is ubiquitous today. In fact, many of the successful post-50 start-ups are in fact tech start-ups. The true present story of Boomers and tech is very different from the mythical present.

The digital performance marketing company iProspect published a study titled "The Ageless Internet: From Silver Surfers to Golden Geeks," which reveals that confidence in technology and Internet usage is as high in the over-50s as it is among the 30 to 49 demographic. Importantly, the findings show that the older group is just as digitally savvy as younger generations. To underscore their conclusion that the digital age divide is a myth, they found a full 80 percent of 50- to 59-year-olds believe their age is no barrier to using the Internet, and they expect to use it more in the future. Mind-blowing is that this percentage rises to 88 percent of 60- to 69-year-olds, and to as many as 92 percent of those age 70 or more.

When it comes to the social edge, 28 million 50-plussers already subscribe to Facebook. The Forrester Research study finds that the Boomer demographic buys twice as much online as younger adults.

Deloitte published a report that concludes that older consumers are likely to continue working, accumulate an ever-greater share of global wealth and become increasingly interested in technology. Ben Perkins, who is head of consumer business research at this Big Four accountancy firm, sees this as an important market for future growth. According to Deloitte's report, smartphone ownership among the over-55ers was predicted double in 2014. With all the large-screen smartphones now on the market, there is no cap in sight on this explosive growth curve.

> When it comes to the social edge, 28 million 50-plussers already subscribe to Facebook. The Forrester Research study finds that the Boomer demographic buys twice as much online as younger adults.

I think Apple's retail service is darn good, although the lines can be tough to maneuver. Yet I've often wondered why Apple doesn't segment its service by training older staff Geniuses and sales staff to serve older customers. Tesco, the UK's largest retailer, is doing just that to sell mobile technology. Perkins at Deloitte raves about this new model: "Basically there's somebody of the same generation who understands the subtleties and differences between what a twenty-five-year-old and what a fifty-five-year-old may be looking for in a mobile device."

But for many of us, technology is a means to an end more than an end in itself. If we are thinking about starting or reinventing a business, technology plays a minimal role—if any role at all—in deciding what kind of business we want to create or transform. If anything, technology comes in at the later stages, when we try to conform the latest advances to our existing ideas. Backing into technology further into the process can be frustrating when we have to jury rig the tech to suit our business model, especially if we are also still learning how to use it in the first place.

Seth Godin discussed an aspect of this after-the-fact insertion of technology in a blog post, giving examples of changes in technology that have required more than just slight adjustments in how businesses are run: mail to email; books to e-books; Visa to PayPal; direct mail to permission marketing, and so on. As he points out: "The question that gets asked about technology, the one that is almost always precisely the wrong question is, 'How does this advance help our business?' The correct question is, 'How does this advance undermine our business model and require us/enable us to build a new one?'"

> Not only must we be lifelong learners of technological advances, but we also must be prepared to look at all the new possibilities for our businesses and continuously reinvent to take advantage of them.

Not only must we be lifelong learners of technological advances, but we also must be prepared to look at all the new possibilities for our businesses and continuously reinvent to take advantage of them. Adapting the technology to our old methods and perspectives simply won't work long term. We are the ones who must adapt.

Ask yourself: What possibilities in the latest technology inspire an entrepreneurial reinvention—or a brand-new business?

The Social Edge

Of course, it also makes sense to take a look at how you can creatively use the technology you're already familiar with, such as social media, which Baby Boomers are using with rapidly increasing frequency in their personal and professional lives. Whether you're thinking of recareering or starting a business, or you just want to rev up your existing career or business, recent trends point to a way post-40 women especially can capitalize on their strengths.

Online recruiter Jobvite has reported that 94 percent of recruiters use or plan to use social media to find candidates. Although the company will obviously have a bias in its numbers because it makes social media recruiting software, even being conservative and lowering this percentage shows a distinct trend.

Couple this with the Hiscox studies showing that female entrepreneurs are experiencing a more rapid rate of growth than male entrepreneurs and that one reason for this growth is women's use of social media in all aspects of their businesses, not just for hiring.

Fast Company recently highlighted stories of women and men using social media to launch new careers or businesses, including the following:

- Kay Roseland, who was laid off in her sixties, decided to get certifications in social media and start a blog. Then through social media contact, followed by face-to-face contact, she ended up landing a job blogging for Infor.com.

- At 50, Gail Dosik went from the fashion industry to culinary school, then started her own Manhattan bakery, building word of mouth through social media and email.

- Attorney Diane Danielson recareered into marketing in her forties, jumping into an on-the-job crash course in social media and web-based marketing, ultimately landing a job when she wasn't even looking for one simply through her online presence.

For women, being social can mean big business, especially for those in midlife and beyond. One of the most persistent stereotypes about Baby Boomers and Matures is that they are unwilling to learn new things and are not on top of the latest technology. The stats show otherwise (see studies by the Kauffman Foundation and Northwestern's Kellogg School of Management mentioned above), but public perception often lags behind reality. One of the best ways to change the stereotype, to change the story, is to be a visible example of its opposite.

On top of this lagging, out-of-date public perception, we are at a critical point coming out of the Great Recession during a time of unprecedented technology and increasing numbers of people putting their money where their values are. This groundswell of value-based action means we are in a position to shape what business looks like going forward, including using our businesses and careers to build genuine connections with others, combine our values with our business practices, and make a profit in innovative, meaningful ways. Social media is also all about storytelling, a place to share the story you are creating for yourself and to co-create stories for the future of the marketplace and the global community.

All of these potential opportunities for a new story capitalize on the current strengths of many women and of social media. Right now, you are in a unique position to redefine business, not only for yourself but also for generations to come, by combining the two.

Perhaps the examples above or other success stories are exactly the path you want to take, or perhaps you will simply follow your own natural path in building relationships and using social media in ways that are comfortable for you.

Whatever you do, from investing in your social media education or business practices to simply increasing or innovating within your existing social media use, remember that online and off, showing up and having presence are essential components to opening yourself up for opportunities, sometimes when you least expect them.

> Today and into the future, building relationships is building your business, even if—especially if—that business is you.

Today and into the future, building relationships is building your business, even if—especially if—that business is you.

The Future of Podcasting

The fast-growing podcasting trend allows all of us to meet our tribe, our audience(s), where they are. Edison Research recently reported that a stunning 39 million Americans have listened to a podcast in a typical month. But clearly this is only a bellwether of what's to come. If we step back to look at why this current trend is growing, it makes total sense. Podcasting is a medium that provides freedom to connect wherever you are (even on technology as small as portable smartphones), and whenever it suits the listener (since it's solely audio content, it is available around the clock). Pretty soon it will be a no-brainer to dial up a podcast, even in our cars. Before we get too excited, there is a big BUT. Women are underrepresented in podcaster land. What an opportunity for we women who love to share our stories, and converse with our peeps!

Ageless Technology

There's one area of technology that often flies under the radar when we're talking about Baby Boomers and tech, yet the impact is profound, as well as demonstrating how technology with purposes specific to this demographic can serve all ages.

Few people think of Bluetooth earpieces or e-readers like Kindle as being technology designed for our needs as we age, yet some earpieces can filter out background noise and boost our ability to hear clearly, particularly in crowds, and e-readers can be adjusted in multiple ways to make the type easier to read for all vision types.

Similarly, technology for fitness and health, financial management, travel planning, and more are advancements useful across generations. Yet they all hit a sweet spot, most notably with the post-50 generations who have a heightened interest in this technology with each passing year.

These products are so ordinary that it's easy to overlook them when we're thinking in terms of our own use of technology as well as in terms of making our products and services friendlier to the enormous Boomer market.

The key is not to look at technology that is only for 50-plussers. This mind-set stems from an Othering of people over a "certain age" that is a relic of our past. Instead, we should be looking at creating and buying technology that is multifunctional and user-friendly so that it ages with us, adapting to our needs over a lifetime.

The future of technology is truly Ageless.

The future of technology is truly Ageless.

Your Visionary Business

All visionaries are Ageless, and we all have a visionary voice inside us. That voice can guide us toward making a difference in the world while simultaneously achieving sustainable, meaningful success in our lives and work.

Many of you are no doubt aware of this voice. Maybe you've had to reawaken it at various times in your life—most of us have to do this—but you know it's there.

Some of you, on the other hand, might not see yourself as ever being a visionary. Visionaries are other people, not you. You have ideas, but you don't see them as earth-shattering. You want sustainable, meaningful success, sure, but nothing you're planning will transform the world.

And that's okay. Your definition of success, of what matters most to you, is yours and yours alone. But if at any point in your life you've felt that you were meant for more, that there's a bigger purpose inside you yet to be realized, then you are selling yourself—and the world—short by not uncovering that purpose, by not doing what you can to awaken your visionary voice and allow it to narrate your future.

This acknowledgement is crucial if your reasons for not doing so are that you think it's too late for you, or that you are not smart enough, rich enough, confident enough, creative enough…that you are simply not enough to lead change.

It is never too late to be a visionary. On the contrary, many of us can't be true visionaries until we have the experience, wisdom, and willingness to focus only on what matters—qualities that tend to ripen with age.

You don't have to wait until you feel you are enough. Awaken the visionary voice inside, and you will find that your doubts become insignificant in light of a vision you will be driven to pursue, with passion, purpose, and, yes, even profit. I have found that awakening our Inner Visionary requires profound inner work along with parallel outer due diligence. Please be sure not to shortcut this endeavor, or you surely will end up going in circles or aborting your efforts. You may even want to proceed with this discovery process under the expert and experienced tutelage of a trained professional who has both the know-how and knowledge of the psyche, as well as the real-world knowledge of careers and business to guide you to find where your gifts intersect with what the world needs now.

And that brings me back to those of you who do not feel driven to uncover your larger Soul's purpose, to discover how your personal and professional success can run parallel to making a difference in the world.

Consider this: The more turmoil our world undergoes—economic, environmental, social—the more everyday people choose to spend their money on products and services that in some way go toward healing our Earth. In other words, when given a choice between two companies with essentially the same offering, consumers are increasingly choosing the one that goes that extra step toward making a difference in the world.

Think about where this trend is going. People and businesses that find a way to combine a larger visionary purpose with their business model will be the most profitable. More people and businesses will follow their lead until visionary business practices will become the norm. Not riding this trend now not only means missing out on a larger market, more money, and greater impact—it could make your ideas and your business ultimately obsolete. ❯

CHAPTER 8 ~ *The Ageless Way Reflections*

The questions and exercises below are to help you find your distinct path on The Ageless Way. Turn to page 28 for more about The Ageless Way Reflections.

1. What story are you in right now with your work? Where do you see that story going in the future? What other preferred future scenarios are possible for you? Which has the best possible outcome? Which story do you want to be living and working in the next year or two? Once you have your alternative futures laid out, you can focus on and manifest the one you most want.

2. What does "retirement" mean to you? Are you planning to retire or partially retire at any age? Are your plans part of an old story, one you are living because you are expected to? What changes would you make to workplaces and the ways businesses are run in order to co-create a new story about working past 65 or 70?

3. How does your existing business or business idea root itself in your values? What are you doing to build and deepen genuine relationships, professionally and personally?

4. What opportunities do you have for multigenerational conversations in the workplace? What can you do to change these conversations, to make them collaborative and based on finding common-ground solutions that work for all ages and stages?

5. What are the ideal elements of a workplace that would serve you now and into the foreseeable future? In other words, what does the new work story look like for you? What can you do to start making these changes? Do they all point to starting your own business, as an entrepreneur or solopreneur?

6. What aspects of technology are ideal for you and/or your business? What aspects are more difficult to work with? What would technology without these difficulties look like? Which of these difficulties reflect potential problems with your current ways of doing things, personally and professionally? Could you change your processes or systems in ways that alleviate these difficulties?

7. Determining the new story for your business takes some deep digging to discover what kind of business you want to create, evolve or reinvent. Consider re-exploring the questions on page 232-234.

Chapter 9

AGELESS REINVENTION

*Tell me, what is it you plan to do with your
one wild and precious life?*

~ Mary Oliver

*It started one day in the spring of 1987 when I looked around my
highly coveted corner office. The sun streamed in, warming me and illuminating the piles of memoranda, research, and unanswered telephone
messages stacked up on my glistening lacquered desk.*

*I had made it. I had all the perks. Making top dollar. Broke all the
industry and company records. I was at the peak of this, my fifth career.*

I leaned back in my executive chair and wondered why I was here….

*It began on another bright sunny day, ten years before, when I was
walking down the Avenue of the Americas with my lover. We were both
running successful businesses and creating a wonderful life together. The
whole world seemed to be ahead of us as we strolled along, sharing our
dreams. I pointed to the top of a cluster of skyscrapers, the bastion of big
business, and proclaimed, "One day I will have an office up there and
I'll be making a six- or seven-figure income!"*

*But the "view from the top" proved to be very different from my
original view from the street. I'd gotten what I'd wanted, but at what cost?*

I thought of:

…the abusive, driven bosses I had put up with along the way.

*…my "real woman" role model; powerful, vulnerable, compassionate,
outmaneuvered and crucified by her most trusted allies.*

...our two "little ones" who would be graduating soon. Custody conflicts had kept me from them when they were small. Now they were home, and I was an "absentee mom."

...my lover and second husband. He was always there for me. He had made my kids his own. Yet I was always at the office, working late, dragging home an enormous briefcase on the weekends...

The sunlight continued to stream through my window, but I felt cold. I felt stuck. Grabbed by the "golden handcuffs." I felt cold all over. If I was honest, I was scared. I was confused. Most of all, I was bogged down, strained to the max, burnt out.

What had happened to my aliveness, my juicy feminine passions, the freshness I had when I started out on this path to "fame and fortune"?

I was in a hurry, but where was I going? Where had the time gone? What was I trying to prove, and to whom?

Crossing the Canyon of the Soul

That day in my office marked the beginning of a new passage for me. Going through it, I called it "menopause." Looking back, I'd call it "Midlife Reclamation," (Sands, 1988). I was undergoing a rewiring, a Soul reclamation and a radical reinvention that would lead to a transformation that still informs who I am today as I live my destiny.

Those questions that day pursued me all the ensuing days, pushing me to set aside my earlier aspirations and plan my departure from those hallowed corporate halls. From all that I had dreamed I wanted. Unexpectedly, I was moving down a path without a known destination. A great inner force urged me toward something that was not yet apparent. On the surface, I thought it was the warmth of my family. A respite. A drink of rejuvenation. I sought healing waters from their loving embraces.

Phase One seemed innocent enough. I'd take a short sabbatical, six months to a year, I told myself, my family, and anyone else who asked. Especially the corporate headhunters! It felt so good to turn down significant opportunities I would have danced in the streets for before.

It was all a reverie until my predetermined deadline came and went. It dawned on me that I didn't know what I wanted to go back to. What was worth leaving my family for? What were my real desires? What was I striving toward?

For the first time I had no goals. I had nothing to prove. But if I had no goals, what was I? Who was I? The not knowing was sheer torture! I fought with it. I wrestled with it. I wasn't a *somebody* anymore! I had no title. I belonged nowhere. I had no place to go anymore. I no longer had a suitable answer to "And what do you do?" Uneasy, I quickly made up business cards with just my name. God forbid I should say, "I'm in between." I clearly had to be a *this* or a *that*.

What I did not know then, I know now decades later. I had bought into our culture's myth of the Goddess Athena–like new breed of women visionary leaders, all seeking the American Dream in the hallowed halls of Corporate America. Ayn Rand, author of *Atlas Shrugged*, one of my adolescent favorites, would have loved my fiercely feminist rugged individualism. I made the mistake of believing the American Dream was my desired reality when it was only a myth.

A Woman's Reclamation of Our True Feminine Power

I ultimately chose to make this midlife crossing…my way. My questions morphed into, "How am I going to experience my menopause?" "How will I age?" "What do I want for my Third and Fourth Age?" All the women in my ancestral lineage had followed a path of Alzheimer's, madness, and death. Could I choose rebirth?

As I tried to force myself into high gear, to go out and get myself going again, I felt the spirit drain out of me. Some connectors had just burnt out. I had no choice, I had to stop and be still. I had to listen to my inner cries. I had to surrender. In some deep recess of my Soul I knew that I was going through a death that had to be. I had to trust that a rebirth would come.

Of course, it takes practice to reprogram the circuitry of a lifetime. I know that this is the gift of the midlife crossing. In menopause, each of us is called inward to pause. We are urged to take time out. To return to the inner spiral, thread-in-hand leading us back to our awaiting Soul in our belly, in our pelvis.

Hot flashes? They were the burning heat surging inside me as new connections, new circuitry were being laid in place.

Fatigue? An enforced quiet that helped me surrender to an energy level more appropriate to this new life phase.

Fuzz brain? Loss of focus? A trick of the feminine, forcing me to move down from my head to connect back into the richness of my Soul's resting place.

Dreamtime? Where I found my Soulspeak, my Soul's calling (Sands, 1988).

It appears that most of us listen for guidance everywhere except from within. Even when I'm coaching savvy, accomplished clients, I have to keep reminding them that the answers are within them...my gift is to ask the right questions and to unveil unconscious patterning! Our Souls reside deep within us. For women, I believe it rests deep in our belly. Don't expect to hear your Soulspeak if you are thrashing and crashing or racing from one thing to the next. Quite the opposite. Your Soul will come calling if you are in a quiet, safe space and you are expansively receptive to what emerges or shows up for you (in a moment and over time). Your Soul will speak in its own language through dream symbols, "ahas" that unexpectedly emerge across the blank screen of your meditating mind, and when you engage in such reflective activities as journaling or taking a walk in the woods.

Native Americans use the spiral to symbolize the continuum of life. The early years they depict as a going out from the center of the spiral, into the external world. Later years are represented as going inward along the spiral. Menopause is the internal "wake-up call." If heard, it beckons us to move toward wholeness by going within returning to our center.

Now I lean back in my chair. I look not at a corporate corner office, but at my own home, filled with symbols of a woman's life. I rejoice in who I am and extend my vision for a new story for our times outward to our world. I see that our planet, too, is in the same dark descent that marked the beginning of my midlife transition...and possibly your own.

We live in a time of what, in 1990, I termed "Continuous Discontinuous Change," which I define as the ongoing organic change process (a force field of its own) that is inconsistent (it erratically shows up and shifts direction unexpectedly) and, to boot, it is always changing vs. incremental over time. That said, we live in a time of intense upheaval and chaos. Our systems have broken down; our infrastructure is in grave disrepair. The homeless are on every corner. Many of our youth are distraught, lost, and suicidal, expecting an imminent demise of our planet and our way of life. Others are graduating in enormous debt for higher education costs. Our elderly are ignored or forgotten. Our middle-aged are out of work in record numbers.

We are besieged with plagues and natural disasters. Substance abuse is rampant. Crime is rising. Unrest is coming out of hiding into Main Street. Barbaric terrorism threatens the globe.

This too is menopause, our midlife passage on a global and societal level. As a society, we can move into the next phase awake, alert, responsible for what we are creating. But, first, we must heed the passwords: time-out, reflection, and awareness. We must be willing to take responsibility for our lives, confront our collective demons, mourn our losses and "if only's," then fully let go.

The Change

It is we PrimeTime peri- and post-menopausal women who will change the tides of our times. We will acknowledge, individually, the onset of our midlife, and our entry into a new Elderhood. By so doing, we will collectively create a space for a long overdue social acknowledgement: our country's midlife is here. We must spiral down and inward so that the wisdom of our Inner Wise Elder Woman Crone will be available to all who follow us.

For so many of us, the past few years have been personally and collectively challenging. We have been calling forth all our strength, demanding we dig deep to find our spiritual well so that we may dive and hone our emergency toolkits and, no matter what chaos touches us, we can return to center. The greatest gift of these times of epoch change has been the call to further unleash our Signature Greatness DNA. Sometimes the call is so silent, it is barely perceptible except to the trained ear. Other times it shakes us up like a cacophonous horn blowing for all the world's Souls to come to attention.

I'm always stumped when asked for simple tips on how to know when your Soul is calling. In my experience, both personally and as an invited witness for others, the call comes in a variety of ways as part of an ongoing process of Soulwork or Soul reclamation and deep transformation. It shows up as messengers in dreamtime and in real time, visitations and synchronicities, as well as chance encounters. The best tip I can give you is to ready your inner soil for the Soul to seed your consciousness with visitations and new awareness. I ask you to remember always that our vocation does not come from a voice "out there," rather it comes from a voice "in here." As I shared about Soulspeak a few pages back, your Soul will come calling if you are in a quiet safe space and you are expansively receptive to what emerges or shows up for you. Self-trust and non-judgment are key to your inner knowing. Do you recall dreams and consider symbolism? Are you paying attention to what attracts you—a color, an activity, a person, certain words or music? Your Soul will speak in its own language through dream symbols, words, and "ahas" that unexpectedly emerge across the screen of your mind, most often while engaged in activities in which you are present to the moment, such as meditating, dreaming, journaling, or walking in the woods.

All of history shows us that true greatness emerges in times of crisis and transition. When I ask folks to share who they think of when they think of greatness, the first answers are always the most notable: Abraham Lincoln, Mahatma Gandhi, Winston Churchill, Golda Meir, John F. Kennedy, Martin Luther King Jr., Mother Teresa, Nelson Mandela, Gloria Steinem, and now our youngest Nobel Peace Prize winner, Malala Yousafzai, age 17. All those leaders are visionaries who answer the clarion call of crisis and tragedy. All were called to meet the challenges of their day, and each rose to greatness.

Unfortunately, most people can't imagine that they also have the potential to reach their own greatness. More often than not, folks respond much like this accomplished woman client: "When I think of greatness, I think of MLK or Mother Teresa or JFK and can't imagine that I am like one of those people." It's not surprising that when surveyed, community

> All of history shows us that true greatness emerges in times of crisis and transition.

college students routinely said they wanted to reach greatness, but when asked what that meant for them they drew a blank.

Truth is whether you are a schoolteacher, a mad scientist, or a driven CEO, we all are made of the same stuff. After all, we have so much more to learn about our brains' capacity and the power of our unconscious mind. Just think, if we only could learn to master the capacity we have now, we would be making quantum leaps for humanity. It is the same with our innate Signature Greatness DNA.

Jim Collins, author of *Great by Choice* and consultant, and I are on the same wavelength when it comes to the source of greatness: "Greatness is not a function of circumstance. Greatness, it turns out, is largely a matter of conscious choice."

We all have enormously untapped reservoirs of our Signature Greatness DNA just waiting to be released. No matter what age, life cycle, or stage we are in, be it a stay-at-home mom or a soon-to-be retiree, we can bring our unique brand of Greatness DNA to whatever we do and to all we engage. It is our divine-given gift, and thus our responsibility as conscious human beings to share it with others so that they too may ignite their own genius within themselves. No matter what you are doing in the moment, whether it's planning for public housing for the elderly, changing diapers, mounting a fund-raiser, sitting on a board, or leading your own business, bring your unique Signature Greatness to it. These times demand it.

> We all have enormously untapped reservoirs of our Signature Greatness DNA just waiting to be released.

In broadest terms, greatness is a vague concept that is almost completely dependent on a person's perspective and biases. Without a clear personal definition, we can be assured to never reach our own greatness, much less catalyze someone else's.

As history teaches us, extraordinary greatness arises when we are faced with daunting challenges. In those harrowing moments, we are called to take emboldened stands for what matters most to us. This kind of greatness may come as if out of nowhere, brought to the forefront by unexpected momentous events.

Whatever the triggering event(s)—a major catastrophe or the normal ebb and flow of this cycle of life, a loss of a friend of forty years to cancer; unexpected divorce after twenty-five years, falling off the career track, or being toppled from the tower of power at age 50—each event thrusts us into transition and presents us with a life-changing challenge for us to meet and to awaken our own Signature Greatness DNA.

Like the mythic Sumerian goddess, Inanna, (called Persephone in later myths), who must first descend to the underworld to disrobe to her true putrefied self on death's hook before re-emerging as her potentiated Queen of the Overworld, or Odysseus, who must resist the call of the Sirens on his obstacle laden journey home—each of us blessed with these challenges will come face to face with our own Signature Greatness DNA encoded in our very cells since our life began.

It is we who are entering, in the midst of, or, like me, leaving our rich middle years, who can most assuredly tap into this reservoir of greatness. As history tells us, change makers and world shakers always deepen their culture and leave a legacy for future generations by confronting the difficulties of their times with invention, insight, and transcendent understanding. Just remember this: Getting from good to great and then to realizing our Signature Greatness is a moment-by-moment endeavor.

Moving in the Direction of Our Destiny

Ours is an era of quantum change,
the most radical deconstruction
and reconstruction the world has seen.

~ Jean Houston

Approaching the apex of our youthful years, disillusionment spreads like molten lava, burning up all that is not real. It is the primary task of midlife to confront our "reality" and to let go of cherished illusions like the childhood motto, "Follow the Golden Rule and nothing bad will happen to you." Or our Pollyannaish belief that our dearest ones will never betray or leave us. Or that good always prevails over evil. Perhaps the hardest of all to swallow are the dreams never realized, the opportunities now lost to our receding youth—the "never will bes" and the "if only's."

Midlife disillusionment is poignantly expressed by a 61-year-old male client who beseeches me with, "I did everything I was supposed to: I rose to the top of my field, earned seven, even eight figures, traveled the world and had my pick of women. I got everything I wanted and I still don't have what I need!"

The choices we now face as human beings, especially those of us in our PrimeTime, will determine whether we become extinct like prior cultures (ancient Egyptians, Romans, and Greeks), species (dinosaurs), and planets (once watered Mars), OR if we will rise to new expanded consciousness. We can make this epoch shift into a new paradigm but only by means of a complete transformation.

Whatever our challenges, both personally and collectively, we are all searching for ways to recognize our Soul's purpose—to find meaning in our everyday lives and to move in the direction of our destiny. Many of us are asking, "What really matters? Is this all there is? What is our purpose here? How can we lead effectively—and keep our Soul intact—during turbulent as well as good times? Visionary Leaders with Wrinkles have a sense of larger purpose and balance as they age and morph from lives of self-accomplishment to an even more enriching life of Soul-based greatness. These visionaries (like you and me) are seeking to not only achieve but to positively transform themselves and their world…locally and around the globe.

Don't get me wrong…finding your Soul's purpose and embracing your Signature Greatness DNA are not solely for the rarefied few. We are all capable of the same precious gift of living our destiny. It's a matter of choice, or staying on your quest to *The Ageless Way* until you embody your own unique Signature Greatness DNA. Now, with the gift of wisdom and a long life lived, I have come to understand that each of us births on this planet with our potential for greatness intact. I see it so boldly and with clarity when I experience the unique wonder of each of my grandchildren (and I recognized it in their parents when they were kids, too.) It's all so obvious early on. (I remember it so clearly in the joy of learning my adolescent students shared with me.) Unfortunately, somewhere along our early

We are all capable of the same precious gift of living our destiny.

life paths, we tend to lose our birthright and most of us miss our calling… only to spend our Third and Fourth Age trying to recover and reclaim our innate greatness.

I recently read that psychologist Rollo May (1909-1994), in describing his times, provided applicable insight and forewarning about our current times. His words caution us that we, like his clients, are reflections of our times: "The signs of the times is that the 'nothingness' (the lack of meaning) in their lives that drives so many of my clients into therapy equals a 'cry for myth, the cry for pattern, for meaning.' "

Through the challenges of our days, we are being called to discover our true purpose, to unleash our unique Signature Greatness and to bring who we are to our communities, workplaces and families. We are being called to find out what is most essential and true to each of us and to share that with the world.

What's Next?

A problem adequately stated is a problem well on its way to being solved.

~ R. Buckminster Fuller

Most of us are asking the same life-altering questions as we find ourselves standing at the precipice of change: How do I make decisions now since I don't know who I'm going to be…or what the world will be like by then?

We are all taking the time to redefine what's really important to us. Most of us, especially at midlife (and most definitely in our Elderhood) are taking stock at every level. We all want our lives to matter because the reality of life's brevity begins to really sink in as we get older. We enter new stages of life as transitions shake us to our roots.

"Life is so short!" writes Bonnie, a 50-something powerhouse caught between elder caretaking and her life passing her by. A 46-year-old family business owner asks, "How do I lead and live in these turbulent times?" A lamenting 38-year-old CEO who seems to have it all pleads, "I'm yearning for something I can't quite wrap my arms around." And a 41-year-old CFO of a Fortune 500 company exclaims, "It's all such BS! No more spin. Teach me how to be real."

Josephine, age 46, came to me because she wanted more intensity and vitality in life. "I've made it to the top. I have more money then I'll ever need, but I feel like I am wasting my life doing work I could do blindfolded or give to someone else to do. I have a great husband and all the toys. Now I want to live a life of value and creativity, to give back."

Just going to work every day to pay the bills or to save for retirement isn't the answer for most of us anymore, certainly not during or post Great Recession. So many of us have strived throughout our youth, driven by extrinsic rewards. We relied on acquisition to make us feel good. However, at midlife and beyond, many of us find the "wizard" of big bucks and corner offices is no big deal. We discover that there's no yellow brick road to the land of peace and abundance. Suddenly, almost everything we've been about no longer holds meaning. As we ponder our crossroads, we seek to find our significance.

A 55-year-old second generation family business owner exclaimed during a recent session, "Oh my G-d, I just got it…I have less time before me with my wife than we have behind us. We have got to change how we are doing things and make more time for what matters to us!"

The timing couldn't be more perfect.

We are in the early days of an epic epoch change. More of us are moving into and out of our midlife passage than ever before. Developmental gerontologists like myself now consider midlife to range from 38 to 70 (give or take on either end.) In fact, almost one half of the United States population is now over 40! By 2020, 78 percent of the United States population will be over 50 (Administration of Aging, 2002)! With these statistics comes the realization that "the fifty and older population from 2000-2050 will grow at a rate 68 times faster than the rate of growth for the total population." ("Beyond Workforce 2020," Hudson Institute).

While the ages may be different for developmental gerontologists, the founder of Jungian psychology Carl G. Jung, as well as developmental psychologists Maslow, Neugarten, and Erikson, left us developmental models and associated tasks to track our growth as we move through our life course. Anyone 38 or older is in what Erikson, in *Identity and the Life Cycle,* described as the last two seasons of life, autumn and winter. Since the majority of our citizenry in developed countries is over age 35, this is important in understanding our times and what moves us to action.

Seasons Of Life
Erik Erikson

© 2009 Karen Sands/Sands & Associates, LLC, adapted from Erik Erikson's model, Seasons of Life.

Understanding these powerful developmental models of successful aging and creative living against the backdrop of "finished by 40," makes it clear that we need a brand-new Ageless Story as well as tools for midlife course correction. Baby Boomers have always been drivers of change. Now they drive a dissipative structural shift as they demand lives filled with significance.

Most of our current leadership, at the helm of our most powerful corporations and governments, are in midlife. Many are now entering or in their later midlife, while more and more are already in early Elderhood. Clearly, they are in one of Erikson's last two seasons.

However, the paradigm is not only shifting for midlifers. Younger and younger people are seeing through the empty promises of a life that is only profit-driven and is not aimed at the betterment of others and the higher good in accordance with contributing to the Triple Bottom Line: People, Planet and Profit.

A hot-shot 33-year-old adamantly told me that she was going into her own business because she didn't want to play by the "not having a life" rules and wants more time for herself and her young family. In their book, *Midlife Crisis at 30*, Lia Macko and Kerry Rubin examine the process of self-evaluation that takes place with younger and younger adults…especially in post Great Recession, when young people are over-burdened with education debts and a lack of desirable jobs.

History proves that even in the worst of times, or even because of these times, we've always moved (been supported) toward our long-term betterment. It's not easy. In fact, it's tough and sometimes quite painful. That is the way of breakdowns into breakthroughs. As reported by Jungian analyst John Perry, who coined the term "renewal process," there is profound meaning and order to the process of transformation. Things may seem like they are falling apart, but there is the possibility for deep and expansive healing and restoration when we re-story.

My client, a 57-year-old married, brilliant international dealmaker, tells me: "Who ever thought at this time of life we'd be living from paycheck to paycheck? I've planted so many new seeds. Any of them taking hold will bring us great rewards. In the old days I'd just keep barreling forward… steam rolling whatever lay in my way to getting things to happen. Now I know better. I have to wait…and wait. So much of all this is pure luck, destiny and, as you say, trusting the process."

A perfect example of someone who has learned from experience and is using her personal history and decades-long patience to find opportunity, satisfaction, and meaning is 91-year-old Barbara Beskind. The title of the

Today Money story about her by Scott Stump (February 25, 2015, Today. com) sums up the story: " 'Age is not a barrier': Tech designer, 91, lands her dream job in Silicon Valley." Beskind's inventiveness began "out of necessity" during the Great Depression in the 1920s. As she tells it, "I wanted to make a hobby horse, and I made it out of old tires. I learned a lot about gravity because I fell off so many times." Though she wanted to be an inventor, she was told that women weren't accepted at engineering school. She, therefore, pursued other avenues and hobbies until, at 89, she followed her dream by applying, and being hired, for a job at the Silicon Valley global design firm, IDEO, working on the design of aging-related (age-friendly) products. While praising the welcoming intergenerational culture and atmosphere at the company, in the Today story Beskind also shared her perspective about hiring someone from her generation for that position. Suggesting that many younger designers "can't put themselves in the shoes of the elderly" and, therefore, often design for fashion rather than functionality, she shared her feeling that "elderly people bring experience that you can't teach."

The key learning for all of us, especially at midlife and into our elder post-70 years, is to allow life to happen, recognizing that many of the transitions that are taking place within and around us personally are also happening on the larger scale. Those of us who are astute will trust the process in front of us and leverage today's powerful changes into new opportunities for tomorrow, regardless of our age, stage, or life cycle. Each of us is being called into a self-renewal process, as is our Mother Earth.

Life is not the way it's supposed to be.
It's the way it is.
The way you cope with it
is what makes the difference.

~ Virginia Satir

The "then" time frame for some people encompasses the next two to five years, and for others, ten to fifteen; however, what is the same for all is that these questions range from the more profound—*Why am I here? Is this all there is?*—to the more fundamental practical decisions about where to go from here in our personal and professional lives.

- When do I step down and pass the baton?
- What's my new passion?
- Should I join some company boards, or rev up and start a new business?
- Can I afford to downshift?
- Is this the relationship I want now?
- How do I turn my empty nest into a launching pad?
- How do I make a lasting impact?

The clock is ticking louder and louder, what I call "Beat the Clock Syndrome," (Sands, 1988). Just as in adolescence, most of us are teetering between in control and out of control. Each "what if?" requires a multitude of compromises and leads to more complicated scenarios without obvious answers. Caught in the race against time, we are confronted with the tremendous terror of not knowing. The million-dollar question is *How do we live in between?*

This living in between is but another phase and skill set to hone on the Ageless Quest I described in chapter four, "Ageless Women." We have to stay in the center of time and wait it out. We have to sit in our worst fears. I know that if I resist, my fear manifests even more. Instead of staving off the fear of the unknown with my favorite numbing tricks (filling myself with extra helpings of carbs, obsessing over roads not taken, buying something I probably don't need), I must instead find a safe middle ground. A place within where time doesn't exist, where it's okay to not know…yet. An Ageless place. That's where real clarity is birthed.

This Ageless place within is filled with trust and patience. Even in the worst of times, I've always known that I'm supported and guided. Oh, my very astute rational mind will make mincemeat out of my deep abiding trusting nature if I let it. I've learned the hard way that if I can get out of my own way and stop pushing the stream in the direction I want it to go, I'll find myself totally in the flow, riding on top of the waves to my destiny. Happens every time. It will for you, too.

"Voice Dialogue" is a powerful deep discovery process I learned years ago and work with to this day. The Voice Dialogue methodology and modality were originally created and taught by Drs. Hal and Sidra Stone, authors of *Embracing Your Inner Critic.* Over the decades, I've morphed my own version of their work to fit the needs of my clients as they wend their way on *The Ageless Way.* This modality and discovery process has worked incredibly well for me to keep my clients attuned to the "wu wei" (Chinese Taoist concept of "action without action" or "effortless doing") to keep flowing in their lives.

Combined with my adaptation of the Voice Dialogue modality, I also employ Expressive Arts therapy (a blending of art, dance/movement, meditation, guided imagery, inner quests, and more). In addition, I provide a variety of empowering exercises (e.g., clients literally trace out their "Life Story Events Map," as well as creating a "Peaks & Valleys Career Map").

None of these modalities and exercises are parlor games, so they should be conducted, created, and analyzed under the guidance of a trained facilitator. I mention them here so that if you want to explore any of these modalities and exercises as you move along on *The Ageless Way*, please send me an email at Karen@KarenSands.com or give me a call at 203-266-1100.

But while I wait, my task is to keep striving for greater consciousness, stretching to unleash my unique Signature Greatness DNA and to reawaken the visionary within.

Now more than ever, it is critical that we remain flexible and adaptable, making friends with change, with not knowing…with certain uncertainty! This is our time to tap our resources—within and without. Seek the counsel of professional coaches, therapists, and advisors as we prepare for a new phase or a totally new cycle. Now is the time to invite change and embrace transformation.

We must create our own eye in the storm of time, a place of inner calm where we look objectively at the possibilities around us instead of being pushed relentlessly forward by the ticking of the clock, which inevitably leads us in haste to make the safe decisions, but not necessarily the right ones.

Once we find that center, that space between time and timelessness, we must anchor ourselves with proper assessment tools and the knowledge and experience of every resource available to us. With this anchor in place we can move forward with purpose, passion, and profit toward what matters most to us, to our communities, and to our world. We can create the new story of our times.

All we have to remember is to stay in motion. That's the key to longevity! As with most things in life, our great learning is to seek both/and vs. either/or. So we must welcome the in-between times to reflect, to hear our Soul-speak in the silence, and to regain new clarity. Because we must remember that heading into action without clarity is as dangerous as it was for King Sisyphus. Otherwise, we may miss the gift of what Bucky Fuller coined as a right-angle precession. Tracing patterns in nature, Fuller uncovered a new truth: We must stay open to what shows up, although it may look like a detour. It may very well be our destiny honking.

All we have to remember is to stay in motion. That's the key to longevity!

What Does "Reinvention" Mean?

I use the word "reinvention" often because it is a necessary process for most of us as we go through transitions: career transitions; life transitions, such as entering midlife or Elderhood; relationship transitions; and the transitions we face in our lives, work, and businesses from the epochal changes the entire planet is undergoing—economic, environmental, social.

What exactly do I mean when I use this word?

People sometimes think that reinvention means dropping everything and starting on a new path. Although this might be what we need to do at times, in my experience that is rare. This misconception can lead people to a cycle of starting new endeavors without ever finishing any of them because when they hit a rough patch they "reinvent" again, rather than reassessing along the way and making necessary shifts while continuing to move forward.

Furthermore, that's not really reinvention at all. It's essentially a cycle of invention without the all-important prefix, just as revising a story is not the same as writing a completely new one. Reinvention is essentially a revision of your story, a re-storying. It's a process of working with who you are, where you are, what you've done, are doing, and are capable of. It means looking at the story you are in right now and all the possible directions for the plot in the future, and then choosing the plot line that you most want to experience in your future story.

Reinvention is a process of building and transforming based on the best of you as well as the core of what really matters to you. Yes, you often have to toss out old definitions of yourself and of success, as well as aspects of your life that do not really matter, that are merely clutter. You have to remove the tangential plot lines, the side stories that distract from the main plot, and sometimes you even have to cut characters who are dragging the story down. Reinvention is a purification process, getting down to your essence, to your Signature Greatness DNA, and to your core values. But you don't toss out the gold with the dross.

This is an important distinction in these uncertain times. If we look at reinvention as an either/or prospect—either I continue doing exactly what I'm doing or I discard it all and do something completely different—many of us will feel stuck, knowing we can't afford to throw it all away. Others will throw it all away and very likely find themselves with nothing to show for it because they also tossed what they needed.

Either/or thinking is not the answer. Reinvention is about both/and. You can continue moving forward on your path, doing what you need to do pragmatically while also getting in touch with your Ageless Visionary voice, with what matters most to you. You can identify what needs to go and develop a plan toward your vision that includes the best of both worlds, the best of who you are now and who you can be.

Emilio Prodo, age 50, president of Life Reimagined, states, "Many fifty-year-olds have twenty to twenty-five years of work ahead of them, and

> Either/or thinking is not the answer. Reinvention is about both/and.

they want another experience, they want to do something more meaningful, but they want to apply the experience they have."

In the words of Nietzsche, "Remember: You will have many stages of life, each a chance to reinvent yourself and contribute to the world in a different way. It's through these experiences that you will learn how to excel in a rapidly changing world." I couldn't have said this any better!

Dreamtime is a rich resource to mine while you travel on your reinvention quest. When I finally allowed my midlife reinvention spiral path to be revealed, I was guided to my renewed work in a dream I had that foretold that I was entering into a new growth period.

> *I am in my cellar workroom, a place where I come to translate my unconscious into collages. To move with the new pulsing within me. I am engrossed in this artistic endeavor. I pause, look to the window…light is streaming. Flowers in the field outside are vibrant with color. I smile to feel so alive! Looking behind, I see a green sprout push through the cellar floor. It unfolds before my eyes! Such a beautiful sight, this new life. It emerges with vigor and grace. I move toward the plant, and it wraps its tender leaves ever so gently around me. Then I hear something metallic fall to the floor, as if falling from the plant's unfurled leaves. I pick it up, hold it in my hand: It is a coin, a very old coin. On one side there is the face of a midlife woman. On the other side, a woman's very ancient face.*

Ancient Future (Sands, 1992) appeared at every significant juncture. I knew then that this archetypal force would continue to teach, heal, and guide from within me. I understood in my belly that having come through this passage, my new work would be to guide other "accomplished women" through their passage into the mysteries of midlife womanhood, as well as Elderhood. That's how my renewed professional life began again in the mid-1990s.

My mythic visions continue to give me hope and the courage to be in the here and now, and to still find meaning no matter how many times I'm asked to struggle. Even the mythic King Sisyphus had to learn that we can't trick death or the gods. So I too honor the ongoing organic cyclic changes which return me to rolling myself up a new mountain each time, always knowing I won't give up the struggle. I'm not in love with it; I just won't let anyone or anything keep me down. You count on this; I will keep showing up triumphantly because my fate is in my hands!

The Difference Between Reinventing and Rearranging

In my years of experience, I have found that there are two approaches to both reinvention and to how we age. We have to make a conscious choice in both cases, or we will be thrust into doing so by forces beyond our control. Most of us are brought to this choice point by one or more, likely a series of major life triggering events. Our choice is either/or. The more commonly selected approach is the more cursory, no-risk, and the surface solution-finding, thereby bypassing the more risky route of transformation. Others, like me, choose to follow the more Radical Reinvention approach, which takes us on a far deeper dive, or into the "descent" into lasting transformation. I've depicted this "either/or" approach in my Evolutionary Spiral of Reinvention model on page 273.

...when I'm talking about reinvention, I'm talking about Radical Reinvention in which the ultimate goal is transformation.

Make no mistake: When I'm talking about reinvention, I'm talking about Radical Reinvention in which the ultimate goal is transformation. There's a danger to being too cautious under the guise of being realistic or practical.

When a room in your home doesn't serve you—the space doesn't work for how you use the room; the furniture is too big, too small, too inappropriate for the task; and the overall atmosphere is too closed, too open, too shabby, too stressful—you have a couple of options. You can rearrange the furniture, maybe throw up a coat of paint, and that will help to a degree in the short term. Or you can knock down some walls, replace the furniture, and completely redesign the decor—basically reinvent the room to serve your purpose, and to serve others who use that room, in every possible way.

We face the same choice in our lives, our careers, and especially in our businesses. For example, established and new entrepreneurs faced with globalization, rapidly changing technology, and the seemingly never-ending fallout from the Great Recession can't simply rearrange our businesses. Restructuring, downsizing, and pinching pennies—these are not enough to survive, much less thrive. We have to transform how we do business, and we have to do it now.

In my work over the decades, I have learned that people say they want change, and then they limit their own sense of what changes are possible for them (especially those who've "been there, done that"). Focusing solely on rearranging our lives feeds the limitations, sucking us back into the status quo—doing more of the same—rather than inspiring us to climb the summit that takes us beyond what we believe is possible to doing what we never thought we could.

We are all different, at various points on the spiral of life. Post-recession, some people by necessity must reenter the workforce or focus on remaining there and, for them, for now, rearranging is absolutely a positive move, a way to improve on the status quo without taking risks they can't afford to take or simply do not wish to take. But this necessity is a means, not an end, a necessary step on the journey to larger transformation.

To mentally close that door to more out of life and work by assuming it is impossible and dangerous to move through is as much a mistake as diving through that door blind and without any preparation.

Yes, reinvention carries risk, but closing the door to reinvention is also risky. The risk is not just to the individual, but to our Mother Earth as a whole and the next seven generations who will suffer if enough of us do not collectively strive for anything short of personal and global transformation.

These insightful words shared by Dr. W. Edwards Deming decades ago have kept me on my path ever since: "The first step is transformation of the individual. This transformation is discontinuous. …The individual, transformed, will perceive new meaning to life, to events, to numbers, to interactions between people." These times demand not the "same as before" approaches; these times demand rather new approaches to meet and thrive in the midst of massive Creative Destruction. Disintegration and reintegration are a necessary part of this evolutionary reinvention now beckoning us into the future.

Reinvention is not a myth, although it may require a mythic call for action…our call to greatness…based on the archetypal hero and heroine's

We have to transform how we do business, and we have to do it now.

journey, which each of us traverses from midlife into Elderhood, what I call "Crossing the Canyon of the Soul" (Sands, 1997). Now is the last chance we get to embrace the gift of turning crises into opportunities.

Myths are stories to help us re-story our own journeys. Now Baby Boomers need to re-story both our generational journey from the 1960s and our own individual stories as we move through midlife into our elder years.

Myths are stories to help us re-story our own journeys.

Not everyone will be called or will answer this call, but those of us who do cannot afford to dismiss it as impossible or even impractical. We all face the same questions, even if our answers may differ. The right questions are far more important than the answers.

What will your/our new story be?

- What kind of human(s) do you/we want to be?
- What future do you/we want? Same old status quo or one that is impactful, even transformative?

Transitions force us, if we hear the call, to sift through the kernels of our prior story like the fairy tales of our childhood, like the corn in the story of Vasilisa and Baba Yaga (see chapter four, "Ageless Women") or Rotten Eyes (see chapter one, "The Ageless Way") weaving the flax thread for the Queen Mother. Under the guidance of the sacred dark feminine, the wise woman Crone (whether portrayed by Baba Yaga or the Queen Mother), each of our heroines gained the skill of discernment, as well as each owning who they fully were, inside and out. These breakdowns and their enormous potential for rebirth, reclamation, and re-storying are classic for the archetypal hero's and heroine's journey and necessary for the future of us all.

We are the Visionaries with Wrinkles on our faces from all we, Boomers and those on the cusp, (on either end of the age spectrum, forties and seventies), have faced as a generation. We are the ones we've been waiting for. We must not miss our cue to reinvent not just ourselves, but our world, now that we have the hard-earned wisdom and experience to do it.

I'd be remiss not to both clarify and underscore here that this new story is not only about Baby Boomers; it is about all generations. Boomers are being called to lead the way. For some, the calling is an inner knowing that comes from deep within, a pulling toward some vision, a mission, a passion…it is the reason each of us is on the Earth at this time. Sometimes a calling arises out of tragic loss or crisis. For others, it may be numinous connection with something far greater than we mere humans. Whatever its source, or what we call it, it can fluctuate between a quiet whispering to a fire inside burning brightly. For me, there have been (and continue to be) synchronicities, messengers, and happenings like the appearance of Ancient Future, the Elder woman in the mirror as she guided me on *The Ageless Way*. There's no denying destiny. What gets my mojo going every day is bringing illumination to our stories, especially those stories we own (as if our own) around what it means to grow older, our place in the future, and how we will show up in the world. Women Boomers are being asked to light the way as Vasilisa was asked by Baba Yaga when given the luminous fiery skull on the stick to light her way to her home and hearth.

You Are Here…Now What?

Once the "what" is decided, the "how" always follows.

~ Pearl S. Buck

Before you can move into a new aspirational future, it is important to know where you are now so you can realistically futurecast possible scenarios or stories as to where you want to end up. As I share a series of models of reinvention and renewal, please take the time to determine where you are now vs. where you want to be going forward.

Many of you are probably familiar with developmental psychologist Abraham Maslow's Hierarchy of Needs, which is typically depicted as a pyramid with our most fundamental needs for food, water, security, love, and so on forming the foundational rows of the pyramid. Without meeting these basic reptilian needs, Maslow theorized, we would not be motivated to fulfill our higher-level needs for esteem and self-actualization.

AGELESS AGING

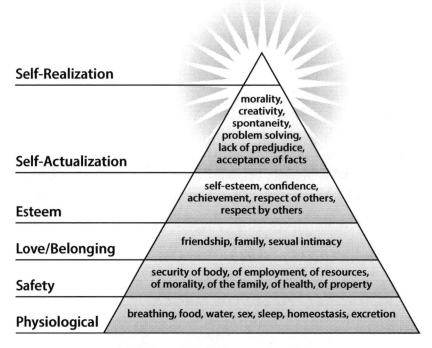

Self-Realization

Self-Actualization — morality, creativity, spontaneity, problem solving, lack of predjudice, acceptance of facts

Esteem — self-esteem, confidence, achievement, respect of others, respect by others

Love/Belonging — friendship, family, sexual intimacy

Safety — security of body, of employment, of resources, of morality, of the family, of health, of property

Physiological — breathing, food, water, sex, sleep, homeostasis, excretion

© 2009 Karen Sands/Sands & Associates, LLC

In his own words, Maslow called us to actualize our own unique Signature Greatness DNA: "The story of the human race is the story of men and women selling themselves short."

I believe there is yet one more level beyond self-actualization, and that is self-realization, the height of consciousness, when we fully realize our connection to all there is, to others, to the Earth, to the universe. I've added self-realization to the tippy tip of Maslow's pyramid on the illustration. Every particle within and without us is interacting as part of larger systems. Truly realizing this connectivity takes self-actualization to a new level, where we can act consciously in ways that ripple out beyond our selves, affecting our world profoundly.

A pervasive craving for transcendence or wholeness is spreading like a viral epidemic. As early as 1990, Christina and Stanislav Grof, M.D.s, forecast that what many of us would be experiencing as a "spiritual bank-ruptcy" or "Soul sickness" were precursors to the dark night of the Soul that ushers in the dawn of healing and transformation.

Another way to format Maslow's pyramid model is as a spiral. We spend our lives circling further and further inward as we meet our basic needs and strive for those that can only be met by delving inside ourselves. Once we reach self-actualization, when we are whole and have what we need inside to bring fulfillment to our outer world, we can radiate outward again as we achieve self-realization, in a spiral whose arms reach out to infinity and back again.

Sidra Stone, author of *The Shadow King* and more, describes our Earth walk as "where we're born and we walk this spiral away from our essential selves. We develop inner selves to protect us, and ways of being in the world that are creative and extraordinarily useful. They make us capable of living and being successful. Then at some point we stop, and we start walking back along the spiral towards our center, and we pick up what we've left, we pick up the opposites, and we stop to dis-identify from whatever it is we've been identified with. The road is back, back to who we are, but carrying with us everything that we've accumulated over the years. It's an enrichment, and it's about keeping the gifts while moving back towards who we are, whom we really are. I think that is for me what conscious aging is about. It's as though each of us comes in with a song to sing, and we have a tendency to lose it, to lose the awareness of it, whereas conscious aging is listening more and more for that song. Moving more and more toward what belongs to us…to what energetically harmonizes with our own song" (*Visionaries Have Wrinkles*, 2012).

Many people have yet to fully reach the higher levels of Maslow's pyramid, or find themselves at either end of the spiral but never long in the center part of the spiral, much less willingly hanging out in their descent represented as the lower end of the spiral! Even those who have reached self-actualization may find themselves slipping—or falling fast—toward the lower rungs of the pyramid, or outer arms of the spiral, because discontinuous change—super storms and other extreme weather events, the economic roller coaster—is ripping apart everything we thought we knew.

Perhaps those who have felt actualized and come close to self-realization may find themselves suddenly at the bottom of the pyramid due to a triggering event or perhaps a combination of multiple events, like job loss, divorce, disease or impairment, natural disasters, or loss of loved ones, to name only a smattering of universally shared triggers. It is difficult to focus on those higher needs when other, more fundamental needs are being unmet. Attempting reinvention based on where you were in the past or where you want to be will likely leave you frustrated, stalled, and ultimately burned out and depressed.

Before you can create preferred futures, based on alternative stories, you have to first assess exactly where you are now. One of the first steps is to examine your current state and then commit to continuously reducing your variations until you are within Six Sigma degrees of variation in every aspect of your life and work.

CONTINUALLY REDUCING THE VARIABILITY

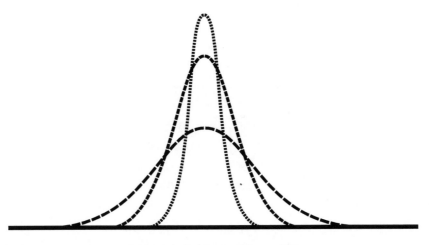

© 2009 Karen Sands/Sands & Associates, LLC

All transitions get kicked off by a triggering event(s). Once in play there's really no turning back. We can vacillate or stomp our feet but there are only two possible routes available once you find yourself, your relationships, or your company in a transition. The most effective model I have come up with to depict these two pathways, I call the Evolutionary Spiral of Reinvention.

EVOLUTIONARY SPIRAL OF REINVENTION

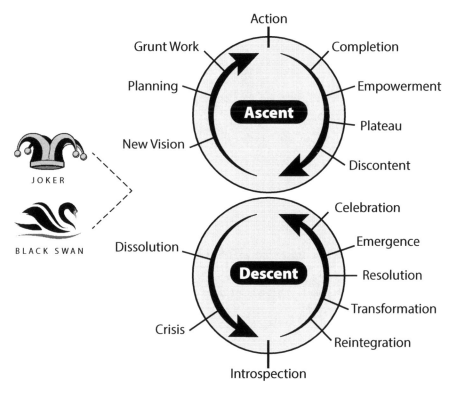

©2009 Karen Sands/Sands & Associates, LLC

The triggering event may not be a surprise. The triggering events that bring us to our knees are what we in foresight call either a "Trickster" or "Joker" event, which is a not-unheard-of or unexpected event, like a lay-off or the death of an aged parent. But the more potent "Black Swan" event is totally unexpected and not in the realm of known possibilities. This category of triggering events gets its name from the sighting of the very first black swan.

A Joker triggering event forces us to take immediate action to rearrange our circumstances so we can quickly find a new vision and implement it using our tried and true know-how and skills perfected to date. A Trickster event requires your current level of problem-solving skills with the help of an outplacement or career counselor.

The more potent Black Swan triggering events force us into a mega-crisis by moving us into breakdown that over time forges a deep and triumphant lasting transformation. The latter descent requires a transformational professional to illuminate the way through darkness into the light.

We don't always get to choose which end of the spiral we traverse. I know for me that the heady route is a surface one that serves us in most transition circumstances. I far prefer the double whammy of moving from descent to ascent, from the bottom end of the spiral around and up the ascent to the top of the spiral that demands an in-body experience where our whole circuitry is rewired.

To make your ascent more of a sure thing ask, "What is my present story?"

The following questions are so critical for a sustainable radical reinvention that I suggest you scan and ponder these as you read on. To make sure you capture your responses, I've included these same questions at the end of this chapter in the Reflections.

- What are your strengths and weaknesses? What would others say are your strengths and weaknesses? (Think of colleagues, clients, family, friends. Even better—ask them!)

- What are your greatest accomplishments? What strengths did you use to achieve them? What weaknesses and challenges did you overcome and how?

- What do you regret doing? What do you regret not doing?

- What basic needs must you fill right now? What desires would you like to fulfill knowing all your basic needs are met?

- What has changed for you in the past three years? What trends can you see in these changes that are likely to affect the next three?

- What were your biggest priorities five, ten, and twenty years ago? What are your biggest priorities now?

- What are your biggest challenges today?

- What legacy do you want to leave for the next seven generations and beyond?

This is just part of the assessment my clients routinely work through from the get-go. Before we can move on to the next step, or onto the next turn on their personal spiral of evolution, or reach their next level of success however they self-describe it—we have to together figure out what the next step is! Most people are unsatisfied with the status quo but are uncertain about what they can do to change it. In David Brooks's column for The New York Times, he talks about these self-assessments, what he calls life reports. One key point Brooks makes is that the biggest regrets people have about their lives are what they *didn't* do. What's more important: "Nobody regretted the life changes they made, even when they failed."

In other words, you may not know exactly what to do next, but you can be sure of one thing: You have to do something. In the words of Aristotle, "Where the needs of the world and your talents cross, there lies your vocation."

> You may not know exactly what to do next, but you can be sure of one thing: You have to do something.

Future Tasks

This time, like all times, is a very good one,
if we but know what to do with it.

~ Ralph Waldo Emerson

Mastering these eight future tasks will transform your transition into an opportunity: 1) Acknowledge accomplishments; 2) Face failures; 3) Resolve what can't be; 4) Let go of the past but don't forget it; 5) Be more conscious; 6) Make better conscious choices; 7) Continually reduce the variability in your life and work; 8) Choose new success goals for your future.

Beyond Mere Success

Most of us have several successes under our belts, such as getting that job or promotion, hitting or exceeding a profit or fund-raising goal, starting and sustaining our own businesses, and so on. Many of us also know how it feels to reach that big goal and think, *Is this all there is?* Somehow, the accomplishment doesn't feel the way we thought it would. We still feel unfulfilled, longing for something more.

This frequently comes down to the definition of success we started with when we first began working toward our big goal. If we did not consciously think through that definition, to determine what success really means to us beyond the superficial achievement, we could easily find that the attainment of our goal is itself superficial. More often than not, we act out the stories our society tells us about success, only to find them two-dimensional.

Often, by the time we achieve what we set out to do, we discover that our dreams have changed, that we have changed. If we did not continuously reassess our path and ourselves along the way, our present story, we could end up exactly where we're headed but not where we want to be.

Sometimes the problem lies in thinking too small right from the start. We strive for visions that are safe and relatively easy to accomplish rather than taking a risk on the BIG dream that our visionary voice is telling us to pursue. The result? Not only do our successes never feel like enough, but we often feel like we are not enough, which only feeds our fears and pushes us even more to take the safe route, to dream small.

Therefore, by giving in to your fears and playing it safe you are feeding your fears, not lessening them. In the process, you are robbing yourself of the passion you would feel every day if you were working toward a big vision of meaningful, sustainable success, of transformation, reinvention—of making a difference in your life, your work, your world.

Sustainable Success

Do what you love. Follow your passion. Live your Soul's purpose. These ideas have an almost universal appeal, and they are, of course, true. Yet how we go about achieving these is where many of us get stuck.

Some people just make the leap—quitting their unfulfilling job, starting a new business, committing to a cause they are passionate about—without any planning. This impulsive decision often stems from reading or listening to something motivational or from a "last straw" event that pushes them to do something—anything—to feel in control of their own destiny again. This initial passion is exciting, but as unplanned-for obstacles emerge, those bursts of motivation quickly give way to frustration and sometimes despair. For some, these experiences seem to provide proof that in the real world, most people simply don't have the luxury of achieving meaningful success in their everyday lives and work.

And that's a shame, because the problem isn't what they are striving to achieve—it's how they are going about it.

Others suffer from the opposite problem, although it has just as much to do with control—an almost addictive habit of planning to the exclusion of taking any action. Often these plans dictate taking action after something happens—after the economy improves, after retirement, after banks start giving small business loans again, after the kids are out of the house, after …life. This type of planning does not tend to include the kind of flexibility required not only to act in the first place but also to course correct along the way. Because if one thing is static in life, it's that discontinuous change will always occur.

A third subset of people are those who plan and take action. They accomplish much of what they set out to accomplish, and most people would say they are successful, yet no matter how much they achieve, they still feel as if something's missing. This feeling usually stems from one of two things: changing priorities and definitions of success or neglecting to define what sustainable success really means to them in the first place. The story they want to live is not in sync with the story they are creating. Working long hours for profit isn't satisfying no matter how much you make if your definition of sustainable success includes having the time and energy to spend with friends and family. Earning that promotion can feel hollow if what you are doing every day feels purposeless, achievement for the sake of achievement.

On the surface, these problems all appear to be very different problems, but the solution for all of them lies in the preparation stage. First, you need to redefine what sustainable success means to you so that you don't sacrifice what's really important for lesser goals or for a definition of success that isn't entirely your own. Part of this definition should include fulfilling your

Soul's destiny—knowing what you stand for—so if you haven't figured out what that is yet, don't rush this stage, no matter how eager you are to start transforming your life, career, or business. Doing this requires awakening (or reawakening) the Ageless Visionary we all have inside and learning to really listen to that voice, cultivating the many characteristics that tend to come with age (but are not guaranteed!) such as wisdom, creativity, and perspective.

Next, determine what's missing today from your present story and what will be needed tomorrow. Take these big issues and choose one problem to solve at a time. Break it down into its smaller components so you can get your head and Soul around them.

Then create a plan that encompasses alternative future scenarios. Play around with old and new narratives, but focus on the aspirational future story that you most want to create. Remember that we are wired to create our future. By envisioning alternative future stories at the outset, you create the best opportunity to realize the future you most desire.

Too often, our plans are rigid, not taking into account how the world might change or how we will change. Do your homework and consider different end scenarios. These alternative outcomes will inform the actions you will need to take. Build flexibility into your best-case plan. Assume you will encounter obstacles and think through what you will do about them. A plan that includes many possible avenues not only makes it more likely that you'll reach your destination; it can also ease much of the fear that keeps you perpetually in the planning stage.

Make the future happen your way! The time is now! It's never too late.

Caution vs. Hesitation

Before making any big change in our lives—particularly before reinventing ourselves, our work, our world—it makes sense to pause and get in touch with our Inner Visionary voice. If we aren't clear about what really matters to us, we risk pursuing goals that leave us feeling empty even if we are successful.

Even once we have a vision for transforming our world, we need to take the time to do our homework, to fill in the gaps in our knowledge—about facts, trends, emerging markets, and so on—and build our game plan based on this solid foundation, this understanding of our present story and probable alternative future scenarios.

Sensible caution, patience, and a whole lot of trust are essential to creating a future of sustainable, meaningful success. But once we have a plan in place, we need to act without hesitation, because as with leaping across a chasm, it pays to determine how far the other side is so that you know exactly what you are leaping toward and how much of a running start you need. Once you start running, you have to leap decisively. If you hesitate even a little, you won't make it across.

We often blur the line between caution and hesitation by over- planning, getting caught in the research, the to-do lists, thinking we need to create a perfect plan before we risk taking action. Of course, there's no such thing as a perfect plan. If we allow our inner perfectionist to overwhelm our Inner Visionary, we might as well never plan at all, for we'll never act. If you build periodic reassessment into your plan, you do not need to hesitate. Just leap and then reassess the next leap after you're on the other side.

In the end, we don't always control when our visions will come to fruition. Along with planning for continuous reassessment, we have to account for lag time between the actions we take and the fruit they bear. But one thing is guaranteed: The longer you take to act, the longer you will wait for your vision to be realized. You do control your actions. You do control every leap you take.

> The longer you take to act, the longer you will wait for your vision to be realized.

Sometimes, we hesitate because we are the first ones to ever attempt the jump. Maybe we should wait until someone else tries it. Then we'll know we can do it. But if we wait, the opportunity may be lost to us forever. Or we might be sitting on this side of the chasm next to everyone else who is waiting for us to go first.

We are the Ageless Visionaries we have been waiting for. Pause to look before you leap—not during. Then go for it with gusto.

No One Wins the Waiting Game

Many of us are waiting out the aftereffects of the Great Recession. We're playing it safe, not taking any risks, putting off our next big steps, the transformations we long to make in our lives and work, until the winds of global economic change die down. We've locked the doors, boarded up the windows, and headed down into the basement.

The problem is that boarded-up windows not only keep the winds from coming in, but they also keep us from seeing out—we close off our perspective, our ability to see the big picture. Sometimes playing it safe and sticking with the status quo is the most unsafe choice we can make.

When we finally venture out from our basements and tentatively open our doors, we are likely to see a different world out there, one created and reshaped by the people who didn't hide away, who instead realized that the only way to survive was to start planning the rebuilding process before the structure collapsed, not after.

Post the Great Recession it's been harder and harder to stay on the job until retirement age. The picture for older workers is mixed. It's true that more older workers are in the labor force, and the good news is that they are experiencing lower unemployment rates than younger workers. But older workers who lose their jobs unfortunately tend to be out of work longer and earn less when they do find a new position.

If you are 50-plus and you want to be in the game, then AARP's latest trends to watch will be of interest:

- Desire to work longer is rising.
- Unemployment is down.
- Length of joblessness is longer.
- Age discrimination remains a major worry.
- Over-70 crowd is pushing the envelope.

We are likely to find that the place we held in the old world, that we so desperately tried to protect, no longer exists. And because we weren't part of creating the new world, the new story for our future, we also weren't part of creating and ensuring our place in it.

Now, I'm not suggesting that you just abandon everything and throw yourself out into the storm. If you are an executive or a business owner, you need to start preparing to lead change by figuring out exactly what that means and how you can stay ahead of the curve of change without abandoning what already works in your organization.

If you are not financially ready to start that new business you've been longing to start, quitting your job today isn't the answer. But as I've said before, the choice isn't either/or. It isn't either you stay at an unfulfilling job or you risk everything and start your business. The choice is both/and.

Stay at the job while you take concrete steps toward starting your business, going beyond just dreaming about it. Commit to taking action every day to build it, and taking into account the bigger world picture as you do. The world is undergoing an epochal shift. Build your business based on what the world needs and will need, based on likely trends as well as the changes you want to see in the world. If you build your future assuming it will look like the past, your business will be obsolete before you even open its doors. In fact, the business of the future might not even have doors, not the way we've always thought of them, anyway.

Waiting on the world to change is the riskiest move we could ever make—not because it won't, but because it will.

In the words of Steve Jobs, founder of Apple, "Your time is limited, so don't waste it living someone else's life. Don't be trapped by dogma—which is living with the results of other people's thinking. Don't let the noise of others' opinions drown out your own inner voice. And most important, have the courage to follow your heart and intuition. They somehow already know what you truly want to become. Everything else is secondary." ❯

CHAPTER 9 ~ *The Ageless Way Reflections*

The questions and exercises below are to help you find your distinct path on The Ageless Way. Turn to page 28 for more about The Ageless Way Reflections.

1. Reflect on this period of your life. How would you change it? When did this time of reinvention start for you? Was there an event or experience that marks the beginning of your current transition? Do you find yourself at the beginning or the middle, or perhaps at the end of this transition at this time? What resources and/or tools are you using to support yourself as you make the trek from what is ending to what is newly beginning?

2. Write down all your either/or choices related to reinventing your life, your career, your business. First, determine which are no-brainers, where one option is clearly superior to the other. Next, look at what's left and think about how you can have both/and instead of either/or in each situation.

3. What does "sustainable success" mean to you? When you envision yourself living every day by what you stand for, bringing your Soul's purpose to everything you do, whether at the company helm or around the kitchen table, what does your preferred alternative future look like, feel like, sound like? With whom, where, and when?

4. Take a moment now to do a spin-off of the life report—the Future Report. Imagine yourself one year into the future, looking back at your life, and answer the same questions above. Now try it again, imagining who you are five years from now. Be honest based on where you are now. What answers are you happy about? What answers do you need to change? What will your future self-regret? What will you do now to change the course you are on? How will you reclaim your future?

5. What's your present story?

    These questions have been asked earlier in this chapter and repeated here so you can take your time to dig deeper.

    - What are your strengths and weaknesses? What would others say are your strengths and weaknesses? (Think of colleagues, clients, family, friends. Even better—ask them!)

    - What are your greatest accomplishments? What strengths did you use to achieve them? What weaknesses and challenges did you overcome and how?

    - What do you regret doing? What do you regret not doing?

    - What basic needs must you fill right now? What desires would you like to fulfill knowing all your basic needs are met?

    - What has changed for you in the past three years? What trends can you see in these changes that are likely to affect the next three?

    - What were your biggest priorities five, ten, and twenty years ago? What are your biggest priorities now?

    - What are your biggest challenges today?

    - What legacy do you want to leave for the next seven generations and beyond?

Chapter 10
LETTING GO

*So I believe that we can't, in late life, get set in our ways—
fixed on what we used to do, on what was accustomed, or on what
others expect us to do. We must always be open to each new day,
to the future. My ability to survive and keep on plugging is an
outgrowth of my passion for hope and change. …We must always
be open to each new day, to the future, to new opportunities.
They're there, but we have to be ready to see them.*

~ Maggie Kuhn, activist and writer
founder, Gray Panthers

Phoenix Rising Redux

*As I escaped the fire, stepping over the front threshold with one foot—
the only way out of the engulfing flames and choking smoke—I heard in
my head, "Call Mark's name!" I shook my head to dismiss the voice, for
my husband, Mark, was at the gym, miles away. But as I brought my
remaining foot forward, the insistent voice clamored, breaking through
my instinct to propel myself over the threshold and far from the flames.*

*I stepped back into the billowing smoke and fire and yelled for Mark
as loud as I could muster through the heat and soot, screaming, "Maarrk!"
Only then, as I turned to save myself, I glimpsed Mark stumbling out,
disoriented, from a back hallway, nearly asphyxiated. A few more seconds
and my love would've been gone, overcome with smoke, and burnt to a crisp.*

*I stood outside in the cold 2001 January air, watching flames devour
my home and office. As the wooden beams and all our possessions crackled
under the heat, I took a deep breath. "It's just stuff…only stuff. Let it go."*

Managing Loss and Renewal

Being a veteran survivor of sudden and prolonged tragic loss, I knew that this fire was the beginning of a major life-shaking and life-affirming journey that would bring us to our knees. "Resiliency" is my middle name, so I knew we would rise again to our feet. What mattered most is that we were alive and unharmed. What kept me going even at the worst moments was deeply knowing the value of tragic events to hone me for some as yet unknown emerging new story chapter. As if on autopilot, I defaulted to what has always worked before. I gave my complete trust to the organically unfolding process in which I suddenly found myself.

I can't believe more than a decade has passed since that day when I watched everything I owned and all my work go up in flames.

To my great disappointment I was just too "burnt out" from the fire's aftermath, and we had no stable place to call "home" or "office." I had to make the hard call that I was unable to keep my commitment to present for the very first time at the prestigious American Society on Aging's annual conference on my new work and to have my books on *Mastering Reinvention* and *The Greatness Challenge* highlighted. It meant a big deal to me.

My 2001 whacks on the side of the head didn't stop here, but no need to pile it on for you. So I'll skip ahead to the upshot. Finally, by end of summer, I was back in my rhythm and our home was being rebuilt from the foundation up. I was thrilled to be heading out to the first Conscious Aging conference held in years, which was being launched in San Diego in mid-September. You guessed it: I was on my way to the Hartford airport to catch my flight on 9/11. The rest is history. None of us have been quite the same since.

I have learned over the years that each transition—no matter how devastating—can be an invitation for greatness. Traumatic events like my home fire, or world tragedies like September 11, the Asian Rim tsunami, Hurricane Katrina, and Hurricane Sandy, force us to look at what really matters. With every transition there is transformation, and often a greater connection to others and to our Soul's purpose. These events refine us and make us look more closely at ourselves, our relationships and our place in the world. True greatness is forged from change.

Carolyn Conger, in her book *Through the Dark Forest*, a personal growth book on death and dying, echoes my belief in the role of transformation in our lives when she shares, "I believe that transformation into wholeness is a person's true work, and that this work can take place over a lifetime or in the few days or hours preceding death. …It's never too late for transformation."

Transitions—however devastating—always invite us to unleash our Signature Greatness DNA and awaken the visionary within (Sands, 2001).

Every decade we live is a new transition. We begin examining what really matters and spark stronger connections with others and with our Soul's purpose. Transitions refine us, making us reexamine ourselves, our relationships, and our place in the world.

Change Forges True Greatness

Fires, natural disasters, layoffs, failed businesses, loss of loved ones. We all experience devastation in our lives and with that devastation, a choice—be consumed with mourning over what we've lost or honor that loss by moving forward with a renewed focus on what really matters.

As more and more of us are being called to align our passion, vision, and intention with action, we discover immeasurable meaning and profitable contributions to the Triple Bottom Line: People, Planet, and Profit.

When I rebuilt my life and my business, I found that having to reinvent everything (yet again) sharpened my edge and reawakened the visionary inside me, my inner voice that had been weighed down under piles of papers and the distractions and tangents they represented. Now those piles were ash, and my mind was lightened, my voice free.

As I've mentioned, the Greek legend of King Sisyphus of Corinth has always intrigued me, for I felt a kindred spirit but I didn't know why. I had long decried (in my Ayn Rand–esque view of modern life) that I was not going to end up spending eternity like Sisyphus just rolling a boulder up a mountain, then having gravity cause it to slip back to the bottom just as it reaches the pinnacle.

Writing this book has compelled me to revisit the old story of Sisyphus and take another hard look in my own life's rear-view mirror. What I have learned has enabled me to more fully grasp the deeper meaning of this myth and its relationship to *The Ageless Way*.

Though he violated natural law by duping death (thus offsetting life's balance and, in so doing, showing immense hubris), ultimately none of us can escape the ongoing cycles of our struggles and existence. He learned, as I have, and we all must, that in order to survive and thrive it is essential to honor and find our flow within these cycles, rather than violating them. So, what is the only solution for Sisyphus, and us? To find meaning and beauty in those natural cycles of up and down. To create our new Ageless story. Every time Sisyphus gets his rock to the top of the mountain, he has a moment of transcendence and triumph in sending the message forevermore: "I have the resilience and fortitude to keep rising and never be kept down! I'll get up again and again. And even if only one time, I just might roll it over the edge and be freed."

The Sisyphus myth teaches us all to decipher and find discernment between just repeating something over and over and "re-cycling," the latter of which allows us to find new perspective and evolve more artfully and sustainably. We, too, need to learn to find significance and joy in our sacred cycles…even if that means returning to trudge up the mountain again and again. Now the eternal struggle story works for me. It has merit because it has meaning and purpose. It reeks of hope and vision.

We need to learn to find significance and joy in our sacred cycles.

I, like King Sisyphus, will stick to my truth guided by my moral compass no matter what transpires, even at great loss with untold grieving and loneliness. Long ago I resolved to never allow the gods to see me defeated by despair. I silently vowed to prove to my kids that it's more than okay—in fact it is imperative—for us each to stand up to abuse, and that it's our given right to be fully alive, empowered, and independent. With that in mind, as a woman and their mom, I knew then (and still know now) that my fate and theirs was in my (and our) hands.

Even Sisyphus came to peace with his eternal burden and he, too, learned to love his struggle. In the end, as he continued to carry his burden into eternity, the gods gifted the king with forever hearing the exquisitely divine music from the flute of Orpheus, a legendary Greek musician whose music was known to charm all living things.

The pages of my personal story have turned. I used to have a lifetime-long struggle with struggle; perhaps like Sisyphus, I fell in love with my struggle. What keeps me going, though, are the words of Helen Keller: "Although the world is full of suffering, it is full also of the overcoming of it." I believe that in the process of writing this book and my digging deep into story, myth, and dreamtime, I now know that my sacred Ageless story is filled with all of my goings—up and down, again and again—rolling my self up each mountain along my quest. I know that my story will end triumphantly—as I illuminate the way for you, and we light the way for those to come.

Like Sisyphus in ancient times, we are faced with choices every day. Sometimes we make the right ones. We take the risk, and we listen to that voice inside telling us to leap—not because we have all the answers but because we're asking the right questions. We know that by doing so we'll be able to recognize the answers when they arise. Yet it's one of life's bittersweet truths that, for many of us, it takes a traumatic event to force us to start asking these questions in the first place.

What really matters to me? Am I doing what I think is right or what other people expect of me? Have I been heading in the wrong direction all this time? I've always known I was meant to make a difference, to leave a legacy, yet what am I doing to make that happen?

These aren't easy questions to ask (and they aren't the only questions to ask). Some are downright painful—especially when we realize there are parts of our lives, and even past personae of ourselves, that we simply have to let go before we can live up to our true potential for greatness.

Yet by letting go of everything that's holding us back, we can move from the pain to the purpose, allowing the Ageless Visionary that we all have inside to start asking the questions that will shape our future and the future of our families, our communities, our world.

Do remind yourself frequently that if Sisyphus needed time to get down the mountain before he started up again, so do we. Our legendary king used his descent wisely as he reveled in his triumphant feat to have reached the pinnacle, accepted his fate to start all over again, and took his

By letting go of everything that's holding us back, we can move from the pain to the purpose.

time to descend so he could enjoy the process by listening to the music that gave him succor.

Only by letting go can we join together in making a difference. Only by letting go can we grab hold of what really matters with both hands.

Breaking Free in Love, Life, and Work

I'm sure you've read about the increased divorce rate among people post-50. One study by Bowling Green State University cited it at more than double what it was twenty years ago. No matter how you look at it, these statistics still mean that millions of Baby Boomers are single.

CNN did an interesting segment ("Divorce Among Baby Boomers") on this trend in which one Boomer divorcee, Margie White, commented that while she was married she thought one of them would get a second chance at love when the other died. Eventually, White realized how sad this thinking was and what it said about their relationship. Her "aha" was that they both deserved second chances. Perhaps Boomers aren't as willing to "settle" for less in love. I didn't. Now after almost forty awesome years together with my true love, my second husband, we are ever more deeply in love with each other than when we first fell in love. Our couple's mantra is "One plus one equals three," the third being the sum of our separate parts.

Reevaluating our past, present, and probable future love stories can be painful yet freeing, especially if we are open to recognizing that our relationships don't have to fit the cultural narrative, that we can create our own love stories that look nothing like the fairy tales in which women are powerless to change their destiny.

What is new is that most divorces among older couples, as in younger ones, are initiated by women. This information was corroborated in a 2004 national survey conducted by AARP. The numbers show that among divorces by people ages 40 to 69, women reported seeking the split 66 percent of the time.

In the fall of 2013, The New York Times reported that, for the first time, more Americans 50 and older are divorced than widowed, and the numbers are growing as Baby Boomers live longer. Sociologists call them "gray divorcees."

The CNN report also referred to the Bowling Green study, which found that more Boomers are remarried, and these marriages tend to end in divorce more frequently than first marriages do. More interesting, I thought, was that longer life spans and changes in what people want from marriage are two key factors in the rising rate of gray divorces.

Many people are realizing in their fifties or sixties that they potentially have several decades still ahead of them, which can lead them to re-evaluate whether the marriage is everything they want it to be, whether they both really want to be together for all that time. Some people realize that they do not want to be married or even spend the rest of their lives with a single life partner.

Most of the reasons for divorce among Baby Boomers are similar to those of people divorcing at any age, such as growing apart or one person falling in love—or just in bed—with someone else. For Boomers, additional factors come into play:

- After the kids leave home or after one or both people are home more often, couples often see their relationship in a new light, one that can reveal weaknesses or complete disintegration.

- Women are more financially independent than in the past, so they are not tied to a marriage for security.

- Boomers in general value independence and personal development, so it makes sense to many that they shouldn't stay married if they are unhappy.

- With the combination of facing mortality, and the potential for a longer, healthier life ahead compared with past generations, people realize they don't want to spend the time they have left with each other if the marriage is now no longer fulfilling.

In a Reuters article called "Gray Divorces Rising as More Baby Boomers Opt to End Marriages," one quote stood out from family lawyer, Lynne Gold-Bikin, who noted that a third person is often the catalyst for someone to end a relationship. "They may need that push to get them out, what I call the springer. You need somebody to spring you from the marriage."

For some people, this "springer" was the third person in an affair, something that usually occurs long after the marriage has started to fall apart. Giving ourselves permission to break commitments made in good faith before reaching this point could save a lot of pain and heartache.

If more couples could end an unhappy marriage by reaching loving closure before reaching the point of finding someone else, both could move on without carrying the painful baggage with them. The would-be cheater avoids the spiral of collusion and betrayal. The person who would be cheated on is saved the hurt and deceit. Both avoid falling into the martyred victim role, giving up power over their life choices by blaming the other (for cheating, for driving the other away, etc.). All easier said than done, of course!

Unfortunately, the presence of a new love interest is a recurring theme in post-50 marital ruptures. This "springer" offers an excuse, a way to free the spouse who is unable to tell the truth that the love is gone and who can't admit the relationship is irretrievable. Unwilling to face the truth head on, denial and avoidance reign. Without a way to find closure, the new love interest becomes the only way out.

Feeling trapped is a recurring theme in life post-50 that goes beyond relationships to other domains as well:

- Feeling trapped in a job you no longer or never did love, just putting in your time until you can retire.

- Feeling trapped by the very idea of retirement when you want to keep working, leading, contributing, making a difference.

- The sandwich generation feeling trapped by the needs of their kids and their parents, wondering when they'll have time to pursue their own visions.

- Feeling trapped in our bodies, which no longer look or work quite as they used to, and the fear of these changes accelerating down the road.

This list could go on and on, as we all know. What I am getting at is this idea that sometimes we need another person to spring us from whatever it is that restricts our Agelessness. How many of us have knowingly stayed trapped because we have deer-in-the-headlights syndrome or we simply do not know which steps to take next?

A third party (or several people) can be our "springer" to empower us to leap into a new future. No need to go through this discovery and dis-engagement, sometimes dis-entanglement, process alone. Be proactive and seek out a springer who will be the catalyst, support, and guidance needed, depending on the situation. For example:

- A mentor or coach to guide you to redefining your career or retirement.

- A caretaker with new ideas or simply hands-on support for sandwich situations.

- A women's group to share your personal, visceral experiences as well as solutions for the trapped feeling (if not solutions for some of the changes in your body, particularly those related to health).

I do not think it is wise to wait around for this person to find you, however. If you know you are trapped, start reaching out. Even if you do not feel trapped, reaching out may open doors you didn't even know existed and could provide the support and guidance you could need down the road.

In the midst of a situation that seems to be all about breaking away and dividing, we can take away a valuable lesson about coming together by reaching out—and up.

If you decide to reach out for support and guidance, then do your due diligence so you find a professional who is a perfect match and has the experience and know-how to get you through your dark night of the Soul, illuminating the way so you can journey forward. If you know trusted sources who can provide a reference, ask for confidential support. Know that the answers and way forward are already within you. All that is needed as you begin your quest is a safe sacred vessel and a trusted veteran to light the way forward. There are a variety of specialists that can help, such as a certified coach, a licensed therapist, a mediator, a career counselor-coach, your religious leader or spiritual guru…whoever will be your anchor and wind beneath your wings until you can fly on your own again. A cautionary note: Never, ever give up your power. Only work with a professional who midwifes your own inner knowing into the light of day.

Being Single ≠ Being Alone

As we age, we may also face the death of our partners. Women tend to outlive men, and being over 50 and single (newly single especially) comes with issues that simply did not exist for most people when they were single in the past. Because so many more of us are living to ripe old ages, single-hood can mean isolation and loneliness. For many who are newly single, career, grown children, and grandchildren can't replace the lost partner. Many single women are considered "cougars" and are feared to be husband thieves, when all they crave is the company of dear friends. Single men may find that the long-dreamed-of "sugar daddy" role appears alluring until it goes bust in real time. We need to change these damaging cultural stories about love and sex in older women and men.

Living alone can be intensely lonely or delicious self-care time. Living alone also means not having someone there if something happens to you. Carrying a cell phone or similar device or making an arrangement with a friend, relative, or neighbor to regularly check in (or check with each other) are common ways for people to offset this vulnerability.

Many people over 50 are caring for aging parents, a responsibility that often falls heavily (and unfairly) on the single children in a family. Emotional and physical exhaustion and time constraints are just a few of the obstacles to dating and socializing in general that can come from being a caregiver.

In general, I think this situation is just one example of why we need to rethink our social networks and communities going forward, so that we include more intergenerational activities in our lives and build self-sustaining, accessible communities of multiple generations, among other attributes (see "Ageless Homes and Communities," chapter eleven).

Being single does not have to mean being isolated and alone.

Losing a Parent

I lost my mom before she died. I could no longer deny that my mom's Alzheimer's was full-blown. She was only 59! There was no retrieving her. After thirty-six years as a mother and housewife, she had just started to work. She never got to find her voice. Her life was never fully lived.

As complicated as our relationships with our parents may be, most people agree that losing a parent has a profound weight all its own. The loss of a presence that has always been there is part of it for some. It's like losing a piece of our own identity. For others, the idea that someone who gave us life is now dead is surreal, a reminder of our own mortality. For many of us it's both.

As Marion Woodman put it when I interviewed her for *Visionaries Have Wrinkles* (Sands, 2012):

> Once my parents died, I felt as if I was in the front line of the shots that were coming from the other side. There was no defense between them and me. There was no generation ahead of me. I had to be who I was; I was no longer a daughter. I had to stand up and say, okay, I'm the adult in this situation now.

When we lose our parents later in life, we often have to deal with the attitude that, although sad, it's expected, as if that should lessen the grief we feel. For some, feeling as though this should be the case can interfere with allowing the bereavement to run its course.

Other troubling emotions can make it difficult to fully grieve. What many people don't talk about or even want to admit to themselves is that the loss of a parent can sometimes be freeing, even a relief, like a weight lifted. This new feeling, along with a range of other emotions, is common among those whose parents were suffering a prolonged illness, especially for those who were active in their parent's care. It is also common when the relationship was strained, difficult, or abusive.

This sense of liberation and relief, of finally being able to be who we truly are, can be mortifying, only adding to the guilt so many of us already feel. Guilt about not doing more to prevent the death, not trying harder to have a good relationship, leaving things unsaid, and so on—the reasons we might give ourselves to feel guilty are truly endless.

It can help to know that no matter what thoughts and feelings you have about the loss of a parent, you are not alone. Even the darkest of thoughts are a natural part of grieving, of processing the pain, anger, guilt, sadness, and relief into insight about our own lives, our relationships, and who we really are at our core.

Although you can learn to let go and you can reach a point where the feelings aren't so raw, the loss will always be a part of you. Too often, we set time limits on grief, especially the "expected" grief of losing a parent, but these artificial limits have nothing to do with reality, and they only weigh the grief down, prolonging our ability to integrate it into who we are.

For me, it helps to step back and see the big picture, such as my place and my mother's place in our lineage, our maternal generational story, and to recognize that even in death we live on in what we leave behind for the generations that follow us. This passing on of our generational story is true whether or not we have children of our own.

In Hope Edelman's book *Motherless Daughters: The Legacy of Loss*, she so aptly draws from Mother Nature's coffers to provide a template for our timeless connections to our maternal roots:

> Nature often offers metaphors more elegant than any we can manufacture. In the redwood ecosystem, all seeds are contained in pods called burls, tough brown clumps that grow where the mother trees' trunk and root system meet. When the mother tree is logged, blown over, or destroyed by fire the trauma stimulates the burls' growth hormones. The seeds release and trees sprout around her, creating the circle of daughters. The daughter trees grow by absorbing the sunlight their mother cedes to them when she dies. And they get the moisture and nutrients they need from their mother's system, which remains intact even after her leaves die. Although the daughters exist independently of their mother above ground, they continue to draw sustenance from her underneath.

This passage struck a chord that resonates to my core. My mother's unfulfilled, prematurely shortened quest for her Womanself inspired my own lifelong journey to fulfill this quest and, to this day, still influences my mission to seed and tend to generations of daughters into the future.

Women form a sacred circle with deep roots in time and timelessness, each woman forming burls of new seeds where their trunks and root systems meet. Together we unearth ancient future wisdom to nurture our new seedlings, creating an ever-widening circle of daughters. My wish is that generations of women everywhere will continue to draw sustenance from our roots.

Losing our parents can leave us feeling rootless and disconnected; in reality, the opposite is true. Our roots, our connections, go far deeper than a generation or two, just as the roots we put down from this day forward, the connections we make, will help to sustain the generations to follow.

The loss of each unique person still leaves a hole in us that will always be there, just as our own deaths will leave holes in others. Perhaps that is why the most mature trees form the forest canopy, so that these holes will let the sunlight through.

Losing Our Kids

Losing my babies at the whim and will of the patriarchal powers that be was the most difficult loss I've ever experienced. I am one of the fortunate ones, because I have my kids back and, to boot, wonderful grandkids. My scarring is healing, albeit slowly even all these decades later. But for those who lose their children to illness, disease, or to horrific tragedies (like the unimaginable massacre at Sandy Hook Elementary School or the devastating losses of Trayvon Martin, Michael Brown, Tamir Rice, and others lost in unimaginable ways), my heart and prayers go out to you. The ravages of war can also take our kids or bring them back so different from when they left. How do we cope with such a loss that's not supposed to happen? I don't know. Truthfully, I don't want to ever have to know. As devastating as any of these losses are, please know that if you are suffering such a loss, you will return to life again buoyed by our unrelenting human resilience to thrive. For many of us who have suffered so much, we transform our loss into a new story to prevent others from experiencing similar pain. In our new story we become the anchor and support for others to return to life.

Losing Our Spouses or Partners

Both in their elder years, Sidra and Hal Stone's efforts to speak aloud about the inevitable are beacons for those of us coming up alongside or behind them. In our interview for *Visionaries Have Wrinkles*, Sidra explained:

> Our goal is to have a practical/spiritual conversation about aging, as well as planning for a spiritual and physical preparation for the ultimate stages of aging. Of course we are also planning for the transition to dying, and the post-death transition. We talk about it a lot. We talk not only of how we will deal with the coming years, the natural process of aging, and of death, but of what happens next as well. We talk about the possibility of the intensification of energetic connections as the physical bodies begin to fade. And we talk of how I will deal after Hal is gone. We talk about both the spiritual consideration of aging and both spiritual and psychological preparation for the ultimate stages of aging and for the transition and the post-death transition. We talk about it a lot.

My husband of almost forty years and I have talked about how fast time is moving, our eventual passing, and how and where we will carry on. But these were theoretical conversations between a trained GeroFuturist and her husband. Now after my beloved's massive heart attack several years ago, which he survived in the face of terrible statistical odds, while thumbing his nose at death, our conversations are much more profound and the eventuality is a very real fact of life for us both. Don't get me wrong. We do not live in a moribund, depressed state by any means, but we do talk the truth, keenly aware of the over- and undertones like we never were before. Our secret remedy is to live our life together to the fullest. How will either of us cope with the other's passing? I can only hope with the same laughter, loving tenderness, and open-heartedness with which we've spent all our years together.

Then there are the realities of what comes next if one of us is disabled or if both of us are? And what happens after one of us does depart? Where will we live? Who will love us? How will we fill the emptiness of our loss? Who will we turn to in our sorrow? And how will we create a new ending without the other? We know the questions; we too are searching for more answers.

Losing Our Friends

Elly Guggenheimer told me in our interview for *Visionaries Have Wrinkles* that she had lost almost all of her close friends by the time she was in her early eighties. She went on to say, "I had a very, very close friend, who was my sister, really. She was the person I spoke to on the phone in the morning and with whom I shared my feelings. She died a year and a half ago." When I asked Elly how she lives with that loss, she shared, her raw truth: "Not terribly well at times. You ask how do you cope with loss? You go on. How do human beings cope with all the things that happen to them? …We just go on day by day. You try not to think ahead. When you get to be my age and think ahead, you think, 'How much of a burden do I become to my children? Do I land in a nursing home or assisted care?'" Even for Elly she admitted that death is the most unplanned-for event in a life where it is absolutely inevitable.

Mourning Our Past

All the clichés about the midlife crisis obscure several realities. One reality is that the crisis happens to women as well as men, and another is that a midlife crisis can come at any time, even more than once—from age 35 to 75, give or take a year or two! The way we trivialize it—with the images of men in new red sports cars with toupees flying, pursuing younger women, or by images of men riding Harleys with their bellies protruding from their Jimmy Dean look-alike black leather jackets—can make it more difficult for us to understand a midlife crisis for what it really is: a grieving process.

299

The details of what we grieve are individual—we might be mourning our lost youth or some other element of our past selves that has changed. We might even be grieving the person we never were and now feel we never can be, the image of ourselves and the accomplishments we always assumed we'd have time for, only to realize (or believe) that time has come and gone. Sometimes, we grieve a past that we are viewing through rose-colored glasses, feeling that we never fully appreciated it at the time. The truth is probably that the past was never as rosy as we remember but that we also probably did take some things and people for granted. The lesson in this reality is that now is another time we don't want to look back on as unappreciated, which is surely what will happen if our present is occupied with mourning the past instead of living in the moment.

By seeing these crises as mourning periods, we have the opportunity to move through them and learn from them. Renowned psychiatrist Elisabeth Kübler-Ross's groundbreaking research in thanatology enunciated five emotional stages of grief: denial, anger, bargaining, depression, and acceptance. Not everyone goes through all stages or in the exact same order. These same emotional stages often apply to the "midlife" crisis no matter when it hits us. Divorce and widowhood also force us through these same stages. In fact, any ending will likely include these stages. We can easily get stuck along the way if we do not face and ultimately accept the loss.

The entire anti-aging industry is founded on a lucrative story keeping people stuck in denial of aging. Relationships can be poisoned by the anger (and its cousin, envy) over the loss, especially if we blame someone else—our children, our spouse, our parents, our colleagues—for lost opportunities. The erratic impulsive behavior most commonly associated with the cliché (attempting to buy youth or success via the new car or new wardrobe or quitting a job suddenly without any game plan) can be a form of bargaining or of denial ("If I do this, I can make up for this or stave off that"). Sometimes bargaining comes in healthy life changes, such as renewed interest in fitness, volunteer work, or restarting an activity that we always wanted to turn into a career but never had time to pursue. Unless we accept the loss motivating even these changes, however, we might not sustain them once we realize they are not bringing back what we lost, which could leave

> **Seeing crises as mourning periods, we have the opportunity to move through them and learn from them.**

us stuck in the next stage, depression, the feeling of hopelessness and the risk of mourning not just our past but the future we believe we can't have.

Accepting the loss and our suffering, on the other hand, can help us to focus on what we have to gain (and have ahead of us in the future), as we are, on new terms. This acceptance is, I believe, at the heart of many of the benefits of aging I detail in the "Positive Aging" chapter, especially the optimism and lack of regret and anxiety found in those who are happiest in their Third and Fourth Ages, not to mention the wisdom that clearly requires insight into the dark and the light of life and ourselves.

It can help to recognize that the crisis is not all in your head and that, in fact, it may serve an evolutionary purpose. A recent study published in the Proceedings of the National Academy of Sciences found that chimpanzees and orangutans also experience a significant dip in happiness around their own midlives. The marked depression and changes in social interactions, distinct from the individual's emotions and behaviors before and after this time of life, were measured using standard surveys by those who knew the animals well. Seeing the same U-shaped curve in happiness from childhood to Elderhood, with the dip occurring at midlife, even in our close evolutionary cousins, supports the possibility that the crisis is genetic and possibly adaptive in our evolution.

Crisis is not all in your head … it may serve an evolutionary purpose.

For the Baby Boomers, we have not only found ourselves in the midst of midlife transition; many of us also find ourselves in an unwanted midlife crisis. The concurrent Great Recession has brought us into a tragic reversal, sending most of us tumbling off our archetypal towers and brought to our knees as our whole generational story collapsed around us, leaving us in a state of "shock and awe." Even with the recession lifting, we continue to suffer in survival mode, unsure of how to navigate the turbulent waters of our midlife and later life in a game with new rules.

If so, what purpose does this adaptation serve? According to the researchers, the most plausible explanation is that the crisis occurs at a time when we are often at the height of our lives—with our children (if we have them) able to fend for themselves without us, our careers in their prime, and financial security at its strongest—a time when the anxiety and depression many of us feel is a reminder not to take all of this for granted.

In Austrian psychologist Viktor E. Frankl's memoir, *Man's Search for Meaning,* he describes his horrific four-year-long Nazi internment and separation from his beloved wife after being sent to the Auschwitz concentration camp during WWII. Frankl's gift to us all is to reveal that our will to transcend our circumstances may be the determiner between life and death, in reality and metaphorically. I can't do justice to Frankl's words, so I share them here so you too can glean the secrets he shares on how to accept and rise above whatever tragedy and loss befalls us, and they will:

> What was really needed was a fundamental change in our attitude toward life. It does not matter what we expect from life, but rather what life expects of us. ...No man and no destiny can be compared with any other man or any other destiny...when a man finds his destiny is to suffer, he will have to accept his suffering as his task; his simple and unique task. He will have to acknowledge the fact that even in suffering he is unique and alone in the universe. No one can relieve him of his suffering or suffer in his place. His unique opportunity lies in the way he bears his burden...the way in which a man accepts his fate and all the suffering it entails, the way in which he takes up his cross, gives him ample opportunity...even under the most difficult circumstances to add a deeper meaning to his life.
>
> *Frankl wrote at a time that used "he" as the generic singular pronoun, which we now recognize as non-inclusive.*

Many of us know intellectually that these days we are living longer and healthier lives than ever before, and that the prime of our lives is likely still in the years ahead, yet the primal fears about death remain and can easily overtake this knowledge.

Research only confirms that our crisis is not a result of some external reality, which we can circumvent or lessen by being proactive in our lives. We can do this by coming to terms with the losses in our lives and focusing less on who we were (or thought we were) and more on who we can be. We can take this time to reimagine our futures, to go from good to great, and to plan our remaining years in our Third and Fourth Age to surpass the first half beyond measure. When we face and accept who we are, the story we have lived and are living, we can create a new story for our future.

What we need to do now is to complete our stories, yet with a new ending of our own making, using the wisdom we've garnered in the process, much like Vasilisa as she journeyed home with her fiery skull, and Rotten Eyes in the old hide as she spun her threads.

Mastering Fear

Do not fear the aging of the body, for it is the body's way of seeking the root.

-Lao-Tzu

Of course, even without being in crisis mode, our everyday fears and our fears about the future can debilitate us, keeping us from taking that next step, from listening to that visionary voice inside. But when we let our fears prevent us from taking action, we only create a future to be afraid of—one full of regrets, irretrievable opportunities, and a "safe" life that is more frightening than anything.

Even though our circumstances change, fear never goes away completely. Even the most successful people in the world are afraid. Instead of blocking their fears from their minds or hiding out from them, they figure out what their fears are trying to say. Then they plan how to guard against what they are afraid of—and move forward anyway.

Similar to the midlife crisis, fear is an evolutionary development. It developed to protect us from harm at a time in human history when avoiding immediate threats was most important to our survival. Those whose fear prevented them from being eaten by a predator lived on to reproduce. This adaptation is not so useful when our fears are about the less immediate future. The fear can debilitate us in the here and now, the time when we can take actions that will benefit us in the long run. Therefore, figuring out what your fear is trying to tell you makes sense, but trusting your fear in its immediacy is often a mistake.

One sure-fire way to stop the fear process from overtaking you is to step out of the situation that feels threatening. Take a few moments to center yourself (even in the moment the fear is gripping you) by taking a few deep breaths. Then, with all your might, move your attention from the immediacy and give yourself this respite so you can take what I call a "god's-eye view" of the situation. Once disengaged from the immediate threat, you will be able to discern that which is truly a danger so you can determine an appropriate response rather than reacting inappropriately.

This present time is a great time to reach out to others, especially those in a similar situation or those who have gone through it and survived (and preferably thrived!). Someone else might also have insight into what your fear is trying to tell you, especially if it's something you don't want to admit to yourself. Sometimes just saying our fears aloud helps diminish them, and sometimes just knowing we have support no matter what can reassure us that, even if our fears come true, we're not alone.

Sometimes a distraction works better than anything, something engrossing that can give us a break from our own anxieties, so we can face them again from a fresh (and refreshed) perspective.

Ultimately, action is the best weapon against our fears. Even small steps can embolden us to take more small steps, then larger steps. Right now, those first steps might be simply writing down everything you are afraid of, and then using your imagination to come up with every possible solution. Just mind dump—don't judge what you write. Sometimes, even the most ridiculous ideas can be springboards to innovative answers you might not have thought of otherwise.

Once you have a game plan in mind, break it down into actionable steps. Then, as much as possible, let the fear go. It has served its purpose. You don't need it anymore.

Old Age Is Not for Sissies

Since, having just turned 70, I have not yet experienced old age, I cannot knowingly write about it from my own life story. Instead, I will share the thoughts and recommendations from those who have passed through their own old age. Bette Davis captures my growing sentiments about later life aging: "Old age is no place for sissies." Edith Wharton wrote about her cure for growing older: "The only cure for growing older is…to make one's center of life inside of oneself, not selfishly or excludingly, but with a kind of unassailable serenity—to decorate one's inner house so richly that one is content there, glad to welcome anyone who wants to come and stay, but happy all the same in the hours when one is inevitably alone."

Last but not least, Rebbe Nachman of Breslov, founder of the Breslov Hasidic movement in the 1800s, writes stirringly of the transient nature of our physical aches and pains and life itself as we enter into old age.

Teach me, God,
to live out my days
focused on
all that is meaningful
in life.
As unaccountable aches and pains
multiply,
as memory and retention fade,
teach me to be related to my physical existence with
an ever-expanding recognition of its transient nature;
teach me to relate to my soul with an ever-expanding
awareness of
her eternal nature and ageless worth.

~ Rebbe Nachman of Breslov, founder of the
Breslov Hasidic movement in the 1800s, "Ageless Aging"

Embracing Our Own Mortality

*From the middle of life onward, only he remains vitally
alive who is ready to die with life. For in the secret hour of life's
midday the parabola is reversed, death is born.*

~ C.G. Jung, "The Soul and Death"

Most of us don't want to think about our own death. Dying is this distant, vague event that is too depressing or frightening or unreal to contemplate, and we don't control it anyway, so why waste time and emotion thinking about it?

Renowned Jungian analyst and prolific author Marion Woodman shared her thoughts with me on her own confrontation with serious illness and possible death: "It is one thing to know that you will die. It is another to experience the terror *in the body* of being extinguished. After all those years of denying my body, and then to wake up in the night and feel the burning fear of *this body* not existing in *this realm* anymore, makes me see and smell and hear and feel in an entirely different way. ...That is why I'm so grateful for this illness. To have a chance to look at everything a second time is huge. HUGE."

What constitutes a good death? Is it the commonly shared wish for dying peacefully and painlessly in our sleep? Or perhaps it's only after a long and fulfilled life? If that's a good death, then what's a bad death? The opposite, being alone and in pain till the end?

Florida Scott-Maxwell also unveils the shadow reality of old age and waiting for death: "I don't like to write this down, yet it is much in the minds of the old. We wonder how much older we have to become, and what degree of decay we have to endure. We keep whispering to ourselves, 'Is this old age yet?' 'How far must I go?' For age can be dreaded more than death. ...It is waiting for death that wears us down, and the distaste for what we may become."

But facing and even embracing mortality has very little to do with death and everything to do with life. The sooner you deal with it, the more time you will have to benefit from the insights you gain into true happiness and fulfillment and the path to accomplishing your true masterpiece, your most visionary achievement yet.

In my interview with Carolyn Conger for *Visionaries Have Wrinkles,* she shared her view of death and dying and her embrace of her own mortality:

> I work with people who are headed toward death. …I am comfortable with the idea of death, and with the procedure of death. I go through periods where it's fascinating to think about death and the simple mysteries that surround it. Adults and even children alike ask about death, such as where do we go? What happens? Is there reincarnation? Truthfully, I am not worried about the act of dying. …I think that one of the reasons that we have death is so that we can appreciate life. Everything is part of a cycle. Elderhood is a cycle. …The cycle of death is just one of those. …I also know that the passage can be easy. I trust that I'll be able to do it well. The things that concern me about death are that somebody's going to have to clean up my mess here.

For tens of thousands of years we accepted death as a natural part of life. But by the end of the nineteenth century, that thinking was eliminated; in its place, death and dying became unnatural, dirty, to be hidden from view. Prior to the 1900s, people were allowed to die a natural death in hospitals or allowed to spend their last days at home with their loved ones in attendance. Ever since the 1900s, medical science has been more dedicated to saving lives at all costs, not in facilitating our passing on.

In our Western world, death and dying have virtually been erased from our view of our life course as a continuum. Even as a youthful teacher of life sciences, it was not okay for me to teach about death as a natural extension of life. The closest I got was to have a menagerie of animal and plant life around the circumference of the classroom so that the adolescents I taught could experience the birth and loss of life as an everyday happening.

Why do we in the United States have more trouble with the idea of death than other cultures? According to studies on death and dying, 72 percent of Americans believe in an afterlife and two percent believe in reincarnation. So what's the problem? Is it our fixation with youth, perhaps? Clearly the better our life, the more we are able to embrace death.

I recently found a quote by Ram Dass in my long ago Omega conference notebook where he states eloquently, "The art of being able to look directly at death and directly at suffering is a function of your ability to find in yourself that which is not changing, which is not separate, which is not vulnerable to time and space. That's the spiritual work. That's the journey of aging."

I am so moved by reading Dass's words again because they reflect my own deepest knowing that we have a choice about how we age, and the stories we tell ourselves about aging, death, and dying will inform our process. I feel this as the mother of a dear friend of mine is in the process of dying, a long, lonely road she has taken in which she was stuck, didn't live her full truth, and remained in denial. The ending to her sacred Soul story is not what she would have wanted. Though it is too late to rewrite her story, those of us still living have the opportunity to find our way on *The Ageless Way* and change the type of ending we will experience.

Cecelia Hurwich (aka Cec) a gerontologist colleague, mentor, and dear friend, whom I also interviewed for *Visionaries Have Wrinkles*, is the epitome of a modern day Baba Yaga to me. Hurwich is as luminous, vital, and full of life in her nineties as she was when I first met her in her late seventies. Hurwich has faced suffering and loss having lost a great deal of sight and some hearing, too, and she lives with a heart that is weak. As Dass stresses, the secret to Hurwich's long, full life is to follow her passions where they lead her. She surrounds herself with loved ones, and dear, dear admiring and loving friends of all ages. Hurwich recently published her book, *92 and Dancing*, which coincided with her hometown of Berkeley, California, naming a day commemorating her.

When Hurwich and I visited last, she shared that she is ready to pass on because she has maxed out on love and lived such a rich, full life of blessings that she'd rather go now than later on. Almost in the same breath she whispered that she is going to start her next book after she returns from traveling with Don, her still-adoring partner of many, many years. My choice is clear: I want to create my ending story much like Hurwich's. What about you?

You might be surprised by what people do usually regret in the last weeks of their lives, according to palliative care nurse Bronnie Ware, author of *The Top Five Regrets of the Dying: A Life Transformed by the Dearly Departing.*

1. I wish I'd had the courage to live a life true to myself, not the life others expected of me.

2. I wish I hadn't worked so hard.

3. I wish I'd had the courage to express my feelings.

4. I wish I had stayed in touch with my friends.

5. I wish that I had let myself be happier.

The top two regrets are unsurprising. The last three also make sense at a glance, but it is a little surprising to see them in the top five. Of all the possible regrets people have when looking back on their lives, these come up again and again as among the most important.

The more I thought about this list, the more I realized something else interesting. Number three is actually at the root of all five regrets, especially for women. Although our society considers it more acceptable for women to express emotion, the range of acceptable emotions is limited. Most women are taught not to express anger, for example, or any feelings that could rock the boat. Even in the most liberated women, our inner patriarch whispers that people won't like us or love us if we are angry or critical or even "too" direct, that our worth as women is tied into keeping the peace and caring for everyone else's happiness—before and often instead of our own.

So why is this such a common regret among the dying? Suppressing our feelings clearly has ripple effects in our lives. In the moment, holding back seems like a minor act that avoids the discomfort of confrontation or the possibility of rejection. The habit of holding back begins to define our relationships with others, as well as defining who we are.

When we hold back our feelings, we create a dishonest foundation for all relationships. We might think we are keeping the peace, but holding back regularly has the opposite effect. Why? Because the feelings don't go away just because we decide not to voice them. And even though we aren't expressing them directly, we are expressing them, whether we like it or not—in our body language, our tone, our choice of words, and so forth. The other person picks up on something but can't respond directly because we aren't being direct.

The more we avoid telling the truth, or avoid expressing ourselves fully, the more distance we put into the relationship because the unexpressed is always there, building up. Intimacy becomes difficult, even impossible, because one or both people aren't honest about how they feel or even who they are. Furthermore, we don't give ourselves a chance to resolve the situations that are causing these feelings, so we set ourselves up to feel this way often and with increasing intensity. Too often, this avoidance leads to bitterness and resentment. The discomfort and rejection we seek to avoid each time we hold back becomes an almost inevitable result of holding back.

This impulse, holding back to please others, is quite clearly tied to the most common regret, living according to others' expectations rather than our own. It is also a large part of regret four, not staying in touch with friends. The healthier our relationships with others, the more likely we are to see their value and to prioritize them in our lives. This value is important as we enter the time of life when we begin to lose more and more friends and family members.

Learning to express our feelings is also key to avoiding regrets two and five because it affects who we are in profound ways. After all, if we don't have the courage to be honest about our emotions, how likely are we to have the courage to take chances on our dreams? How likely are we to make necessary changes in our lives for our own happiness, including being honest (with ourselves, our colleagues, our bosses) about our work and what matters most to us? The habit of holding back our feelings becomes a habit of holding back. Period.

One caveat, of course, is to recognize that you don't need to express how you feel about every little thing to every single person you encounter. The closer your relationship with someone (or the closer you want to be), the more you should share with that person. Even then, learning to prioritize what's important to express and what isn't, an ability I call discernment, is essential to being honest without being cruel or self-centered.

Embracing your mortality is really about embracing the truth of who you are and what you are capable of, no matter what your age or stage. You can't make a difference in the world, and leave a legacy, if you don't have the courage to see it—and tell it—like it is.

Now is the time to face the fact of our mortality so that we can glean the truths from it that can guide our lives now and into the future.

Embracing your mortality is really about embracing the truth of who you are and what you are capable of, no matter what your age or stage.

Watching a peaceful death of a human being reminds us of a falling star; one of a million lights in a vast sky that flares up for a brief moment, only to disappear into the endless night forever.

~Elisabeth Kübler-Ross, "On Death and Dying"

Near-Death Experiences and the Afterlife

People have long been curious about ghosts, visitations from spirits, seances, and more. It appears there is a resurgence of curiosity and exploration into connecting with the "other side." Perhaps this is because so many of us have lost those near and dear and, as we enter into our middle and later years, the reality of our own crossing over becomes impossible to deny.

Or is it because there is a crack between our world and the Overworld and perhaps even the underworld? Whatever the causal factors, more and more educated and successful adults are coming out of the closet and sharing their abilities and experiences in contacting and connecting with those who have passed on.

Not being an aficionado on near-death experiences, nor having experience connecting with loved ones who have departed, I'm going to defer to those far more adept in this field. Dr. Raymond Moody, Jr., M.D., Ph.D., is known around the world as a scholar, lecturer, author, and to this day, researcher into consciousness. In the 2001 updated edition of his 1975 groundbreaking book, *Life After Death,* Moody explores what lies beyond death. He investigates more than one hundred case studies of people who experienced "clinical death" and later were revived. Dr. Moody shook up the establishment about the existence of life after death and the process of crossing over to the other side of our conscious reality.

Recently I was introduced to the work of Diane Corcoran, Ph.D., of the International Association for Near-Death Studies (IANDS.) Corcoran is a lieutenant-colonel Vietnam-era nurse who tended to countless soldiers and heard their near-death experiences. These soldiers' stories compelled her to earn a Ph.D. in the field of near-death studies. Corcoran continues to devote her life to the study of near-death experiences.

Although I have had experiences that seemed from another plane, I have not consciously attempted to contact or converse with the afterlife. I invite you to send your stories and recommended readings to me at Editor@ KarenSands.com so I can share them with other readers on my blog at www.KarenSands.com/ageless-beat-blog.

A fitting closing for this chapter is a humorous take on death and dying by Katharine Hepburn: "I think we are finally at a point when we've learned to see death with a sense of humor. I have to when you're my age, it's as if you're a car. First a tire blows, and you get that fixed. Then a headlight goes, and you get that fixed. And then, one day, you drive to a stop and the man says, 'Sorry, Miss, they don't have this make anymore.' " >

CHAPTER 10 ~ *The Ageless Way Reflections*

The questions and exercises below are to help you find your distinct path on The Ageless Way. Turn to page 28 for more about The Ageless Way Reflections.

1. Ask yourself: What really matters to me? Am I doing what I think and feel is right or what other people expect of me? Have I been heading in the wrong direction all this time? I've always known I was meant to make a difference, to leave a legacy, yet what am I doing to make that happen?

2. At what times in your life have you been forced to let go of something or someone? What did you learn about yourself? What did you gain from this experience? What could you gain from consciously letting some things go now? What would those things (or people) be?

3. What stories have you been living in your relationships—with partners, friends, family, colleagues? What do you see as the probable future story for these relationships if they continue on the same course? What is your preferred aspirational story for these relationships? Do you need to let any of them go? Do you need to focus more on any of them? Do you need a "springer" to help you gain perspective? Perhaps it's time to work with a professional so you don't burn your bridges as you move forward.

4. Have you lost a parent or a spouse? Did you have feelings you didn't expect? Were you ashamed of having any of these feelings? How has this loss changed the way you look at your own aging and mortality?

5. In what ways do you see your parents and yourself in the larger picture of generations and your ancestral lineage, as well as future generations of your family?

6. Imagine you have been given a one-time gift. You are on your deathbed, reviewing your life, and then you are given the chance to go back in time, to where you are now. What would you do differently?

Chapter 11
AGELESS HOMES AND COMMUNITIES

How does one keep from "growing old inside"?
Surely only in community. The only way to make friends with time is
to stay friends with people. ....Taking community seriously
not only gives us the companionship we need, it also relieves us
of the notion that we are indispensable.

~ Robert McAfee Brown

Making big relocation decisions is very different post-50 than it was in our twenties, thirties, and forties. Even putting aside the effects of the Great Recession on the housing market, most of us are acutely aware that time is a diminishing asset. In the past, it wasn't such a big deal to change our minds and move on...even to return again. Now, most of us want to limit the number of relocations ahead, to find the perfect place or to decide whether to create that perfect place right where we are. Or maybe the option will be two locations, one for the difficult to navigate harsh weather, (be it beating the heat or snowstorms), and the other to be where you love it the most, with your loved ones nearby and with outdoor fun.

And by "perfect place," I don't mean perfect for retirement. Most of us, deep down or quite consciously, want to find the perfect place to live our greatest decades yet.

Baby Boomers are redefining their next life phase, including housing preferences. These new Boomer lifestyle preferences are creating a structural change in the housing industry, bringing with it new challenges and opportunities for architects, home builders and developers, as well as renovators, while at the same time birthing a new specialty of age-friendly design—creating a new partnership with sustainable "green" building. There is a consensus among experts that the 50-plus demographic is, by and large, seeking six key elements in their housing choices:

- Bonding and connection
- Convenience
- Safety and security
- Eco-friendliness
- Age-friendliness
- Customization

These preferential elements come down to low-maintenance, high-tech customization and plenty of entertainment areas inside and out, single-level homes with multipurpose flex rooms, wide doors and hallways, accessible bathrooms with no "lips" to traverse and attractive grab bars, and more.

We're talking about end-of-life care and the transition itself with friends too. In fact, we're in the early stages of evolving a shared plan to find a way that we can all stay living here on the coast of rural northern California. We are envisioning a shared end-of-life-care community that will support us. We're doing things already to keep us in our own homes, like chipping in and paying for people who will drive us places, or cook for us all.

Most of us don't have any of our children here. There isn't anyone who has a child near here. Those of us who have adult children don't live near them, and the thought of having to go into a more urban area is not very attractive. Many of the people around here had experiences in communes when they were younger. We are trying to weave a new way of aging together as a community. We'll see what happens.

~ Dr. Sidra Stone

Boomers Still in Love with the White Picket Fence

According to a recent Fortune.com article, the anecdotal evidence and the actual data don't agree, yet the media keep telling us that Boomers are moving from the burbs to urban landscapes. Patrick Simmons of Fannie Mae gives us the real scoop: "Contrary to the downsizing perception, the percent of Baby Boomers residing in single-family detached homes was at least as high in 2012 as at any time since the onset of the housing crisis. Even the oldest members of the Boomer generation, who have largely exited the child-rearing stage and begun to retire in large numbers, show no major shift away from single-family residency." The reality appears to be that the long-term trend within older households shows downsizing is getting far less common, and happening much later in life.

Boomer Flight Out of Big Cities

Contradicting Fannie Mae's view of Baby Boomers staying in place is an article on NASDAQ.com that states that Baby Boomers are proving to be a force to be reckoned with. This claim is based on survey results provided by AARP New York, which show that many 50-plus New Yorkers plan to leave the city when they retire. The bad news is that, because of skyrocketing costs and a desire for a slower, less stressful life, the segment of New York Boomers (and those in other cities around the country) most likely to leave is the middle class. In many bustling large cities folks feel priced out, and as we age, concerns like safety, high taxes, infrastructure, mobility, and age discrimination loom large.

WHAT ARE OUR CHOICES AS WE AGE?

Fortunately, more and more innovative quality options for where and how we live into our elder years are emerging. Dr. Bill Thomas of www.changingaging.org has been declared by The Wall Street Journal as one of the top ten Americans shaping aging. Thomas is internationally known for his health care system innovations and is an outspoken advocate for "life beyond adulthood." I commend Thomas for taking his message of "The

Age of Disruption" on tour as he crisscrosses the American countryside to change our conversations and assumptions about these options. As stated on his site, Thomas "has built a reputation as one the most eclectic and creative thinkers working in the field of medicine." Additionally Thomas is an author, entrepreneur, musician, teacher, farmer, and physician. His wide-ranging work explores the terrain of human aging. Another voice in senior housing is Steve Moran, author of the fastest-growing senior housing industry blog; www.seniorhousingforum.net is another great resource to help you stay on top of what's new in 50+ housing. Ron Kauffman, founder of www.seniorlifestyles.net, actively writes and podcasts on senior lifestyles and resources for successful aging. Kauffman believes that "it is important to reach our Boomers and seniors with the messages and information needed to properly plan for aging and the issues and challenges that surround aging and family caregiving." Lastly, a name I recommend you track in senior care and related housing issues is Carol Marak of www.SeniorCare.com. In her own words, "At SeniorCare.com, I explore and investigate the latest studies and trends by top health care research companies, then ask thought leaders how seniors and family caregivers can make sense of that research and put it into actionable strategies and deliverables that solve their challenges."

Aging in Place

For some, staying put is the ideal solution. Maybe you live near family or in an area or home that you love, or maybe moving simply isn't an option right now because of the economy, work, or other factors. The age in place phenomenon is leading to rapid growth in home improvement spending, according to Harvard's Joint Center for Housing Studies. Baby Boomers who have different needs or tastes than they did when they first bought their homes don't want to (or can't) sell, so as the economy improves they are investing in remodeling.

Aaron D. Murphy is owner of ADM Architecture and managing editor at EmpoweringTheMatureMind.com. ADM's architecture firm and residential design focus as an NAHB (National Association of Home Builders) CAPS "Certified Aging in Place Specialist" is to advocate for and give independence to those Baby Boomers and their families to stay in their own homes for as long as it is possible. Murphy states that "Good design and planning can accomplish exactly that successful outcome, and it's astronomically more affordable to plan ahead with good design modifications at home when compared to the alternative costs of facility care in an assisted living or nursing home setting." Murphy's first book is titled *Aging In Place: 5 Steps to Designing a Successful Living Environment for Your Second Half of Life.* For more information, visit www.ADM-architecture.com.

A remodel that you can live with into the future ideally combines function, foresight, and fashion. Look at your existing needs and anticipate future possible needs so that you can remodel now to serve them but without sacrificing aesthetics. For example, designing wider hallways, eliminating lips, providing open spaces, and installing recessed floor lighting and modern-looking features that double as grab bars without looking the part—these are ideal for toddlers in the house as well as for accommodating the needs of residents and guests who've suffered illness or injury.

The concept of universal design rests on this idea of combining accessibility with beauty in building and remodeling rather than tacking on necessary items, as they are needed, which can quickly make a beautiful home resemble a hospital. In other words, universal design means customizing your home now to suit the present and the future. You don't have to choose one or the other. Not to mention the added property value of making your home more livable for anyone, at any age or stage.

Downsizing

Baby Boomers are once again a driving force that will determine the future demand for different types of housing and the stock of homes for sale when—or if—they downsize.

According to Fannie Mae, Boomer downsizing is not happening as fast as we thought it would, as shown by the share of Baby Boomers in single-family detached homes being roughly stable from 2006 to 2012.

While the share of 50- to 69-year-olds living in multi-unit buildings rose slightly in 2012 and 2013, the long-term trend among older households shows downsizing getting rarer and happening later in life.

The long-term trend suggests that older households are less likely to downsize than older adults did in the past.

Relocating

If you are thinking about relocating, you can still look for or remodel a home with an eye toward universal design to suit your present and multiple possible futures, but first come the decisions about where that home would be located.

So what now? Take time to assess what truly matters.

For example, if like many people you long to live on the coastline, be sure to factor in the risks of flooding and increasingly severe weather resulting from climate change. Tools like Climate Central's sea level rise analysis can help. You can plug in a ZIP code and assess the likelihood of flooding in your dream location. Weather is a serious consideration, especially along the coast, where it threatens homes, financial security, and lives, not to mention the effects on the family members of those hit by disaster.

Why take the chance of having to rebuild your home and your life? Even if the market improves, having to sell and move again seems like a waste of time in the years when we could be realizing our greatest visions yet.

Another consideration is whether to live in the city or the country or somewhere in between. The city often has the advantage of more transportation options, walkable neighborhoods, lots to do to stimulate mind and body, and convenient stores and health care options. Social networks are often easier to build and maintain in a city.

Outside the cities, however, we have nature, low crime, low cost of living, more space, clean air and plenty of clean water, smaller communities, farm-to-table options (especially important as the planet warms)—factors that for many offset the fact that the nearest hospital is an hour or two away and that getting around can be more difficult and time consuming.

Retiring the Retirement Community

One way around the urban vs. rural question is to move to a retirement community with onsite care, transportation options, and so forth, but this relocation can be a painful compromise for those who would rather not be isolated from other generations, living only among those with whom they may not have anything in common beyond their age. Some people who make this choice see a retirement home and 50-plus community of some kind as inevitable, so they decide to choose the place themselves rather than leave it to their children or grandchildren.

Defaulting de facto to a retirement community stems from a combination of past realities and present stereotypes about aging that do not have to be true for us. One such stereotype is that we grow needier as we age and have less to offer. This ageist stereotype is far from true. Every generation has needs; this doesn't automatically mean less to contribute. These needs simply change. And with each passing year, we have more to offer, not less—more wisdom, more experience, more skill, more connections… the list goes on.

The retirement community is dated in a world where many will choose not to retire at all. Ever. Longer, healthier lives are coinciding with increasing specialization in business, making people with experience ever more in demand. Many Baby Boomers will not only work past retirement age—full time, part time, as entrepreneurs, professionals, consultants, trainers, volunteers, and so forth—but they are likely to be active contributors to society.

Those Boomers seeking a planned community are savvy consumers, so they are forging a whole new shift in retirement housing and assisted living for their parents (if they are caretakers), but also they are looking ahead to what they will need as they age. What were once acceptable expectations, features, and amenities of retirement communities for prior generations, (now renamed and rebranded as "active adult communities"), will not fly with Baby Boomers. This generation and Matures on its cusp want bigger rooms; privacy; Wi-Fi and the latest high tech; exercise rooms; hip salons; and of course places to hang out, like a local Starbucks, shopping, arts and entertainment; and services to support their encore business or newfound careers.

Continuing to work is not only a necessity for many in this economy; it is also a desire. The 55 to 64 age group is the fastest-growing, most successful group of entrepreneurs. Post-50 women and men would rather reinvent work to adapt to their changing lives, their changing bodies, and a renewed focus on what really matters. So why shouldn't we do the same with where we live?

> Many Baby Boomers will not only work past retirement age--they are likely to be visible, active contributors.

> The 55 to 64 age group is the fastest growing, most successful group of entrepreneurs.

321

Reinventing Home

No matter where we choose to live, we do have to consider the reality that our bodies and minds will continue to age. The solution isn't a community to take care of us. We need a community in which we all take care of one another.

Some Leading Edge Boomers have suggested a modern twist on the communal living ideal of the 1960s, with Boomers living in their own homes but sharing a cook, a housekeeper, a driver, a doctor, and so forth. There's another new model emerging with one in every three Baby Boomers single and approaching retirement or simply an extended long life. Many of the women I've spoken with about alternative housing models are turning to shared housing. Some of these shared situations include "Snow Bird" arrangements where six months of the year they share residences in warm-weather winter climates (e.g., Florida) and then return to another desirable location when it gets too hot where they winter. This new rendition of the 1980s sitcom *The Golden Girls* is beginning to take hold.

These new housing models are close to what I'm talking about, but one key element is missing: other generations.

In an intergenerational community, we can get whatever help we need while returning the favor, helping younger generations with our networks, expertise, childcare, or the services we offer through our own businesses. Rather than seeking help from strangers, paid or volunteer, which raises very real fears about safety and crime, in a multigenerational community, the people who help you, who spend time with you, are the people you help in return. They aren't strangers. They are your neighbors. Some may even feel like adopted family. Does this eliminate the possibility of crime or of someone taking advantage of another? No, it doesn't. But it greatly minimizes the chances when the people you interact with aren't strangers, when they live in the same community day by day, receiving as well as giving.

Not only does a multigenerational community help buffer the intense loss and loneliness we tend to encounter in later life, but it also enables mentorship in both directions. The legacies of older generations and the new perspectives of younger would ensure a stronger community, where no one is swept under the rug. Further, a stimulating active community prevents many health problems related to growing older and ensures that someone is always watching out to catch a problem early.

I do think it's high time that we figure out how and where we want to live and what we want that to look like and then come together, all generations, to reinvent our communities—rural, suburban, urban, and everything in between. I've been exploring this idea for years with futurist colleagues and in my journalistic research. More recently it's becoming a discovery conversation among my cohorts. Here are just a few of the ideas buzzing among Baby Boomers and Matures:

- Intergenerational cooperatives (apartments, condos, grouped housing) in which the residents trade services—younger neighbors helping with driving, running errands, checking in on people, and so forth, and the older neighbors helping with childcare, cooking meals, business consulting, and other areas of professional expertise (particularly from the many Boomers who will still be working).

- Multiple generations living under the same roof with separate entrances and kitchens providing privacy and convenience for the new extended family.

- Self-sustaining "communes" of like-minded folks of all ages, people in our "tribe," that are farm-to-table accessible (even in suburban and urban communes).

- Regular visiting health care specialists who see everyone in a building or small community in a single visit.

- Homes built or remodeled according to universal design principles to meet existing needs as well as future possible needs for all ages and stages.

- Community-owned vans or buses for regular trips to far-off grocery stores, clinics, and so forth.

- "Granny flats," where a resident stays in her or his home and rents out the rest to a young family.

- More rest areas, such as benches, and rest rooms in communities.

As some of us face this decision first for our own parents, we have the opportunity to start there in rethinking our communities and our families.

For some of us, the extended family under one roof might continue to make a comeback. This scenario is certainly happening with the children of Boomers and their families staying with their parents because of the economy. In the past, it was common for Elders to live with their children and grandchildren. Reinventing home for some might mean finding new ways to work the multigenerational household.

No matter how or where we choose to live, now or in the future, we all need to question our assumptions about who we will be—who we can be—tomorrow. Our lives and our futures are more than just a new coat of paint on the lives of our parents and grandparents. The communities we create cannot only provide for us into the next age, but they can also mirror the collaboration we need in the world as a whole and be rich soil for the growth of the generations who follow.

A Space for All of Us

City officials in Vienna, Austria, have been taking a novel approach to urban planning for almost two decades: asking people how they use the city, and then redesigning public spaces and housing based on actual needs.

The impetus for this is an official policy approach called "gender mainstreaming," which the city uses to take gender equality to a new level, including equal access to city resources. By surveying the population, they discovered the actual needs of women, including women with families, and redesigned parts of the city to make fulfilling these needs much easier.

What struck me (beyond the unprecedented governmental care for women) is that many of the renovations not only help women and families but also women and men of all ages and abilities. A few examples:

- More streetlights to make walking at night safer
- Wider sidewalks
- A huge staircase with a ramp in the middle near a major intersection
- A series of apartment buildings with courtyards, on-site kindergarten, pharmacy, and doctor's office, all near public transit

What makes city living easier for women and families also makes it easier for people who want to age in place in the city, not to mention people with disabilities. Accommodating strollers also means accommodating wheelchairs and walkers. More streetlights not only aid in safety from crime but also in physical safety for those with weak night vision. Easy access to nature, medical care, and public transit in living spaces makes life much easier and more enjoyable for all ages and stages.

Universal design principles apply in our homes, as well as in our cities, the idea of design that makes life easier and safer without losing aesthetic appeal. That we have a working example in real life, in Vienna, only shows that this is no utopian ideal. It can be done, and the results are astounding.

I would love to see more cities take notice of this model, and we can all make this happen by asking it of our local and state officials as well as encouraging it in our conversations and our writing and art (the Vienna project got started from public attention garnered through the "Who Owns Public Space" photography exhibit.

Redesigning our homes and communities in this way can also combat the societal tendency to isolate and sweep aside our aging population, instead creating spaces that bring all generations together.

We have an opportunity to not only change the story about aging, but also the space where that story takes place. It can be done. It has been done. ❯

What we need is a radical reinterpretation of longevity that makes elders (and their needs) central to our collective pursuit of happiness and well-being.

~ Dr. Bill Thomas, founder of ChangingAging.org

Chapter 11 ~ *The Ageless Way Reflections*

The questions and exercises below are to help you find your distinct path on The Ageless Way. Turn to page 28 for more about The Ageless Way Reflections.

1. Take time to research universal design ideas, jotting down any that appeal to you. You'll find ideas that you never even considered before. Keep this list in mind and use it as a foundation to which other ideas can always be added as discovered for remodeling your own home if you plan to age in place, or as what to look for if you plan to relocate.

2. Take time to assess what truly matters to you in a home and community. Make a list of MUST HAVE criteria for your dream location, and then look at your options to see which ones intersect with your list. Of these options, use all tools and information available to you to narrow down your list realistically. If you feel overwhelmed by this, consider hiring an International Coach Federation (ICF) Master Certified Coach to help.

3. What does your ideal community look like? Where could you see living out the rest of your years? Is it urban, rural, or somewhere in between? What does it look like physically? Who is there? In what ways do all of the people living there (even if just you and a partner) work together based on each person's strengths and abilities? How is the space set up for you to engage in activities you want to do, whether running a business or taking time for activities such as gardening, painting, or community activism, etc.?

4. How do you envision you want to live during your post-forties and beyond? How might that vision change if you are (or become) single, divorced, or widowed? What impact will having someone else (adult child, caregiver, friend) move in with you have on your vision? What matters most to you of the six preferential elements

listed below, and in what ways can/will you ensure those priorities are met in your life going forward?

- Bonding and connection
- Convenience
- Safety and security
- Eco-friendly
- Age-friendly
- Customization

She said, "I'm so glad that you
finally made it here
With the things you know now,
that only time could tell
Looking back, seeing far,
landing right where we are
And oh oh oh, you're aging,
oh oh oh, and I am aging
Oh oh oh, aren't we aging well?

~ Dar Williams
"You're Aging Well," written and
performed by Dar Williams, 1993,
Honesty Room, Razor & Tie
(lyrics owned by Dar Williams)

Chapter 12

AGELESS ELDERHOOD

*It is an accepted myth that when people grow older they
fall apart and don't do anything. I don't think that is altogether true.
I think it is absolutely up to the individual. I mean, if you feel over
the hill, you are over the hill. Each of us must do whatever
we have a passion to do. It is our decision.*

~ Jessica Tandy, actress

A lot of people just think if you're old, you're an Elder, and that's just absurd. There's a huge difference between old people and Elders. This is true for the transformation into Elderhood vs. moving into old age. The true Elder has made that transformation where she's opened up into a vast inner range that's arcing over space and time. Elders are actually accessing some of the wisdom dimensions of consciousness. As Elders we draw from our life experience. Even more significantly, we've opened up into a new interiority where we're in touch with the transcendent in a way that's very different from when we are beginning and moving through our earlier life stages. An Elder has a container of consciousness wider and deeper than that of someone who's just old.

The author of *Avalanche,* W. Brugh Joy, was a transformational, masterful teacher and mentor and a guiding force in my Ageless Quest to understand what it means to age and become an Elder. As I moved into my early middle years, we had several conversations about the significance of Elderhood and what it takes to embrace the Elder within. He cautioned me that my quest to take on Elderhood as my cause célèbre would demand a maturation of consciousness. We were both in our early to mid-forties when he shared his thoughts about our crossing the bridge into Elderhood: "Most of the material that I might have to share about Elderhood is either material that I've run across that I don't know the source of, and most of all the ideas that I might have, I would have to reflect back to others who already have passed through as they crossed the bridge into Elderhood…but Elderhood definitely has been a creative idea coming through me."

In 1993, Joy shared a dream with me that he had not too long after he wrote his own chapter on Elderhood. In his dream somebody he revered as an Elder had fallen off a very high plateau, which he interpreted to mean that his psyche was asking him to consider the underbelly or the downside, the shadow of Elderhood. Joy supported my quest to write about this topic with a caveat: "I think in order to really give a wonderful 360-degree view on aging and Elderhood, you need to not only engage the average reader (who is actually quite naive about these topics) and then really offer them something both exciting and shocking so you can shake their psyche out of its comatose states, where they are caught in the spell of the collective, steeped in the collective values and the collective consciousness. Only then will you break through their veils of denial of aging, death, and dying."

At another time, Joy shared an earlier dream he had when he was age 45, which portended his future Elder self arising from the depths of his psyche: "I am facing a deep, dark pool of water. Slowly, from its depths, rises the body of a man. At first, he is floating facedown and seems to be dead. He then becomes animated and I see that he is actually a healthy older man in his seventies or eighties. He stands on the water's surface, smiles, and embraces me as I smile and embrace him."

When I shared my notion with Joy that Elders were the visionaries we've been waiting for, he encouraged me to continue on my Ageless Quest, which informed and laid the groundwork for my book *Visionaries Have Wrinkles* (which unfortunately he never got to see, as he passed on before it was published). Descriptors of the Elder are reminiscent of the attributes of Agelessness described in this book's Introduction. As described in chapters one, "The Ageless Way," and four, "Ageless Women," Baba Yaga and the one called "Rotten Eyes" are personifications of the Inner Elder Wise Woman (Crone).

The universal Elder, whether Crone or Sage, is arcing over a huge range of human-being-hood, and isn't just confined to one woman's life and what

Elder descriptors are reminiscent of the attributes of Agelessness.

she has learned. An Elder has broken into the realization that she is a part of a larger fabric and that she has access to the Overworld range, so that there's a transcendental quality to Elderhood.

According to Maggie Kuhn, founder of the Gray Panthers, "We are not 'senior citizens' or 'golden agers.' We are the Elders; the experienced ones; we are maturing, growing adults responsible for the survival of our society. We are not wrinkled babies, succumbing to trivial, purposeless waste of our years and our time."

There's no preconceived image of what the Elder ought to be doing and what she ought to look like, because once she's touched whatever is intrinsically true for her, the luminosity she owns begins to radiate. What's important to stress is that what these individuals are doing in the world may differ greatly from Elder to Elder. Elderhood honors the uniqueness of each individual's inner being, as it radiates out into life through him or her.

A word to the wise…don't be fooled by charlatans who hold up images of what Elderhood ought to look like. Unfortunately we're given a lot of clues and posturing on what Elderhood is, yet I think this veils a deeper transformation. I have to resist creating an image of Elderhood for you and, rather, encourage you to find your own image in your deep self-discovery process. If you are asking, "How can you know who is the charlatan versus the real-deal Elder?" the simplest counsel I can offer is that Elder presence cannot be feigned. When you see a true Elder, or you're next to one, you realize she's come into her Soul, because she's emanating from a deeper place.

How we show up in the world as Elders varies from person to person. Some Elders may be political, others may be involved in the healing arts, or making a difference in the profit or nonprofit world, while still others may be involved in the home and keeping the hearth fires burning, and many may be involved in serving humanity in myriad ways.

What's important to keep in mind is that there are many threads that make up "the Elder," so any one image won't capture the essence of what it means to be an Elder. What is so across the board is that Elderhood is all about awakening into the vast transcendental dimensions. Elders share the wisdom of these realms by fully expressing our Signature Greatness DNA. Thus, our individual expression is solely our own and is related to

Elderhood is all about awakening into the vast transcendental dimensions.

the time and the context of our lives. Yet the process and the patterning of Elderhood enfoldment are universally shared. In the second half of life, most certainly in our elder years, our primary life task is all about surrendering to the mystery of who and what we are and why we incarnated.

Truly understanding Elderhood has nothing to do with the end of life. It has to do with being in the now and embodying the attributes of Agelessness so that we are a living expression of the transcendent mystery, which will move between temporal or more eternal, allowing the Elder to always be aware of them simultaneously.

The primary task we must accomplish to become a true Elder is to validate our life as it has been lived. We cannot attain Elderhood unless we first acknowledge and own that all of our different life experiences have led us to this realization of Elderhood, which some would call enlightenment.

At some point we hear the call that is the bridge to our potential Elderhood and, at minimum, the bellwether of old age in the offing. We are called out of our usual life and perspective, forced like Innana to drop our persona and all our worldly positional possessions as we, like her, descend into the underworld. Our descent is triggered by illness, through an actual call, some sort of awakening (e.g., illumination or an event) that shocks us enough so that we begin to catch a glimpse that there are other dimensions from the one we've called our own. This is truly what a midlife crisis is all about. Whichever triggering event starts our journey into our interior world, it forces us to make contact with the depths of our being.

When the call comes, we either realize it's time for our journey inward, and we're willing to make the sacrifice for it, or we're not. You can read more on this journey inward, or what I've coined as "Crossing the Canyon of the Soul," in chapter nine, "Ageless Reinvention."

Crone Time

The onset of midlife accelerates the emergence of the Crone aspect of womanhood. Menopause may be the initiatory bridge into "Crone Time." But it is in our sixties and seventies that she turns up the heat. Like puberty, before we got our periods, and now as we leave midlife, we are again moving into uncharted territory. As young pubescent girls, the prize was becoming a highly desired woman. But the prize of becoming a wise woman has not yet been embraced by our society and by ourselves.

In our forties, fifties, sixties, seventies, and beyond, we have the ability to come into our fullness. Something's shifting in the deep bedrock of our Souls—it's the Crone rising. This potent archetypal energy force will not come to all of us as we age, but those to whom she reveals herself are being asked to speak their truths like never before.

Florida Scott-Maxwell, author of *The Measure of My Days*, shares her Crone-like truth-telling perspective on being a wise Elder woman:

> Age puzzles me. I thought it was a quiet time. My seventies were interesting, and fairly serene, but my eighties are passionate. I grow more intense as I age. To my own surprise I burst out with hot conviction. Only a few years ago I enjoyed my tranquility; now I am so disturbed by the outer world and by human quality in general that I want to put things right, as though I still owed a debt to life. I must calm down. I am far too frail to indulge in moral fervor.

The Crones are the culmination of greatness. They are the future of aging. Through the full expression of their passions, their presence, their truth, they will lead us all into a new consciousness, and they will embody and model *The Ageless Way*.

There's no more time to waste, for now is the time of our generational phoenix rising so we too can sing our final song of creation into existence. Make no mistake; we are the Visionaries with Wrinkles we've been waiting for. ❯❯

We turn not older with the years,
But newer every day.

~ Emily Dickinson, 1830-1886

CHAPTER 12 ~ *The Ageless Way Reflections*

The questions and exercises below are to help you find your distinct path on The Ageless Way. Turn to page 28 for more about The Ageless Way Reflections.

1. Imagine you have been given a one-time gift. You are on your deathbed, reviewing your life, and then you are given the chance to go back in time to where you are now. What would you do differently? I'm repeating this critical question here again (also included in chapter ten, question six) because in our Elderhood this question is even more poignant and time-sensitive to how we live out our greatest Elder years.

2. If you were to leave the Earth within the next six months, what would you regret not doing?

3. If you knew you were to pass on tomorrow, what would you be sure to do or say, and to whom? Do you feel that you can do this right now?

4. What do you believe are the most serious physical, technological, social, spiritual, or emotional threats to humanity and our planet that, unless reversed, endanger our future? In what ways do/will you make an effort to offset those odds (e.g.: recycling, making time for in-person connection with loved ones, spending time in nature, getting involved in local and national and even global sustainability efforts, etc.)?

5. What old story do you want to change (yours, humanity's, or our planet Earth's?) How are you going to live your triumphant Ageless life so you can look back at every decade and say, "YES! I did it! I've lived my life to the fullest and made a difference I'm proud of!"

Chapter 13

AGELESS FUTURE

*The future belongs to those
who believe in the beauty of their dreams.*

~ Eleanor Roosevelt

The 1976 movie *Logan's Run,* based on the premise of the novel by William F. Nolan and George Clayton Johnson, depicts a future in which humanity lives in a dome, shielded from the destroyed, poisoned world outside. The dome is a hedonist utopia of sorts except for its dark side—no one lives past age 30. The society is run by a central computer that tracks an implant in the hands of the citizens, which changes color with age, alerting the computer to the approach of a citizen's last day, when he or she is killed.

Runners, who try to escape their fate by running to a mythical place outside the dome (called Sanctuary), are chased by Sandmen, the society's enforcers. Logan 5 is one of these Sandmen, who begins to question the society after meeting Jessica 6, who plans to become a Runner.

Logan is tasked by the computer to seek and destroy Sanctuary by pretending to be a Runner, so he leaves the dome with Jessica 6 only to find that the world outside is not destroyed and poisonous but lush and overgrown. In the ruins of the U.S. Senate chamber, they encounter an elderly man who explains the outside world and tells them there is no Sanctuary. They bring him back to the dome, intending to show people that it is possible to live much longer, intending to overthrow the computer's control.

This story of an alternative future is clearly more cautionary than aspirational! Yet I see in this story so many themes that resonate with where we are in our story today and what that means for our future story.

The society in this mid-1970s movie mirrors views of the Boomer generation at the time—hedonistic, not trusting anyone over 30. Now, many would just as easily see the Millennial generation depicted here, which more than anything shows us that the stories we tell about youth are based more in stereotype than reality. Similarly, the man Logan and Jessica discover outside the dome demonstrates the falsity of the myth that life ends after 30 (or 40, 50, and so on).

In this story, we have a woman, Jessica 6, leading the way out of a society limited by ageism, just as women will lead the way into our own Ageless Future. We also have a livable Earth only when we choose to break free from an ageist society's constraints, only when multiple generations come together, instead of isolating themselves from one another. The central computer is our society, churning out the same old story about age and the world to the point where few think to question it. This is just the way it's always been. In the end, when the computer captures Logan and learns from him that Sanctuary doesn't exist, that there's just the world out there, the computer—the old story—self-destructs. Then Jessica and Logan lead everyone out of the dome, showing them the man they met outside, and they all see what is truly possible for them. For the man who had lived alone and isolated for decades, this is a moment when he becomes visible.

Creating a new story for our times, for our future, is a powerful act. On its own, it's not enough. We have to question the old story, as well, the past story and the present story that was shaped by that past. This process isn't linear. We don't do one and then the other. We need to examine all of our stories and begin creating a future story, and then go back to see how that future story impacts the old story (does it make it self-destruct?), and then adjust our future story again. Ultimately, and perhaps most importantly, we have to share our future stories with each other, leaving our comfort zone, multiple generations coming face to face in the real world we share. Together, we can move forward, creating a new story based on our shared values, including our shared concern for the Earth and one another.

But is this how our story will unfold?

> Creating a new story for our times, for our future, is a powerful act.

Tipping Point

The future of the world economy rests in the hands of our aging population. Our country is behind much of the world in recognizing this. World leaders from Japan to Mexico are actively looking into the key role in economic growth that is and will be played by people over 60, who will soon number 2 billion. Europe even made 2012 the Year of Active Aging. In the United States, more and more voices are joining the chorus (from Jane Fonda to Pfizer), but most of our leaders have yet to pick up the refrain.

Yet without our leaders taking active, visible, vocal steps toward policies that take advantage of an active, productive, powerful element of society—our 40, 50, 60, 70, and our Elder population—the story of our planet Earth will not have a happy ending.

Elizabeth Isele, an indomitable voice for senior entrepreneurship, has been preaching about this for years. Isele's tireless work is finally getting more traction after she testified at a 2014 Senate hearing on this very topic and implored our government to be more age- and senior-friendly.

No matter what age you are while reading this, the issue affects you, and not just because our national (and world) economy affects everyone. It affects us all because as long as we live we all age. People are living longer and healthier. We have the unprecedented opportunity to reinvent our own futures in ways that make midlife through Elderhood just another transition into new or reimagined ways of doing and being, rather than a time of retiring…and waiting to pass on.

There are parallels to the women's movement and the economic growth we experienced through practices that enfranchised women. We can experience the same growth by essentially empowering (or re-empowering) this huge chunk of our population that, in the past, we as a society dismissed as useless or even as burdens. Not only do we need to recognize that the post-40 and post-50 generations are the near- and mid-term future, and that Millennials are the future leaders, we also need to recognize that women are still in the process of changing our economy. Post-50 women are especially poised to do nothing short of saving the world.

> The future of the world economy rests in the hands of our aging population.

What do we do next? Today, I want to ask every one of you, women and men, at every age and stage, to reach out to the leaders of our nation, our companies and nonprofits, academia, our communities—and ultimately transform the conversation about aging. Ask them what they are doing to take advantage of what we have to offer in our fifties, sixties, seventies, eighties, nineties, and beyond. Don't forget to ask if the pre–Great Recession demarcation of "over the hill at forty" is still operative, or if the newer "fifty is the age of the tipping point, with age sixty the end point!" espoused by today's HR executives is the new game rule. It's apparent that our aging Boomer leadership is forcing a shift in the over-the-hill mind-set of current leaders, employers, and even our electorate. But where does it stop? At what age are we truly over the hill?

At what age are we truly over the hill?

Those of you who are these leaders are in an even better position to guide this conversation and, even more, to go beyond lip service and act. How will you change your business, your community, your country to incorporate an active aging workforce, to harness the wisdom and experience of the people who just might be the only ones who can jump-start our economy and protect our Earth (and harness other planets) for generations to come?

The future of the world is in the hands of our aging population, and ultimately that describes all of us. So how about it? Are you ready to save the planet and our way of life?

The Time Is Now

In 1826, as soldiers marched across a bridge that spanned the River Irwell in England, the bridge began vibrating in time with their steps, ever more violently until the bridge collapsed. From that point on, British soldiers were ordered to break step when marching across a bridge.

What happened was a physics phenomenon called "resonance." Not only were all of those soldiers vibrating the bridge at the exact same time, but their steps created a vibration that just happened to coincide with the bridge's own frequency of vibration, magnifying it to tremendous effect.

Resonance occurs in the mechanical and the natural world. Think about pushing a child on a swing. The swing's motion is its resonance frequency. If you push at the right time and with the right force to match that frequency, the child will swing higher and higher. But if your timing is off, if you push too soon or too late, you'll slow or stop the swing.

This same principle applies to great movements and epochal transitions. The First Wave Feminist movement (as mentioned at the book's outset, this is better known as the Suffrage movement, which extended voting rights to women across the United States), civil rights, the 1960s peace movement, the Second Wave Feminist movement, and so on. The Occupy Wall Street movement was a perfect example of this phenomenon: People who were essentially vibrating on the same frequency came together at the right time and magnified the frequency collectively, until it grew in impact and in size all over the globe. When our timing is right and we are able to come together with like-minded people, members of our tribe, those who are on the same frequency, we can reshape the world beyond our imagination.

The big question, then, is how do we know when the timing is right?

You simply have to keep acting in some way on your vision. The bridge never would have collapsed if the soldiers hadn't been moving forward in lockstep across it. Each of us must determine when we are in sync with what truly matters vs. going over the cliff like lemmings running amok or soldiers not choosing to break their step.

Collectively, however, timing takes an interesting twist, which again relates to physics, specifically "dissipative structures." Ilya Prigogine first coined the term to describe higher or more evolved ordered structures that arise out of chaos, out of a system that is not in equilibrium. Cyclones, hurricanes, and dissipative Bénard cells (which are formed when a viscous fluid is heated between two planes or plates to eliminate surface effects in the gravitational field) are examples of dissipative structures, self-organizing systems. So are we!

In 2011, Occupy Wall Street emerged because of the economic chaos we are in as a nation and as a world. The greater the chaos and uncertainty, the more likely an ordered movement will emerge. In fact, every self-organizing system, including our own human system, planetary system, organizational system, is affected in the same way. Each can move from

How do we know when the timing is right?

the triggering event to collapse, dissipate into nothingness, or reorganize into a new, higher-ordered structure.

This effect is why now is the time for us to pursue our greatest visions yet. Now is the time for visionaries to come together, particularly Ageless Visionaries, to pursue individual re-storying of our lives and work that makes a difference in the world. Order will emerge from the chaos—economic, environmental, and social. We can either watch it happen or we can make it happen and, by doing so, create the aspirational or preferred future we want to live in and leave behind a legacy for generations to come.

Unstoppable Vision

When people are ready to, they change.
They never do it before then, and sometimes
they die before they get around to it.
You can't make them change if they don't want to,
just like when they do want to, you can't stop them.

~ Andy Warhol

A colleague of mine, another coach and consultant, recently talked about why people so often do not take that next step and act on their vision. He said they are fearful, and those fearful thoughts bring them nothing but things to fear. There is some truth to this. Perhaps you've heard it phrased another way, made popular by the 2006 film and the companion book, *The Secret* (Simon & Schuster, 2006) This concept has been around for much, much longer. I state it this way: "Our thoughts create our reality."

The truth, of course, is much more nuanced than this—and much grander.

For one thing, the universe is a pretty big place. Earth alone, although infinitesimal in the scale of the universe, is itself an elaborate and complex entity. Did my thoughts create the increasing hurricanes, earthquakes, and tornadoes sweeping the globe? That's a little arrogant, don't you think? Billions of people on Earth, and my thoughts are producing large-scale weather events?

On the other hand, our collective actions have certainly contributed to the climate changes that have led to these events. Their general occurrence was predictable (and predicted), even if the specific times and places were not. Not to acknowledge this would also be a tad arrogant.

Our actions are a direct result of our thoughts, and even small actions can have a large effect. The Butterfly Effect is alive and well—one small action, the flapping of a butterfly's wings, can cause a chain reaction of other small actions that build up into monumental events. Consider this as well: The absence of those flapping wings also has an effect. That particular chain reaction doesn't happen, but another one does.

In other words, even our inaction has an effect on our world.

We all have an Ageless Visionary inside us, but for some, it lies dormant in its chrysalis while their lives go on quietly around it. Imagine what the world would be like if we all completed our personal transformation, broke free from the chrysalis, and allowed ourselves to fly? What kind of chain reaction could we start with thousands, even millions, of visionary wings flapping? Even the small steps we take toward reinventing our lives to have more meaning and impact could have a significant effect on our Earth.

I think my colleague and *The Secret* have it half right. Our thoughts do create our reality. But we are complicated beings with multiple inner voices giving rise to an elaborate web of thoughts. Before we start thinking our vision into existence, we need to make sure it's the Ageless Visionary within us who is dominating the conversation and informing the stories we tell others and ourselves. Even then, all the visionary thoughts in the world do not produce change if we simply sit around thinking and waiting for change to come to us. When you think over all you've accomplished in your life, you know this is true. Your attitude and thoughts played a huge role, but you couldn't have done any of it without one thing—action.

What keeps many of us from awakening that visionary voice and listening to it is that we are unsure of the actions we need to take. We want to make such a monumental impact on our lives and on the world that we can't help but think every step must also be monumental—and that's a little overwhelming. That is where we're wrong. Those first steps must be meaningful, but they can be as small as the flapping wings of a newly emerged butterfly. The results, if you just keep flying, can be nothing short of world changing.

You are not alone in wanting to fulfill your purpose on Earth and realize your destiny encoded in your Signature Greatness DNA. The more of us who flap our wings, the bigger the effect we can have on our lives, the lives of our families and communities, and ultimately the planet. We can create an Ageless world.

The New Story of Our Age

Our past, present, and future stories are the three-legged stool upon which our lives rest. Ignoring or denying any of them is like cutting a leg off the stool, throwing our lives, our organizations, our communities, and collectively, our Earth, off balance.

A final story apropos to our writing our new story is *The Princess and the Goblin* and its sequel, *The Princess and Curdie* by George MacDonald, 1872. These stories are more than fairy tales because they are filled with multiple layers of symbolism.

> *An 8-year-old princess Irene had explored her castle unattended by her nurse, and in the attic, sitting in a shaft of sunlight, was an old, old Crone woman, a beautiful old woman with silver hair, long silver hair. The old, old woman was spinning thread from spider webs. As she spun, she told Irene that she was her great-great-grandmother. Her newfound Grandmother told Irene that she must always keep her finger on the thread, and that Irene should allow it to roll out ahead of her so it would lead her where she needed to go. Grandmother cautioned Irene that she should keep her finger on this magic twine, for it is the thread of her life, and it is the thread of meaning for her life.*

We accumulate knowledge over a lifetime, bits, bytes, and pieces of it, but the wisdom of age is the sum total that comes with experience and with having lived a full life. There are things that we know very clearly, particularly when we're very young, before we've been totally socialized. But at the middle, and even more so at the end of life, we've collected so many stories and so many experiences that the actual words or concepts may still be the same as in our youth, but they're clothed in much richer adornments.

Just as we are simultaneously the young girl and the old, old woman Crone, and everything in between, our past, present, and future stories exist simultaneously within us. We need to recognize and embody the shadow and the light, the myth and the truth, the strengths and the flaws—of our stories, of who we are at every age and stage, of our place in a much bigger picture of humanity, our planet, our universe. We need to carry it all within us, and find our balance as we walk along the thread in the hands of the Fates and the old, old ones, as we shine the light now in *our* hands.

My woman's story is a Boomer woman's story. We can't be kept down. We are the portal to *The Ageless Way.* We are being called to light the way to a new triumphant Ageless Story for our times. Our Ageless Future doesn't stop with Baby Boomers! It starts with Boomers! It finishes with all of us of every age, stage, and cycle.

Our Ageless Future doesn't stop with Baby Boomers! It starts with Boomers! It finishes with all of us of every age, stage and cycle.

I beseech you not to be content solely with the stories that precede you. Instead, re-story your own myths for your Ageless Future. The new story for our times transcends time while simultaneously carrying past, present, and future deep in its bones. The new story for our times is Ageless.

The new story for our times is Ageless.

It is my hope that this book provides you with that ball of twine, so you can see your own life thread for yourself…that golden thread that goes through all of our lives and connects us to those (and that) which we love. It is the thread that leads you where we're supposed to go, so you can help others to find and hold their thread and show them how to fling it ahead of themselves. Together we will weave a new Ageless story for our times. ❯

As the world turns, you feel young and restless.
Remain bold and beautiful because these are the days of our lives.
And we only have one life to live?

~ NBC's *Days of Our Lives* soap opera

CHAPTER 13 ~ *The Ageless Way Reflections*

The questions and exercises below are to help you find your distinct path on The Ageless Way. Turn to page 28 for more about The Ageless Way Reflections.

1. Imagine you could visit the future to see what society looks like after we have all adjusted to increasing longevity. What do you see? How much of what you see could be our reality now if we weren't so caught up in our old stories about aging? What does your aging utopia look like?

2. What is your vision for yourself over a longer life span? Your work? Your family, now and for generations to come? What is your vision for your community, our nation, and our world? How do these intersect? What can you do at this intersection to begin co-creating new stories for these times? What is your Ageless legacy?

3. Now see yourself five years from now. You are dressing to go to work or to go out for the day. Notice how you are dressed. What are you wearing? How do you get to where you are going? What does your workplace or where you are look like? Who else is there? Now prepare to meet a journalist who is writing an article about your Ageless life to date and your Ageless Legacy. What will the journalist's article say about your story?

We are the visionaries we've been waiting for, so let's, together, transform the conversation around aging and create a future legacy across generations we can all be proud to leave behind for the future. Please send me your questions or reflections at Karen@KarenSands.com, and let's send ripples of positive change out into the world.

If you enjoyed this book, please leave a review on Amazon. It matters a great deal if this book has been valuable for you.

Afterword by Harry R. Moody, Ph.D.

Agelessness: In Shadow and Light

I t happened to me recently when I was talking with a 20-something and I casually mentioned a story about comedian Jack Benny, someone famous to me in my youth (I grew up on radio). My young friend had never heard of Jack Benny, and he had no idea what I was talking about. It was a surprise, and it made me think, made me realize my age. But what does that really mean?

"I don't feel like I'm 70," (I say to myself). And, as someone said to me recently, "You don't look 70." What do we make of these statements? What about my 97-year-old friend, Larry Morris, who has said to me, on more than one occasion, "I feel the same as I did at 18…"?

It is obvious that we live in a society that does not promote Agelessness, unless it is achieved by cosmetic surgery. In short, we are engulfed by stereotypes, and they come at us from all sides, from the time we are young to the time when we are old. How then do we escape stereotypes and, instead, acknowledge the inherent richness in growing older? How do we change our own attitudes, so that we're not (secretly) pleased to be told, "You don't look your age"? How do we change the wider society so that we no longer waste the talents and life experience of what will soon be one in five of America's population over the age of 65?

As you now know, having come to the end of this book, there is no better place to begin pondering these questions than *The Ageless Way*. But taking this book seriously and traversing this path means coming to understand just how difficult, and how important, it is to see the way that stereotypes and language of ageism hold us in their grip and to know, as with any movement, that it's up to all of us to envision and create a better way, a new story. Karen deftly illuminates the New Story of Our Age so that together we can radically reinvent growing older. *The Ageless Way* is just the guide we need right now whether we are 18, 40, or 101-plus.

I am of an age at which I am retired or, as I sometimes put it, "practicing retirement." Practicing retirement may take a long time for me to master, because retirement today is not what it was when I entered the workplace (around 1970). Retirement has changed. Aging has changed. In fact, everything has changed, despite my enthusiastic feeling of Agelessness. T.S. Eliot put it well: "The pattern is new in every moment, and every moment is a new and shocking valuation of all we have been." Rather than cowering from that change, this book invites a new perspective of multiple possibilities and opportunities and provides tools to begin that journey with renewed vitality.

Why are we so sure about what aging is, anyway? Gerontologist Robert Kastenbaum addressed the question "When does aging begin?" He answered, "…in infancy, much earlier in life." Aging begins whenever we become more and more bound by habits. Habituation was Kastenbaum's answer to the question of when aging begins. When I consider this idea, the word that comes to mind is the Buddhist term upaya, from Sanskrit, which is a form of skillful means, even a path to liberation. To discover the ageless part of ourselves is not to deny age, which would only perpetuate the illusion in which we too often find ourselves. The illusion of "living in the moment" is something our media and culture celebrates, but for all the wrong reasons. It is another version of youth culture, of cheerful denial: "Have a nice day." It is not the place we need to go. "Be here now" (as Ram Dass would put it and Karen Sands would confirm) requires much, much more of us. It offers not the escapism of media culture but the fullness of reality.

What then about "positive aging," a goal to which I have given many years of my own life? I can spin out all the variations: successful aging, productive aging, conscious aging. These are all ways of defying the stereotypes and illusions of our ageist society. Thus, when told, "You don't look your age," I can respond, with Gloria Steinem, "Yes, this is what 70 looks like."

Karen Sands, in this book, understands the complexity and dilemma inherent in mixed meanings, adhering to old ideas, and forging new possibilities, and she insists that we need to be vigilant about not reinforcing damaging stereotypes under the guise of "staying positive." The point is precisely what geriatrician Bill Thomas underscores, when he calls attention to our use of the word "still," as in, "She's still driving," "He still goes to work each day," and so on. We do not escape stereotypes by turning them into their opposite, or even by (secretly) feeling pleased about "defying" them.

As you have likely discovered—perhaps rediscovered—in reading this book, to experience Agelessness, then, is not to deny age. But realizing, and accepting, one's age can actually be the other path to transcending it. What we in our culture desperately need, and what *The Ageless Way* provides, is a positive vision for the second half of life, but it must be a vision different from "magical thinking," which is ultimately destructive denial. Think only of the power of so-called "anti-aging medicine" (a big business) and you get the point.

Going into the shadow means avoiding the false illusions of the light, which is not light at all. Think of the Turkish story of Mulla Nasr Idin. Someone found him crawling around under a street lamp and asked what he was doing. "Looking for my key," Mulla replied. "Where did you lose it?" "Back there in the dark alley," replied Mulla. "Then why are you crawling around under the street lamp?" he was asked. "Because there's so much more light here," answered Mulla.

It is in the shadow that we must look in order to find illumination, and conscious aging must inevitably be "shadow work." It begins as overcoming the false dualism between the "well-derly" and the "ill-derly," the positive and negative poles of later life. It is in the shadow part of ourselves that we will find the vision we need. What Karen Sands has done by interweaving Herstory and history with mythology and modern-day story, trend-spotting, resources, and each chapter's clarifying questions (in this book and in her ongoing online sharing of postings, guest experts, resources and offerings) is to shine a light on what we need so profoundly to understand and to see.

Harry R. Moody, Ph.D.

Visiting Professor, Creative Longevity & Wisdom Program
Fielding Graduate University

THE
AGELESS
WAY

Resources

You've Always Known You Were Meant for More

Reading about what is possible for you and for our world can spark your own realizations, discoveries, and BIG ideas. Don't let them slip away! **No matter your circumstances or your age or life stage, you can start acting now to fulfill your potential to transform your life, your work, and your world.**

And you don't have to go it alone. You will find books, card decks, and coaching services available for purchase, as well as numerous **FREE** tools for taking the next steps, at www.KarenSands.com. Check back regularly for ongoing information about the future and a continuous stream of new offerings. (You can also follow Karen on Twitter, LinkedIn, Facebook and Pinterest to get the latest updates.)

Here are just a fraction of the resources you will find at KarenSands. com today and in the near future:

- If you're 40-plus or serve the Boomer market, Karen's **Ageless Beat blog** offers a wealth of information, strategies, and guidance for you to make **the next several decades your most visionary yet** (at www.KarenSands.com/ageless-beat-blog).

- Download **FREE and low-cost e-books and mini print books**, such as *A Glimpse of Tomorrow's Future, The Greatness Challenge, Mastering Reinvention, An Ageless Story,* and *Crossing the Canyon*, at www.KarenSands.com/bookstore. Many more are in development.

- Also download **video and audio interviews, reports, how-tos**, and much more at www.KarenSands.com."

- Get your copy of ***Visionaries Have Wrinkles*** (print & e-book) which continues receiving rave reviews for conversations with women visionaries who share their no-holds-barred inspirational points of view on growing older boldly, wisely, and visibly to reshape the future of aging for all of us. Or download a pdf chapter to get acquainted with these visionaries. Make sure you check out the companion card deck, ***Visionaries Have Wrinkles Reflections Card Deck***, and the companion workbook, ***Visionaries Have Wrinkles Reflections Journal.*** Available at www.KarenSands.com/bookstore and Amazon.

- Sign up for the **FREE monthly Ageless Beat newsletter** (www.KarenSands.com/ageless-beat-newsletter) to follow the latest conversations about how post-40 women and those who serve them can transform their lives, businesses, and the world.

- Browse **Ageless Experts** at www.KarenSands.com/ageless-experts for articles by professionals who offer expert wisdom on various aspects of the future for and by women 40-plus (also the men in their lives) and for those who serve this market by offering services, products, and opportunities.

- Find out more about **FREE interactive forums, webinars, upcoming podcasts, workshops, and retreats**.

- **Expand the new language of our evolving Ageless Story by sharing words and phrases** you find or create as you make your way on your Ageless Quest. Send them to Karen@KarenSands.com for inclusion in our continuously expanding Glossary at KarenSands.com/glossary.

- Check back regularly for **new readings and links** at KarenSands. com/ageless-reads-links, or share your own recommendations at Karen@KarenSands.com.

- Find out about **coaching tailored to 40-plus women and men** for creating **sustainable Ageless businesses** and **full, meaningful Ageless lives** at www.KarenSands.com/ageless-coaching. Get one-to-one and group coaching, career, retirement, or semi-retirement planning to monetize what matters most to you and your clients. For details, contact Karen@KarenSands.com.

- Learn **how to stay in sync with the people who keep you in business,** especially those entering and moving through midlife and beyond. Read more at KarenSands.com/Media.

- Contact Karen about **corporate trainings and speaking,** especially on how to **leverage Boomer knowledge workers,** prepare for **post-50 futures,** and promote **intergenerational collaboration and innovation in the workplace.** Read more at KarenSands. com/Media.

- You are invited to send **your stories and recommended readings** to Karen at Karen@KarenSands.com so she can share them with other readers on her site and her blog at www.KarenSands.com/ageless-beat-blog. »

Before you go, don't forget to DOWNLOAD YOUR FREE GIFT of **The Ageless Way Reflections Journal** *at KarenSands.com/the-ageless-way/workbook to support your ongoing reflections. Thanks for joining me on The Ageless Way.*

Please share your experience reading this book and invite others to join us on this journey to Ageless longevity and futures as yet unimagined. If you are ready to rock your age and our globe's future, give me a call or write me at Karen@KarenSands.com.

– Karen

P.S. A gentle reminder: If this book is of value to you, please leave a review on Amazon. It matters a great deal to share **The Ageless Way** *with you and those you will share it with.*

HOW TO CREATE YOUR AGELESS WAY
GROUP, POD, OR CIRCLE

You can bring *The Ageless Way* home to roost in your own neighborhood, work team, classroom, or your favorite virtual platform. Invite other Ageless Visionaries to join you in traversing *The Ageless Way*. Use this book as a guide and text for your gathering of seekers, entrepreneurs, nine-to-fivers, book bloggers, and people like you with a unique purpose to create a new story for our times.

Here are some ideas on how to organize your *The Ageless Way* grouping, whether it's you and a friend or a larger gathering.

Meet in person or go virtual using Skype group video calls, Facebook groups, Google Hangouts, or free conference call lines. If you are part of an already-established group, consider bringing *The Ageless Way* to them, or selecting and sharing a particular chapter or relevant discussion point that resonates.

When creating a group, organize an introductory meeting using the Preface and Introduction as a prerequisite for your exploratory meeting. Then, I suggest a twelve-week process with a weekly gathering of two to three hours focusing on one chapter and its associated Reflections. Ask each participant to download the *Ageless Way Reflections Journal* for their personal use as the group moves through the book. Download the journal at www.KarenSands.com/the-ageless-way/workbook.

I welcome your feedback and contributions about how you are gathering and running your pod, cluster, study group, or sacred circle. Please keep me posted and share your stories, ideas, and questions on traversing *The Ageless Way* by emailing me at Karen@KarenSands with "TAW Groups" in the subject line. I'd love to hear from you!

"AGING VS. AGELESS" COMPARISON CHART

*Compare your list with a list that
came out of recent workshops*

AGING	AGELESS
End	Beginning
Final stages of life	NEW stages of life
Borrowed time	Decades to go
Running out of clock	Revving up the engine
Old = decrepit	Old = active
Ugly	New dimensions of beauty
Decline	Thriving in new ways
Disease	Wellness
Sexless	Oh, really?
Retirement/retired	New path, roles, encore careers
Burden on others/dependency	New freedoms and independence
Death and dying	Just another life stage
Wills	Legacy, creative possibilities for
Future	I create NOW
Invisible	Visible
Timidity	Adventurous/risk takers
Gullible	Savvy
Losing it	More with it than ever
Clipping coupons	Not yet begun to spend

DAR WILLIAMS LYRICS
You're Aging Well

Why is it that as we grow older and stronger
The road signs point us adrift and make us afraid
Saying, 'You never can win'
'Watch your back', 'Where's your husband?'
I don't like the signs that the signmakers made

So I'm going to steal out with my paint and brushes
I'll change the directions, I'll hit every street
It's the Tinseltown scandal, the robin hood vandal
She goes out and steals the king's English
And in the morning you wake up and the signs point to you

They say, "I'm so glad that you finally made it here
You thought nobody cared but I did, I could tell
And this is your year and it always starts here
And oh, you're aging well"

Well I know a woman with a collection of sticks
She could fight back the hundreds of voices she heard
She could poke at the greed, she could fend off her need
And with anger she found she could pound every word

But one voice got through, caught her up by surprise
It said, "Don't hold us back we're the story you tell"
And no sooner than spoken, a spell had been broken
And the voices before her were trumpets and tympani
Violins, basses and woodwinds and cellos, singing

"We're so glad that you finally made it here
You thought nobody cared, but we did, we could tell
And now you'll dance through the days while the orchestra plays
And oh, you're aging well"

Now when I was fifteen, oh I knew it was over
The road to enchantment was not mine to take
'Cause lower calf, upper arm should be half what they are
I was breaking the laws that the signmakers made

And all I could eat was the poisonous apple
And that's not a story I was meant to survive
I was all out of choices but the woman of voices
She turned round the corner with music around her
She gave me the language that keeps me alive, she said

"I'm so glad that you finally made it here
With the things you know now, that only time could tell
Looking back, seeing far, landing right where we are
And oh, you're aging, oh and I am aging oh, aren't we aging well?"

Written by Dar Williams | Lyrics published with permission from BMG Rights Management US, LLC

INDEX

A

acceptance 301–303
   role in happiness 169
   Viktor Frankl on 302
advertising
   advances in 186–187, 190–191
   ageism in 188–189
   models breaking the age barrier 187
   transcending ageism in 123
afterlife 311–312
   Americans' belief in 308
age-friendly ideas 72
   business opportunities in 200, 205
   defined 225
   in housing and communities 315–327
   in the workplace 225–230
   product design 259–260
   universal design 319
ageism 17–19
   and sexism 18, 54
   defined 53
   directed at Baby Boomers 142–143
   facing in ourselves 40–42
   in advertising 188–189
   in fashion industry 186–187
   in financial services 189–190
   in higher education 64, 191
   in movies 185–186
   in product development 184–185
   in the workplace 60–64
Ageless Aging
   and Maslow's Hierarchy of Needs 270
   crucial questions 47–48
   introduction to 13–27
Ageless Attraction 119–139. See also Ageless
      Beauty, sexuality
   Who are we if we're no longer young?
      137–139
Ageless Beauty 119–139
   and our identities 137–139
   and the fashion industry 186–187
   and the silver screen 123–124
   anti-aging industry 120–121
   defined 126
   defining it ourselves 126–128
   dispute over 126–127
   Sharon Stone's view 126
   vs. Agelessness 122
Ageless Future. See Aspirational Ageless Future
Agelessness 122–126
Ageless Quest
   defined 42
   for women 109–112
   introduction 20–27

resources for 349–351
   to Elderhood 329–333
Ageless Technology. See technology
Ageless Women 109–118
   caretaking 115–118
   embracing the Crone 112–115
Ageless Workplace. See workplace
Age of Greatness
   defined 91
aging in place 318–319
   defined 318
   in the workplace 220–222
Aging vs. Ageless" Comparison Chart 353
Amos, Tori 72
Ancient Future. See Inner Ageless Visionary
Angelou, Maya 137
Aniston, Jennifer 20
anti-aging industry 120–121
Aristotle 275
Aspirational Ageless Future 48–50, 335–344
   acting on our vision 340–342
   defined 49
   quest for 24–29
   rewriting our stories 342–343
   role of Boomer women 142–143
   the power of resonance 338–340
   Venn diagram 22
Atchley, Robert C. 195
   Conscious Aging 42–48
   on Conscious Aging 45, 196
   "Spirituality and Aging" 45

B

Baby Boomers
   ageism in advertising 188–189
   Ageless Aging 35–37
   and financial services 189–190
   and technology 237–238
   and the future of leadership 222–225
   Boomer Values Realignment Study 220–221
   Boomer women's story 142
   careers serving 191–193
   consumer power 173–207
   definition 9
   entrepreneurship 230, 230–231
   housing trends 317, 323–324
   in the workplace 60–64
   Leading Edge vs. Later Edge 176–178,
      177–179
   leaving the workforce 182–184
   mentoring younger workers 222–225
   role in Ageless Future 142–143
Barletta, Marti
   "PrimeTime Women" 188

"Beat the Clock Syndrome" 144, 261
benefits of aging 72–106
    creativity 101–104
    discernment 86–87
    invisibility 91–94
    less regret 76–77
    optimism 74–75
    presence and luminosity 94–100
    truth telling 77–86
    wisdom 88–91
Bitter, Lori 185
Black Madonna 58, 141
"Black Swan" events 273–274
Brown, Robert McAfee 315
Brush, Candida 157
Buck, Pearl S. 269
business of aging 234–236

C
"Canyon of the Soul" 248–249
careers. *See also* entrepreneurship, workplace
    in aging 191–193
    job losses after recession 155–156
    reinvention of 247–283
    retirement age 213–215
caregiving
    among women 115–118
    caring for yourself 116–117
Cher 211
Clinton, Hillary
    and ageism 18
Clio Feminists
    defined 4
coHERency
    defined 99
Collins, Jim
    business research 90, 92
    "Great by Choice" 253
communal living 322–324
community
    and moral support 168–170
    collective wisdom 168–170
    communal living 322–327
    intergenerational 64–66
Conger, Carolyn 37
    on Crone energy 114
    on dying 307
    on transformation 287
    "Through the Dark Forest" 287
Conscious Aging 42–48
    accredited course 43–44
    conferences 195–196
    defined 41–42
    vs. Positive Aging 196
consumerism 173–207
    advertising 188–189
    among Matures 236–237
    beauty and fashion 186–187
    shift to relationships 220–222

Continuous Discontinuous Change 251
Continuous Quality Improvement movement 89
Corcoran, Diane 312
Cousineau, Phil
    "Once and Future Myths" 25–26, 31
Creative Destruction
    defined 203
creativity 101–104
    Creative Destruction 203
    tips for developing 103–104
Crone. *See also* Inner Ageless Visionary,
    Visionaries with Wrinkles
    as a symbol for women 112–115
    as truth-teller 113
    creativity 101–104
    defined 113
    discernment 86–87
    entering "Crone Time" 332–334
    lack of regret 76–77
    optimism 74–75
    personified in goddess myths 113
    presence and luminosity 94–100
    reclaiming the term 58
    the power of invisibility 91–94
    truth-telling 77–86
    wisdom 88–91

D
Dass, Ram 308
death and dying. *See also* loss and letting go
    and the afterlife 311–315
    facing our own 306–312
    of a child 297–298
    of a parent 295–297
    of a spouse 294, 298–299
de Beauvoir, Simone 112
Deming, W. Edwards 89, 228
    fourteen points 228
    on reinvention 267
    "Out of the Crisis" 227, 228
    "System of Profound Knowledge" 228
    theories on the workplace 227–229
denial of aging 70–72
Diana Project study 158
Dickinson, Emily 333
discernment 86–87
disillusionment 254–256
divorce 290–294
    role of a "springer" 291–293
downsizing 319
"Dragon of Aging" 144
"Dragon of Midlife"
    defined 144
Dychtwald, Ken and Maddy
    "Age Wave" 194, 219

E
Edelman, Hope
    "Motherless Daughters: The Legacy of Loss"
    296–297

educational gerontology
    challenges 198
    defined 197–198
Elderhood 329–334
    and the world economy 337–338
    defined 329
    physical challenges of 305
    uniqueness of Elders 331–332
Emerson, Ralph Waldo 275
encore careers
    defined 221
entrepreneurship 153–169
    and Baby Boomers 230, 230–231, 237–238
    and social media 239–240
    and women 153–165
    backlash 162–163
    Boomerpreneurs 230, 230–231
    Boomers and technology 237–238
    considerations and first steps 231–234
    downsides 157–158
    Entrepreneur Barbie 166–168
    grannypreneurs 236–237
    ideas for businesses 234–237
    podcasting 241
    reinventing business 231–234
    solopreneurs 230, 230–231
    trends 205–206
    upsides 159–160
    women of color 160–161
Erikson, Erik
    "Identity and the Life Cycle" 258
    Seasons of Life diagram 258
    Seasons of Life model 258–259
Estés, Clarissa Pinkola
    "Women Who Run with the Wolves"
        109–112
Evolutionary Spiral of Reinvention 272–273
    Black Swan event 273–274
    Joker event 273
Expressive Arts therapy 262

F
fear
    mastering 303–304
    of failure 144
    of the unknown 261
feminism
    and our bodies 133
    Clio Feminists 4
    definition 54
    First Wave 2
    history 2–4
    in business 164–166
    Ms. magazine 2
    Second Wave 3
    Third Wave 3
Fike, Katy 154
    Tech Savvy Daughter blog 100
finances. *See also* entrepreneurship,
    Longevity Economy

financial confidence 150–152
    services for Boomer women 189–190
    Social Security 215
    women's contribution 165–166
First Wave Feminism
    defined 2
Frankl, Viktor E.
    "Man's Search for Meaning" 302
Freedman, Marc
    encore careers 23, 219
Friedan, Betty
    "The Feminine Mystique" 133
    "The Fountain of Age" 13
Fuller, Buckminster 15, 24, 36, 256
    "emergence through emergency" 202
    right-angle precession 263
Furlong, Mary 165, 181

G
Gardner, John 69
gender mainstreaming
    defined 324
generations. *See also* Baby Boomers, Matures
    different marketing messages for 177–178
    Generation X 56
    Generation Y/Millennials 56, 65
    Generation Z 56
    legacy for our daughters 166–168
    reducing conflict between 218–219
    role in redefining aging 54–57
    the future of collaboration 64–66, 65
    together in the workplace 60–64, 217–219
geriatrics
    vs. gerontology 193–194
GeroFuturist
    defined 19
gerontology
    decline in educational programs 199–201
    vs. geriatrics 193–194
glass ceiling
    and entrepreneurship 153–157
    and "silvered" glass ceiling 183–184
Godin, Seth 238
"Gray Tsunami" 173. *See also* Baby Boomers
Great Depression
    defined 218
greatness. *See* Signature Greatness DNA
Great Recession
    defined 74
    effect on higher education 198–201
    effects on entrepreneurship 176
    effects on women's careers 155–156
    shift to a focus on relationships 220–222
Grof, Christina and Stanislav 270–271
Guggenheimer, Elly 109
    on end-of-life planning 45–46
    on loss of friends 299

H

happiness
  dip in midlife 301
  distorted perceptions 69–70
  three common factors 169–170
Helen of Troy 167
Herstory
  defined 2
higher education
  and the 50-plus demographic 191
  challenges since the recession 198–201
  decline in gerontology programs 199–201
housing 315–327
  age-friendly design 324–325
  aging in place 318–319
  communal living 322–324
  discussion of options 318–325
  downsizing 319
  relocating 320
  retirement communities 320–321
  six key elements 316
  trends among Boomers 317
Houston, Jean 254
Howard, Beth 121
Hughes, Dorothy Pitman 2
humanility 89–90
Hurwich, Cecelia 308–309

I

Inner Ageless Visionary
  first encounter 10–12
  getting in touch with 95–96
  listening to its voice 146
  reinventing the future 341–342
  role in reinvention 265–266
inner feminine
  role in invisibility 93
  strengthening in menopause 180
inner masculine
  role in presence 99–100
inner patriarch 309
  defined 144
  re-storying 147–150
inner voices 39, 143–145
Intergenrationsl 53-62
  Venn 55
invisibility 91–94
Irving, Paul 54
Isele, Elizabeth 337

J

Jobs, Steve 281
Jong, Erica
  on Ageless Attraction 132
Joy, W. Brugh
  "Avalanche" 329
  on Elderhood 329–331
Jung, Carl G. 306

K

Kauffman, Ron 318
Kent, Muhtar 141
Kerouac, Jack i
Kübler-Ross, Elisabeth 311
  on beauty 123
  stages of grief 300
Kuhn, Maggie 195, 285
  on Elders 331

L

Lao-Tzu 94, 303
leadership
  fostering a shared vision 222–225
Lessing, Doris 91
  on invisibility 92
Levine, Suzanne Braun 2, 14
Longevity Economy 211–245
  defined 211–212
  financial planning 212–213
  role of Elders 337–338
Longfellow, Henry Wadsworth 36
loss and letting go 285–313
  accepting suffering 301–303
  as a fresh start 286–287
  as a path to greatness 287–290
  breaking free 290–294
  death of a child 297–298
  death of a parent 295–297
  death of a spouse 298–299
  death of friends 299
  divorce 290–294
  facing our mortality 306–311
  losing a partner 294
  mastering fear 303–304
  mourning our past 299–303

M

Manning, Margaret 169
  Boomerly blog 169
  www.Sixtyandme.com 169
Marak, Carol 318
marriage
  losing a partner 298–299
  re-evaluating in later life 290–294
Maslow's Hierarchy of Needs
  higher needs 269–270
  viewing as a spiral 271–273
Matures
  ageism in advertising 188–189
  defined 56
  housing and community options 323–324
  spending habits 236–237
McClusky, Howard 198
Mead, Margaret 85
Meir, Golda 1
menopause
  and sexuality 131
  as force for change 179–181, 248–249
  re-storying 249–251

sexist view of 134–135
"The Change" 179
"Trick of the Feminine" 179
mentorship 222–225
midlife crisis
as a bridge to Elderhood 332
as a time of mourning 299–303
Midlife Reclamation 248–251
midlife transition 250
Millennials
characteristics 65
Monroe, Marilyn 119
Moody, Harry, Ph.D.
afterword 345–347
Conscious Aging 42–45, 42–48
"The Five Stages of the Soul" 41
Moody, Raymond Jr.
"Life After Death" 311
Moran, Steve 318
Moss Kanter, Rosabeth 191
"When Giants Learn to Dance" 181
movies
"Logan's Run" 335–336
roles for older women 185–186
Ms. magazine 2
multigenerational leadership 65, 222–225
multigenerational workplace. See workplace
Murphy, Aaron 318–319
myths. See stories

N
NASA 182–183
near-death experiences. See afterlife
O
Occupy Wall Street movement 339
Oliver, Mary 247
Omega Institute 85, 195
online resources
Ageless Beat newsletter 350
Ageless Experts 350
Boomerly blog 169
coaching 351
dodsonandross.com 134
EmpoweringTheMatureMind.com 318
Encore.org 219
http://voicedialogueinternational.com 148
Karen Sands's mini books 350
Relationships @Work 63
StrengthsFinder 63
The W. Edwards Deming Institute 229
Transition.org 85, 154
W. Edwards Deming Institute 229
What's Underneath Project 125
www.70candles.com 169
www.ADM-architecture.com 319
www.changingaging.org 317
www.KarenSands.com 349
www.KarenSands.com/ageless-beat-blog 349
www.maryfurlong.com 185
www.SeniorCare.com 318

www.seniorhousingforum.net 318
www.seniorlifestyles.net 318
www.Sixtyandme.com 169
www.StyleSociety.com 204
www.theworldcafe.com 218
optimism 74–75
oracles 48–50
O'Shaughnessy, Jacky 124–125, 187
"Our Bodies, Ourselves" 16, 133

P
Papyrus 50
Pastore, Fran 164
Peterson, David A.
educational gerontology 197
podcasting 241
Pogrebin, Letty Cottin 2
Port, Michael
"Book Yourself Solid" 147
Positive Aging 69–106. See also benefits of aging
an example 104–105
benefits of aging 72–104
defined 69
roots of movement 194–195
vs. Conscious Aging 196
what's next 196–197
Prigogine, Ilya
dissipative structures 339
"PrimeTime" demographic 182

R
Rand, Ayn
"Atlass Shrugged" 249
Rebbe Nachman of Breslov 305
Reflections
about 28–29
chapter 1 51–52
chapter 2 67–68
chapter 3 107–108
chapter 4 118
chapter 7 208–209
chapter 8 244–245
chapter 9 282–283
chapter 10 313–314
chapter 11 326–327
chapter 12 334
chapter 13 344
regret
and Positive Aging 76–77
and reinvention 274–275
of the dying 309–311
reinvention 247–283
business 231–234
caution vs. hesitation 278–281
defined 263–266
Evolutionary Spiral of Reinvention 272–273
finding your starting point 269–275
future tasks 275
going beyond success 275–276
Midlife Reclamation 248–251

Radical Reinvention 266
    sustaining the change 276–278
    triggering events 272–274
    vs. rearranging 266–269
relocating 320
resources 349–353. *See also* online resources
re-storying
    aging 69–106
    entrepreneurship 153–169
    menopause 249–251
    our sexuality 128–136
    the Boomer story 174–181
    the future 342–343
    the inner patriarch 147–150
    the power of myths 268–269
    the workplace 220–222
    women 109–118
retirement 213–217
    retirement age 213–215
retirement communities 320–321
Roddick, Anita 168
role models 1
Rometty, Virginia 145
Roosevelt, Eleanor 335
Rumi 27

S
Sacks, Oliver
    "The Joy of Old Age" 104–105
Sands, Karen
    about the author 362
    career turning point 247–248
    Conscious Aging 42–48
    early history 4–12
    house fire 285
    role in Second Wave Feminism 6
    "Visionaries Have Wrinkles" 20–21
    work as Educational GeroFuturist 19
    work in Educational Gerontology 197–198
Satir, Virginia 260
Scott-Maxwell, Florida 88
    on being a wise Elder 333
    on old age and death 306
Seasons of Life diagram 258
Second Wave Feminism
    defined 3
self-esteem 143–150
    and invisibility 92–94
    "Dragon of Midlife" 144
    steps to improving 145–146
sexism
    and ageism 18
    surrounding menopause 134–135
sexuality 128–136
    and menopause 131
    "female hysteria" 133
    satisfaction increasing with age 136
    sexual health 132
shadow self
    defined 39

Sham Syndrome 144
Signature Greatness DNA
    defined 5–6, 14
    tapping into 252–256
silver ceiling
    defined 183–184
Silverman, Sarah 17
Six Sigma
    defined 227–226
Sladek, Sarah
    on "aging out" 218
social media
    as a business tool 239–240
Soul
    and money 147
    finding its purpose 97–100, 276–278
    listening for Soulspeak 252
Soulspeak
    defined 250
    hearing 252, 263
    in dreams 250
stages of life 257–258
    contrasted 44–45
    Third and Fourth Age achievements 44
Steele, Allison 13
Steinem, Gloria
    founding of Ms. 2
    on aging 137
    on Elder sexuality 131–132
STEM (science, technology, engineering,
        mathmatics) 164
Stone, Hal and Sidra
    "Embracing Your Inner Critic" 262
    Voice Dialogue model 148, 262
Stone, Sidra 316
    on planning for aging 298
    "The Shadow King" 271
stories
    Artemis and Actaeon 134–135
    Baba Yaga and Vasilisa 109–112
    Inanna 254
    "Logan's Run" 335–336
    myth of Sisyphus 287–289
    Odysseus 254
    Skeleton Woman 129–130
    "The Old Woman's Hide" 31–35
    "The Princess and the Goblin" 342
storytelling
    and self-esteem 143–150
    and the Ageless Future 48–50
    and The Ageless Way 16–17
    mythology 38
    re-storying 37–38
    to understand the future 42–45
    to understand the past 38–40
    to understand the present 40–42
Straker, David
    on leadership 92–93
sustainable success 276–278

T

Tandy, Jessica 329
technology
    age-friendly 241–242
    and Boomerpreneurs 237–238
    podcasting 241
    social media 239–240
terminology for aging 57–60
    Crone 58
    Elderhood 329
    redefining "seniors" 57
"The Secret" 340
Third Wave Feminism
    defined 3
Thomas, Bill 35, 317–318, 325
"Trick of the Feminine"
    defined 179
Triple Bottom Line
    defined 156
    diagram 156
    for the new economy 222
    shift to values 176
truth-telling
    and Baba Yaga 112
    and Crones 112–113, 333
    and loss 310–311
    and Visionaries with Wrinkles 112–113
    and wisdom 332–334
    power of 77–86

U

universal design 319

V

Visionaries with Wrinkles
    and Elderhood 111
    Baby Boomers 268
visionary business 242–243
"Voice Dialogue"
    defined 262

W

Ward, William Arthur 95
Ware, Bronnie
    "Top Five Regrets of the Dying" 309
Warhol, Andy 340
Warren, Elizabeth
    leadership of 93–94
widowhood 294
Williams, Dar 1, 11, 31, 109, 119, 329
Winfrey, Oprah
    on the culture's youth obsession 122
Winterson, Jeanette 128
wisdom 88–91
    and "humanility" 89–90
    defined 88
Wolfe, David 173
    "Ageless Marketing" 57, 179, 194
    on advertising 87
    on the gray market 174
    "Serving the Ageless Market" 57
women
    and agelessness 109–118
    and community 168–170
    and entrepreneurship 153–165
    caregiving 115–117
    embracing the Crone or the
        Wise Woman Elder 112–115
    future of the workplace 163–166
    roles in Hollywood 185–186
    shaping the future 141–171
    spending on fashion and beauty 186–187
Woodman, Marion 15
    Conscious Aging 42–48, 195
    on losing a parent 295
    on mortality 306
workplace
    age-friendly adaptations 225–230
    dealing with generational differences 60–64
    embracing multiple generations 217–219
    exodus of Baby Boomers 182–184
    future of women 163–166
    importance of friendships 63
    mentorship 222–225
    Workforce 2000 182
    Workforce 2020 182

Y

Yancey, Sandra 160, 165
    foreword iii–v
Yousafzai, Malala 53

www.KarenSands.com

About Karen Sands

Karen Sands has spent decades transforming conversations about Positive Aging, women, and the future, culminating in paving a more vibrant age-friendly way forward for age 40-plus women in the twenty-first century. In ushering in *The Ageless Way*, Sands capitalizes on tomorrow's trends today to illuminate a new story, a narrative fostering a life of unlimited meaning, satisfaction, impact and legacy-making, as well as money-making futures that matter. Karen shakes up limiting perceptions and outmoded thinking, transforming them into new possibilities transforming aging and ageism on its head. Her work aims to catapult women to the forefront of the business of aging as innovative social entrepreneurs, change-makers, visionary leaders, and discerning high-value consumers. By bringing together the best practices of sustainable business with avant-garde approaches to timeless living and unlimited Ageless Aging. In doing so, she prepares us to rock our age by generating and utilizing innovative, intergenerational conscious gero-businesses and services partnered with civic engagement and sacred activism. She is a "Visionary with Wrinkles," a CCE-BCC and ICF-MCC certified Master and Mentor Coach, a TED support Master Coach, the leading Educational GeroFuturist on the Longevity Economy, and author/creator of *Visionaries Have Wrinkles*, *Gray is the New Green* and *The Ageless Way* book, services, and program. Sands is also an online entrepreneur, speaker, publisher, and multi-book author/ blogger. Karen Sands propels women and men across generations to usher in *The Ageless Way* and radically reinvent the true meaning of growing older at any age—in life and in business."

Made in the USA
San Bernardino, CA
08 December 2016